W9-ARB-333

Please remember that this is a library book,
and that it belongs only temporarily to each
person who uses it. Be considerate. Do
not write in this, or any, library book.

Dialogues of the Great Things of Brazil

(Diálogos das grandezas do Brasil)

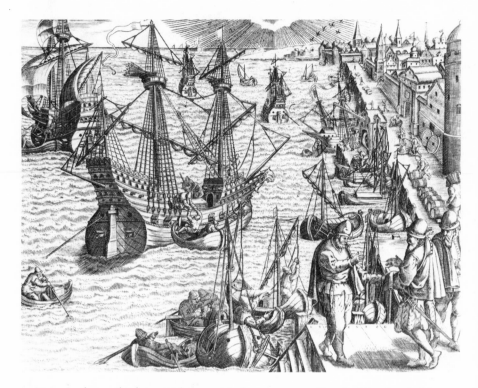

Hans Staden embarks at Lisbon on his first voyage to Brazil. Theodor de Bry, *India occidentalis* . . . (Frankfort, 1590–1634), III, 1. *Courtesy of The Edward E. Ayer Collection, The Newberry Library, Chicago.*

Dialogues of the Great Things of Brazil

(Diálogos das grandezas do Brasil)

Attributed to

Ambrósio Fernandes Brandão

Translated and annotated by

Frederick Holden Hall

William F. Harrison and Dorothy Winters Welker

University of New Mexico Press

Albuquerque

This publication has been supported by the Newberry Library's
Lester J. Cappon Fund and by the National Endowment for the Humanities.

Library of Congress Cataloging-in-Publication Data

Brandâo, Ambrósio Fernandes, b. ca. 1555.
Dialogues of the great things of Brazil.

Translation of: Diálogos das grandezas do Brasil.
Bibliography: p.
Includes index.
1. Brazil. I. Hall, Frederick Holden, 1915–1972. II. Harrison, William F.,
1934–   . III. Welker, Dorothy Winters, 1905–   . IV. Title. V. Title: Diálogos
das grandezas do Brasil.
F2508.B7713   1986   981   86-16044
ISBN 0-8263-0885-6

Design by
Barbara Werden

iv

Contents

Illustrations   vi

Foreword by José Antonio Gonsalves de Mello   vii

Preface   xi

Introduction   3

Dialogue I   15

Notes to Dialogue I   49

Dialogue II   85

Notes to Dialogue II   113

Dialogue III   131

Notes to Dialogue III   163

Dialogue IV   191

Notes to Dialogue IV   220

Dialogue V   247

Notes to Dialogue V   279

Dialogue VI   304

Notes to Dialogue VI   326

Appendix   341

Bibliography   349

Index   369

Illustrations

1. Hans Staden embarks at Lisbon for Brazil   Frontispiece

2. Map of Brazil in 1618   2

3. A water-powered sugar mill in Pernambuco   21

4. Indians cutting down brazilwood trees   26

5. Portuguese ships attack   34

6. Natives attack a Portuguese settlement   38

7. Map of Brazil ca. 1519   86

8. Map of Brazil and Africa in 1618   101

9. Older type of cane press   141

10. *gangorra*   142

11. Newer type of cane press   143

12. A Brazilian jangada   155

13. Manioc plant   194

14. Manioc grating wheel   195

15. The *maracuja*   214

16. Gathering cashews   218

17. Sapucaya   219

18. Piranhas   258

19. Howler monkeys and peccary   267

20. *Guaxinim* and *tamandua*   271

21. Sinimbu and *teguacu*   273

22. Sloth   274

23. Execution of a prisoner   319

24. Corpses   320

Foreword

José Antonio Gonsalves de Mello,

University of Recife

❧

IT WAS IN THE FIRST HALF OF THE EIGHTEENTH CENTURY that the public was made aware through the press of the existence of two texts of a work entitled *Diálogos das grandezas do Brasil* (*Dialogues of the Great Things of Brazil*). Andrés González de Barcia Carballido y Zúñiga, editor and annotator of the second edition of the *Epítome de la Bibliotheca Oriental y Occidental, Náutica y Geográfica* of Antonio Rodríguez de León Pinelo, in three volumes, published in Madrid in the years 1737 and 1738, made it known that in the library of the University of Leyden, in the Netherlands, and in the library of the counts of Vimieiro, in Lisbon, there were preserved manuscripts of that work. The manuscript of the Leyden library had been purchased in 1690 from the estate of Isaac Vossius (1618–1689); that of the library of the Vimieiros probably disappeared in the fire that followed the Lisbon earthquake of 1755, but there is a possibility that this is the one which, at an unknown date, was acquired by the National Library of that city. This supposition is based on the identity in the number of folios: Diogo Barbosa Machado, in the first volume of his *Bibliotheca lusitana* (Lisbon, 1741), states that the manuscript of the Vimieiros consisted of 106 folios, which is exactly the number that the manuscript in the Portuguese capital contains.

The Lisbon manuscript, which bears the slightly variant title *Diálogo das grandezas do Brasil,* retains traces, in a typical mid-seventeenth-century hand, of a reader who tried to establish its authorship, annotating some autobiographical references made by one of the interlocutors of the *Diálogos.* From these annotations, Barcia attributed the work to one "Brandão, a Portuguese, a resident of Pernambuco"; Barbosa Machado assigned it to

vii

Bento Teixeira, the poet of the *Prosopopéia* (Lisbon, 1601). The latter attribution received general acceptance until the end of the last century, when Capistrano de Abreu, upon comparing the autobiographical references with various documents, proposed another name: that of Ambrósio Fernandes Brandão. This suggestion received new documentary reinforcements from Rodolfo Garcia (1930) and from the writer of these lines (1955, 1962, 1966). Such an attribution of authorship combines in its favor the perfect agreement of the autobiographical references with what we know of the life of Brandão from reliable documents. He must have been born about 1555 and was dead by 1634.

The Leyden manuscript received interlinear additions and corrections, which were incorporated into the text of the Lisbon manuscript; it may be concluded from this fact that the latter is a copy of the former. How did that Portuguese manuscript come to find a home in the Netherlands? Unhappily, nothing is known on this point for certain to this day. But it may be considered that Brandão was a sugar plantation owner in Paraíba in the year in which he wrote the *Diálogos,* 1618; and that it was in Paraíba that there lived, in 1634, a Jesuit father, Manuel de Moraes, a native of São Paulo, Brazil. Father Moraes, during the occupation of Paraíba by the forces of the Dutch West India Company (1634–1654), abandoned his religion, became a Calvinist, and traveled to the Netherlands, under a subvention from the governing body of that company in Amsterdam. It is established that he wrote (or began to write) a description or history of Brazil and a dictionary (apparently of the Tupi language, in which he was fluent). For either of these works the text of the *Diálogos* was of obvious utility, and possibly he brought it with him or had it brought to the Netherlands in 1635 or 1636, when he was devoting himself to the two projects mentioned above. This is mere supposition, however, based on the two men's residence in Paraíba and the identity of their interests.

Not until 1848–1849 was the publication of the *Diálogos* undertaken. (The title was put in the plural in conformity with the Lisbon manuscript, since the dialogues number six.) In 1877, in a daily newspaper of Recife, the first and part of the second dialogue appeared. Between 1883 and 1887 the dialogues were published for the first time—in a historical review—as a whole but with the text incomplete. In 1930 the first edition in book form appeared, likewise incomplete. This deficiency having been pointed out in 1960, the University of Pernambuco brought out the first integral edition two years afterwards. In 1966 the University published a second edition, based on the text of Leyden compared with that of Lisbon.

Frederick Hall admired the anonymous work, attributed, with solid documentary support, to Ambrósio Fernandes Brandão, and dedicated himself with perseverance and competence to the task of translating it into the English language. Unfortunately, he was prevented by death from completing this work. The project thus initiated was brought to a successful conclusion by two dedicated and equally competent scholars, friends of Hall: William F. Harrison and Dorothy Winters Welker, who are jointly responsible for the edition. Thus the *Diálogos* have attained publication in English, enriched with precious annotations, which clarify in detail the subjects discussed by the interlocutors. We all remain indebted to the editors and annotators of this publication for an inestimable contribution to Brazilian history.

Preface

THE PRESENT TRANSLATION AND EDITION OF THE *Dialogues of the Great Things of Brazil* is in a very real sense the achievement of Frederick Arthur Holden Hall, Luso-Brazilian bibliographer of the Newberry Library in Chicago. During the last years of his life Hall prepared a preliminary draft of the translation and began the accumulation of material for the annotations. The intention of the present editors is but to complete Hall's project in a form that will constitute a worthy memorial to him.

After his graduation from the University of Michigan, Hall resided in Brazil for nine years, first as a student and later as cultural attaché for the American Embassy in Rio de Janeiro. He admired and loved everything about the country—its people, its scenery, its language, its history and literature. After his return to the United States in 1946 he prepared himself for a career in library science, a career that culminated in his appointment as Luso-Brazilian bibliographer for the Newberry Library. But he never lost his nostalgia for the "great things" he had known in Brazil. Eventually he determined to prepare a memorial of his affection for his second fatherland: he would translate and annotate the memorial composed by another ardent lover of Brazil, author of a work whose worth had long been recognized by scholars but which was still inaccessible to readers unfamiliar with Portuguese: the *Diálogos das grandezas do Brasil* (*Dialogues of the Great Things of Brazil*).

Hall began his studies of the *Dialogues* at the Newberry Library, pursued them further at the University of Texas, where he studied for two years, and then went to Brazil to consult original sources. He carried on correspondence about the edition with Brazilianists all over the world. But death overtook him before he could complete the translation or begin the writing of an introduction and notes. In 1972, he died of malaria just at the beginning of a sojourn in Portugal, where he would have continued his research.

Frederick Hall was ideally suited to the task he had undertaken. Besides

xi

his deep feeling for things Brazilian and his unique understanding of them, Hall had a rare gift for translation. His knowledge of world history, culture, and literature was exhaustive, his taste flawless, his command of both English and Portuguese masterly. His approach to the *Dialogues* was deeply sympathetic, yet keenly critical. He was able to trace with amazing fidelity the erratic and often puzzling course of the *Dialogues*. As if by natural affinity he succeeded in conveying the distinctive flavor of the work—or rather its flavors, for the style of the Colonial chronicler varies from the familiar to the flowery, from the lyrical to the sententious, from the piquant to the pedantic. When one of the speakers in the *Dialogues* got stuck in a grammatical or logical quagmire, leaving the reader at a loss for his intention, Hall could extract the meaning and yet preserve the effect of momentary disarray. He understood his author's need for occasional friendly assistance, but always kept his own contribution ancillary to the writer's intention. Few translators can have been so much at one with their authors as Frederick Hall.

The two editors who took up this task, so brilliantly begun and so tragically left unfinished, have tried to edit Hall's translation with all the rigor he would have exercised had he lived to perform the final critical scrutiny of his work. At the same time they have been at pains to preserve so far as possible Hall's graceful, sensitive style and his fidelity to the spirit of the original.

In his copies of the Brazilian editions of the *Dialogues*, Hall left many a question mark and not a few exclamation points. In addition, there are a number of marginal notes. Some of these point to implications in the text so subtle that they would escape any but the keenest and most sympathetic reader. Others record Hall's gentle amusement at the logical and stylistic difficulties the author so readily got himself into. Still others express appreciation of lively or moving passages on which Hall would have the reader dwell as he had done. And numerous comments point out textual, historical, or scientific difficulties that needed to be explored. Thus Frederick Hall pointed the way for what his continuators have tried to accomplish.

Brazilianists across the world had eagerly awaited the completion of Frederick Hall's projected edition and had generously offered him their assistance. All of them were his friends and associates, for he had been of inestimable assistance to them when they came to pursue their own research at the Newberry Library. After Hall's death, these scholars promptly offered their help to the present editors to the end that the completed edition might be worthy of Frederick Hall. This ready help from Hall's colleagues is not the least of the debts owed by the present editors to the initiator of the English translation.

It would be impractical to name all the people who have had a part in making this edition possible, much less to acknowledge their contributions adequately. There is only room to mention briefly those to whom the editors are most deeply indebted.

Our greatest debt of gratitude is to Frederick Hall himself, who thought deeply and constructively about the problems of the text and left us a rich fund of information, interpretation, suggestions, and questions to be resolved. His correspondence with scholars and his notes on interviews with specialists in varied fields supplied valuable data and pointed to important paths for investigation.

Among the living scholars who have helped us, the first to be mentioned must be Dauril Alden, of the University of Washington, who freely shared with us his vast knowledge of Colonial Brazil and of bibliographical sources. Professor Alden carefully read the entire manuscript, making criticisms and suggestions that have greatly enriched the translation and annotations.

José Antonio Gonsalves de Mello, of the University of Recife, in his Brazilian edition of the *Diálogos* furnished not only exhaustive information about the authorship of the work but also a superlative editorial model. Professor Gonsalves de Mello had spent many hours in personal consultation with Frederick Hall, offering suggestions which were carefully preserved by Hall and of which the present editors gratefully made use. Finally, Professor Gonsalves de Mello graciously consented to read the completed manuscript and to write the Foreword.

Chandra Richard de Silva, of the University of Sri Lanka, read all the portions of the edition that deal with India and neighboring lands and with economic matters, and made many valuable suggestions for interpretation and for bibliographical sources. This edition is deeply indebted to him.

Donald Simpson, formerly assistant curator of botany, Field Museum of Natural History, Chicago, was so kind as to investigate for us some of the problems connected with Brazilian flora. Additional information on both flora and fauna was obtained from other scientists of the Field Museum, which is especially strong in its Brazilian holdings and in the staff who have charge of them.

Sincere thanks for other information and suggestions and for advice on editorial matters are richly due to the following scholars: Ruth Lapham Butler, former Custodian of the Edward E. Ayer Collection, the Newberry

Library; Francis A. Dutra, University of California at Santa Barbara; Kathleen Hill, Eastern Kentucky University; Lloyd Kasten, Professor Emeritus, University of Wisconsin; Benjamin Keen, Professor Emeritus, Northern Illinois University; Frederick W. Murray, Northern Illinois University; and Aurora Maria Soares Neiva, Federal University of Rio de Janeiro.

Our deep appreciation is due to Lawrence W. Towner, former President and Librarian of the Newberry Library, who encouraged us throughout our endeavor and aided us in ways too numerous to mention; to James Wells, former Vice-President of the Library, who made available to us important library services that speeded and facilitated our work; to John Aubrey of Special Collections, who freely put at our disposal his wide professional knowledge and scholarly judgment; to Robert W. Karrow, Jr., Curator of Maps, who helped us in many ways far beyond the location and evaluation of maps; to Karen Skubish, the obliging and infinitely resourceful Supervisor of the Main Reading Room; and to many other members of the Library staff whose competent and cheerful assistance has been an unfailing support, notably that most indefatigable of pages, Michael Kaplan. Finally, our profound gratitude is due to the Newberry Library, sponsor of the edition, and to the National Endowment for the Humanities, for their generous subventions toward the publication of the work.

This edition was planned to accomplish two purposes which are perhaps incompatible: to provide an annotated text that will be useful to Brazilianists, and to supply to beginning students of Brazilian history and literature the information they need in order to read the *Dialogues* with understanding and pleasure. The editors apologize to the first group for telling them many things they already know, and to the second for telling them some things they may not find interesting.

The Introduction and annotations to the edition, as well as all translations unless other sources are named, are the sole responsibility of the present editors.

W.F.H. and D.W.W.

Dialogues of the Great Things of Brazil

(Diálogos das grandezas do Brasil)

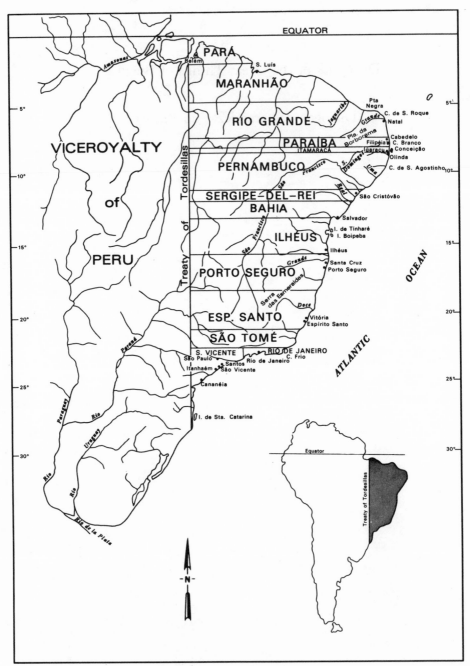

Map of Brazil in 1618.

Introduction

§

The Historical Background of the Diálogos

WHEN THE *Diálogos das grandezas do Brasil* WERE WRITTEN, IN 1618, Brazil had been a part of the known world for 118 years. It was the most precious rarity in the Portuguese imperial crown, as one contemporary put it. But few people, even in the government, had yet realized that this was true. Portuguese eyes were turned primarily to India, where Portugal during the sixteenth century had built up a vast and profitable commercial empire. Most Portuguese, like Alviano in Dialogue III, were convinced that India, and not Brazil, was to provide the unlimited riches that they hoped would flow into the metropole from the far-flung Portuguese Empire. In this belief the Portuguese were mistaken, and the author of the *Dialogues* was one of the few far-sighted persons who saw the truth.

In fact, Brazil had been added to the Empire almost as a footnote to India. In 1498 Vasco da Gama rounded the Cape of Good Hope and opened the ports of India to Portuguese trade. Two years later Dom Manuel, King of Portugal, sent a follow-up expedition to India under Pedro Álvares Cabral. For a reason about which scholars still disagree, Cabral, on his voyage south along the coast of Africa, veered to the west far out of his course—so far that he sighted the coast of Brazil. The fleet touched land there on April 22, 1500, and a few days were spent exploring the region and observing some friendly Indians. When Cabral sailed off to the Orient, one of his ships was sent back to Portugal with an official report of the discovery. This report, written by the scribe of Cabral's fleet, Pero Vaz de Caminha, vividly reflects the explorers' joy of discovery and the wonder of the new land. It is the first of a long series of enthusiastic tributes by Portuguese to their most valuable overseas possession.

Portugal had a firm legal basis for its claim to Brazil, and therefore it regarded any other nations that tried to trade or to establish settlements in the area as intruders. Portugal's claim was based on its discoveries and

3

on the Treaty of Tordesillas (1494), in which both Spain and Portugal accepted a settlement proposed by Pope Alexander VI. By this settlement Spain was assiged all lands discovered west of an imaginary line 370 leagues west of the Cape Verde Islands, and Portugal all the land east of this line. The terms of the treaty were so vague, however, that they led to further disputes between the two countries. Furthermore, other nations of Europe—mainly England, France, and the Netherlands—were reluctant to accept the papal settlement, insisting on their own right to claim lands in the western hemisphere on the basis of discovery or exploration. France especially made several attempts to establish permanent settlements in Brazil (see Dialogue I). The Netherlands was to do so a few years after Brandão's time. Nevertheless, a measure of order had been introduced, at least for the time, into the struggle for territorial rights in the newly discovered lands.

Caminha had noted that the only economic resources readily available in Brazil were parrots, purges, and brazilwood. But the first crop to be harvested, the writer averred, was the souls of the Tupi heathen. In practice, it was brazilwood that got priority, for the reddish dye it yielded was in great demand in northern Europe for the manufacture of dyestuffs. To exploit this valuable resource, the Crown contracted with merchants who undertook to establish trading posts, or "factories" (feitorias), along the coast. The merchants bartered with the Indians to cut and chop the brazilwood trees and load the logs onto ships (see Dialogue III), which transported them to Lisbon. Thence the wood was shipped to European centers and even to the Orient.

But the traders were soon plagued by foreign competitors, especially the French, who as early as 1503 were reported to be cutting brazilwood along the coast. To defend Portugal's possessions against the interlopers, the King in the 1530s divided the new land into fifteen parallel captaincies, each stretching straight west into the interior to the still vaguely defined boundary of the Spanish holdings, the Viceroyalty of Peru. The fifteen captaincies were distributed among twelve donataries, or proprietors, each of whom was given the titles of governor and captain major along with extensive rights of taxation and control. In return, the donataries undertook to defend their captaincies and to colonize and develop them at their own expense.

The cutting of brazilwood became less and less profitable as the great stands of timber near the coast were exhausted and the producers had to move inland (see Dialogue III). By 1550 brazilwood had been largely replaced as the staple of commerce by sugar cane, the cultivation of which became during the colonial period Brazil's prime economic activity as well as the basis for Brazilian society, with "sugar barons" occupying positions of power and prestige comparable to those enjoyed in European countries by the hereditary nobility (see Dialogue III).

From the very beginning, the new settlements faced the problem of obtaining an adequate labor supply for the sugar mills. Portuguese immigrants were few, and these, in accordance with Portuguese tradition, regarded it as beneath their dignity to perform manual tasks. For a time the Indians exchanged their labor for such foreign novelties as glass beads and scraps of metal, but these trinkets soon lost their appeal, and the Indians returned to their free forest life. The Portuguese then resorted to enslaving the Indians, a procedure that triggered numerous Indian uprisings. To complicate this situation, French interlopers gained allies among the Indians and did everything they could to inflame them against the Portuguese. It was not long before the French and Indians had terrorized and ravaged vast sections of the Brazilian coast. By 1548 most of the colonies were economically and defensively in a desperate situation.

There was one exception to this chronicle of disaster (if we disregard São Vicente, which enjoyed some modest success). This was the captaincy granted to Duarte Coelho—Pernambuco in the Northeast. A strong and able administrator, Duarte Coelho had gained the friendship of many Indian tribes, and though there were occasional conflicts, in general he was able to secure a high degree of cooperation from them. Moreover, he had built up an immensely profitable sugar industry in his captaincy. When the Indians proved unsatisfactory as field hands, Duarte Coelho imported blacks from Africa. The Africans were a valuable work force because they were already familiar with agriculture, cattle-raising, and working with iron. The capture of slaves in Africa and their sale in Brazil quickly became a thriving industry, one in which great fortunes were acquired by individual Portuguese. Olinda, the capital of Pernambuco and home of many of the slave-owning sugar barons, became a place of lavish display and luxurious living as well as an "academy" of good manners, as it is called in the *Dialogues* (I, VI). New Christians and crypto-Jews, then the most successful members of the commercial class, were encouraged to come to Pernambuco to find a refuge from the Inquisition, which threatened them in Portugal. It may have been for this reason that the presumed author of the *Dialogues* chose Pernambuco as his Brazilian home.

By 1549 it had become apparent to the monarch, Dom João III, that apart from the Northeast the Brazilian settlements were foundering, and that he had no recourse but to take on a large part of the responsibility for developing and defending the colonies himself. He repossessed the Captaincy of Bahia, and sent out Tomé de Sousa to be the first governor general of Brazil, with orders to found a capital in this centrally located captaincy. Along with Tomé de Sousa came Jesuit missionaries, who devoted themselves with dedication and skill to the conversion and education of the Indians. Under Tomé de Sousa's capable leadership the city of Salvador, or Bahia de Todos os Santos (Bay of All Saints), was built and the surrounding lowlands turned over to sugar plantations, which soon made Bahia second only to Pernambuco as a sugar producer. Thus as early as 1580 there were two cities of some importance in Brazil—Olinda and Salvador, both centers for sugar exportation. Rio de Janeiro had been founded in 1567, but gave as yet little hint of its future glory. As time went on, the King took over other captaincies that were faltering, and when new captaincies were created, they were mostly royal captaincies.

In the meantime a new threat was looming. In Europe, Protestant Netherlands had been fighting Spain for independence since 1568. The union of Spain and Portugal in 1580 gave the Dutch a justification for infringing on Portugal's monopoly of trade with the Portuguese colonies in both the East and the West Indies. Dutch fleets began to sail to the Orient, looking to buy spices directly at their source rather than through Portuguese middlemen. So successful were these ventures that in 1602 Dutch merchants, with the support of the Dutch government, organized the Dutch East India Company to trade for spices in the East. Though Spain and the Netherlands signed a twelve-year truce in 1609, the Spanish were unable to ban the Dutch company from the Orient. By the time of the writing of the *Dialogues* (1618), Portugal was using up all its revenue from the spice trade in defending its eastern interests. It was in this economic crisis that the author of the *Dialogues* sought to draw attention to the immense potential of Brazil as a source of income for the Crown. He insisted, correctly, that Brazil was capable of producing as much revenue as India, with none of the expenses attendant on the India enterprise (see Dialogue III).

But it was too late to save Portuguese India. Not long after the *Dialogues* were completed, the English moved in on the India trade, already threatened by the Dutch, and eventually the Portuguese had to give up their ambition to dominate commerce in the East. Moreover, the Dutch had cast an acquisitive eye on Brazil as well as on India. Even during the time of the *Dialogues* Dutch scientists were making studies of the Brazilian flora and fauna in preparation for economic exploitation of the country when the

Dutch should take it over by force of arms. Especially attractive were the rich returns to be had from sugar, for Brazil was at that time the main source of this product for practically all of Europe, and the great sugar refineries were located in the Netherlands.

The Dutch did attack Bahia in 1624, but they were driven out a year later. In 1630 they began a series of invasions that for varying lengths of time put them in possession of the seven captaincies from Maranhão to Alagoas. The occupied area included Pernambuco, Paraíba, and Itamaracá, the three captaincies upon which the *Dialogues* are centered.

The Dutch did not enjoy their Brazilian conquests for long. They were driven out of the occupied captaincies one after another; all had been lost by 1654. The Dutch invasion caused a great deal of upheaval and destruction, but it left valuable information, systematically accumulated and carefully preserved, that laid a solid basis for future scientific exploitation and research.

In the middle of the Dutch occupation the union between Spain and Portugal came to an end (in 1640). The Portuguese now began to concentrate on developing their Brazilian resources. There was no dearth of self-appointed advisers to tell the government how this should be accomplished. Among these advisers a very large place must be assigned to the so-called chroniclers of Brazil, each of whom had his own ideas about the virtues of the new land and how these could be used to build the future. True, government officials were often deaf to their counsel, as the author of the *Dialogues* laments (Dialogue III), but with the passage of time it has transpired that our author, and others among the chroniclers, saw further ahead and more accurately than the administrators who made the decisions—or left them unmade. This is not surprising. Well informed about the land in which they had lived or traveled, personally involved in the country and its future, visitors or immigrants to Brazil were often in a position to make better judgments about its management than administrators in distant Portugal.

The Chroniclers

No sooner had the new land been discovered than the bold spirits who had ventured there began to write about their experience for the information and entertainment of their compatriots back home. Throughout Brazil's first two centuries—the sixteenth and seventeenth—there was an outpouring of travelers' accounts, mostly on the model of earlier chronicles published by voyagers to India and Africa. The earliest of these accounts simply described the land or related the writers' experiences there, but as time passed and the country began to be colonized, the history of the European settlements came to be set down.

Most of the writers were Portuguese; but others were Spanish, French, German, Dutch, and English, for adventurous or ambitious men came from all over Europe to seek their fortunes in the land of promise. Some were official reporters to the King, like Pero Vaz de Caminha in the year of the discovery and Campos Moreno in the time of the *Dialogues*. Others were admitted fortune hunters, like Hans Staden, survivor of hairbreadth escapes among the cannibals. Several were missionaries, zealous to convert and educate the Indians or to set up religiously oriented colonies. Most of these were members of religious orders, like André de Thevet, José de Anchieta, Fernão Cardim, Claude d'Abbéville, Vicente do Salvador, and Simão de Vasconcellos; one, Jean de Léry, was a Lutheran. There were men of learning and culture among the chroniclers, like Magalhães de Gandavo, bent on serious study of the characteristics of the new land. And there were speculators, come to build a personal fortune and, in most cases, determined to return to Portugal as soon as they had done so; Gabriel Soares de Sousa was a representative of this group. Some were scientists, like Georg Marcgrave and Willem Piso, brought to Brazil to study the botanical and zoological possibilities of the country by the Netherlands government, which hoped to realize rich profits from their researches. Many must have been impelled by a mixture of these motives. Some must have come to establish a new life in Brazil and play a responsible part in developing the country. Among these, the author of the *Dialogues* is surely to be numbered.

The term *chroniclers*, though strictly speaking is appropriate only to the historians among these authors, is generally given for convenience to all the early writers about Brazil—even when they wrote primarily description rather than history. In a sense, this use of the term chronicler is fully justified, for every writer chronicled his own experience of Brazil, whether he expressed it in a personal narrative, a study of Indian languages, a sermon on the settlers' mistreatment of the Indians, or a botanical or zoological study.

Some of the narrators falsified their information, some exaggerated, some filched material from each other without acknowledgment, some accepted too uncritically what they heard or read; but by far the largest part of the information they recorded proved carefully collected and considered, detailed, accurate, and truly valuable. Together these men built up a vast store of information based on observation, conversation, reading, and travelers' tales. Several of the chronicles are of excellent literary quality, even when their primary purpose is utilitarian. What all share is an endless curiosity about Brazil. Most show unbounded confidence in a great future for the land.*

The Author

The *Diálogos das grandezas do Brasil* are a description of Brazil as the country appeared to a successful Portuguese businessman in 1618. The work has been attributed at different times to various authors, but scholars now generally agree that it was written by Ambrósio Fernandes Brandão, a merchant and sugar planter who operated enterprises in Paraíba and Pernambuco, in the Northeast of Brazil. A detailed analysis of all the theories of authorship, an account of the known facts of Brandão's life, and a history of the various editions are provided in José Antonio Gonsalves de Mello's definitive Brazilian edition of the *Diálogos* (Recife: Imprensa Universitária, 1966).

The biographical details are scanty. A few are given in the *Dialogues* themselves; others have been gleaned from contemporary documents. Born in Portugal about 1555, Brandão arrived in Brazil in 1583 and settled in Olinda, Pernambuco. Here he obtained employment as a factor (agent) for Bento Dias de Santiago, who held the contract for collecting tithes in the captaincy. Within only a few years after Brandão's arrival he had risen to become a wealthy sugar planter and consequently a person of the highest social standing. As a sideline, he engaged in agricultural experiments and pursued an extensive interest in the flora and fauna of the country.

When the neighboring Captaincy of Paraíba had to be defended against the French and Indians, Brandão played an active part in military operations. In 1585 he was chosen captain of a company of merchants who marched against the French and their Indian allies. In 1591 he took part in a foray against the Petiguar Indians in Pernambuco, as he relates in Dialogue I.

Like most of the wealthy merchants of Brazil at this time, Brandão was

---

*The chroniclers named above and many others are cited frequently in the notes to the present edition. For the reader who wishes to become better acquainted with these authorities, a brief sketch of the life and work of each of the principal chroniclers is provided in the Appendix. The best editions and translations of their works are listed in the Bibliography.

a New Christian—a term properly applied to recently converted Jews, but in popular usage often extended to their descendants over several generations. Many New Christians were crypto-Jews, practicing in secret the religion that persecution had forced them, or their ancestors, to renounce in public, and this may have been the case with Brandão. Both he and his friend Nuno Álvares, who like Brandão served as a tax collector, were denounced before the Inquisition in Brazil for heresy and related offenses, but fortunately both were cleared of the charges. The *Dialogues* provide little information about Brandão's religious faith. Almost pointedly, it seems, the author refrains from discussing religious matters. True, he admires the fine monasteries erected by various religious orders; he commends the learning of the Fathers; and he observes with apparent approval that the Jesuits "are reaping a rich harvest of souls" among the heathen. But there is a notable scarcity of those references to the Virgin Mary and to Jesus that are so plentiful in many contemporary writings, and virtually all his scriptural allusions are to the Old Testament. The few points of doctrine that he mentions are common to the Jewish and the Christian faith (there was only one creation; all men are descended from Adam; God can do anything). These facts are, of course, too scanty to provide a conclusive answer to the question of Brandão's religious beliefs.

In 1597 or earlier Brandão set sail for his native land, where he resided for about ten years with his family in a house and garden that he owned in Lisbon. There he performed public services as treasurer general of the Office of Deceased and Absent Persons, and was acquainted with high government officials. He was, however, once more denounced before the Inquisition (by a gardener who reported that he engaged in the dangerous practice of reading books). Again cleared of the charges, he returned in 1607 or later to Brazil, where he had retained family and business ties during his absence. He was writing the *Dialogues,* as he tells us himself, in 1618, when he was probably some sixty-three years old. Most likely he himself is the Brandônio of the *Dialogues;* Alviano, the "straight man," may be Nuno Álvares, Brandão's friend and fellow tax collector. It is not known when or how Brandão died, but he was no longer living in 1634, when Paraíba was occupied by the Dutch.

The Dialogues

"The *Diálogos das grandezas do Brasil* is one of the fundamental documents of the history of the Brazilian Northeast in the first quarter of the seventeenth century," says Gonsalves de Mello in his masterly Brazilian edition of the work. It is also one of the first significant works of Brazilian literature. The treatise was apparently undertaken to encourage immigration and to promote exploitation of the colony's resources. To this end the author sketched the history of the colonization and described the outstanding features of the individual captaincies, especially those of the northeastern coastal region, where he himself resided. With an expertise derived from long and successful experience in trade and industry, he showed how the riches of the new land could be turned to the advantage of the individual settlers, of Brazil itself, and of the mother country, Portugal—or more properly, Spain, since Portugal at this time was part of that country, though it retained certain rights to the independent administration of Brazil.

To celebrate the great things of Brazil Brandão represents a long-time resident of the colony, Brandônio, as extolling the merits of his adopted country for the benefit of Alviano, a skeptical newcomer from Portugal. At first contemptuous of everything about Brazil, the doubter is overwhelmed by Brandônio's arguments and eventually capitulates completely.

The argument between the two interlocutors typifies a conflict that extended over several centuries between men who saw the New World as a land of either innocence or promise and men who condemned it out of hand as savage or degenerate. The controversy gave rise to a vast literature on both sides of the question. This literature has been superbly summarized and evaluated by Antonello Gerbi in his *La disputa del Nuovo Mondo: Storia di una polemica, 1750–1900.* In the present study this work is cited in the English translation by Jeremy Moyle: *The Dispute of the New World: The History of a Polemic, 1750–1900.* (For complete citations of these two works see the Bibiography.) Gerbi's admirable study examines in detail not only the period defined in the title but also the antecedents of the dispute in earlier centuries as far back as classical times. Strangely, Gerbi omits even to mention the *Dialogues,* which so aptly recapitulate this historic controversy.

The choice of the dialogue as a device in exposition and argumentation was, of course, not original with Brandão. The dialogue form had been widely used by both classical and medieval writers. Brandão's models were, however, most likely contemporary works that used the dialogue to extol the glories of favored lands, especially the newly-discovered ones. Examples are Garcia d'Orta's *Colóquios dos simples e drogas da Índia* (1563) and Luiz Mendes de Vasconcellos's *Diálogos do sítio de Lisboa* (1608).

In spite of the artificiality that inevitably attends the dialogue form, it serves Brandão's purpose well. The arguments for and against Brazil are treated exhaustively and convincingly. At the same time, a surprising effect of reality is achieved, mainly through the compelling impression made by the author's enthusiasm and his delight in the new land.

Brandão loved his adopted country and tried to advance it in every possible way: by extolling its beauties, describing its opportunities, and promoting the development of its resources. He was curious about all its features, including the inhabitants both Portuguese and Indian, and he described these things as faithfully as he could, dispensing praise and blame where he thought each was deserved. The information he collected is voluminous and immensely valuable, ranging from geography and history to products, industries, flora and fauna, sports, scenery, and the quality of life in Brazil. The account is enlivened by anecdotes, personal recollections, and speculations on a wide diversity of subjects.

Certainly the most interesting feature of the *Dialogues* is the information they contain about the newly discovered continent. The second most interesting feature is the faithfulness with which Brandão's discussions reflect the ideas of the post-Renaissance period. It was a fascinating time to live in, full of new discoveries and new concepts, but also of stoutly held traditions and what today we consider to be superstitions. Conflicts between the new and the old had not yet been resolved. Authority had given way to observation, but traditional ideas were hard to let go. Thus the ancients were wrong in believing that the torrid zone was uninhabitable, as experience had proved; but they "nonetheless based their argument on such a plausible foundation that, though today we are seeing and discovering the contrary of what they affirmed, almost everyone still holds this to be doubtful" (p. 87).

Reading Brandão's descriptions and speculations, one is constantly reminded that the sciences were in their infancy or yet unborn: black skin and kinky hair must be caused by the heat of the sun; certain fishes appear by spontaneous generation in the flooded fields in springtime; there is a bird that lives on air. Yet observation and reasoning are suddenly all-important: Brandônio doubts the existence of the mythical salamander, supposed to live in fire, for the very good reason that he has never yet seen one of the creatures in the fires of Brazil's sugar mills. His natural history is, by and large, natural. True, he believes in the existence of a creature that is half goat and half sheep—in fact, he is certain that he has owned some specimens himself (Dialogue V); yet he has the good judgment not to repeat any of the fantastic stories about sea monsters that other chroniclers relate with unwavering credulity.

Brandão stands at the meeting place of the ancient and the modern world, but he faces into the future. He sees clearly what needs to be done to develop the country, and just as clearly how tradition blocks these practical measures. He has produced a vivid picture of the transitional era in which he lived. This picture is sometimes dazzling, sometimes horrifying, sometimes grotesque, and sometimes strikingly anticipative of the world of today. Essentially it is a true picture, worthy of the great country that has so brilliantly realized many of the hopes and dreams of one of its earliest patriots.

No one has yet been able to establish with certainty a single literary source that is known to have been used by Brandão. Other chroniclers describe some of the same phenomena and relate similar anecdotes, but there are no convincing verbal parallels. The chronicler who in some passages stands closest to Brandão, Vicente do Salvador, wrote nine years after Brandão presumably completed his *Diálogos*.

Probably Brandão picked up most of his data about Brazil from his own observations and experiments and from conversations with the settlers, the Indians, and perhaps the ever knowledgeable missionaries. He may have had access to manuscript sources preserved in the libraries of the Jesuit *colégios* or circulated privately among his acquaintances. To accumulate the vast store of information that was obviously at his command, Brandão must have had a consuming interest in his subject, an unflagging curiosity, inexhaustible energy and patience, and a highly retentive mind.

Like many another successful businessman before and since, Brandão liked to think of himself as a man of culture and even of some pretensions to scholarship. He refers to a few of the stock figures of classical mythology and to the best-known stories of the Old Testament. He seizes on every excuse to hold forth on philosophy, political economy, history, and what passed at the time for science. But except in matters related to trade and industry—the area in which he had made his fortune—his learning is superficial and his opinions secondhand. He cites authorities, but sometimes misrepresents their views. He shows no acquaintance with Latin or any other foreign language. His knowledge of Brazilian flora and fauna does not go beyond that of a lay observer. Both his information and his ideas on subjects other than Brazil were most likely derived from popular literature or from conversations with educated men—for instance, the learned clergymen of the Brazilian missions, or the highly placed politicians with whom, as he takes pains to let us know, he was acquainted in both Brazil and Portugal. There is no evidence that he had had the benefit of a university education before migrating to Brazil.

Nor does Brandão's literary style show the effect of an exposure to the classical disciplines. It varies from the stiffly formal and ornate to the engagingly conversational. It is sometimes pretentious, but it does not reflect the Gongorism fashionable at the time. He becomes hopelessly involved in his own sentence structure, often to the near despair of a translator. His overlong sentences lead to innumerable mistakes in matters of grammatical agreement. He has an inveterate habit of telling first the thing that happened last. He unknowingly says the exact opposite of what he means. Though he has taken pains to structure the entire work and each individual dialogue, his schemes of organization frequently break down or are forgotten. He repeats himself in different parts of the *Dialogues*. He promises to describe something later on and never gets around to doing so.

Yet with all his lapses, Brandão stands out among the so-called chroniclers because he covered so many areas of the northeast Brazilian scene and covered them, on the whole, so well. He maintains for the most part a sprightly, conversational style. He is capable of warm feeling, even for the Indians, and occasionally of a heavy-handed humor. In spite of the obscurities and eccentricities of his style, his boundless enthusiasm for and wide knowledge of the country come through effectively. In a few passages he rises to poetic heights as he extols the beauty and grandeur he sees around him. Above all, his writing is suffused with an infectious sense of wonder and delight, and with the fervor of unbounded expectations. He loves his adopted country with both heart and head, and he celebrates its splendid future as it lies hidden in the great things of the present. A sensitive modern reader cannot but fall victim, as Brandão did, to the magic of Colonial Brazil.

There have been several editions of the *Diálogos* in the original Portuguese, culminating in the definitive Brazilian edition of José Antonio Gonsalves de Mello, described above (see the section on *The Author*). The reader is referred to Gonsalves de Mello's Introduction for a comprehensive digest of all that is known about the history of the *Diálogos* and their manuscripts and editions; for a useful summary of their historical content; and especially for a close examination of the question of authorship, with summaries and evaluations of the various theories that have been proposed.

Dialogue I

[The Settlement of Brazil[1]]

§

The "bit of fluff" that occupies the two friends, Brandônio and Alviano, at the beginning of Dialogue I is an extraordinarily appropriate literary device. Not only is the reader's curiosity piqued by the "trinket" itself and by the odd site of the parent tree, but the fluff both illustrates and symbolizes the fertility of Brazil and its yet untapped natural resources, the subject that is to occupy the speakers throughout the six dialogues. The opening exchange presents an engaging picture of Brandônio, the curious and knowledgeable observer of the Brazilian scene. A reflective man, he has nevertheless a keenly practical turn of mind, and at this moment is bent on finding a use for the fluff to which his attention has been directed. Alviano, on the other hand, reveals himself as a "heretic in things Brazilian," as Brandônio calls him later on. The episode is a happy introduction to Brandônio's grand plan: to describe the "great things of Brazil" so convincingly that a skeptic like Alviano will become "better informed . . . and able to change {his} opinion."

Brandônio's account begins with a brief but systematic survey of the Brazilian settlements, arranged in geographical order from north to south. He identifies each settlement as to location, origin, and principal economic resources, though he has little to say about the southern captaincies, since he has lived only in the North. As in all the dialogues, Brandônio is full of practical suggestions. He has plans for shipping goods up and down the Amazon River, for ending the illegal traffic in sugar between Paraíba and Pernambuco, for reforming the High Court in Bahia. He would like the settlers to stop being lazy and develop the natural resources of the land, a theme that recurs throughout the work.

When the question of the habitability of tropical climates comes up, Brandônio readily seizes on a topic which is ripe for speculation and which has occupied many a writer before him. It affords a graceful transition to Dialogue II, where the question is to be discussed in detail.

ALVIANO   What is that little trinket, Senhor Brandônio, that you are turning over on that piece of paper? From the way you are looking at it so carefully, I should think that it must be made of diamonds or rubies.

BRANDÔNIO   It is nothing like that, but just a bit of fluff that looks rather like wool. That tree right there in front of us has a fruit about the size of a peach, and the fluff grows inside it. A short while ago a little girl found it on the ground where it had fallen. She brought it over to me, and I was just thinking how many things it could be used for.

ALVIANO   The tree itself seems no less remarkable than its fruit, for it looks to me as if it's growing right out of the upper story of this house. It must be rooted there, for it seems to be part of the house.

BRANDÔNIO   The humidity that all the soils of Brazil enjoy makes them produce so abundantly that any kind of stick thrust into the earth will send forth roots and soon bear fruit. This tree, which looks to you as if it is growing out of the house, was a pile driven into the ground—one of several that support the house. The pile took root, and from it grew the tree that seems to be part of the wall.

ALVIANO   It must look strange to people who don't know the explanation. But tell me now about that bit of fluff you were examining: what do you think it could be used for?

BRANDÔNIO   It seems to me that certainly it could be used to stuff pillows and cushions, and even to make mattresses, and also—if it were spun—to make cloth. And as for hats, why, I think there is no question but that it would make very good ones.[2]

ALVIANO   You must be joking. If it had been any good for such a purpose it couldn't possibly have gone undiscovered for so long without people having tried to do that.

BRANDÔNIO   That's no reason for thinking that this wool or fluff could not be used as I say, for there are still many things to be discovered—about plants as well as minerals—whose properties and nature have not been figured out.

ALVIANO   I would take the contrary view, for the world is so old and people so keen on new things that I should think there is nothing left in it to be discovered, and no experiment that hasn't yet been tried.

BRANDÔNIO   You deceive yourself roundly on that score, Senhor Alviano, for there are still many things to be discovered, and unsolved mysteries that will be solved in the future.

ALVIANO I can't bring myself to believe that, for everything has already been so much explored that it seems to me that all those mysteries have been investigated and tried out by men, who have availed themselves of, and put to use, only those things that they found really to be of some value.

BRANDÔNIO That is an uninformed opinion and as such obviously mistaken. For if anyone had shown you, three hundred years ago today, a piece of the cane from which sugar is made and had told you that with human industry there would be made from that cane as fine a loaf of sugar as we see made today, you would have thought that ridiculous. And, further, if a piece of old linen cloth had been shown to you and you had been told that from that cloth was to be made the paper on which we write, who doubts that you would have thought that absurd?[3] And, likewise, if they had put before you a little bit of saltpetre, sulphur, and charcoal, while swearing to you that from those materials would be made a substance which, when fire was touched to it, would knock down walls and fortresses, and kill men at a great distance, I doubt not that the more they asserted it could be done the less you would have believed it.[4] For you must know that the first discoverers of things stumbled onto them by chance, through ill-defined principles, but their successors continued to refine them until they brought them to their present state of perfection.

ALVIANO I admit what you say, but still you will not deny that those things which we make use of are grown and cultivated by the industry and assiduous effort of the farmers and master inventors who discovered them. This is not the case with your fluff, which is taken from a tree growing wild in the fields. For the wheat, flax, and other plants that men use or consume are carefully tended and cultivated, and thus they give perfect fruit. So true is this that we never see wheat, flax, or vegetables growing in the fields by themselves, without being cultivated by man.

BRANDÔNIO If that opinion of yours were true, it seems that one would also have to grant that men were the creators of those plants, which would be tantamount to denying that God created everything, and by the same token would be a blasphemy. For well do we know that God created the wheat, the flax, and the plants of the field, and that later on human industry cultivated them in order to make better use of them. Because the Scriptures say that Noah planted vines we need not understand that he was their creator, but rather that he took the vine where it was growing wild, created by God in the fields, and put it to use, cultivating it so that it bore more perfect fruit. And if wheat and other plants do not grow by themselves in the fields, it is because the seeds are lacking for that. When a seed falls to the ground, cattle and birds tread on it or eat it. But if the wheat had been sown in a place where it could not be destroyed by beasts, it would reproduce from its own seeds dropping around it, as other plants do.

ALVIANO That I admit, for I know very well that all things issue from a single beginning, which was God's primary creation of them. And although we do see some fruits that seem not to have been so created, such as the sweet limes, grapefruit, and others like them, which human industry has managed to produce by grafts and other means, still those plants which God first created are the essence from which these derive. But this is not the subject on which we began our talk, but rather the fact that that fluff, which you say looks to you like wool, appears to me to be of little use; for if it had been good for anything our ancestors would already have made use of it. Nor am I confounded by the examples that you cited, of sugar cane, paper, and gunpowder, for these are so many laborious developments that time produces in the course of long years. Therefore, I will once again assert what I said earlier, that it would be better if that pretty little bauble were made of diamonds or rubies, which men have known and held to be precious stones since the beginning of the world.

BRANDÔNIO Well, who would deny that if this were made of diamonds or rubies it would be of greater value, because of the esteem in which the world holds them for their glitter and show, and because they delight the eye with their beauty? For I know no other virtue that they have. But I myself was never inclined to have my money tied up in such goods, for if it had been I would have considered it an unsafe investment.

ALVIANO Your opinion is a strange one, and it runs counter to that held by all men of good judgment. They always make it a point to put some of their money into precious stones because of the great value that the world puts on these, and also because they are one thing that can be hidden in any place, no matter how small, and thus escape detection. That way, in sudden emergencies that arise, they prove most useful to their owner, for in them he carries capital sufficient for his needs, according to the value of the stones and the demand for them.[5]

BRANDÔNIO   All that is true, and I grant further that precious stones delight the heart at the sight of them, and are a marvelous restorative for the melancholy. And they say it is true that if a person wearing an emerald commits an act of sensuality the emerald will shatter by itself, so much does it love chastity.[6] However, I repeat that I would not want to have my money tied up in such merchandise, for just as the emerald was the most coveted of precious stones but suffered a loss in value because of the many mines that were discovered in the West Indies,[7] and that produce them in great quantities, similarly so many mines of diamonds and rubies may be discovered that those stones may lose their value, and the people who possess them find themselves without the wealth they thought they had.

ALVIANO   Your opinion does not seem unsound to me, for I have seen many fine, large emeralds that came from those Indies. In our own time, others have turned up that Azeredo discovered in this Brazil of ours.[8] At first they seemed very promising, but their fragility soon showed up, for they were not true emeralds. Whence I infer that gold, silver, and precious stones are only for the Castilians, and reserved for them by God. For we Portuguese, inhabiting the same land as they do, and occupying the more eastern part (wherein, according to reason, there ought to be more mines), cannot discover any at all in as long a time as this Brazil of ours has been settled,[9] whereas they discover many every day.[10]

BRANDÔNIO   One cannot deny that the Castilians are good conquistadors and explorers, for in their conquests they have ranged from Cartagena to Chile and the Rio de la Plata,[11] which is land beyond measuring. Everywhere they found a great number of mines of gold, silver, copper, mercury, and other riches, which they enjoy today and make good use of. But that's no reason to call our Portuguese bad conquistadors.

ALVIANO   But why not, if we see that in all the time that they have lived in this Brazil they have not spread out into the back country so much as to settle ten leagues[12] of it, contenting themselves merely with making sugar on the seashore?[13]

BRANDÔNIO   And do you consider that an occupation of little account? For myself, I consider it a much greater thing than working mines of gold and silver,[14] as on some future occasion I shall clearly prove to you. But so that you may not hold our Portuguese to have little talent for conquest, thus embracing an erroneous opinion, I must tell you that of all the nations in the world it was they who made the greatest conquests. If you do not agree, just cast your eyes over that Orient where our forefathers, at the cost of their blood, won by conquest so many rich kingdoms, famous cities, and wealthy provinces, reducing the mightiest kings to tributaries of the Lusitanian Empire.[15] That did not happen with the Castilians, for their conquests in the West Indies and in Peru were over a weak and timorous people, whose hands were always tied against their own defense, for they lacked both the weapons and the will to resist, so much so that four ill-armed Castilians could shackle powerful kings in their own cities and houses—kings who possessed great riches and many subjects in their kingdoms, but subjects without the spirit, persistence, or wit to defend them.[16]

Now that was not the case with our Portuguese in the Orient, for they conquered the most warlike nations, which were very well armed and had cavalry as well as foot soldiers, countless pieces of artillery and other firearms which even today startle the world by the size of the balls they hurl, and which our people did not fear to breast, though many of them lost their lives in the fray as they scaled the walls of the cities they were capturing.[17] Consider also the many islands,[18] lying in the center of the ocean deeps, which they discovered and settled; those kingdoms of Angola and the Congo;[19] the islands of Cape Verde[20] and São Tomé;[21] and this great land of Brazil. Thus to our Portuguese may rightly be given (because of their many conquests on land and sea) the fitting name of Hercules and the Argonauts.[22]

ALVIANO   Who can have any doubt of that? But what I am saying is that in this Brazil they are cutting short the conquest when they might expand it far and wide.

BRANDÔNIO   It is true that they have not gone deep into the bush, but as for that, you must know that all the conquistadors who recently discovered these lands that now lie open to us were inclined to put their hands to that occupation from which they first derived a profit. Whence I see that our Portuguese who settled the islands of the Azores have persisted in wheat growing right up to the present simply because the first comers had launched into it; the Castilians who settled the Canary Islands[23] took to growing grapes, and they have stuck to that occupation up to this very day; and those who settled the Cape Verde Islands found profit trading in slaves and make their living from that, just as in the Kingdom of Angola they are still engaged in the subjugation of the tribes. On the island of São Tomé they took to making

A water-powered sugar mill, Pernambuco. Kaspar van Baerle, *Rerum per octennium in Brasilia . . . Historia* (1647), between pp. 24 and 25. *Courtesy of the Edward E. Ayer Collection, The Newberry Library, Chicago.*

a very dark sugar which even now they manufacture, and though they have the equipment to turn out a better product they don't want to bother to do so. Some of those who settled in the West Indies busied themselves in pearl fishing, others in making indigo dye, others in collecting cochineal,[24] others in raising cattle, still others in working mines; and all of them still practice the very first occupation they engaged in. In this Brazil of ours, the first settlers took up sugar making; many of those who came later followed their example, and that—as I have indicated—is the general custom of the world. So what wonder that the inhabitants of Brazil concern themselves only with growing sugar cane, even though they might take up many other things?

ALVIANO   I don't see it that way, but rather I certainly think that the reason why the inhabitants of Brazil produce only sugar is that they have found the land good for nothing else; hence I consider it the most worthless in the world, for those who live on it spend their lives in continual discomfort, and have neither rest nor—above all—any of the good things to eat that are commonly had elsewhere.[25]

BRANDÔNIO   I certainly pity you, seeing you hold so unreasonable an opinion. So that you will not persist in it, or make so crass an error,

I want to show you the contrary of what you believe. But for me to do so properly, you must first tell me, Does Brazil's being a worthless land arise from a deficiency in the land itself or in its inhabitants?

ALVIANO   How can you blame the inhabitants for the bad quality of the land? For obviously they cannot supply what it lacks or render its sterility productive!

BRANDÔNIO   Then you are telling me that it is the land that must be called—to use your word—worthless?

ALVIANO   That's what I said.

BRANDÔNIO   Well, then, you are wrong. Every type of agriculture in the world could be practiced here, for this land is blessed with great fertility, excellent climate, benignant skies, general wholesomeness, healthful air,[26] and a thousand other virtues that must be added to these.[27]

ALVIANO   If the land really had all those qualities, I think that in as long a time as Portuguese folk have been living here they would have discovered them; but they have not as yet, because they don't exist!

BRANDÔNIO   I feel obliged to make you retract the error into which you have fallen. Do you not see that Brazil produces such an abundant quantity of meats, both domestic and wild, and of every kind of tame fowl, raised at home, and an infinite number of others to be found in the fields; and such great abundance of most excellent fish of different sorts and names; so many shellfish and crabs that are taken with very little effort; so much milk drawn from the cattle; so much honey found in the trees of the forest; eggs without number; marvelous fruits grown with little labor and others with none at all, for the fields and forests liberally supply them; so many different kinds of vegetables; so much of the staples manioc and rice; and an infinitude of other things healthful and nourishing for humankind that I hope to describe to you in detail later on! Now, how can a land that abounds in all these things be said to lack them? Surely I see no province or kingdom, among those in Europe, Asia, or Africa, that has such an abundance of all those things, for we know very well that if they have some of them they still lack others; and thus you are very much mistaken in the opinion that you hold.

ALVIANO   Then why are all those things so scarce, if there is, as you say, an abundance of them?

BRANDÔNIO   The blame lies with the settlers, who are negligent and do not want to work.[28] For you should know that this whole State of Brazil is made up, in general, of five classes of men,[29] to wit:

Seafaring men, who are engaged in maritime commerce and come to the ports of the captaincies of this state, their carracks and caravels[30] laden with freight. Here they unload and caulk their ships, take on another cargo, and make the return voyage laden with sugar, brazil-wood, and cotton for the Kingdom.[31] At any time of year many men of this category can be found in the ports of the captaincies.

The second class of men is made up of traders who bring their wares out here from the Kingdom and realize a great profit when they sell or barter them for sugar. And thus it happens that there are many men in this category who have opened shops here filled with goods sent to them by merchants who are their correspondents in the Kingdom. Since the sole purpose of the men of this class is to enrich themselves through trade, they are not concerned with benefiting the land, but rather they aim at stripping it of all they can.

The third class of men comprises craftsmen and mechanics, of whom there are many in Brazil of every specialty. They seek to employ their skill for their own profit, without giving any thought to the common good.[32]

The fourth class is made up of men who work for others for wages, and are employed in crating sugar, acting as overseers in the cane fields and sugar mills, raising cattle (these men are called cowboys), and accompanying their masters as wagon drivers. There are many such people[33] throughout all this state, but not one of them gives a thought to the common good of society.

The fifth class comprises those engaged in agriculture. These are further divided into two categories. The first category embraces both the richer members, who own sugar mills and to whom His Majesty in charters and letters patent grants the title of *senhores de engenho* [sugar mill owners], and those who are not so rich, who are planters but do not own mills.[34] The second category, men whose resources do not permit so much, are engaged in truck gardening. And all of them, in both categories, work their plantations or farms with Guinea slaves,[35] whom they buy at a high price[36] for this purpose. And since all that they have to live on is what their slaves can raise, they cannot bear the thought of having even one of the slaves do anything except work in the fields, for they think it a great loss of time to plant a tree, which would bear fruit in two or three years, because that seems to them too long a time to wait. And add to this that every last one of them thinks that in a very short time he will embark for the Kingdom, there to end his days.[37] Yet the thousand difficulties that obviously prevent them from doing so are not enough to rid them of that notion. So with this idea that all of them in general have of going back to the Kingdom, and their greed to make four more sugar loaves and plant four more hills of beans, there is not a man in this whole state who tries to plant, or is disposed to plant, fruit trees or to make any of the garden improvements that are made in Portugal. Likewise, they are not inclined to raise cattle or poultry, and if anyone does try to do so it is on a very small scale, and he raises so little that all of it is consumed by himself and his family. And this explains the scarcity or absence of those things and the fact that in Brazil we do not see farms, orchards and gardens, irrigation reservoirs, and large outbuildings, such as we have back in our Spain[38]—not that the land is unsuited to these things! Whence I conclude that the lack of them is to be laid to the settlers' not caring about having them.[39]

ALVIANO   Being still a newcomer in this state makes me unaware of those great things which you maintain could be had here. In order that I may be better informed on them and be able to change my opinion, I ask that you explain in just what way all those things may be had which you claim Brazil is capable of producing. So tell me about its location, its benignant skies, its salubrious air, and the other things that you say are abundant here.

BRANDÔNIO   The world knows this province of Brazil by the name of America, but it might better be known as the Land of Holy Cross,[40] for it was thus first named by Pedrálvares Cabral,[41] who on that day discovered it,[42] on the second expedition that the King, Dom Manuel[43] of glorious memory, sent to India. By chance he came upon this great land, previously neither seen nor known to the world. Since the discovery seemed noteworthy to him, he at once dispatched a caravel[44] to the Kingdom with the news of what he had found, and about that subject an elderly nobleman, well known in Portugal, told me several things of great importance.

ALVIANO   And what did the nobleman tell you?

BRANDÔNIO   He told me that he had heard his father say—as a matter that admitted of no doubt—that the news of so great a discovery was much celebrated by the great king; and that a famous astrologer,[45] who was in our Portugal at that time, in this connection cast a horoscope, basing his computations on the season and hour in which this land was discovered by Pedrálvares Cabral, and on the season and hour in which the King received the news of its discovery; and that the astrologer reckoned that the newly discovered land would become a rich province, the refuge and asylum of the Portuguese people.[46] Now, even though we should not take any stock in those things,[47] still they are signs of the greatness which every day it is acquiring.

ALVIANO   God forbid that the Portuguese nation should suffer such evils that Brazil would be their refuge and shelter! But tell me, if Pedrálvares Cabral gave this province the name of the Land of Holy Cross, what is the reason for the name that had first been given it being so forgotten and for calling it Brazil in more recent times?

BRANDÔNIO   The name is not forgotten by His Majesty and the lords of his councils, for when they refer to this state in the patents and charters that they grant they call it the Land of Holy Cross of Brazil. This name of Brazil was added because of a wood of that name, which gives a red dye[48] prized by all Europe, and which is shipped there from this province only.

ALVIANO   Well now, tell me—as you have already threatened to do— about the great things in this province called Brazil, or the Land of Holy Cross.

BRANDÔNIO   That part of this land which today is inhabited by the Portuguese begins at the River of the Amazons,[49] sometimes called the Pará, and extends to the Captaincy of São Vicente, the last of the captaincies south of the equinoctial line [the equator]. The line runs right through the middle of Pará.[50] Between this first[51] settlement and the last one, São Vicente, there are many notable towns,[52] much very fertile country, famous rivers, and ports and bays that can easily accommodate great fleets.

ALVIANO   Now tell me about each one of them.

BRANDÔNIO   Pará, or River of the Amazons,[53] is situated, as I have said, on the equinoctial line. Proceeding south, it is the first of the Portuguese discoveries and settlements one encounters. There as yet we do not have (for it was settled only recently) more than a small fort[54] garrisoned by a few poorly equipped soldiers. The river is more than eight leagues wide at its mouth, and within the confines of this broad gulf there are countless islands, some large and some small, heavily wooded, with most excellent sites where large settlements could be made, and all surrounded by fresh water, for all the water of this vast bay is of that quality.

Inland along the river the land is extremely fertile; it enjoys very good air and hence is free from fevers. It has much excellent timber,

Indians cutting down brazilwood trees to be shipped abroad by Europeans.
André Thevet, *Les singularitez de la France Antarctique* . . . (Paris: Héritiers de
Maurice de la Porte, 1558), fol. 117ʳ. *Courtesy of the Edward E. Ayer
Collection, The Newberry Library, Chicago.*

suitable for heavy construction, many foodstuffs native to the region, a great deal of wild game—the open country is full of it—lots of various kinds of fish,[55] nourishing and delicious and easily caught, and quantities of shellfish. Yet so far, because of the short time that they have been settled here, our people have made no improvements on the land,[56] which is inhabited by dark-skinned heathen with long straight hair, who speak the same language as do the others of Brazil.[57]

ALVIANO   Do you know by any chance where that great river has its source?

BRANDÔNIO   The local people claim that it issues from a lake which they say lies deep in the back country, and which they also make the source of the other majestic, fast-flowing rivers that we find all along this Brazil coast.[58] They buttress their argument by showing that the flow increases in all the rivers at the same time,[59] though the weather is calm and equable at the point on the coast where they empty into the ocean. But I have heard enough from a certain *peruleiro*,[60] an honorable and wealthy man, very well informed, to induce me not to put the Pará River (which we are considering) in the same class with the others, swelling its flow when they do.

ALVIANO   And what did the *peruleiro* tell you?

BRANDÔNIO   In the year '86 [1586] this man of whom I speak came to Pernambuco. He told me that a brother of his had to flee the city of Lima because he had gotten into some serious trouble, for which the Viceroy was making every effort to arrest him and punish him severely, in order to make an example of him. Since they were searching for him everywhere, he feared that if he went along the coast he might be found. Wishing to be free of this fear, he struck out inland with two companions who wanted to accompany him. Having walked some fifty leagues, as he calculated, he came upon the source of a stream which, judging from the appearance of its bed, he suspected would become a mighty river. Adding to this that its waters were seen to flow to the east, he thought that perhaps it discharged them on this other side, on the Brazil coast, which he was most anxious to reach. Whereupon, supplying himself with some foodstuffs, which he bartered for with the Indians who dwelt thereabouts, and obtaining from them in addition some fishhooks,[61] he and his two companions got into a canoe that they found right in the river. Always following the current downstream, with the river growing wider and deeper at every turn, they at last came to some falls. The waters hurled themselves down from a great height between large rocks. To get past these, they had to make a portage, taking the canoe out and carrying it on their backs along the river's edge until they had gotten down past the rocks. Then, farther down the river, something like one hundred and fifty leagues as they figured it, they found another waterfall, which they negotiated in the same way. From then on they traveled without meeting any other obstacles until they came to the mouth of the river we are considering, that of the Amazons. From there, it being summertime,[62] they traveled in the same canoe right up the coast to the West Indies.[63] For food they always caught lots of fish, and they carried water, storing it in calabashes.[64]

ALVIANO   If such a voyage is possible, then His Majesty[65] could save himself great expense by shipping his silver down that river.

BRANDÔNIO   That's just what the *peruleiro* claimed. He said that his brother had noted with great interest that if two settlements were established at the two waterfalls up river, not only could His Majesty send his silver {from Peru} down the river, but the merchants as well could send their goods to Peru up the same river, and spare themselves the great expense they are put to in sending them by the long route over which they carry them now.[66]

ALVIANO   But those falls which you say are in the river, wouldn't they be an obstacle to navigation?

BRANDÔNIO   It was because of them that he said that His Majesty would have to form three ship's companies: one to carry merchandise and fetch the silver and other things from the river's mouth up to the first waterfall; another that would fetch and carry the same way from the first to the second waterfall; and still another from there to the point where the river rises. Since there would be settlements at the places where the transfer of cargoes would have to be made, it would be an easy matter to get the system going.

ALVIANO   If things really are the way the *peruleiro* described them to you, I suppose not many years will go by before that shipping route is developed, and with great benefit to the traders and settlers in Peru. But now, beyond the River of the Amazons, or the Pará, what is the next settlement toward the south?

BRANDÔNIO   There comes next the Maranhão, a celebrated river that lies two degrees to the south of the equinoctial line. It was King Dom João [III] of glorious memory who commanded that this settlement be made.[67] For that purpose, he ordered the preparation of an expedition, but because of misfortunes and various disorders (after they had reached land), everything was lost without their achieving the purpose for which they had been sent.[68]

And lately, in our time, Gaspar de Sousa,[69] who was governor of this state [Brazil], received news, which he could not doubt, that the French had seized that great river and were erecting a fort [São Luís]. In the year '615 [1615], by order of His Majesty, he prepared a fleet of which Jerônimo de Albuquerque[70] was captain. Albuquerque with great good luck landed there and gave battle to the French, who were garrisoned at the fort under their governor, Monsieur de la Ravardière.[71] Albuquerque overcame and conquered them, expelling them from their fort and the river, with many of their men killed.[72] The place passed into the hands of our soldiers, and today it is settled and fortified by them and brought under the rule of His Majesty.[73] And in that way the French were deprived of a most ample harbor on that river for their trade, and of a port of refuge for the pirate ships that came out from France every year to plunder this Brazil coast.[74]

ALVIANO   You say the Maranhão country has already been settled by our people and because of that the pirates no longer have a sheltered port where they can repair their ships. Beyond that benefit to the State of Brazil, does Maranhão offer any other advantages to its inhabitants, as do the other captaincies of this state?

BRANDÔNIO   Up to now we are not sure, for it has been settled such a short time, but it gives great hopes for future progress. Our people for the present have settled on an island [São Luís] at the entrance of the harbor, about twenty leagues wide and as many long, because it is a position which can be fortified, and which in fact was fortified by the French, since from there they could block the entrance to the bay. But up the river, which is a tremendous one, much very fertile land has been found along its banks. This could be settled and many mills built to produce sugar, and a great quantity of foodstuffs might be raised. There one also finds ever so many kinds of timber, of very good quality and of a size that would astonish you. For all these reasons it seems to me there is no doubt that in the new settlement a great volume of trade can develop in the future.[75]

ALVIANO   And what do the people who are taking part in that new settlement have for food?

BRANDÔNIO   The very same foodstuffs the rest of the inhabitants of this state [Brazil] have, for they all grow there in great abundance. And—

above all—there is no end of excellent fish, which are caught with very little effort.

ALVIANO   And just how are the fish caught, without, as you say, any work?

BRANDÔNIO   At a certain time of year they send two or three canoes, or as many as they wish, to cross over the width of the river at night. They tip the canoes so that the lower side faces the flood tide. To do this, the Indians who man the canoes simply sit down[76] on the side that they are going to tip. And at other times they tip it in the same way toward the ebb tide. Riding tipped this way for the space of two hours, and without any other help, the canoes are filled with the most excellent fish, which jump right in by themselves.[77] When they have caught in this way all they need, they head back to land, where they divide the catch among all the villagers.

ALVIANO   If fishing is as easy as all that in the river, the colonists must have all the fish they desire! If they could only get meat in the same way they could say they were living in that Golden Age about which the poets spun their fables of rivers of honey and butter that issued from the earth.[78]

BRANDÔNIO   If enjoying the Golden Age consisted of that, I could tell you also that they do enjoy excellent meat all the time, which they obtain just as easily.

ALVIANO   And how is that?

BRANDÔNIO   They send some canoes up the river, and in them men trained for this job, armed with harpoons. In certain stretches, in bays that are formed by the shifting of the river, in sidewaters and lagoons extending inland, they find a great quantity of fish which they call sea cows,[79] much larger than their namesakes and of very strange shape and appearance. In these places they are all together as in a fishpond, and there the men kill them with a simple thrust of their harpoons. These fish are easily found without a search, because they swim on the surface of the water.

No matter how they are prepared, these sea cows are no different from beef. Indeed, their flesh is so similar to beef that I have seen many persons eat it for such, and afterwards, when they were told it was fish that they had eaten, they would not believe it. The sea cows, which are caught this way in great numbers, can be of use to the people of Maranhão when they are suffering a shortage of meat, though later on they will have plenty of meat because the land is most suitable for raising cattle. Furthermore, much game and many wild animals, delicious to eat and very nourishing, are found in the fields and forests.

ALVIANO   From what you tell me of Maranhão's recent settlement, I think that it will come to be a captaincy (as they call the divisions of Brazil) of great importance.[80] But, leaving it aside now, please tell me about the location and the importance of the other settlements that follow one another along the coast toward the south.

BRANDÔNIO   The next settlement, which is small both in population and in area, is Jaguaribe.[81] It lies four degrees south of the equinoctial line. Jaguaribe does not hold out much promise of future greatness, for the land round about is good only for food crops, though the coast is rich in very fine ambergris,[82] great chunks of which appear along the shore at regular times of the year. It is collected and sold to merchants and other persons, who carry it or send it to the Kingdom, where it is much prized because it is perfect and very white just as it is.

ALVIANO   If ambergris rises from the sea along there in large quantities, the wealth from it will make up for the poverty of the sterile soil, and that settlement will surely prosper.

BRANDÔNIO   In the past, before the coast was settled, the captains of Rio Grande made a great profit on the ambergris, which they had their men barter for with the heathen. But since the place is settled now and they have given this up, the three-year term of the captain of Rio Grande (which is contiguous to Jaguaribe) is of little importance.

ALVIANO   Well, tell me about that.

BRANDÔNIO   The Captaincy of Rio Grande lies six degrees south. In 1597, by order of His Majesty, it was settled and fortified by Manuel Mascarenhas Homem, who was captain major of Pernambuco, and Feliciano Coelho de Carvalho, who was captain major of Paraíba.[83]

At the entrance to the bay stands a fortress, very well supplied with soldiers paid from His Majesty's Exchequer and with artillery. Thus the French pirates[84] are prevented from coming into that port. The French used to go in there to careen their ships, take on food and water, and load up with brazilwood, which they bartered for with the natives. A captain of His Majesty lives in this captaincy, a new one being sent out every three years.

Even now, in this year of 1618,[85] there is only one sugar mill, for the land is better suited for cattle pastures, of which there are many right up to the border of the Captaincy of Paraíba, which lies next to this one.

ALVIANO   Let us take quick leave of that poor land of Rio Grande and pass on to the Captaincy of Paraíba, which I have heard praised as very fine and fertile. I have also heard that its conquest and settlement were a heavy drain on His Majesty's Treasury, and cost the colonists of Pernambuco no little labor and money.

BRANDÔNIO   The Captaincy of Paraíba is situated seven and one-half degrees south [of the equator]. Between it and the Captaincy of Itamaracá is Cabo Branco,[86] well known to mariners. This captaincy belongs to His Majesty[87] because it was settled at the expense of his Exchequer, as is likewise the case with the captaincies which lie to the north and with which we have already dealt. Because it is very fertile and produces much sugar—there are many mills[88] in its territory—Paraíba occupies the third place in greatness and wealth among the captaincies of this state. For, after the Captaincy of Pernambuco, which rightfully holds the first place of all, and after it, Bahia, to which second place is given—inasmuch as it is the capital of all the Province of Brazil, seat of the Governor General,[89] the Bishop,[90] and the High Court[91]—Paraíba, then, holds third place. From the tithes that are paid on the sugar crop, on cattle, and on manioc and other vegetable crops, every single year it renders somewhat more than twelve thousand cruzados[92] to His Majesty's Treasury.[93] And this is beyond what is paid on the great quantity of sugar produced in this captaincy[94] that enters the customhouses of the Kingdom. I have no doubt but that, if it were not right next to the Captaincy of Pernambuco, its growth would have been greater, for it began to be settled from the year 1586 on down.[95] The colonists were few and poor, but they were valiant soldiers. I remember having seen in that year the site where the city stands,[96] now full of houses of stone and mortar[97] and many churches, but then covered with forests.

ALVIANO   And what harm does the Captaincy of Pernambuco do the other by being its neighbor? It seems to me that it would be, rather, an advantage, for thanks to its proximity the settlers of Paraíba could easily supply all their needs from Pernambuco.

BRANDÔNIO   On the contrary, that is the reason that it has not prospered more. Since Pernambuco is so close by, the settlers [of Paraíba] are accustomed to supply their wants there. For this purpose they send over much of their sugar and exchange it for the articles they need.[98] Thus they continually enrich the Captaincy of Pernambuco and diminish their own. That is the reason that the ships have stopped calling, but they would come if the colonists would await their arrival and buy from them the goods they need, reserving their sugar for that purpose and having it all ready to be stowed aboard. But since the settlers have already spent their sugar to buy provisions in Pernambuco, the ships that come into their port [Filipéia][99] find no outlet for the goods they carry; still less can they take on cargo as quickly as they require. And that is the reason that very few ships come in here,[100] although the captaincy could easily lade twenty great ships every single year.

ALVIANO   His Majesty can easily put a stop to that by decreeing that no sugar shall be shipped from here to Pernambuco, and with that the damage will be checked.

BRANDÔNIO   He has so decreed,[101] but carelessness on the part of the captains, and the little forethought and less desire on the part of the local officials to enforce the decree—besides the fact that it is very easy to get a dispensation to the contrary from the governors general—upset everything, so that the only man who doesn't take his sugar to Pernambuco is the man who hasn't got any!

ALVIANO   That isn't right; since the Captaincy of Paraíba belongs to His Majesty, his vassals and ministers should work for its prosperity and not contribute in this way to the aggrandizement of the Captaincy of Pernambuco, whose proprietor is a private individual. The loss must be very great for the King's captaincy, the settlement of which has put him to such great expense.

BRANDÔNIO   Yes, it cost him a lot, with the many captains and fleets he sent out from the Kingdom to secure possession of it. There was even a contingent of Castilians who helped to garrison its fortresses—something that was never seen in any of the other conquests in this whole state.[102]

ALVIANO   And what was the reason for His Majesty's putting more capital into the conquest and settlement of this Captaincy of Paraíba than he was accustomed to invest in the others?

BRANDÔNIO   It was on account of its fine harbor, into which the French pirates used to go to repair their ships.[103] They also took on cargoes of brazilwood, which they bartered for with the Petiguar[104] heathen. With the wood, and other prizes captured along the coast, they would make the return voyage to France. This resulted in considerable damage to the whole State of Brazil, but a stop was put to it all when His Majesty took possession of the harbor and its roadstead. These

Portuguese ships attack a French vessel encountered in Brazilian waters.
Theodor de Bry, *India occidentalis* . . . (Frankfort, 1590–1634), III, 10. *Courtesy of the Edward E. Ayer Collection, The Newberry Library, Chicago.*

were energetically defended by the French pirates, who had made allies of the Petiguares. These heathen, of ferocious disposition and much given to war, ruled all the back country. To reduce them to friendship with us and turn them against the French entailed infinite trouble and expense. In order to accomplish this, our people had to send many armed expeditions deep into the interior, particularly to a range of mountains that is called Copaoba.[105] The heathen were gathered there in great numbers, since the land thereabouts was exceedingly fertile. Indeed, it has been claimed that it will produce much wheat, good wine, and other fruits of our Spain.

ALVIANO   Why do not our own people take advantage of those highlands which you say are so fertile?

BRANDÔNIO   They have not done so yet because the region is somewhat out of the way in the back country and the tribes that lived there were restless. But His Majesty has now sent orders to settle it. For that purpose, he has appointed Duarte Gomes da Silveira[106] captain major of the highlands. Even now some religious of the Order of the Patriarch St. Benedict[107] are evangelizing the Indians, reaping a rich harvest of souls. In those same mountains, according to what I, and some other people too, heard from a reliable man who is a friend of mine, there was found some time ago something so strange and curious that it astonished me.

ALVIANO   Well, do not hide from me what that man told you had been found in the mountains.

BRANDÔNIO   He gave it to me as a true story that when Feliciano Coelho de Carvalho, who was captain major of the previously mentioned captaincy,[108] was marching through those same mountains, making war on the Petiguar heathen, he found himself on the 29th day of the month of December of the year 1598 at a river called Araçuagipe. The river had gone dry; so there were only a few pools of water that the heat of summer had not yet dried up. Going down the river, some of his soldiers came upon a cave on the western bank. This was formed by three rocks standing together in such a way that fifteen men could get inside. Now this cave, on the east side, was seven to eight palms high, and on the west side thirteen to fourteen palms high.

Over all the curving face of the rocks were some outlines whose form showed that they had been made by human hands. First of all, on the highest part of the west side of this cave were fifty indented marks, which started at the bottom and ran upwards one right after the other. In size and arrangement they resembled the way Our Lady's rosary is painted in altar pieces. Where these indentations ended, the outline of a rose was formed in this manner:[109] It should be pointed out that most of the characters seen in the cave were arranged on the west side. There, to the right of the fifty indented marks, in an elbow angle formed by the rock, were found thirty-six more indentations like the others, nine of which ran lengthwise toward the top while the others ran crosswise toward the left. And above them all was another rose like the one I have drawn, and just a little bit below was another rose just like it. Next to this was a figure that looked like a dead man's skull. Next, at the left, were twelve indentations like the others, and above them, near the first fifty marks, were some figures like skulls. To the right of the elbow angle was a cross, and then, to the left, on the face of the rock, fifty indentations were arranged in six groups. And in one of these groups was a rose—not very plain, for it appeared to be worn with time—and right after this were nine more marks just like the first ones. And in the whole cave could be seen six more roselike figures.

On the rock that stood in the middle between the other two were twenty-eight signs or characters, which I shall diagram below, divided into three groups, with three more roses beside them.

The most remarkable thing of all was that one rock, which was between the other two large ones, thrust its edge out over the other two in the manner of an arch, and they were all so close together that nowhere could you wedge an arm in between them. On the lowest part of the rock in the cave appeared twelve indented marks just like those that we have shown. In the center of them was a round figure like this: ◯ , with one more rose perfectly drawn. It should be noted that all the roses were just alike, except for one that had twelve petals, counting the one in the center. And around the inside of the cave were the outlines, or characters, which I have told you about, made in the following manner:

All of these characters were sketched for me just the way I am showing them to you here.[110]

ALVIANO From a look at the marks you have shown me, I should certainly take them to be symbolic signs of things to come,[111] which we cannot understand, for I cannot believe that nature itself has carved those dots, roses, and other things without any human intervention. And since we cannot understand such mysteries, leave these tracings of them for more enlightened minds, and let us go on to the rest of what is to be said concerning the Captaincy of Paraíba.

BRANDÔNIO It is governed by a captain major appointed by His Majesty for a three-year term. At the entrance to the harbor is a fort garrisoned by soldiers,[112] paid by his Exchequer, under the command of a captain. The place is not strongly fortified, and this is the fault of the governors general, who carelessly do not give the necessary orders. The city,[113] which is up river a way,[114] is built on the bank. Although it is small, it has many houses, all of stone and mortar.[115] It is favored with three religious orders, which have convents there, namely, the Order of the Patriarch St. Benedict,[116] the religious of Our Lady of Carmel,[117] and those of the Seraphic Father St. Francis of the Province of St. Anthony,[118] who have a sumptuous convent, the best of all that belong to that order in the entire State of Brazil. In matters spiritual, this captaincy is the head of all the others in the northern zone (from Pernambuco north), for which reason the prelate bears the title of Administrator of Paraíba.[119] From its own resources, the captaincy is capable of lading twenty great ships with sugar every year.[120] On the south it borders the Captaincy of Itamaracá.

ALVIANO Well, then, tell me about it.

BRANDÔNIO The Captaincy of Itamaracá lies eight degrees south of the equinoctial line, and its proprietor, under His Majesty, is today the count of Monsanto.[121] Its settlement [Conceição], situated on an island, lies near the port and the bar to the harbor. The island is called Itamaracá, and from it the captaincy as a whole takes its name. It has much good land, throughout which are sugar mills that pay a land rent to the lord proprietor. No such payment is made by the colonists in the captaincies belonging to His Majesty.[122] These rents bring the proprietor a lot of money, along with the retithe [redízima] due to the proprietor by the terms of his grant—being a tenth part of the total amount His Majesty collects from the captaincy. Formerly the captaincy had fifty leagues of coastline, including the district of Paraíba,

Natives attack a Portuguese settlement in Itamacá. Theodor de Bry, *India occidentalis . . .* (Frankfort, 1590–1634), III, 7. *Courtesy of the Edward E. Ayer Collection, The Newberry Library, Chicago.*

which His Majesty cut off from the rest, since he had settled it at his own expense. It borders on the Captaincy of Pernambuco, and markers have been placed between the two to divide their respective territories.[123]

ALVIANO   Let us go on to the Captaincy of Pernambuco, for I am very anxious to hear about it, particularly as it is famous the world over for being great, rich, and abounding in everything.

BRANDÔNIO   The riches and bounty of this captaincy are what one would anticipate from the glowing reports of those who have seen it with their own eyes. It is a proprietary colony,[124] and at present the captain and governor of it, under His Majesty, is Duarte Coelho de Albuquerque.[125] To him go the taxes, the retithes, and other rights, which every year bring him some twenty thousand cruzados. As things stand today, the tithes, customs duties, and brazilwood bring His Majesty's Treasury close to one hundred thousand cruzados.[126] And this is in addition to the shipments of sugar that pay the regular duty at the customhouses of the Kingdom. The captaincy is situated eight and two-thirds degrees south of the equinoctial line. The chief town of the district, where all business activity is concentrated, is Olinda. The first settlers gave it this name when they caught sight of the beautiful view to be had from the hill on which it now stands and, in their enthusiasm, they exclaimed "Oh! Linda!"[127] ["Oh! Lovely!"] The town is located on an inlet from which two promontories jut out into the sea. One of them forms Cape St. Augustine,[128] so well known throughout the world; the other is called Point Jesus, after the beautiful church of the same name which the Fathers of the Company[129] built there.

The entire captaincy has fifty leagues of coastline, running from the latitude of the island of Itamaracá to the São Francisco River. Between these limits there are numberless sugar mills,[130] many farms growing all kinds of food crops, countless herds of beef cattle, goats, sheep, swine, game birds and domestic fowl, and various kinds of fruit, and all in such abundance that he who contemplates it and has the curiosity to observe it is struck with wonder.

Innumerable merchants live in the town of Olinda, and keep open shop. Their shelves are filled with costly goods of every kind, in such quantity that the place seems to be a miniature Lisbon. The entrance to the harbor could not be finer. It is defended by two forts, well armed and garrisoned.[131] Ships anchor off the near shore, absolutely secure in any weather that may come up, even the heaviest, for they are protected by enormous reefs on which the sea breaks. There are always more than thirty ships anchored there at any time of year. For every single year the captaincy exports more than one hundred and twenty shiploads of sugar, brazilwood, and cotton.[132] The town is quite large and has many good buildings and fine churches. Among these are the one belonging to the Fathers of the Company of Jesus,[133] the one of the Fathers of St. Francis of the Order of St. Anthony,[134] the monastery of the Carmelites,[135] and the monastery of St. Benedict, with religious of the order.[136] In all these monasteries are priests of great learning, letters, and virtue. A short while ago His Holiness separated the captaincies of Pernambuco, Itamaracá, Paraíba, and Rio Grande from the Bishopric of Bahia de Todos os Santos.[137] He put in charge of them Antônio Teixeira Cabral, a prelate of consummate learning and virtue, with the title of Administrator of Paraíba.[138] There is also in the town a house of retirement for gentlewomen, which is called a nunnery although as yet they have no special rule of life.[139]

The entire Captaincy of Pernambuco is able to put into the field six thousand men-at-arms, with eight hundred cavalry,[140] for all the folk of gentle birth are superb horsemen. Because of the great pride they take in this, their horses are always handsomely caparisoned.

The Fathers of the Company have public schools in which they teach reading, writing, and Latinity.[141] In the other monasteries scholars read theology and liberal arts and emerge consummate theologians.

Although the settlers have not spread out much into the bush, there are many things up country worthy of note because of their size: for instance, torrential rivers, trees of tremendous height, marshlands, and other things. I remember in '591 [1591] coming back from the pursuit of some hostile Petiguares—I went with an armed force that was giving them chase, for they had attacked and killed some white men in a stand of brazilwood—I remember coming upon a cave that the heathen called a *camucim*,[142] and it was something that made you think!

ALVIANO   Well, tell me what you saw in that cave.

BRANDÔNIO   I reached the spot at nightfall and rested there with my men, for a river of exceedingly cold water that flowed nearby made it an inviting campsite. After we had made our camp, the Indians showed the greatest fear of going near the mouth of the cave. Their fear increased and spread even to the *mamelucos*,[143] who are sons of white men. They maintained that anyone who dared to go inside the cave would die. This fear was so deeply rooted in them that I could not dispel it by telling them not to be afraid to go up to the cave. I told them that it was ridiculous and nonsensical to be worried about being killed in this way. Seeing that this had little weight with any of them, I desired to see the cause for such great fear. To satisfy my curiosity, I entered the mouth of the cave accompanied by two soldiers who wanted to go with me, each carrying a flaming torch. The bats that lived in the cave were a great obstacle, for, frightened by the light, they started to come out, and struck us hard buffets as they collided with us. We went forward just the same, walking deeper into the cave, which widened out in some places and in others grew narrow again, until we came upon a small stream, which ran underfoot, of the most frigid water. Beyond the stream the cave widened out in the form of a chamber around which (oh, wondrous thing!) were arranged countless earthen vessels. There were so many of them that I wouldn't dare to guess at their number. Inside each one was a complete skeleton of a dead man, with the skull on top.[144] It seems that the cave had served the heathen as an ancient burial place. What struck me most was that the Indians claimed—though I did not put it to the test— that many white persons had already gone into the cave and smashed some of the earthen vessels, but that when they had gone back inside the next day they found the urns sound and all in one piece and the skeletons back inside them.

ALVIANO   I would consider that a fable, although the form of the cave does sound strange to me. I would certainly like to know if there appeared to be in the neighborhood any signs of ancient settlements that might have stood there. In that case we could suppose that the skeletons had been brought from them to be entombed there in that fashion. But if there were no such signs of settlements, it would seem curious indeed that they should have been brought from a distance to be placed inside the cave.

BRANDÔNIO   All around the cave there was nothing but thick forest. Judging from the appearance and size of the trees, they must have taken root there right after the universal deluge.

ALVIANO   You have told me enough of the wonders of the Captaincy of Pernambuco, and they do not surprise me, for I have often heard a great deal of praise for it. But to get on down the coast, tell me what colony lies next to it on the south.

BRANDÔNIO   Right after it come the settlement and fort of Sergipe-del-Rei, situated at _____ degrees,[145] a wee thing whose only riches are in cattle, which are raised there in great numbers. The captaincy belongs to His Majesty and has a fort[146] with a captain and soldiers who defend the harbor against pirates, preventing them from coming in to take on water and necessary stores as they used to do before there was any fort there. It borders on the Captaincy of Bahia, the capital of this whole State of Brazil.

ALVIANO   Well, tell me about the great things of that captaincy. Since His Majesty has made it the capital of so large a state, they must be great things indeed.

BRANDÔNIO   The Captaincy of Bahia lies 13 degrees south of the equinoctial line. It is the property of His Majesty and, as such, is the
capital of the State of Brazil[147] and the seat of the Governor General,
for His Majesty commanded him to establish his official residence
there. However, this command has been openly flouted during the
last several years, for the governors prefer to live in the Captaincy of
Pernambuco, either because they get more profit out of it or because
there they are closer to the Kingdom—I can't say which is the reason.[148]

Bahia is also the seat of the Bishop [of Brazil],[149] who attends sacred
functions in his cathedral, with his canons, clergy, and other dignitaries, all paid by His Majesty's Exchequer from the income of the
tithes. Likewise, in the city, which bears the name of Bahia de Todos
os Santos [Bay of All Saints], sits the High Court,[150] with many judges:
the Chancellor, the judge for cases involving the interests of Crown
and Exchequer, the Secretary of the Exchequer, and the Superintendent
of Probate and Intestacy. These officials hear all lawsuits in Brazil
involving personal property up to the value of three thousand cruzados.
If more than that amount is involved, the case goes to the High Court
in Lisbon. The salaries of all these judges and other officers of the
Court in Bahia are paid by His Majesty's Treasury.

ALVIANO   I have heard it said by many men experienced in Brazilian
affairs that the High Court that sits in the City of Bahia does more
harm to the state than good to its citizens.[151]

BRANDÔNIO   The truth is that the High Court in Bahia might very well
be done away with. I have always been of that opinion, and many
times I said as much to the Bishop of Coimbra, Dom Afonso de
Castelbranco, when he was a governor of Portugal.[152] That court is a
great drain on His Majesty's Treasury, and the money spent on it
might well be reserved for other things more useful to his service.
The presence of the Court in Brazil has not had the effect that was
anticipated. The error in judgment arose because the inhabitants of
the whole state were aggrieved and harassed by the arbitrary procedures
of the superior crown magistrate [ouvidor-geral], who—before the Court
was established—had the administration of justice in his hands. The
colonists petitioned His Majesty to free them from so great a burden,
beseeching him to send a High Court out to Brazil, which should sit
in Bahia de Todos os Santos, just as a like court sat in the State of
India, in the city of Goa. They were ill advised to do so, for they
might have improved the quality of justice in a better way.[153] Because

they did not consider well of the matter at that time, they now find themselves exposed to the present harm.

ALVIANO   I should like to know how the High Court in Bahia harms the inhabitants of the state, for I believe that, if His Majesty understood that it was of no benefit to them, he would spare himself the expenditure of all the money that he disburses to maintain it.

BRANDÔNIO   The harm is this: all the inhabitants of this state are bound by ties of blood or friendship to everybody else in the captaincies where they live. They rarely press their suits to the point of being obliged to have recourse to the High Court in Bahia; before that happens, friends and relatives intervene to patch up matters and put an end to the lawsuits. Hence few of them are appealed to Bahia. If those cases that are taken there had been appealed to the Kingdom instead, it would be far better for all the inhabitants of Brazil. For it has been my experience, not once but many times, to send some papers to be handled in Bahia and at the same time to send others like them to be processed in the Kingdom, and the papers sent to the Kingdom came back long before the others returned from Bahia. Since all navigation along this coastline depends on the monsoons,[154] the dispatch of business is greatly delayed by a contrary wind. Furthermore, there is no colonist in this whole state so forsaken that he does not have some relative or friend in the Kingdom to whom he can send his papers to be taken into court. And if he sends a chest of sugar[155] along with the papers, that is sufficient to meet the expenses involved. This is not the case with Bahia, for not everyone has relatives or friends there. When these are lacking, then people must of necessity follow up their own affairs in person. For the cost of their daily keep they must take cash with them, and this is hard to accumulate in Brazil. As I have said, this is not the case with papers that are sent to the Kingdom, for they can be entrusted to relatives or friends, and a chest of sugar sent along to meet expenses. In my opinion it would have been better if His Majesty (so far as this matter of justice is concerned) had adopted another, more beneficial, means, which would have redounded to the common good of the state.

ALVIANO   And what might His Majesty have done instead?

BRANDÔNIO   Withdrawing and completely abolishing the High Court in Bahia, he could in its place create in this state three magistrates with judicial districts like those in the Kingdom and with the same jurisdiction. And if their jurisdiction were broadened somewhat, it would not be a bad idea. They ought to send one of these magistrates to serve in Paraíba, for it is a royal city [captaincy]. This magistrate would have competence in all judicial processes appealed to him from the justices and judges of the Captaincy of Pernambuco and its districts, of the Captaincy of Itamaracá, of the Captaincy of Paraíba itself, of the Captaincy of Rio Grande, and of the towns in Maranhão and Pará, so long as His Majesty made no other provision concerning them.

The second of the three magistrates should sit in the City of Bahia de Todos os Santos, hearing cases appealed to him from the justices and judges of Sergipe-del-Rei, of Bahia itself, and of the captaincies of Boipeva, Ilhéus, and Porto Seguro, and their environs.

The third magistrate should sit in Rio de Janeiro and in like manner have competence in all cases appealed to him from the justices and judges of the Captaincy of Espírito Santo, of Rio de Janeiro itself, of the Captaincy of São Vicente, and of the town of São Paulo[156] and its environs. And when, because of the sums involved, the cases escape the jurisdiction of these magistrates, recourse should be available to the High Court in Lisbon. It should be stated expressly in the instructions to each magistrate that he could enter the captaincies within his jurisdiction only for the administration of justice, and that he could remain in them for only thirty days, after which time he need not be obeyed. By such means, an end could be put to the great damage that would result otherwise, and the settlers of this state would be relieved of the heavy burdens that they now bear.

ALVIANO   I should like to know what their difficulties are.

BRANDÔNIO   They are many and serious. If a person is indicted on any charge, no matter how trivial, he must hie himself to Bahia for a letter of safe-conduct.[157] Since only there can that be granted, it is a great nuisance and costs him ever so much time and money—and until he secures it he is a fugitive from justice.

Moreover, any case that is appealed from a lower court must be taken to Bahia, with great inconvenience and expense for the appellant. During the interval of the appeal, the Court goes right on with the case, which is very prejudicial to the litigants. This would not be the case if they had a magistrate nearby. Since the captaincies that would be within a magistrate's jurisdiction lie close together, appeals to that magistrate could be made quickly and without much expense.

But I don't know how we got started on this and strayed so far from the subject of our conversation, for we are discussing matters beyond our power to remedy!

ALVIANO Do not regret having discussed them, for it yet can happen that our conversation may come to the hands[158] of someone who will make it known to the gentlemen of His Majesty's Council[159] so that they may employ the proper remedy.[160]

BRANDÔNIO God grant that it may be so! Leaving that matter aside, I shall go on to discuss the other great things of Bahia de Todos os Santos.[161]

Its port is on a vast bay well able to hold any number of ships, even those of the greatest draft. Because it is so big, many whales seek shelter in it. A colony of Basques, who live nearby, wreak a fearful slaughter of these whales to get their oil.[162] They process a great quantity of it, and it is taken to the other captaincies in this state to be sold.

Many islands lie in this great, broad bay, into which—amidst inlets and marshlands—a number of rivers empty. On the banks of these rivers, all around the great bay, are many mills for making sugar.[163] Their cane and firewood are transported in large boats, for most of these mills, or almost all of them, are approached by water, which greatly facilitates everything connected with sugar making.

The city is situated on a hill of medium height and is protected by three forts built on sites well adapted for its defense.[164] It has its cathedral, with dignitaries, clergy, and canons, where the Bishop lives. There are four more religious houses, namely, those of the Fathers of the Company of Jesus,[165] of the Order of St. Benedict,[166] of the Carmelites,[167] and of the Franciscans of the Province of St. Anthony.[168]

The income from the tithes of this captaincy amounts to about sixty thousand cruzados every year for His Majesty. The settlers are of aristocratic stock and are wealthy people. Its territory begins at the São Francisco River and extends to the Captaincy of Ilhéus.

ALVIANO Let us go on to consider the other captaincies and settlements.

BRANDÔNIO The first settlement on the coast beyond the captaincy [of Bahia] is Boipeva.[169] It has very little trade. Its owner is also the owner of Ilhéus, Francisco de Sá de Menezes, who is lord proprietor of both of them, under His Majesty.

ALVIANO Well, tell me about Ilhéus.

BRANDÔNIO The Captaincy of Ilhéus is situated 14 degrees south of the equinoctial line. At present it is of little account and produces a scanty income, though its land is most fertile and many sugar mills might be established there. But frequent attacks by the heathen, who are called Aimorés,[170] prevent that and do great harm to the settlers. Yet there is hope of its turning out well in the future because of its good location and the quality of its soil.

ALVIANO   I have heard that said—and most emphatically—by many people who boasted to me of its fertile lands. But, since there is nothing more to be said of this captaincy, let us go on to that of Porto Seguro, which adjoins it.

BRANDÔNIO   The Captaincy of Porto Seguro[171] is situated _____ degrees south of the equinoctial line.[172] It belongs to the duke of Aveiro, who is proprietor of it under His Majesty. It has only a few sugar mills, and therefore His Majesty collects only a small income from its tithes. For the same reason, the lord proprietor receives little from the retithes and land rents. And this because the same Aimoré tribes, which I told you plagued the Captaincy of Ilhéus, do great damage here too. Thus it does not grow as it might, despite having most fertile soil and plenty of room for development. It comes to an end at the border of the Captaincy of Espírito Santo.[173]

ALVIANO   Now tell me about that captaincy.

BRANDÔNIO   The Captaincy of Espírito Santo is situated 20 degrees south of the equinoctial line. It is a proprietary colony, and at present Francisco de Aguiar Coutinho holds the title of captain of it, under His Majesty.[174] It has a few sugar mills. Its territory is extensive and abounds in foodstuffs and balsam.[175] This latter the inhabitants make into beads and other trinkets that they send to Spain, where they are greatly valued for their pleasant aroma.

It was from this captaincy that Marcos de Azeredo[176] set out to discover the emerald mines that were rumored to exist in the back country. As a matter of fact he did find them, and brought back a great quantity of stones which at first were judged perfect, but later were found to lack many of the qualities of true emeralds.

ALVIANO   It was bad luck for that explorer that the first valuation of the stones proved incorrect, for otherwise they would have been a great treasure for him. But now let us go on, running down the rest of the coast, for I already know that the Captaincy of Espírito Santo also has monasteries of religious that do it honor.

BRANDÔNIO   South of the Captaincy of Espírito Santo is that of Rio de Janeiro.[177] It was given that name because it was discovered on New

Year's Day; and it lies at 23 degrees south latitude. It belongs to His Majesty, and has a gallant fortress[178] well supplied with artillery, munitions, and soldiers, and a captain who is appointed by him every three years. It has a city, small but well situated, which at present does a good trade because many ships come there from the Rio de la Plata. They bring lots of *patacas*[179] to pay for the goods which they buy and which they carry back on their return voyage. Great quantities of manioc flour are produced in all parts of this captaincy, and ships coming out from the Kingdom put in at Rio de Janeiro to take on cargoes of it, which they carry to Angola, where it is sold at a high price.

The captaincy has several mills for producing sugar. For some years now it has been a capital and the seat of a governor, for when Dom Diogo de Menezes was governor of Brazil,[180] His Majesty detached three captaincies from the jurisdiction of the governor general at Bahia—namely, Espírito Santo, Rio de Janeiro, and São Vicente— and incorporated them into a new government. Of this he made Dom Francisco de Souza[181] governor, charging him to discover the gold deposits of São Vicente. Dom Francisco was promised the title of marquess if he should discover them. But with his death those high hopes came to naught.

There also lives in Rio de Janeiro an administrator who has charge of religious matters in that captaincy and in those of Espírito Santo and São Vicente. He is exempt from the jurisdiction of the Bishop,[182] who may take cognizance only of those cases that are appealed to him. Like the other captaincies, Rio de Janeiro also has monasteries of religious, which lend it great honor.

ALVIANO From what you have now told me, I am well informed on this Captaincy of Rio de Janeiro. Therefore we can pass on to the Captaincy of São Vicente, which I gather is the one that lies next to it.

BRANDÔNIO The Captaincy of São Vicente is the last of our settlements along this great Brazil coast.[183] It is situated 24 degrees to the south of the equinoctial line. It is a proprietary colony, and the captain and governor of it, by royal grant, was Lopo de Souza, and on his death Dom Francisco de Faro succeeded him.[184] It has two towns, one lying along the harbor, which is named São Vicente, and another up-country, called São Paulo. Little sugar is produced in this captaincy, but it abounds in meat and many fruits of our Spain, which are easily grown there, especially quinces. From these much marmalade is made, which is shipped all over the State of Brazil. Nowadays, with the gold mines that have been discovered in it, this captaincy is growing. And it would grow much more than it already has done if our Portuguese who settled there were more interested in mining than they are. For I have seen a gold nugget taken from its mines, just as nature made it, which weighed out at seven milreis.[185]

ALVIANO   The mine that creates so large a nugget cannot be a poor one, even though it is a placer, as those mines are. And that being the case, I cannot see what reason there is for not exploiting them.

BRANDÔNIO   The poverty of the settlers who live in the captaincy, and their being but little inclined to hard work, are the reasons more gold is not taken from the mines.[186] The men who could work the mines, by importing a stock of slaves and other necessary things, will not trouble to do so. And for this reason the mines are almost deserted. But it is my opinion that another reason for this is that they began where they ought to have finished. The first thing that should have been done, before fiddling around with the mines (once they were certain of their value), is to plant food crops all around the place where the mines are.[187] Afterwards, when they had an ample supply of food, they should have started to work the mines. But just the opposite was done, for, without any food supplies on hand, they thought only of extracting the gold. But as the mines lie far in the interior, those who go out to them have to lug along[188] the food that they require, and, when it is consumed, they have to turn back and leave the works that they started. And this is, I think, the true reason that the mines produce so little gold.

ALVIANO   Well, it is my opinion that those mines will come to be of great importance in the future.[189] And since we have now reached the southernmost captaincy of those settled by the Portuguese, tell me what is the length of coastline of all these settlements that you have discussed.

BRANDÔNIO   From Pará, or River of the Amazons, which is situated on the equinoctial line, to the Captaincy of São Vicente, there are almost seven hundred leagues {about 2,400 miles} of coastline, or, in a straight line from north to south, four hundred and twenty leagues {about 1,450 miles}, far more than enough land to hold great kingdoms and empires. In some places the coastline runs from north to south; in other places from northwest to southeast, or from east to west. And what is most astonishing is to see that all of this vast coast, inland as well as near the ocean, has the most beneficent heavens and a temperate climate, rendering it most salubrious and well suited to the preservation of humankind.

ALVIANO   Now on this I should think just the contrary; for, unless the ancients were mistaken, the greater part of the Brazil coast lies within the torrid zone, which was judged uninhabitable because it was so hot. Because of that same fact, the inhabitants of the Guinea Coast and of the other coasts that lie opposite Brazil have a bad climate, which is the cause of much sickness there. Now if that be true, I do not see how those who live in Brazil, being within the same parallel and underneath the same zenith, can enjoy a good climate and kindly heavens when all that is lacking on the opposite coast.

BRANDÔNIO   It is already growing late, and the question that you raise is difficult to answer. Thus it seems to me a good idea to reserve our discussion of it until tomorrow. I shall be waiting for you in this same place so that we can consider the subject, which is indeed a curious one.

ALVIANO   So be it; and I shall take care to be on time.

Notes to Dialogue I

1 · In the Lisbon manuscript the first dialogue has only the numerical designation. It is the only dialogue in that manuscript that lacks a descriptive title. The Leyden MS has no titles for any of the dialogues.

2 · Brandônio tells us later (p. 206) that the fluff comes from the *mungubeira* [*munguba*], a silk-cotton tree. It consists of silky grayish-yellow fibers that grow around the seeds. As Brandônio surmises, the fibers are excellent for stuffing pillows and mattresses and for use in the manufacture of [felt] hats. The material was not commercially exploited at this time in Brazil as it was in the East Indies. Rodolfo Garcia, ed., *Diálogos das grandezas do Brasil*, I, n. I.

3 · China is credited with the invention of paper making about the first century A.D., but the art did not reach Europe until the twelfth century, when the Moors brought it to Spain. By the second half of the fourteenth century paper was used throughout western Europe, and in the following century it gradually replaced vellum for manuscripts. Its general use was still recent enough to make Brandônio think of paper as a modern invention.

4 · The invention of gunpowder is lost in the mists of antiquity; it has been

claimed by the Chinese, Hindus, Greeks, Arabs, English, and Germans. After guns were invented, in the fourteenth century, gunpowder became more important, and in the following century great improvements were made in its manufacture. Perhaps it was these last two facts that caused Brandônio to list gunpowder among recent inventions.

5 · One may speculate whether Alviano's remark reflects the uneasiness of a New Christian (or a crypto-Jew), haunted by the fear of sudden persecution. New Christians from the Iberian Peninsula were at this time scattered in great numbers along the coast of Brazil. Many of them traded in precious stones with Venice, Turkey, and other places, and their operations must have been well known to Brandão. It is to be remembered, too, that Brandão had twice been denounced to the Inquisition. M[eyer] Kayserling, *Christopher Columbus and the Participation of the Jews in the Spanish and Portuguese Discoveries,* p. 129.

6 · Traditions about the supposed magical properties of precious stones existed since classical antiquity and were widely current throughout the Middle Ages. One of many superstitions attached to the emerald was that wearing this gem made a woman more discreet and chaste. Another was that it revealed adultery by shattering spontaneously, as Brandônio notes. Though such beliefs were still current in Brandão's time, some skepticism had developed with respect to them; see Garcia d'Orta, *Colóquios dos simples e drogas da Índia* (1891–1895), 2:206–213, n. 1.

7 · "West Indies" was a term of varying meaning in Brandão's day, but our author apparently reserves it for the Spanish as distinct from the Portuguese possessions in the New World. He never clearly uses "West Indies" to designate Brazil or any part of it; rather, that country is "this Brazil" or "the Brazil coast." Alviano in his next speech plainly distinguishes between "those Indies" [of the Castilians] and "this Brazil of ours."

The emerald deposits "discovered in the West Indies" were those found in 1564 in present-day Colombia, the city of Musó being the center of the mining activity. "Such a great quantity of emeralds was extracted up to the first quarter of the 17th century that just the [royal] fifth brought the royal Treasury more than 300 thousand pesos," says Rafael Antonio Domínguez, *Historia de las esmeraldas de Colombia;* see pp. 32–38.

8 · About 1614 Marcos de Azeredo found what he took to be emeralds in the mountains of the Captaincy of Espírito Santo, now called the Emerald Mountains [*Serra das Esmeraldas*]. Specimens were sent to the King, whose lapidaries examined them and reported that the gems were from the surface and had been scorched by the sun. If Azeredo dug deeper, they said, he would find first-quality emeralds. Accordingly, the King financed

an expedition by Azeredo for this purpose, promising that, if he should succeed in his effort, he would be rewarded by membership in the Order of Christ [*Ordem de Cristo*], the prestigious Portuguese military order of knighthood. But no emeralds were found. Vicente do Salvador, *História do Brasil, 1500–1627*, pp. 65–66. The known facts about Azeredo are amply detailed by Manoel Cardozo, "Marcos de Azeredo, descobridor de esmeraldas," *Revista do Instituto Histórico e Geográfico Brasileiro* 212 (Jul.–Sept. 1951):47–55.

9 · The first settlers came in 1532—nearly 100 years before Brandão wrote. They were brought over by Martim Afonso de Sousa for the express purpose of establishing farms, towns, and plantations in Brazil.

10 · The search for gold and other riches was a principal or even the only goal of most of the earliest explorations in the New World. Peru had yielded to the Spaniards a fabulous treasure in gold and silver, and the Portuguese hoped that Brazil would quickly prove to be an equally rich source of precious metals. Indeed, it was held that Brazil should be even richer in mineral deposits than Peru, partly because it was believed, as Alviano indicates, that the eastern regions of the world were by nature richer than the West in precious minerals, and partly because Brazil was thought to be much nearer to the mines of Peru than was actually the case, the width of the continent being vastly underestimated. See Vicente do Salvador, *História do Brasil*, p. 65; Giovanni Pico della Mirandola, *De astrologia disputationum* lib. 12, in *Opera Omnia*, 2, fols. 482–483; Sérgio Buarque de Holanda, *Visão do paraíso; os motivos edênicos no descobrimento e colonização do Brasil*, p. 108. Though gold had been found from early times in small amounts in the district around São Paulo, it was not until the end of the seventeenth century and the early years of the eighteenth that rich sources of precious metals and precious stones were discovered in Brazil. See below, n. 189.

11 · Brandônio is roughly defining the boundaries of the Viceroyalty of Peru. Cartagena is in the northern part of present-day Colombia. The estuary known as the Rio de la Plata (Brandônio uses the Portuguese form of the name, Rio da Prata) meets the Atlantic Ocean at Buenos Aires.

12 · A league was originally the distance that an average ship would sail in an hour under average conditions. With such a vague definition, it is not surprising that the notion of a league varied greatly. Usually, it was about 3 modern nautical miles, or 3.45 standard miles. John Horace Parry, *The Age of Reconnaissance*, p. 88.

13 · Campos Moreno (1612) declared that the whites lived along the coast rather as guests than as settlers. Vicente do Salvador (1627), in a famous passage, called the Brazilians "crabs" because they clung to the coast and only reluctantly moved into the interior of their country. It was explained,

reasonably enough, that the presence of hostile Indians prevented settlements in the backlands and that the colonists needed to live near the coast in order to facilitate overseas trade and to maintain easy communications with the Kingdom. Diogo de Campos Moreno, *Livro que dá razão do Estado do Brasil—1612*, p. 114; Vicente do Salvador, *História do Brasil*, p. 61; Pero de Magalhães de Gandavo, Prologue to *Treatise on the Land of Brazil*, in his *Histories of Brazil*, 2:129–130. The Brazilian reluctance to live in the interior has not wholly disappeared even today: it was in part to promote the settlement of the back country that Brazil's new capital, Brasilia, was built in 1960 in Goiás, 575 miles from the Atlantic coast.

14 · Cf. the famous statement of Diogo de Menezes, governor general of Brazil, in a letter written in 1609 from Salvador to King Philip III of Spain (II of Portugal): "Your Majesty may believe me when I say that the true mines of Brazil are sugar and brazilwood of which Your Majesty has such great profit without its costing his treasury a single penny." "Correspondência do governador D. Diogo de Meneses 1608–1612," *Anais da Biblioteca Nacional [do Rio de Janeiro]* 57 (1935):54.

Brandônio will state his arguments for the high profitability of sugar on pp. 132–146. An equally favorable case will be presented for brazilwood on pp. 150–152.

15 · The Portuguese conquests in the Orient were indeed numerous, but they were widely dispersed. See III, n. 62.

16 · Hernán Cortés's soldiers took the Aztec emperor, Moctezuma, prisoner in his own palace in Tenochtitlán, and for some time thereafter the Spaniards ruled the city through the captive monarch. Similarly, Francisco Pizarro governed the Incas in the name of their captured king, Atahualpa. Probably both Cortés and Pizarro are to be included in Brandônio's group of four heroes, but the other two could be any of a number of famous conquistadors, for instance Vasco Núñez de Balboa and Pedro de Alvarado.

That the American Indians were spiritless was a common assumption of Brandão's time. Modern historians think the assumption is not justified, and hold that the Indians were defeated principally by horses and guns, advanced military tactics, and certain psychological advantages enjoyed by the invaders. Alberto Mario Salas, *Las armas de la Conquista,* pp. 12–17, 417–418. Another force weakening the natives was the recurrent epidemics, smallpox being one of the principal offenders. "Most historians now agree that introduced disease was the major killer of New World Indians. . . . Single epidemics reduced villages by half or more, and the people of many tribes were completely wiped out in a few decades." William M. Denevan, ed., *The Native Population of the Americas in 1492*, pp. 4–5. See Daniel E. Shea, "A Defense of Small Population Estimates for the Central Andes in 1520," in ibid., pp. 157–180.

17 · Cf. Diogo do Couto (1612), who marvels that the Portuguese conquered great kingdoms in Asia with forces little practiced in war, and with many of their recruits taken from Portuguese prisons. *O soldado prático*, p. 234. Both Diogo do Couto and Brandônio appear to have had a higher opinion of Oriental military power than was justified by the facts. The Portuguese possessed a distinct naval and military superiority, based on their technical knowledge of navigation and on fifty years of experience along the coast of Africa. "Non-European countries never succeeded in filling the vast technological gap that separated them from Europe," says Carlo M. Cipolla, *Guns and Sails in the Early Phase of European Expansion, 1400–1700*, p. 129. Cf. Marie Antoinette Petronella Meilink-Roelofsz, *Asian Trade and European Influence in the Indonesian Archipelago Between 1500 and About 1630*, pp. 118–124.

Cipolla admits, however, that the European rate of fire "could be easily overcome by masses of people. This was a serious drawback, especially overseas where the Europeans were few and their opponents were many." Cipolla, op. cit., p. 138.

18 · Brandão is no doubt thinking of the Madeiras and the Azores, discovered ca. 1419 and ca. 1439 respectively.

19 · Diogo Cão discovered the Congo (Zaire) River in 1483. At the King's wish, Cão made friends with the inhabitants of the region, who welcomed the Portuguese and Christianity and helped the traders to secure slaves. As a result, in the sixteenth century the Congo became a prime source of slave labor for New World plantations. Cão also sailed the entire coast of Angola. At that time the Portuguese had little interest in this area because of its sparse population, but when at the end of the century the number of slaves available from the Congo decreased, Luanda, the capital of Angola, became the focal point of the South African slave trade. To supervise this trade, royal government was established in Luanda in 1592. James Duffy, *Portugal in Africa*, pp. 37–51; Charles E. Nowell, *A History of Portugal*, pp. 53–55; Bailey W. Diffie and George D. Winus, *Foundations of the Portuguese Empire, 1415–1580*, pp. 154–156.

20 · The Cape Verde Islands are situated 300 miles from the mainland of Africa, off the coast between Senegal and Sierra Leone. They were discovered in 1457 by Alvise da Cadamosto, a Venetian sailing for Prince Henry of Portugal. The islands became a base for export of slaves from the Guinea Coast to the New World. Charles E. Nowell, *The Great Discoveries and the First Colonial Empires*, p. 30.

21 · The island of São Tomé, in the Bight of Biafra, was discovered in 1471 by João de Santarem and Pero Escobar. It became the major slave entrepôt

between Guinea and the Congo on the one hand and the New World on the other, and was also an important sugar-producing area. Duffy, *Portugal in Africa*, p. 35; Nowell, *History of Portugal*, p. 47.

22 · In early Greek legend, Jason was accompanied on his quest of the Golden Fleece by warriors of his own locality who were little known elsewhere. But as the story spread and developed throughout Greece, almost all the great heroes of classical tradition came to be included in the crew of the Argo, and among these Hercules was one of the most commonly mentioned. It is to be noted, however, that Brandônio does not actually say Hercules was an Argonaut: he merely sets Hercules alongside these mythological figures. Brandão was certainly familiar with the legendary attributes of Hercules, for on p. 148 he makes Alviano refer to the hero's traditional club.

23 · The Canary Islands were known to the classical world but were virtually forgotten during the Middle Ages. The Portuguese rediscovered them under Afonso IV (1325–1357) and thus established a claim to their ownership, but in 1402 the Castilians began to conquer and occupy the islands. After vain efforts to maintain their ancient claim, the Portuguese were forced to abandon the islands to Spain. Nowell, *History of Portugal*, pp. 14, 32, 34.

24 · For indigo see III, n. 9, and pp. 208–209. Cochineal is a red dye made from the dried bodies of female cochineal insects. Throughout the colonial period Mexico enjoyed a natural monopoly of the product. Dauril Alden, *Royal Government in Colonial Brazil*, p. 376.

25 · Alviano's view was a common though not a universal one. "The whole land of Brazil has no more than two or three handbreadths of good land," said the "Summário das armadas que se fizeram e guerras que se deram na conquista do rio Parahyba . . . ," *Revista do Instituto Histórico e Geográfico Brasileiro*, tomo 36 (1873), pt. 1 (Jan.–Mar.):10.

Many of the disparaging voices were those of foreign travelers in Brazil. "It is an unprofitable land," declared a Frenchman in 1610, "and does not produce enough to maintain the Portuguese, who import all kinds of food from Portugal, the Azores, and the Canary Islands. . . . This Brazil is so poor a country that it would be impossible to live there for long if it were not for the trade in sugar and wood. . . . The Portuguese admit that . . . the land [is] too full of hardship and toil for men who like to have their tables spread for them." François Pyrard de Laval, *Voyage de François Pyrard, de Laval*, pt. 2, pp. 331–333.

Thus Alviano takes up his role as a spokesman for those Europeans who denigrated the New World and all its products and peoples. His criticisms open the way for Brandônio to undertake the defense of his adopted land—a topic that quickly emerges as the principal theme of the *Dialogues*. The two interlocutors thus reflect two conflicting attitudes toward Brazil that were current before, during, and after colonial times. See Introduction, p. 11. In fairness it should be said that from time to time Brandônio mentions some of the drawbacks of the new land as well as its advantages, though he usually plays the former down as much as possible.

26 · In common with most of the other chronicles, the *Dialogues* frequently praise the "good airs" and other climatic advantages of Brazil as well as its auspicious skies. See pp. 25, 104, and many other passages. "Good air" was generally regarded as one of the principal elements of a healthful climate. "If the air is corrupt," says Acosta, "it kills in a short time; if it is healthful, it restores the forces; finally we can say that it is the whole life of man. . . . If the air and the sky are healthful, pleasant, and tranquil, even if there is no other wealth it gives contentment and pleasure." Joseph [José] de Acosta, *Historia natural y moral delas Indias,* bk. 2, p. 114.

27 · Brandônio's tribute to Brazil is reminiscent of Caminha's words in his famous letter of 1500 to King Manuel of Portugal announcing the discovery of the country: ". . . The land has such good air, as cool and temperate as that of Entre Douro e Minho. . . . And it is so well favored that if anyone wishes to profit from it, everything will grow in it because of its waters." Pero Vaz de Caminha, *A carta de Pero Vaz de Caminha,* ed. Jaime Cortesão, fol. 13ᵛ. Caminha's sentiment echoed for 400 years in almost every description of Brazil.

Neither Brandônio's nor Alviano's view of Brazil presents a complete picture. The lush fertility that enraptured Brandônio did exist, but only in favored areas, such as the sugar-growing regions of Pernambuco and Bahia. In other places, after the tropical jungle had been cleared away the soil was left without needed chemical elements, especially calcium, so that food plants would not grow. Then, there were the insects, especially the ever-present ants; there were fevers and tropical diseases, long-continued droughts along with excessive rains and floods, poor soil in some parts, cannibal tribes, *quilombos* [forest settlements of runaway African slaves], corrupt and inefficient courts, and heavy imposts on prime exports and imports. Nevertheless, as Boxer concludes after reviewing the evidence, "Brazil was still a land of genuine opportunity, not only for the hardy, the lucky, or the unscrupulous." Charles R. Boxer, *The Golden Age of Brazil, 1695–1750,* pp. 13–14.

28 · Brandônio here introduces one of his favorite themes—the settlers' neglect of the opportunities offered by their land. Cf., among many other passages, pp. 48, 199, 203, 204, 205, 211, 212, 220, 265, and 305. This

was a common criticism among the chroniclers. For example, Father Anchieta observed: "The land is slack and remiss and somewhat depressing, and for this reason the slaves and the Indians work little and the Portuguese almost not at all, and the whole time is passed in festivals, banquets, and songs, and some are very fond of wine. . . . The feasts that are given in this land, besides being frequent and common, are very costly, and at these feasts they indulge in many excesses of exotic food." Joseph [José] de Anchieta, *Cartas, informações, fragmentos históricos e sermões* (1554–1594), p. 425. Cf. Vicente do Salvador, *História do Brasil,* p. 61, and Magalhães de Gandavo, Prologue, *Treatise,* p. 129.

29 · Brandônio's classification includes only the white population: he provides no categories for the Indians, who were mainly hunters and fishermen, or for the blacks, who as slaves were engaged in domestic and field labor or in the manufacture of sugar. This exclusiveness, of course, reflects the universal prejudices of his day.

30 · Carracks [*naus* or great ships] were merchant vessels of the largest size, 600 tons on the average, though some ran as large as 1,600 or even 2,000 tons. (It should be noted that the shipping ton is a measure of capacity, not weight. The term is imprecise, varying from place to place; roughly, it is the space available for a cargo of about 60 cubic feet. Hence a carrack of 2,000 tons could hold about 120,000 cubic feet of cargo.) On the average, the Portuguese carrack could carry some 7,600 quintals of spices. (A quintal is equal to about 132 pounds.) Braudel quotes a traveler who saw in 1604 a carrack of 1,500 tons under construction in Lisbon. "The amount of wood which goes to make one," he said, "is quite incredible: A forest of many leagues would not suffice for two. Three hundred men working on a single ship can hardly finish it in a year. . . . It requires a crew of 900 men." Pyrard de Laval says the carrack usually had a crew of from 1,000 to 1,200, or at least 800 to 900; he gives an illuminating account of life on board such a vessel in the seventeenth century. Carracks were used mainly for the India trade, many of them following a three-cornered route between Lisbon, India, and Brazil.

Caravels were smaller vessels (sixty to seventy tons), which because of their easy maneuverability were well suited to African and trans-Atlantic trade and to coastwise trade in Brazil. Thus Brandônio will recommend that a caravel run along the Brazilian coast and deliver pepper to the settlers (p. 139).

Fernand Braudel, *La Méditerranée et le monde méditerranéen à l'époque de Philippe II,* 1:277; Pyrard de Laval, *Voyage,* pt. 2, pp. 196–209; Jean Baptiste Labat, *Nouveau voyage aux isles de l'Amérique,* 1:chap. 2; Charles R. Boxer, "Admiral João Pereira Corte-Real and the Construction of Portuguese East-Indiamen in the Early 17th Century," *Mariner's Mirror*

26 (1940):388–406; Vitorino Magalhães Godinho, *Os descobrimentos e a economia mundial*, 2:79; Niels Steensgaard, *Carracks, Caravans, and Companies: The Structural Crisis in the European-Asian Trade in the Early 17th Century*, p. 165; Frédéric Mauro, *Le Portugal et l'Atlantique au XVIIᵉ siècle (1570–1670)*, pp. 71–87.

31 · "The Kingdom" is one of Brandônio's customary designations for Portugal.

32 · Brandônio may have given the mechanical workers of Brazil somewhat less than their due. The craftsmen already made up a conspicuous segment of Brazilian society, and the trade guilds filled an important role. For example, when in 1614 the Jesuits in Pernambuco founded a congregation of workers—the Brotherhood of Our Lady of Peace [*Confraria de Nossa Senhora da Paz*]—"many principal citizens" applied for membership, including wealthy sugar mill owners. But the applications of these industrialists were refused on the ground that the society was only for workmen. The worthy burgesses retorted that they *were* workmen, since they ran mills! Ironically enough, these same sugar barons had on other occasions cited their status as mill owners for the purpose of making themselves appear more aristocratic—and with good reason, since "such people are, for the most part, the great men of Brazil." *Artes e ofícios dos Jesuitas no Brasil (1549–1760)*, Lisbon, 1953, cited by Serafim Leite, *Suma histórica da Companhia de Jesus no Brasil 1549–1760*, pp. 134–135. Cf. J. F. de Almeida Prado, *Pernambuco e as capitanias do norte do Brasil (1530–1630)*, 4:65. Boxer points out, however, that the trade guilds in Brazil during the colonial period never equaled those of Peru in status, perhaps partly because the Brazilian economy was so heavily dependent on slave labor. Charles R. Boxer, *Salvador de Sá and the Struggle for Brazil and Angola, 1602–1686*, p. 15.

33 · That is, skilled laborers.

34 · Brandônio will explain on pp. 144–145 the status of the planters who were not mill owners.

35 · The author commonly refers to all African slaves in Brazil as Guinea slaves, or as people from Guinea, as in this passage and on pp. 91 and 306. The same is true of his contemporary, Diogo de Campos Moreno; see *Livro que dá razão do Estado do Brasil—1612*, p. 112 and n. 22. "The terms used to describe Africans in contemporary sources and subsequent scholarship are frequently so general as to be meaningless as a basis for comparison," notes *The Cambridge History of Africa* (4:616), citing as one example the use of "Guinean" in the general sense of "African." Probably this loose usage simply reflects the fact that the blacks captured in various parts of Africa were collected at ports on the Guinea Coast and from there shipped to Brazil. See also João Lúcio d'Azevedo, *Elementos para a história econômica de Portugal (séculos XII a XVIII)*, pp. 164–165. Brandônio

was well aware that slaves came from other areas as well as Guinea; see, e.g., p. 158.

36 · The price of slaves varied greatly, depending on the ports of departure and arrival, the vagaries of speculation, and the fluctuation of supply and demand, factors which in turn were affected by the production of sugar, the incidence of famine, and epidemics that killed slaves. But high cost was a common complaint. Campos Moreno ascribes it to the heavy duties that had to be paid on slaves in Angola. Another cause was the short life of the blacks in Brazil: some authorities have estimated the average life of African slaves on the plantations at only seven to ten years after their arrival in Brazil. Even though the blacks tolerated captivity somewhat better than the Amerindian slaves, they were decimated by its rigors. In the sugar mills, for instance, the usual work day was of eighteen hours; and in what little free time they were allowed, the slaves often had to raise their own food. See Campos Moreno, *Livro que dá razão*, p. 112; p. 113, n. 23; and p. 119, n. 52. See also Stuart B. Schwartz, "Free Labor in a Slave Economy," in Dauril Alden, ed., *Colonial Roots of Modern Brazil*, p. 176.

37 · Brandônio frequently complains about the settlers' self-serving determination to go home to Portugal as soon as they can become rich, a sentiment expressed by several other chroniclers: "Everyone wants to go home," says Vicente do Salvador, "not only immigrants from Portugal but also native Brazilians: both use the land, not like its lords, but like usufructuaries, only to despoil it and leave it destroyed." Vicente do Salvador, *História do Brasil*, pp. 58–59. Cf. Manuel da Nóbrega, *Cartas do Brasil (1549–1560)*, pp. 131 and 134, and Campos Moreno, *Livro que dá razão*, p. 115 and n. 29. Boxer observes that in the present passage Brandão was exaggerating: the great majority of the settlers had to remain in Brazil, where most of them married and had families, thus contracting strong ties with the country and the people. Charles R. Boxer, *The Portuguese Seaborne Empire, 1415–1825*, p. 91. It is noteworthy that of the four critics of the settlers whose views are given in this passage only one—Vicente do Salvador—was born in Brazil. The other three—Nóbrega, Campos Moreno, and Brandão—were natives of Portugal, but were as loyal to their adopted land as Vicente do Salvador to his native country. Brandão himself went back to Portugal and remained there for some ten years, but eventually he returned to Brazil.

38 · Even before the union of Castile and Portugal in 1580, "Spain" was a geographical designation, not a political one. Consequently, when Brandônio speaks of "Spain" or "our Spain" he refers to the entire Iberian Peninsula. When he wishes to distinguish between the two peninsular peoples, he says "Portuguese" and "Castilians." See p. 19.

39 · Brandônio has criticized four of his "five classes of men" in Brazil for their selfish intentness on enriching themselves to the detriment of the land. The single exception is the men engaged in maritime commerce, whose motives he does not discuss. But the men of the last group are only visitors to the ports of the country, not permanent residents like those of the other four classes. It is primarily the latter who, Brandônio thinks, should be building up the country.

40 · The discoverer of Brazil, Pedro Álvares Cabral, originally called the new land Vera Cruz [True Cross]—not Santa Cruz [Holy Cross], as Brandônio has it. It was a common practice in the sixteenth century to name a newly discovered territory for a church festival that coincided with the date of the discovery. In this case the festival (that of the Discovery of the True Cross; see below, n. 42) fell almost two weeks after the discovery, but perhaps Cabral simply anticipated the event. Vera Cruz soon gave way to Santa Cruz, perhaps borrowed from the name of a trading post established near Porto Seguro in 1503. The name Brazil, derived from the popular wood as Brandônio says, appears as early as 1503 and soon became general. The dropping of the religiously significant Santa Cruz was bitterly opposed by the clergy, and for many years clerical writers persisted in using the old designation. As late as 1761 the Franciscan Jaboatão deplored the change, attributing it to the "foolish policy of men, or their imprudent ambition," which caused them "to value brazilwood more highly than the precious wood of the cross." The name Santa Cruz is still used poetically in Brazil today. Bernardino José de Souza gives a list, with dates, of the early names for the country that appear in maps, letters, and official documents during the first quarter of the sixteenth century. António de Santa Maria Jaboatão, *Novo orbe seráfico brasílico*, 1:5; Bernardino José de Souza, *O pau-brasil na história nacional*, p. 97; Pero de Magalhães de Gandavo, *The Histories of Brazil*, 2:194, n. 14; William Brooks Greenlee, ed. and trans., *The Voyage of Pedro Álvares Cabral to Brazil and India from Contemporary Documents and Narratives*, p. 7, n. 2, and p. 33, n. 4.

41 · It is possible that Pedro Álvares Cabral in his voyage to Brazil had been preceded by one or more Spanish explorers, but it was Cabral's expedition that led to the opening up of the new land. Little is known of Cabral's life. He was only about thirty years old when in 1500 King Manuel (Manuel I of Portugal, 1495–1521) sent him on an expedition to India to follow up Vasco da Gama's successful first voyage of two years earlier. Scholars are not agreed as to whether Cabral came upon Brazil by chance (as Brandônio says he did), after sailing or being driven out of his course, or whether he was carrying out a secret mission to seek new lands to the west. There is a whole library of treatises on the question. For a good

summary of the controversy see Greenlee, *Voyage of Cabral,* pp. xlvi–lx. See also Max Justo Guedes, *O descobrimento do Brasil* (Rio de Janeiro, 1966); Rubens Viana Neiva, "Ensaio de crítica náutica sôbre a viagem transatlântica de Pedro Álvares Cabral," *Revista do Instituto Geográfico e Histórico Brasileiro* 287 (Apr.–June 1970):36–76.

42 · "That day," in Brandônio's mind, is evidently the Feast of the Discovery of the True Cross (no longer included in the Church calendar), which fell on May 3. Actually, Cabral did not discover Brazil on that day but on April 22, 1500. Sérgio Buarque de Holanda, ed., *História geral da civilização brasileira,* tomo 1, vol. 1, p. 48; Samuel Eliot Morison, *The European Discovery of America: The Southern Voyages A.D. 1492–1616,* pp. 210–217.

43 · Manuel I of Portugal.

44 · See above, n. 30.

45 · King Manuel was said to have been "much given to judicial Astrology." (In judicial astrology the character of a man is foretold from the celestial configurations at the time of his birth, or, according to some, of his conception. W. P. D. Wightman, *Science of the Renaissance,* 1:101.) When ships were sailing for India or were due back from there, it was the King's habit to consult "a great Portuguese astrologer who lived in Lisbon named Diogo Mendes, . . . and after Mendes's death Tomás de Torres, the King's physician, a man highly skilled both in astrology and in other sciences." Damião de Góes, *Crônica do Sereníssimo Senhor Rei D. Manoel* (Lisbon, 1749), pt. 4, p. 598, cited by Garcia, ed., *Diálogos,* I, n. 6, along with additional references.

46 · Cf. Vicente do Salvador: "If it should ever happen (God forbid) that Portugal should fall into the power of foreign enemies, as has happened in other kingdoms, so that the king was forced to flee to another land he could find none better to go to than this one." *História do Brasil* (1627), p. 162. This recourse was considered on several occasions after the sixteenth century, and in 1807 Alviano's presentiment was actually realized. In that year Napoleon's army marched on Lisbon, and the Prince Regent, João (later João VI, 1816–1826), migrated with the court to Brazil to begin a sojourn that lasted for thirteen years.

47 · The reader may speculate whether Brandônio means that a belief in astrology would be out of keeping with the rationalism of the new age, or that the belief is unchristian.

48 · Several woods are known by the name brazilwood. Three species, all of which are sources of dye, are found in the western hemisphere: *Caesalpinia crista* L., *C. brasiliensis* L., and *C. echinata* Lamb. The last of these is the species from which the country takes its name; it is a very hard, deep red wood. The coloring matter, brazilin, which is extracted by boiling,

imparts a bright red hue, but this is not permanent and is immediately damaged by acids. Because of this effect the brazilwoods have now been largely replaced by other dyes. Samuel J. Record and Robert W. Hess, *Timbers of the New World,* pp. 238–239, s.v. *"Caesalpinia";* Isaac H. Burkill, *A Dictionary of the Economic Products of the Malay Peninsula,* s.v. *"Caesalpinia."*

For a detailed account of the economic aspects of the brazilwood industry within the Portuguese Empire, see Mauro, *Portugal et Atlantique,* pp. 118–145; for the role of the wood in Brazilian history, Souza, *Pau-Brasil.*

49 · The main stream of the Amazon River rises about 100 miles from the Pacific Ocean in a chain of glacier-fed lakes lying near the western edge of the Andes, in central Peru. The river flows across Peru and Brazil for 3,015 miles and empties into the Atlantic Ocean at the equator. Though the whole reach of the river is popularly called the Amazon, the various sections have their own names, as Marañon, Salimões, and Pará.

The Amazon River was first explored in 1541–1542 by Francisco de Orellana, a member of the forces of Gonzalo Pizarro (a half-brother of Francisco Pizarro), who was searching for the land of El Dorado. With some companions, he separated himself from the main body of the troops that had set out from a base in Quito, and traveled the entire length of the Amazon by boat, reaching the Atlantic on August 24, 1542. In the course of his journey Orellana fought with some natives, who he thought were women. Hence he gave to the river the name River of the Amazons, in allusion to the mythical Greek female warriors.

50 · What Brandônio actually says is "[Pará] is situated in the middle of the equinoctial line." As often, he has said just the reverse of what he means. His true meaning is evident from his statement on p. 105 that "the [equinoctial] line cuts right through the middle of the area of [Pará's] port and settlement."

51 · That is, the first settlement counting from the north, not the first in date of founding.

52 · The principal towns and cities that lined the Brazil coast, together with their captaincies and founding dates, were as follows, proceeding from north to south: Belém, Pará, 1616; São Luís, Maranhão, 1615; Natal, Rio Grande do Norte, 1599; Filipéia, Paraíba, 1585; Igaraçu, Pernambuco, 1536; Olinda, Pernambuco, 1537; São Cristóvão, Sergipe, 1590; Salvador, Bahia, 1549; Ilhéus, Ilhéus, 1536; Santa Cruz, Porto Seguro, 1536; Porto Seguro, Porto Seguro, 1535; Vitória, Espírito Santo, 1551; Espírito Santo, Espírito Santo, 1551; Rio de Janeiro, Rio de Janeiro, 1565; São Paulo, São Vicente, 1558; Santos, São Vicente, 1545; São Vicente, São Vicente, 1532; Itanhaém, São Vicente, 1561; Cananéia, São

Vicente, 1600. Of these, Belém, São Luís, Filipéia, Salvador, and Rio de Janeiro were designated as cities. Buarque de Holanda, *História geral,* tomo 1, vol. 1, p. 196. For the distinctions among village, town, and city see Magalhães de Gandavo, *Histories of Brazil,* 2:211, n. 34.

53 · In his description Brandônio fuses the settlement with the river, as he does later with Maranhão.

54 · The eastern reaches of the Amazon early attracted adventurers and explorers. Well before the Portuguese arrived there, the English, French, and Dutch had founded trading posts on the banks of the river. Portuguese expeditions to expel the interlopers followed closely upon the military actions in Maranhão. (Brandônio will describe the campaign in Maranhão later, on p. 29, since he is following a geographical and not a chronological arrangement.) Francisco Caldeira de Castelo Branco, captain major of Rio Grande and a veteran of the Maranhão expedition, led a force into the territory and in 1616 began the construction of a wooden fort, the one mentioned by Brandônio. Castelo Branco named the fort "Forte do Presépio de Belém" [Fort of the Stable at Bethlehem]. The fort was to become the nucleus of the city of Santa Maria de Belém. Subsequent attacks by hostile Indians were repelled, but the English and Dutch were not so easily driven off. It was not until some years after the *Dialogues,* in 1625, that Jerônimo de Albuquerque achieved decisive victories for the Portuguese in Amazônia, and only in 1648 was the last Dutch position in the area destroyed. The conclusion of the action in Amazônia secured for the Portuguese the last disputed stretch of territory on Brazil's East-West Coast and gave them control of the vast Amazon basin. See Buarque de Holanda, *História geral,* tomo 1, vol. 1, pp. 233–234, 257–259; Garcia, ed., *Diálogos,* I, n. 7; Serafim Leite, *História da Companhia de Jesus no Brasil,* 3:206.

55 · The fish species in the Amazon River are almost infinite in number. Attempts to count them have resulted in estimates all the way from 500 to 2,000 species. Only a few species have any economic importance.

56 · For once, Brandônio excuses the settlers, and with justice: the first permanent settlement in the Captaincy of Pará—Belém, at the mouth of the Amazon—was only two years old; see above, n. 54.

57 · Surprisingly, Brandônio appears to be unaware that the various Brazilian tribes spoke many different languages, though he does recognize (on pp. 325–326) that the Tapuias spoke a unique tongue, a "crack-jaw language." Probably whatever familiarity he may have had with Indian speech was derived from Tupi-Guarani, which predominated along the coast and was used as a common language [*língua geral*] for communication between Indians and whites.

58 · The legendary inland lake was mentioned by many chroniclers. Its lo-

cation was variously given, but usually it was at the head of one or more swift rivers. Thus Monteiro asserts that, according to Indian lore, both the São Francisco River and the Rio de la Plata originated from a large lake somewhere in the interior. Jácome Monteiro, *Relação da Província do Brasil,* 1610, in Leite, *História,* 8:394. The legend of the lake was studied by Jaime Cortesão: "O mito da Ilha Brasil e a integração territorial do Estado," in his *História do Brasil nos velhos mapas* (2 vols. Rio de Janeiro: Instituto Rio Branco, 1965–1971), 1:339–363. Cf. Buarque de Holanda, *Visão do paraíso,* p. 70, and see below, n. 64. For the true source of the Amazon, see above, n. 49.

59 · Presumably, in the inhabitants' view, because there were heavy rains over the lake in the interior, and these caused it to overflow.

60 · Here, a wealthy Spaniard from Peru. For *peruleiro* in the sense of Portuguese smuggler, see III, n. 101.

61 · Presumably, native fishhooks, which were made of thorns. After the Portuguese came, the native hooks were rapidly replaced by the European variety. John Hemming, *Red Gold: The Conquest of Brazilian Indians,* pp. 17, 102; Alfred Métraux, "The Tupinambá," in Julian H. Steward, ed., *Handbook of South American Indians* (hereafter cited as *HSAI*), 3:101; Jean de Léry, *Histoire d'un voyage faict en la terre du Brésil,* 2:4; Nóbrega, *Cartas (1549–1560),* p. 54.

62 · Why the season was important is explained in n. 154 below.

63 · See above, n. 7.

64 · Stories similar to Brandônio's are told by several chroniclers. For instance, Padre António de Araújo passed on an account he heard in 1613 from a backwoodsman named Pero Domingues, who told how a certain Spaniard, condemned to death in Peru, fled by boat on "that famous lake called Paraupaba, whence various and beautiful rivers take their course," and sailed down the Grão-Pará (Amazon) to the sea. Serafim Leite, *Páginas de história do Brasil,* pp. 103–104.

65 · King Philip III of Spain, II of Portugal (1598–1621).

66 · The regular trade route to Peru was long, arduous, and expensive. (For a shorter but illegal route used by smugglers, see III, n. 101.) Trading ships sailed from Spanish ports to Nombre de Dios, a trading post at the narrowest point of the Isthmus of Panama and on the Caribbean side. To this place came merchants from Lima to spend their Peruvian silver for European goods. "The merchandise was lightered up the Chagres River to its headwaters, and thence packed by mule train to Panama [City]; loaded again into ships on the Pacific coast, and after a long and difficult passage landed at Callao [the port of the city of Lima]. Goods for Cuzco had to be packed from Lima over high mountain passes; for

Potosí, carried on by sea to Arica and packed from there via Arequipa."
John Horace Parry, *The Spanish Seaborne Empire*, p. 130.

Clearly, Brandônio's suggestion is a sensible one. A similar proposal
was made in 1624 by Symão Estaço da Sylveira, *Relação summária das
cousas do Maranhão*, signature A5ʳ, but for various reasons no such plan
was ever put into effect.

67 · João III was king of Portugal from 1521 to 1557. The settlement was
actually not on a river but on a bay, now called Baía de São Marcos.

68 · Three men—Fernão Álvares, Aires da Cunha, and João de Barros, the
famous Portuguese historian—were granted the entire East-West Coast
of Brazil to explore and to divide among themselves as they saw fit, but
their every attempt to explore these lands ended in disaster in the form
of shipwreck or of harassment by the Indians or the French. Finally the
promoters abandoned the territory, which eventually reverted to the
Crown. Buarque de Holanda, *História geral*, tomo 1, vol. 1, pp. 105–
106.

69 · Gaspar de Sousa, eleventh governor of Brazil (1613–1617), though of-
ficially stationed in Salvador, spent more than three and one-half years
of his governorship in Olinda. From that place he undertook to oust the
French from Maranhão, probably hoping to carve out a captaincy for
himself in the new region. Francis A. Dutra, "Centralization vs. Donatarial Privilege," in Dauril Alden, ed., *Colonial Roots of Modern Brazil*,
p. 27.

70 · Jerônimo de Albuquerque was a *mameluco,* the son of Duarte Coelho's
brother-in-law and a Tabajara woman. He learned Tupi from his mother,
and this knowledge, along with his other abilities, made him an invaluable asset both in expeditions against the Indians and in the paci-
fication of the tribes. With Manuel Mascarenhas Homem, captain major
of Pernambuco, he battled the French and the Petiguar Indians in 1597
in present-day Rio Grande do Norte, and as a reward for his services
was named commander of the fort of Santos Reis Magos [Holy Magi
Kings, i.e., the Three Wise Men], near the site of present-day Natal,
and captain major of the Royal Captaincy of Rio Grande. Buarque de
Holanda, *História geral*, tomo 1, vol. 1, pp. 195–197; Flávio Guerra,
História colonial do Nordeste, pp. 30–32.

71 · Daniel de la Touche, Seigneur de la Ravardière, an able French naval
officer, along with Charles des Vaux, with the permission of the French
Crown organized a company to colonize Maranhão. João Francisco Lisboa,
Crônica do Brasil Colonial (Apontamentos para a história do Maranhão), pp.
87–88; Carlos Studart Filho, *O antigo Estado do Maranhão e suas capitanias
feudais*, pp. 101–109.

72 · Brandônio is mistaken about the date of Albuquerque's expedition into

Maranhão. He sailed not in 1615 but in 1614, on June 22. In describing the engagement with the French, Brandônio is vague to the point of inaccuracy. Albuquerque's attack resulted not in a victory but in a truce, which lasted for a year. After this indecisive action the governor general, Gaspar de Sousa, sent a new fleet under Alexandre de Moura, which arrived at the fort of São Filipe (the former São Luís) on November 1, 1615. It is probably this date that Brandão was thinking of when he wrote that Albuquerque's fleet was prepared in 1615. The French surrendered to Alexandre de Moura on November 4, 1615. Albuquerque was rewarded for his services by being named captain major of Maranhão, a post he held until his death in 1618. Buarque de Holanda, *História geral,* tomo 1, vol. 1, pp. 230–233.

73 · Six years later there were in Maranhão four fortresses, in the shadow of which lived more than 300 Portuguese. In addition, there were nine native villages, whose inhabitants worked for the Portuguese. Estaço da Sylveira, *Relação do Maranhão,* signature A5ᵛ.

74 · The French pirates illegally cut dyewood along the Brazilian coast, as well as endangering Portuguese shipping to and from Brazil.

75 · Cf. Symão Estaço da Sylveira, who says Maranhão is fertile and produces grains, game, fish, shellfish, fruits, honey, and other foodstuffs, with which the settlers live "in the greatest plenty." He adds that it has a very pleasant sky, and healthful air that makes it seem always spring; there are many great trees, numerous springs, and fertile soil. Some think the Earthly Paradise must be here. "Of all the places to which the Portuguese go, the best is Brazil, and Maranhão is the best of Brazil," he concludes. *Relação do Maranhão,* fols. 5ᵛ–12ʳ. Cf. also Candido Mendes de Almeida, *Memórias para a história do extincto Estado do Maranhão,* 2: 19–31, especially p. 21.

Brandônio's and Estaço da Sylveira's favorable view is in contrast to the opinion of some French immigrants who had apparently been attracted to the region by promises of a land of plenty. Several of these Frenchmen, taken prisoner by the Portuguese in the battle for São Luís (see above, n. 72), freely voiced their disillusionment: instead of the silver, gold, and lapis lazuli that they had expected, they found in Maranhão only tobacco and fustic wood, along with a little ambergris, cotton, and pepper. Buarque de Holanda, *História geral,* tomo 1, vol. 1, p. 220.

76 · The Indians regularly paddled their canoes standing up.

77 · Estaço da Sylveira says that mullet leaped into the canoes in such numbers that the occupants had to throw them back into the sea in order to avoid foundering. Similarly, Métraux tells how in August, when the mullet were swimming upstream in great numbers to spawn, the fish would

jump into empty canoes after the men struck the water with sticks. Estaço da Sylveira, *Relação do Maranhão,* fol. 10ᵛ; Métraux, "The Tupinambá," in *HSAI,* 3:101.

78 · In thoroughly contemporary fashion Brandônio mixes a classical and a scriptural allusion. To the classical Golden Age he adds the biblical rivers of honey and butter, Job 20:17: "He shall not see the rivers, the floods, the brooks of honey and butter" (Authorized Version).

79 · Brandônio will give additional details about the sea cow on p. 256. The animal, which is also called manatee, is a mammal of which one species exists in Brazil, *Trichochus manatus.* It lives in salt water and in adjoining freshwater rivers, feeding on vegetation that grows at the water's edge. Sea cows attain a length of six to nine feet, and the largest weigh nearly two tons. When pursued, they submerge for long periods of time before surfacing to breathe; it is perhaps this surfacing that makes Brandônio think they swim on top of the water. For a vivid description of the sea cow and the method of its capture, see Gonzalo Fernández de Oviedo y Valdés, *Oviedo dela natural historia delas Indias* (1526), chap. 83.

The sea cow probably furnished the basis for many of the contemporary stories about sea monsters and mermen. See Magalhães de Gandavo, *História da Província Sancta Cruz,* in idem, *Histories of Brasil,* vol. 1, fol. 28, with illustration fol. 32ᵛ; Fernão Cardim, *Tratados da terra e gente do Brasil,* pp. 78–79; Gabriel Soares de Sousa, *Notícia do Brasil* (1945), 2: 190 and n. 1; P. J. P. Whitehead, "Registros antigos da presença do peixe-boi do Caribe no Brasil," *Acta Amazônica* 8(3) (1978):497–507. It is typical of Brandão's realistic approach to the wonders of nature that he does not repeat here or elsewhere any of the legends about sea monsters that are reported by his fellow chroniclers.

80 · Three years after the expulsion of the French from Maranhão, the order was given for the creation of a separate State of Maranhão, which was to include the captaincies of Maranhão, Ceará, and Pará and was to be independent of the State of Brazil. (The actual decree establishing the new state was not issued until 1621.) Ceará did not long remain a part of Maranhão, but was placed under the jurisdiction of Pernambuco. One reason for the separation of the State of Maranhão from the rest of Brazil was the vastness of the northern territory; another was that communication between Maranhão and Bahia was difficult at certain seasons because of contrary winds and currents. Maranhão never attained much economic importance during the colonial period. Tristão de Alencar Araripe, *História da Província do Ceará desde os tempos primitivos até 1850,* p. 76; Buarque de Holanda, *História geral,* tomo 1, vol. 1, pp. 266–267; Studart, *Antigo Estado do Maranhão,* p. 232.

81 · Jaguaribe was the earlier name of the territory that became the Royal

Captaincy of Ceará. Because of the arid climate, the absence of precious metals, the lack of good harbors, and the constant Indian threat, the area was long unattractive to colonizers. In 1609 Martim Soares Moreno, nephew of Diogo de Campos Moreno, led an expedition into the territory to establish a fort from which to seek out French interlopers. Because of his success in accomplishing this mission with only a handful of men, Moreno in 1619 was appointed captain major of Ceará for a ten-year period. In the nineteenth century he was made the hero of José de Alencar's famous romantic novel, *Iracema*. Alencar Araripe, *História da Província do Ceará*, p. 67; Buarque de Holanda, *História geral*, tomo 1, vol. 1, p. 202; Studart, *Antigo Estado do Maranhão*, pp. 86, 93.

82 · Ambergris is a biliary concretion that forms in the intestines of the sperm whale. It is found in sea water, particularly of the tropics. Fresh ambergris is soft, black, and ill smelling, but on exposure to air and sun it quickly hardens, fades to a light gray, and becomes pleasantly fragrant. In ancient times ambergris was valued as a perfume and a drug. Nowadays it is used in the East mainly to spice foods and wines; in the West, in the manufacture of perfumes. Burkill, *Economic Products of the Malay Peninsula*, s.v. "ambergris."

83 · Manuel Mascarenhas Homem in 1597 led an expedition against the French and Indians in what was to become the Royal Captaincy of Rio Grande do Norte, the purpose of the action being to protect Paraíba and Itamaracá from the French and their Petiguar allies. He was accompanied by two noted Indian fighters: Jerônimo de Albuquerque (see above, n. 70), who later became captain major of the new captaincy, and Feliciano Coelho de Carvalho, captain major of Paraíba. Feliciano de Carvalho's command was halted on the frontier of Paraíba by an epidemic of smallpox, and it was only in April 1598 that his contingent arrived at the scene of the action. In the meantime, Mascarenhas Homem had established in 1597 the fort of Santos Reis Magos, presumably the fort referred to in Brandônio's next sentence. Next to the fort grew up the city of Natal. Basílio de Magalhães, *Expansão geográphica do Brasil Colonial*, p. 34; Flávio Guerra, *História colonial*, pp. 30–31; Buarque de Holanda, *História geral*, tomo 1, vol. 1, p. 196.

84 · Cf. p. 29, and n. 74 above. Campos Moreno (1612) says this bay had been one of the principal bases for French pirates, who used it for the very purposes Brandônio mentions, and in addition as a place in which to recover from the "ailments of Guinea," presumably acquired when they went to Mina to barter for slaves. The principal ailment may have been scurvy, as with the so-called "Luanda sickness." Campos Moreno, *Livro que dá razão*, pp. 207–208; Charles R. Boxer, ed. and trans., *The Tragic History of the Sea, 1589–1622*, p. 199, n. 2; Prado, *Pernambuco,*

4:215; Francisco Guerra, "Aleixo de Abreu (1568–1630), Author of the Earliest Book on Tropical Medicine . . . ," *Journal of Tropical Medicine and Hygiene* 71 (March 1968):59, 63; Mauro, *Portugal et Atlantique,* p. 76.

85 · This statement of Brandônio's establishes a date at which Brandão was composing the *Dialogues.*

86 · The Captaincy of Paraíba extended south from what was later Rio Grande do Norte to Cabo Branco [White Cape], as Brandônio says, and included two-thirds of the territory formerly belonging to the Captaincy of Itamaracá. Cabo Branco is just south of João Pessoa (formerly Filipéia), the capital of Paraíba.

87 · In other words, it was a royal and not a proprietary captaincy (see Introduction, pp. 4–6).

88 · Campos Moreno said that in 1612 there were twelve mills in Paraíba, with others under construction. *Livro que dá razão,* p. 280.

89 · The incumbent was Luís de Sousa, who held office from 1617 to 1621. Stuart B. Schwartz, *Sovereignty and Society in Colonial Brazil,* p. 193.

90 · The first bishop of Brazil, Pedro Fernandes Sardinha, was appointed in 1551. The incumbent in Brandão's time was Constantino Barradas. Buarque de Holanda, *História geral,* tomo I, vol. I, p. 114; Braz do Amaral, *Resenha histórica da Bahia* (Bahia: Typografia Naval, 1941), p. 104.

91 · The High Court [*Relação*], created in 1609, was the supreme judicial body in Brazil. Appeal from the High Court was only to the Court of Appeals [*Casa de Suplicação*] in Lisbon. Schwartz, *Sovereignty and Society,* pp. 95–96. Brandônio will discuss the High Court—especially what he considers its shortcomings—on pp. 42–44.

92 · The cruzado was an old gold or silver coin of Portugal, the equivalent of 400 reis. Thus, according to Brandônio the tithe paid on sugar by Paraíba amounted to 4,800,000 reis (4:800$000).

93 · Campos Moreno says the tithe from Paraíba in 1612 amounted to 4:000$000, or 10,000 cruzados. If Brandônio's figure of 12,000 cruzados is correct for 1618, the tithe from that captaincy had increased by 20 percent during the six years. *Livro que dá razão,* p. 200.

94 · Each year the Captaincy of Paraíba exported twenty-two shiploads of sugar through Pernambuco to Europe. Loc. cit.

95 · The Portuguese in Paraíba were early faced with the need to expel the French and to subdue the natives with whom the interlopers had allied themselves. This was an urgent task, because the French were depriving the Crown of immense revenue by carrying off brazilwood, and also because they threatened the safety of the settlers in Itamaracá.

In 1585 the Portuguese concluded a peace treaty with the Petiguar Indians in Paraíba. On November 4 of that year the superior crown magistrate [*ouvidor-geral*], Martim Leitão, arrived with an expedition to expel the French and the Tabajaras from the captaincy so that it could be settled. Vicente do Salvador relates how Brandão himself was one of two "merchant captains" selected for this expedition. After the completion of his mission, Martim Leitão began the construction of the city of Filipéia de Nossa Senhora das Neves [Filipéia of Our Lady of the Snows], now João Pessoa. The first sugar mill in the captaincy was set up in 1586, and in the same year the Crown's revenue from brazilwood amounted to 1:600$000. Irineu Ferreia Pinto, *Datas e notas para a história da Parahyba*, 1:20–23; Vicente do Salvador, *História do Brasil*, pp. 265–266.

96 · When he took part in Martim Leitão's expedition. See above, n. 95.

97 · The most common materials for Brazilian houses of the well-to-do were white stone and mortar [*pedra e cal*], which made handsome and comfortable buildings. Often the lower part of the structure served as a store, the top as a dwelling. The houses of the poor had earthen floors and were much less livable and attractive. See J. F. de Almeida Prado, *A Bahia e as capitanias do centro do Brasil (1530–1626)*, 3:191.

98 · Coins were scarce in Brazil until gold was found in quantity in the country at the end of the seventeenth century; so barter among the colonists was common, as often happens in undeveloped economies. Various local products were used as media of exchange, one of the most popular being sugar. Thus in 1612 sugar was established by the governor of Rio de Janeiro as legal currency; its value was fixed at 1,000 reis per arroba for white sugar and at a lower figure for the inferior grades. In São Paulo, besides sugar, cotton cloth, wax, hides, and salt pork were exchanged.

Barter also had its place in transactions between the colonists and traders from Portugal and between the colonists and their business correspondents in Europe (see pp. 23 and 43). It was extensively practiced, too, in the African slave trade; the common media of exchange were tobacco, of which the Africans were especially fond, and *zimbos*—tiny white cowrie shells that were gathered in Porto Seguro and elsewhere.

But barter between the whites and the Indians was the most common of all, being the ordinary means by which goods and services were obtained by the Europeans. The principal product bartered for was brazilwood; others were parrots, monkeys, purges, and slaves, all acquired in order to be shipped to Portugal. The *Dialogues* mention barter with the Indians in connection with the exchange of foodstuffs for fishhooks on p. 27; the transactions in ambergris on p. 31; and the traffic in brazilwood carried on by pirates on p. 33. The subject of barter with the Indians is exhaustively treated by Alexander Marchant, *From Barter to Slavery: The Economic Relations of Portuguese and Indians in the Settlement of Brazil, 1500–1580.* For further information about barter in Brazil see Vicente do Salvador, *História do Brasil,* p. 122; Vivaldo Coaracy, *O Rio de Janeiro no século dezessete,* p. 39; Fernando de Azevedo, *Canaviais e engenhos na vida política do Brasil* (2d ed., São Paulo: Edições Melhoramentos, 1958), p. 58; Richard McGee Morse, *From Community to Metropolis: A Biography of São Paulo, Brazil,* p. 12.

99 · In 1630, boats of up to 300 tons could go up the Paraíba [São Domingos] River to the city of Filipéia (a distance of some fourteen miles). Farther up, the river was navigable only by small boats with a capacity of 100 chests of sugar, the type of craft used in the coastwise trade. These vessels could sail eleven miles above the city, where a *passo,* or warehouse, held the sugar awaiting shipment to Lisbon. António Gonçalvez Paschoa, "Descripção da cidade e barra da Paraíba," in *Documentação ultramarina portuguesa,* 1:17–19; Campos Moreno, *Livro que dá razão,* p. 203. See also Francisco Augusto Pereira da Costa, "O Passo do Fidalgo," *Revista do Instituto Arqueológico, Histórico e Geográfico Pernambucano* 10 (March 1902):53–74, 171–173.

100 · The word "here" in this passage and in Alviano's next speech shows that the author has chosen Paraíba as the scene of the *Dialogues.*

101 · In the instructions issued on May 9, 1609, to Feliciano Coelho de Carvalho as incoming governor and captain major of Paraíba. Garcia, ed., *Diálogos,* I, n. 17.

102 · From 1574 on the Portuguese based in Pernambuco had sent out expedition after expedition to free Paraíba from the Petiguares and the French, but it was not until the Spanish admiral Diego Flores Valdés lent the support of his ships and men to the campaign that the Portuguese were able, in 1584, to build a fort against their double enemy as a protection to future settlers. This fort was the Cabedelo [Sand Spit], originally São Filipe and later Santa Catarina, at the mouth of the Paraíba River. When Flores Valdés departed, he left Francisco Castejón, a Spaniard, in charge of the fort with 110 Spanish and 50 Portuguese soldiers. Quarreling soon broke out between the Spanish and the Portuguese, and before long both contingents abandoned the fort. Even a short-lived cooperation between Spanish and Portuguese was unusual, for, as Brandônio notes, relations between the two peninsular peoples were traditionally strained, in spite of their formal union under the Spanish Crown. Buarque de Holanda, *História geral,* tomo 1, vol. 1, pp. 191–192; Basílio de Magalhães, *Expansão geográphica do Brasil Colonial,* pp. 32–33; Campos Moreno, *Livro que dá razão,* p. 201 and n. 7; Ivan Guimarães, "A verdade histórica sôbre a fundação da Paraíba," *Revista do Instituto Histórico e Geográfico Paraibano* 10 (1946):123–137.

Later on, Brandônio will discuss Flores Valdés's earlier efforts to establish settlements on the Strait of Magellan (II, n. 50).

103 · Cf. the defense against pirates undertaken in Maranhão and Rio Grande do Norte, p. 29; n. 74 above; and p. 31.

104 · The Petiguares were a numerous tribe of cannibals of the Tupi stock who inhabited the coast between the Parnaíba and Paraíba rivers as well as areas inland as far as the Copaoba Mountains. At the end of the sixteenth century they were expelled from a large part of the coastal region by the Portuguese and their Tabajara allies (see VI, n. 55). Thereafter they allied themselves with the Dutch and warred against the Portuguese till 1654, when the survivors were placed in missions by the Jesuits. In this setting they eventually became staunch allies of their former enemies. Métraux, "The Tupinambá," in *HSAI*, 3:95–103; João Pereira de Castro Pinto, "A Parahyba nos tempos coloniaes," *Revista do Instituto Histórico e Geográfico Paraibano* 1 (1909):12–38.

105 · The Copaoba Mountains, now called the Raíz, consist of spurs of the Borborema range. Situated between fifty and sixty miles from the coastal settlements of Pernambuco and Paraíba, as Brandônio will indicate later (p. 215), the chain marked the western limit of Portuguese expansion in the Captaincy of Paraíba. The region is united geographically to Paraíba, but historically to the conquest of Rio Grande do Norte. The fringes of the Copaoba Mountains offered some of the best sites in Brazil for plantations and towns. As the present speakers indicate, the area had not yet been settled, but the governor general, Diogo de Menezes, was endeavoring to make peace with the natives so that its development could be undertaken. Leite, *História*, 1:513; Campos Moreno, *Livro que dá razão*, pp. 199–200.

106 · Silveira, with Feliciano Coelho de Carvalho, captain major of Paraíba, had led an expedition in 1596 that subdued the Indians in the Copaoba Mountains, thus permitting the region to be opened to cattle ranching. The governor rewarded Silveira for his services by granting him large tracts of land in Paraíba, where he set up sugar mills and corrals that made him one of the richest men in the captaincy. João Pereira de Castro Pinto, "A Parahyba nos tempos coloniaes," p. 26; Garcia, ed., *Diálogos*, III, n. 11.

107 · The Benedictines were one of four major religious orders active in Colonial Brazil, the other three being the Jesuits, the Franciscans, and the Carmelites. These orders, in addition to ministering to the spiritual needs of the people, performed important educational services for whites, Indians, and Africans. They also accumulated and preserved much valuable information about animal and vegetable species.

The Benedictines came to Paraíba to teach the Indians in 1599, at

the invitation of the Governor. It was said that the Benedictines owed
the invitation to a suggestion of some sugar barons, including the historian Gabriel Soares de Sousa, and that they were preferred to another
order because they were thought to get along well with the colonists.
In truth, the aristocratic and scholarly Benedictines did not show the
combativeness with which the settlers had charged the Jesuits and Franciscans. The mission promptly received from the Governor a grant of
land for the monastery and church of São Bento. In 1612 the Benedictines
and the Franciscans between them were administering in Paraíba eight
aldeias [villages for Indians], where they gave instruction in religion and
in certain elementary subjects. J. F. de Almeida Prado, *A conquista da
Paraíba (séculos XVI a XVIII)*, p. 129; Ferreira Pinto, *Datas*, 1:29–31;
Campos Moreno, *Livro que dá razão*, p. 204; Heretiano Zenaïde, "As
ruinas da Praia do Poço," *Revista do Instituto Histórico e Geográfico Paraibano*
10 (1946):130.

108 · See p. 31 and n. 83 above.

109 · Brandão forgets that his protagonist is supposed to be speaking, not
writing.

110 · Again Brandão forgets that Brandônio is not writing but speaking. There
are a number of such petroglyphs throughout Brazil, but little is known
of their age, origin, or signification. See Annette Laming-Empiraire,
"Problèmes de Préhistoire Brésilienne," in *Annales: Economies, Sociétés,
Civilisations* 30 (5) (Sept.–Oct. 1975):1249–1256, "L'art rupestre bré-
silien." Angyone Costa's speculation that several of Brandão's designs are
phallic representations seems fanciful. *Migrações e cultura indígena*, pp.
69–87, especially the illustration on p. 70.

111 · Alviano's remark reflects the fact that men's minds were still subject to
ancient superstitions, which moved them to ascribe anything incompre-
hensible to a supernatural cause.

112 · The Cabedelo: see above, n. 102. Campos Moreno said that in 1611 the
fort had a garrison of twenty soldiers, with their officers. Like Brandônio,
he reported that the place was not easily defensible. *Livro que dá razão*,
pp. 200–201 and n. 7.

113 · Filipéia; see above, n. 95.

114 · Four leagues (fourteen miles), according to Campos Moreno, *Livro que
dá razão*, p. 203.

115 · See above, n. 97.

116 · See above, n. 107.

117 · The Carmelites, last of the religious orders to establish themselves in
Paraíba, arrived after 1600. They erected a monastery and founded the
Church of Our Lady of the Rosary [*Igreja de Nossa Senhora do Rosário*].
In contrast to the Jesuits and the Franciscans (see below, n. 118), these

fathers were peaceful and adaptable; they also proved to be excellent teachers. Little is known of the apostolic activities that were the principal function of the mission, because during the Dutch invasion the Carmelites hurriedly buried their records to keep them from falling into the hands of the Calvinists, and when the documents were dug up later on, they had deteriorated so much that they were illegible. Prado, *Conquista da Paraíba*, pp. 129–130. See also Zenaïde, "Praia do Poço," pp. 129–131, and Ferreira Pinto, *Datas*, 1:132.

118 · The Franciscans were the first religious to come to Brazil. They arrived in 1503, either in Porto Seguro or farther north. In 1589 they came to Paraíba and began to build a monastery. They found in the area a settlement of Jesuits, who had accompanied the founder of the city in 1585 and had aroused opposition among the settlers by what the latter regarded as the Fathers' excessive protectiveness toward the Indians. The Jesuits soon came into conflict with the Franciscans as well, and in 1593 the former were expelled from the captaincy (to return at the beginning of the seventeenth century). The Franciscans took up the Jesuits' work and began to administer five *aldeias,* but they encountered the same difficulties with the settlers as the Jesuits had done, so that they in turn were temporarily expelled in 1597. Zenaïde, "Praia do Poço," pp. 129–131; Ferreira Pinto, *Datas*, 1:26; Prado, *Conquista da Paraíba*, p. 128; Estêvão Pinto, *Introdução à história da antropologia indígena no Brasil (século XVI),* p. 18. See Ernst Gerhard Jacob, *Grundzuege der Geschichte Portugals und seiner Ueberseeprovinzen* (Darmstadt: Wissenschaftliche Buchgesellschaft, 1970) and Venâncio Willeke, *Franziskanermissionen in Brasilien 1500– 1966* (Schoeneck: Neue Zeitschrift für Missionswissenschaft, 1973).

119 · The Pope had grouped the northern captaincies into a new ecclesiastical unit in 1615. They were returned to the bishopric of Bahia in 1624. Brandão's information is up-to-date, since he was writing only three years after the separation. Francisco Adolfo de Varnhagen, *História geral do Brasil antes da sua separação e independência de Portugal,* 2:192, 221– 222.

120 · This capability was not realized, according to Brandônio, because the settlers persisted in illegally sending their sugar to Pernambuco; see pp. 32–33.

121 · Álvaro Pires de Castro e Sousa, sixth count of Monsanto and later marquess of Cascais, was adjudged heir to the Captaincy of Itamaracá in 1615, after considerable litigation. Campos Moreno, *Livro que dá razão,* p. 119, n. 47, and p. 193, n. 1.

122 · I.e., the royal captaincies, as distinguished from the proprietary or private captaincies. See Introduction, pp. 4–6.

123 · Brandão is mistaken in thinking that Itamaracá's area had been reduced.

The captaincy had from the beginning only twenty-five leagues of coastline. Probably Brandão was confused by the fact that the initial grantee of the captaincy, Pero Lopes de Sousa, received, in addition to the twenty-five leagues in the Northeast, another twenty-five leagues on the extreme southern coast (the Captaincy of Santo Amaro). Vicente do Salvador, *História do Brasil*, p. 138. It was from Itamaracá's twenty-five, not fifty, leagues that a part was cut away to help form the Royal Captaincy of Paraíba.

One of the markers between Pernambuco and Itamaracá is preserved in the Instituto Histórico de Goiana. It is the only dividing marker of the captaincies known to exist. Mário Melo, "A primeira feitoria de Pernambuco," *Revista do Instituto Arqueológico, Histórico, e Geográfico Pernambucano* 33 (1935):18.

124 · Pernambuco remained the one fully successful private or proprietary captaincy in Brazil. All the others foundered, with the partial exception of São Vicente. Several were converted into royal captaincies, as happened with Paraíba.

125 · Correctly, Duarte de Albuquerque Coelho. Names of members of this family are often confused. The captain majors of Pernambuco from its founding in 1534 were as follows: (1) Duarte Coelho, died 1553; (2) Duarte Coelho de Albuquerque, son of (1), died 1581; (3) Jorge de Albuquerque Coelho, brother of (2), died 1601; (4) Duarte de Albuquerque Coelho, the man referred to here, son of (3), died 1658. Campos Moreno, *Livro que dá razão*, p. 173, n. 1, lists these members of the family but is wrong about some of their dates. The correct dates are given in Charles R. Boxer, "Jorge de Albuquerque Coelho," *Anais da Academia Portuguesa da História*, Series 2, vol. 15 (1965):140 ff. See also João Peretti, "O donatário Jorge de Albuquerque Coelho," *Revista do Instituto Arqueológico, Histórico, e Geográfico Pernambucano* 39 (1944): 132–143; J. Costa Porto, *Tempo de Duarte Coelho* (Rio de Janeiro: Ministério da Educação e Cultura, Serviço de Documentação, 1961), pp. 115–117; and Edgar Prestage and Pedro de Azevedo, *Registro da Freguesia da Sé desde 1563 até 1610* (2 vols. Coimbra: Imprensa da Universidade, 1924–1927), 2:461.

126 · Comparable figures are given by Vicente do Salvador (1627), who says that Pernambuco brought its lord proprietor nearly 20,000 cruzados. The King received in just the tithes 60,000 cruzados, not to mention the duties on brazilwood and sugar. *História do Brasil*, pp. 133–134.

127 · The city, one of the oldest in Brazil, was founded in 1535 by Duarte Coelho, first proprietor of the captaincy. The story related by Brandônio is told about several different historical figures, and is documented by Rodolfo Garcia in his edition of the *Diálogos*, I, n. 22. Like most Brazilian

towns, Olinda was built on the model of Lisbon and other cities of Portugal, which did not follow a rigid plan like the cities of Spain but grew up at random in picturesque confusion. So far as the settlers in Brazil followed any design at all, they appear to have adopted the medieval concept of defense through height or through water barriers. By preference, settlements were built on hills overlooking a river or the ocean, as with Olinda, Salvador, São Paulo, Rio de Janeiro, and Filipéia. Churches and convents were erected on the heights, and around the hills wound the narrow streets leading down to the business center at the water level. Robert C. Smith, "Colonial Towns of Spanish and Portuguese America," in Lewis Hanke, ed., *History of Latin American Civilization: Sources and Interpretations,* vol. 1, *The Colonial Experience,* pp. 289–291.

128 · Cape St. Augustine [*Cabo Santo Agostinho*] projects into the Atlantic about twenty-five miles south of Recife.

129 · I.e., the Company of Jesus, as the Society of Jesus [Jesuits] is popularly known in Spain and Portugal. Two years after the first Jesuits landed at Bahia (see p. 45 and n. 165 below), the fathers came to Pernambuco, where they founded a *colégio* (in Olinda) that attained great prestige. (*Colégio* was the word for any Jesuit mission, whether it was a school, a monastery, a hospital, or some other type of institution. The term included every element in the installation—the buildings, the real estate, the members of the order, the employees, and the people served.) The Jesuits unquestionably constituted the most important religious and educational force in early Brazil. For the history of the Company in Brazil the standard authority is Serafim Leite, *História da Companhia de Jesus no Brasil* (10 vols.), or idem, *Suma histórica da Companhia de Jesus no Brasil, 1549–1760.* See also Flávio Guerra, *Evolução histórica de Pernambuco,* 1: 156–157.

130 · Ninety-nine in 1612, according to Campos Moreno, *Livro que dá razão,* p. 175.

131 · According to Campos Moreno, these forts had a garrison of ninety-eight men between them. Dutra thinks Brandônio's picture of the forts is unrealistic: only two years after the *Dialogues* were written, the governor, Matias de Albuquerque, wrote letters reporting that Fort São Francisco was falling to pieces and would soon be useless, and that Fort São Jorge was in a state of almost total disrepair. The Dutch intercepted these letters, and the information thus gained may well have contributed to their decision to attack Pernambuco in 1630. Campos Moreno, *Livro que dá razão,* p. 118 and n. 43. Francis A. Dutra, "Matias de Albuquerque and the Defense of Northeastern Brazil, 1620–1626," *Studia* 36 (July 1973):125–126; Charles R. Boxer, *The Dutch in Brazil, 1624–1654,* p. 32.

132 · More European ships went to Pernambuco in Brandão's time than to any other port in Brazil, to carry away its riches in the three products Brandônio mentions. Marchant, *From Barter to Slavery*, p. 130.

133 · Presumably the church of the Jesuit *colégio* of Olinda, begun in 1584, and called the most beautiful church in Brazil. It was situated in a picturesque park with a reservoir, fountain, arbors, and innumerable fruit trees. Leite, *História*, 1:453–457.

134 · The Franciscans [*Capuchinhos*] established themselves in Pernambuco in 1585 at the invitation of the lord proprietor, Jorge de Albuquerque Coelho. Between 1585 and 1613 two monasteries were built, one in Olinda with the church referred to by Brandônio, and a second in the port settlement of Recife. Flávio Guerra, *Evolução histórica de Pernambuco*, 1:158. See also Odulfo van der Vat, "The First Franciscans of Brazil," *The Americas* 5 (July 1948):18–30.

135 · The Carmelites came to Brazil in 1580. Their monastery in Olinda, dedicated to St. Anthony and St. Gonzalo, was built from 1584 to 1590 on invitation from the lord proprietor of Pernambuco. Flávio Guerra, *Evolução histórica de Pernambuco*, 1:157–158; *Dicionário de história de Portugal*, ed. Joel Serrão, s.v. "Brasil."

136 · The Benedictines came to Brazil in 1584 and to Pernambuco in 1596. In 1597 they purchased lands in Olinda on which they constructed a monastery. Flávio Guerra, *Evolução histórica de Pernambuco*, p. 158.

137 · See p. 37 and n. 119 above.

138 · Cabral is known to have been in the exercise of this office in 1616. He died in 1621. Varnhagen, *História geral do Brasil*, 2:192, 221–222; see Monsenhor Manoel de Aquino Barbosa, *Freguezia da Conceição da Praia* (Bahia, 1973), pp. 77–79.

139 · The house of retirement [*recolhimento*] was that of Our Lady of the Conception [*Nossa Senhora da Conceição*], which was in existence as early as 1569. As Brandônio indicates, this house of retirement was not a true convent. That priority must be assigned to the convent of Santa Clara of the Exile [*Santa Clara do Destêrro*], in Salvador, which was founded in 1677 and was the only nunnery in Brazil for more than fifty years. Our Lady of the Conception dispensed religious instruction to the unmarried daughters of the aristocracy of the captaincy and taught them to sew sacred vestments and also to make delicious sweetmeats, which had a great reputation among foreign visitors. Flávio Guerra, *Evolução histórica de Pernambuco*, p. 21; Susan A. Soeiro, "The Social and Economic Role of the Convent: Women and Nuns in Colonial Bahia 1677–1800," *Hispanic American Historical Review* 54 (May 1974):210, 214.

140 · As early as 1587 Olinda, along with the city of Cosmos [Igaraçu], could muster 3,000 men, among them 400 horsemen, an auxiliary force of

4,000 or 5,000 African slaves, and many natives. Soares de Sousa, *Notícia do Brasil* (1945), 1:110.

141 · See above, n. 129.

142 · MS *camuci*. This Tupi word means both a clay funerary urn and the cave in which such urns are stored.

143 · The sons of Indian women by Portuguese men often became noted fighters. Some, given education and opportunity, rose to high position in the white man's world, e.g., Jerônimo de Albuquerque (see above, n. 70). In general, however, the *mamelucos* bore a reputation for being bold but arrogant, ruthless, treacherous, and unscrupulous. "The Spaniards, who are better supplied [with *mamelucos*] than all the other Europeans who live in America, have no better soldiers and no more wicked men," said Labat. Hemming, *Red Gold*, p. 77; Boxer, *Salvador de Sá*, p. 23; Labat, *Nouveau voyage*, 2:121.

144 · Urn burial was widespread among the Indians of Brazil, especially the Tupi tribes. See Robert H. Lowie, "The Tropical Forests: An Introduction," in *HSAI*, 3:38.

145 · The space for the number of degrees of latitude is left blank in both the Lisbon and the Leyden MS. The latitude was 11²/₃ degrees south according to Vicente do Salvador (*História do Brasil*, p. 302), but 11 degrees south according to the anonymous author of the "Discripción de la Provincia del Brasil," (*Documentação ultramarina portuguesa*, 2:4). The settlement lay between the São Francisco and Real rivers, the latter being the boundary of Bahia to the south. Sergipe was won after Cristóvão de Barros defeated the Indians fighting under the famous chief Boipeva from 1587 to 1590. Barros was made captain major, and his soldiers were given land grants in the captaincy. These were largely devoted to raising cattle, which were worked in the mills of Pernambuco and Bahia and also used as food for those captaincies. In addition, much lumber was produced. Sergipe-del-Rei was a royal captaincy and was subordinate to the Captaincy of Bahia during the colonial period. Campos Moreno, *Livro que dá razão*, pp. 161–163; Basílio de Magalhães, *Expansão geográphica do Brasil Colonial*, p. 33.

146 · A fort on the harbor, erected by Cristóvão de Barros, was in ruins when Campos Moreno wrote, six years before Brandão. *Livro que dá razão*, p. 162. Apparently a new fort had been constructed by the time of the *Dialogues*.

147 · Of course it was not the captaincy but the city (Salvador) that was the capital of Brazil. It was chosen for this distinction in 1549 mainly because of its central location but also because, with the death of the donatary, the captaincy had reverted to the King, who could thus establish direct control. Another motive for establishing a central government for Brazil

was that the coast could now be defended more effectively against the French and Indians. The King appointed Tomé de Sousa (1549–1553) as the first governor general of Brazil. A former captain in the wars of Africa and India, Tomé de Sousa proved to be one of America's great colonial governors.

By 1612 the district around Salvador (the Recôncavo) had become the most popular site on the coast, with 3,000 white settlers, though they were crowded into an area extending only some twenty miles inland. In addition to sugar, the Recôncavo produced cotton, ginger, rice, corn, and lumber. Bailey W. Diffie, *Latin-American Civilization: Colonial Period*, pp. 649, 741; William Brooks Greenlee, "The First Half-Century of Brazilian History," *Mid-America* 25 (April 1943):116; Campos Moreno, *Livro que dá razão*, p. 140.

148 · During the first twenty years of the seventeenth century there was growing objection to the governor generals' practice of residing during much of their term of office in Pernambuco instead of in the capital, Salvador. For example, Gaspar de Sousa spent most of his term in Pernambuco; see above, n. 69. It was not until February 21, 1620 (thus two years after Brandão was writing), that the King issued an order that "the governors of the State of Brazil shall reside personally in the city of Salvador da Bahia de Todos os Santos or they will not earn a salary or have any jurisdiction whatsoever." This order ended the gubernatorial sojourns in Pernambuco. Dutra, "Centralization vs. Donatarial Privilege," pp. 27–40; Garcia, ed., *Diálogos*, I, n. 25.

149 · See above, n. 90.

150 · See above, n. 91.

151 · Like other wealthy sugar planters of Pernambuco, Brandão felt that the High Court was merely an encumbrance on the Brazilian economy. Severe criticism of the court also came from the Franciscan priest Vicente do Salvador (author of the *História do Brasil*), who resented the Court's attack on the Bishop and the ecclesiastical courts, and from the professional soldier Diogo de Campos Moreno (author of the *Livro que dá razão do Estado do Brasil—1612*), who considered the educated civilians who staffed the court corrupt and their labors superfluous. As to Brandão, in addition to the reasons given in the *Dialogues* he may well have been influenced by sympathy for New Christians in Bahia. Many of the New Christians were engaged in the contraband trade with Buenos Aires (see III, n. 101), and the court, all of whose members were Old Christians, had the authority to enforce control of this trade. The court had the task of collecting the tribute levied on New Christians in 1605 in return for a general pardon. It was even under study for a time as a possible permanent board of the Inquisition in Brazil. But if Brandão did have

these considerations in mind, he was silent about them. "For all its failings," says Schwartz, "the *Relação* probably provided justice to a wider range and larger proportion of the colonial population than ever before." Schwartz, *Sovereignty and Society*, pp. 110–112, 232–235. Cf. Dutra, "Centralization vs. Donatarial Privilege," pp. 58–59.

152 · Properly, viceroy of Portugal. Afonso de Castelbranco occupied the post from August 22, 1603, to December 26, 1604, a period during which Brandão was presumably in the metropole. José Antonio Gonsalves de Mello, ed., *Diálogos das grandezas do Brasil*, pp. viii, xix. The governors had a different function; see below, n. 159.

153 · For a discussion of the difficulties experienced by and with various officials who occupied the office of *ouvidor-geral*, see Schwartz, *Sovereignty and Society*, pp. 28–42. Brandônio will explain later on (pp. 43–44) what he thinks would be a "better way" than the High Court.

154 · The monsoon is properly a wind of the Indian Ocean, but the term was vulgarized in Brazil to refer to any wind favorable to long voyages and even to land journeys. Here Brandônio refers to the *suis* [south winds], which blew from October to January and greatly facilitated coastwise navigation northward. On the other hand, they made it impossible for ships coming from Europe and Africa, already held back by a contrary current, to reach Pernambuco during the season in which they blew. Accordingly, such ships usually steered for the West Indies. Bernardino José de Souza, *Dicionário da terra e da gente do Brasil*, s.v. *monção;* Campos Moreno, *Livro que dá razão*, p. 208 and n. 5.

155 · There was considerable variation in the size of a sugar chest, but according to Boxer, at this period it usually contained 20 arrobas, or about 640 pounds. If the price set for sugar by the governor of Rio de Janeiro (see above, n. 98) is taken as a norm, such a chest would be worth twenty milreis (20$000). Boxer, *Salvador de Sá*, p. 180 and n. 48; Coaracy, *Rio de Janeiro*, p. 39.

156 · In 1553 Father Manuel da Nóbrega sent three of his colleagues to found a mission on the plateau of Piratininga, some forty-five miles from the town of Santos. This mission became the site of the city of São Paulo. The settlement was subjected for three decades to attacks by the Tamoios and their French allies, as well as by freebooters cruising along the coast. By the beginning of the seventeenth century, conditions had stabilized somewhat, and the Paulistas began to make incursions into the interior to capture Indians to be worked as slaves, or to search for gold and, later, for gems. Many of these incursions, or *entradas*, were extensive, some lasting years at a time and ranging as far north as the Amazon, west to the Andes, and south to the Rio de la Plata. The raiders, called *bandeirantes*, became widely famed and feared. Though they established

only temporary settlements, they actually succeeded in pushing back at some points the boundary between the Portuguese and the Spanish holdings—the Line of Tordesillas. Morse, *Community to Metropolis,* pp. 3–14.

157 · After a person's arrest and before the beginning of his trial, he might (unless the charge was extremely grave) obtain a letter of safe-conduct [*carta de seguro*]—a document giving him temporary immunity from arrest in order that he might enter a territory or present himself before a higher authority. See *Enciclopédia brasileira Mérito,* s.v. "carta," and Schwartz, *Sovereignty and Society,* pp. 248–249.

158 · Another oversight, since Brandônio is ostensibly not writing but conversing.

159 · The Council of Portugal, which was established in 1593 by Philip II of Spain (I of Portugal) to work with him on administrative supervision and policy. The Council was made up of five Portuguese noblemen with the title of governors of the Kingdom. The Council's decisions on important matters were subject to ratification by the King. A. H. de Oliveira Marques, *History of Portugal,* 1:316–317; Garcia, ed., *Diálogos,* III, n. 2.

160 · The High Court was to be abolished in 1626 after a series of conflicts. It was not replaced, as Brandônio wished, by magistrates operating within a system similar to that in Portugal. Instead, the Crown appointed a superior crown magistrate, thus reinstating the system that had existed in Brazil before the creation of the High Court. In 1652 the High Court in Bahia was in its turn reinstated. Schwartz, *Sovereignty and Society,* pp. 227–232, 234–235. A second High Court was added in 1751, with its seat in Rio de Janeiro. See Dutra, "Centralization vs. Donatarial Privilege," pp. 58–59.

161 · Brandônio has spent so much time on the High Court that he has little left for the other "great things" of Bahia. This deficiency may be supplied by referring to Soares de Sousa, *Notícia do Brasil* (1945), the second volume of which is mainly devoted to Bahia.

162 · The whaling industry in Brazil began in 1602 under the governorship of Diogo Botelho, who introduced the industry in order to provide oil for the settlers. At his direction Pedro de Orecha, a Biscayan, brought in two shiploads of his countrymen to start the industry and train Portuguese for it. Because this enterprise filled such an important need, the whalers at first were not required to pay any taxes, but later this exemption was withdrawn. For four centuries, until the advent of petroleum in 1859, the oil obtained from whales was used in Brazil for illumination, though it furnished but a dim and murky light. Whatever oil was not needed for this purpose was used in the manufacture of leather and in the treatment of skins.

A detailed account of all phases of the whaling industry in Colonial

Brazil is provided by Myriam Ellis, *A baleia no Brasil Colonial;* for the activities in Bahia referred to by Brandônio, see especially pp. 31–45 and p. 136. Dauril Alden gives a succinct summary of the development of the industry in his "Yankee Sperm Whalers in Brazilian Waters, and the Decline of the Portuguese Whale Fishery (1773–1801)," *The Americas* 20(3) (Jan. 1964):267–288.

163 · Campos Moreno wrote in 1612 that in the district around Salvador there were fifty sugar mills, some of which brought their owners an income of 8,000 to 10,000 cruzados a year. Two of these mills that belonged to a single individual brought him 20,000 cruzados clear annually. *Livro que dá razão,* p. 139.

164 · The three forts were Santo Antônio, Itapagipe, and Água dos Meninos. Campos Moreno, writing in 1612, hence shortly before Brandão, says these forts were in such a state of disrepair as to be totally useless for defense. Ibid., p. 143. Campos Moreno's opinion is to be treated with respect, since he was sergeant major in charge of defenses for all of Brazil.

165 · The Jesuits came to Brazil after they were chosen by the Crown to accompany Tomé de Sousa in the founding of the city of Bahia (Salvador) and the introduction of royal government into Brazil. Six members of the Company, including the famous Father Manuel da Nóbrega, arrived in Bahia in March 1549. One of their first acts was to set up Indian villages [*aldeias*] to protect the Indians from exploitation by the colonists and to facilitate the salvation of their souls. Another was to start a school to train Indian children for the lower clergy in order that they might help carry Christianity to their people. Leite, *Suma,* pp. 3–5. See above, n. 129.

166 · The Benedictines were invited to come to Bahia from Rio de Janeiro. They started a monastery in the capital in 1581. Francisco Vicente Vianna, *Memória sobre o Estado da Bahia,* p. 301.

167 · Shortly after the Carmelites founded their first monastery in Brazil, in Olinda (see above, n. 135), they founded another in Salvador. Ibid., p. 302.

168 · In 1587 the Franciscans of the Province of St. Anthony arrived in Bahia at the invitation of the Bishop of Brazil. Their monastery was completed by 1596. Ibid., p. 300.

169 · Boipeva is an island just south of Bahia, at the mouth of the Prêto River. Vicente do Salvador stated in 1627 that the island of Boipeva, along with the island of Tinharé, was part of the Captaincy of Ilhéus. *História do Brasil,* p. 124. But for trade and defense the settlement of Boipeva, like the Captaincy of Ilhéus, was a dependency of Bahia.

170 · The Aimorés (also known as Botocudos) in the sixteenth century were found all along the Atlantic coast from the Captaincy of Ilhéus to that

of Espírito Santo. Considered the most ferocious of the Brazilian Indians, they left a long and bloody record of pillage and killings. "Stout fierce men," said Anchieta, ". . . they always travel through the forest, where four are enough to destroy a great army, which they accomplish without your seeing what kills you." Anchieta, *Cartas*, p. 308. Cf. Vicente do Salvador, who described how the Aimorés did not fight in the open, but "move like lions and tigers through the forest and burst out to attack on the roads, or concealed among the trees shoot their arrows." Their depredations continued for more than 100 years. Alfred Métraux, "The Botocudo," in *HSAI*, 1:531–540; Vicente do Salvador, *História do Brasil*, pp. 333–334; Campos Moreno, *Livro que dá razão*, p. 126.

171 · Porto Seguro was the first part of Brazil that Pedro Álvares Cabral discovered (1500). In 1534 the King granted this captaincy, extending along fifty leagues (172 miles) of coast, to Pero de Campo Tourinho. In Brandão's time it was owned by Álvaro de Lencastre, third duke of Aveiro. Porto Seguro produced a quantity of brazilwood and *zimbos* (see above, n. 98). About 1560 the Aimorés were driven into the back country by Mem de Sá, governor general of Brazil, but later in the century they laid waste the towns of Porto Seguro, Santo Amaro, and Santa Cruz. Many sugar mills in the colony failed because of these attacks, and also because the cattle that worked the mills were killed by feeding on a plant that grew in the pastures there. See Campos Moreno, *Livro que dá razão*, p. 123, n. 1; Vicente do Salvador, *História do Brasil*, pp. 121–122; Métraux, "The Botocudo," in *HSAI*, 1:531–532.

172 · The figure for the latitude of Porto Seguro is omitted from both manuscripts of the *Diálogos*. Soares de Sousa located the northern boundary at 16²/₃ degrees south. *Notícia do Brasil* (1945), 1:153.

173 · Espírito Santo was separated from the Captaincy of Porto Seguro on the north by the Rio Doce [Sweet River] at 19 degrees, according to some; by the Cricaré (today São Mateos) according to others, said Campos Moreno in 1612. *Livro que dá razão*, p. 123.

174 · Coutinho became the donatary of the captaincy in 1593, but he did not assume its direction till after 1605. The colony suffered from attacks by the Goitacá Indians (a tribe related to the Aimorés), who also harassed the settlers in the captaincies of Ilhéus, Porto Seguro, and São Tomé (Paraíba do Sul) for many years. José Teixeira de Oliveira, *História do Estado do Espírito Santo*, pp. 120–122; Gabriel Soares de Sousa, *Notícia do Brasil* (1974), pp. 40, 41, and 330 (n. 183).

175 · I.e., *cabriúva*. See II, n. 83.

176 · See above, n. 8.

177 · Rio de Janeiro was the name originally given to Guanabara Bay, on which the city was to be erected. It was discovered on January 1, 1502. This

immense body of water could easily be mistaken for the mouth of a river, but in the sixteenth century the word *rio* was commonly applied not only to rivers but to bays and estuaries that were good harbors. Maps of the time show that people were well aware that Guanabara Bay was not a river but a bay or gulf. Though the French made a practice of trading in this area, it long remained unsettled. In 1555 French Huguenots under Nicolas Durand de Villegaignon, a French admiral, undertook to establish a settlement there. The Huguenots built a fort in the bay, from which they were driven in 1560 by order of the governor general of Brazil, Mem de Sá (1558–1572). Savage warfare followed, with the Indians aided by the French, but Mem de Sá finally triumphed. In 1566 he ordered the construction of the city of São Sebastião do Rio de Janeiro. See Vicente do Salvador, *História do Brasil,* pp. 175–176; Coaracy, *Rio de Janeiro,* p. 2; Pedro Calmon, "O Rio de Janeiro, da conquista à fundação dos franceses (1567–1700)," *Revista do Instituto Histórico e Geográfico Brasileiro* 276 (Jul.–Sept. 1967):11–23.

178 · Presumably the original fort of Santa Cruz; certainly not the modern fort of that name. The old fort, built in 1605 by Martim Correia de Sá, governor of the Royal Captaincy of Rio de Janeiro, was situated on the spot where the former church Cruz dos Militares had stood. Coaracy, *Rio de Janeiro,* p. 22.

179 · Silver coins of various values from Peru.

180 · From 1608 to 1612.

181 · The new administrative unit remained judicially subject to the High Court in Bahia. Francisco de Souza, who held the office from 1591 to 1602, eagerly promoted schemes for exploring the mining possibilities of the area around São Paulo both during and after his term of office, but like all his predecessors in this endeavor he died without finding any treasure. The southern captaincies were reunited with the rest of Brazil in 1612. Coaracy, *Rio de Janeiro,* pp. 27, 35–36; Schwartz, *Sovereignty and Society,* pp. 124–127.

182 · The Bishop of Brazil, whose seat was in Salvador. See above, p. 32 and n. 90.

183 · There were actually two captaincies to the south of São Vicente—Santo Amaro and Itanhaém—but disputes were constantly erupting among their *donatários;* so in order to facilitate administration they were treated as a single captaincy with São Vicente. Boxer, *Salvador de Sá,* p. 19.

184 · Lopo de Souza was the grandson of Martim Afonso de Souza [Sousa]. On Lopo de Souza's death the Captaincy of São Vicente was claimed by Francisco de Faro, count of Vimieiro, but it was finally adjudicated, along with the Captaincy of Itamaracá, to the count of Monsanto. See above, n. 121.

185 · Brandônio will tell us later (p. 265) that six or seven milreis was about the price of a calf "old enough to be harnessed to a wagon."

186 · Cf. Antonil's complaint against the settlers on the same ground. André João Antonil [João António Andreoni], *Cultura e opulência do Brasil por suas drogas e minas,* p. 342 and n. 1.

187 · At the time of the gold rush in Minas Gerais (at the end of the seventeenth century) this lesson was yet to be learned. "In their frantic haste to exploit the existing diggings, or to find new ones, the pioneers neglected to plant sufficient manioc and maize, with the result that they suffered acutely from famine in 1697–1698 and again in 1700–1701." Boxer, *Golden Age,* pp. 47–48.

188 · The goods had to be packed by mules or Indians except where there were rivers or streams that were navigable by canoe.

189 · Brandônio's prediction never came true for São Vicente, but gold was discovered in large quantities in Minas Gerais in 1693–1695, and by the end of that period the gold rush was on. During the next three decades additional strikes were made in the interior of Brazil. The total production of gold in the captaincies of Minas Gerais, Mato Grosso, Goiás, and São Paulo up to 1820 has been estimated at about one million kilograms. Hélio Vianna, *História do Brasil,* 1:301–302.

Dialogue II

Which Treats of the Climate and of the Sicknesses

in Brazil and the Medicines That Cure These

༄

Dialogue II takes up the question posed at the end of Dialogue I as to whether the torrid zone is habitable. Many of the ancients had declared that it was not. Brandônio's remarks show an ambivalence common enough in his time: the ancients were wrong, he admits with some regret; but their opinion was fully logical in view of the inadequate facts at their disposal.

Brandônio's description of Brazil's climate and its effect on the population is fitted into the framework of the Ptolemaic cosmography, still generally accepted in the seventeenth century even by scholars. Yet, again, the authority of the ancients is not absolute. Where Ptolemy's theory does not square with experience, Brandônio readily amends or rejects it; and his own theories about climate, unscientific as they inevitably are, at least rest on observation and not tradition.

This discussion leads to the question of the origin of the Brazilian Indians, a subject that occupied a number of Brandâo's contemporaries. Several current theories are brought up and rejected, with Brandônio casting his own vote for Israelitish origin.

Returning to the climate, Brandônio credits it here, as he does in many another laudatory passage, with health-giving qualities that account for the robustness and longevity he claims for the natives. Information is given about both native and imported ailments and about native remedies.

With the background supplied in this dialogue, Brandônio feels that his listener is ready for the next day's discussion of the riches of the new land.

ALVIANO   It seems to me that the same thought must be what has brought both of us to this place at the same moment. For my part,

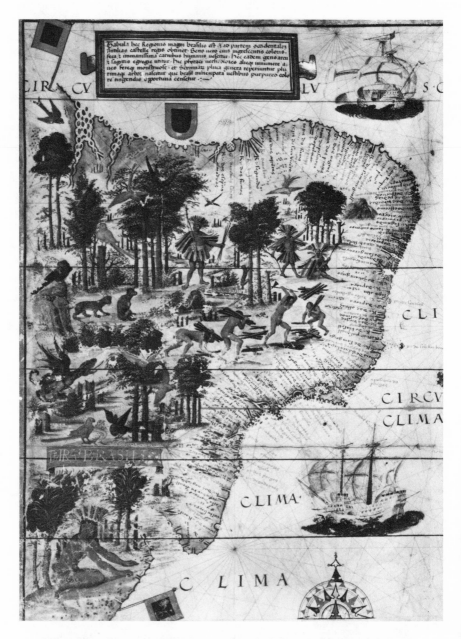

Map of Brazil ca. 1519. Courtesy of the Bibliothèque Nationale, Paris.

I will confess to you that the conversation which yesterday we left unfinished—because of the question I raised—kept me awake all night.

BRANDÔNIO   Repeat your question, so we can pick up the thread of our conversation.

ALVIANO   I expressed a doubt that this land of Brazil could have as good a climate as you claimed, since the greater portion of its coastline falls within that torrid zone which the ancients feared so much for its heat that they declared it uninhabitable. And great doubts were raised in my mind by your telling me that a land that was uninhabitable because of its wretched climate was so healthful for humankind.

BRANDÔNIO   It is true that the torrid zone, into which falls a great part of this Brazil coast, was judged uninhabitable by the ancients, because of the excessive heat which they imagined must exist there. Regarding this, we have in our day learned the contrary;[1] for we find it so temperate and suitable for humankind that the two others—the temperate zones—might well be abandoned, because of the discomfort and harm which their changing climate brings upon their inhabitants and which are the cause of so many sicknesses; and this zone might well be sought as a most suitable dwelling place, where the evenness of heat and cold is so well regulated that we never see it altered more in one season than in another.[2]

ALVIANO   At that time there were very few men in the world who had explored and traveled on their own two feet in these parts, then hidden but today revealed to us. So now you must give me license to believe that the ancient philosophers dreamed up those fantastic things, spinning fancies which in their writings they publicized as true and not to be doubted, and which were accepted as such. Nonetheless, the knowledge that we have today of those things has not shown everything to be contrary to what the ancients taught.[3]

BRANDÔNIO   It is true that Ptolemy,[4] Lucan,[5] Averroës,[6] and other philosophers declared the torrid zone to be uninhabitable, although Peter of Padua,[7] Albertus Magnus,[8] and Avicenna,[9] on the other hand, held it to be habitable. But the former, although they erred in declaring unconditionally that the so-called torrid zone is totally uninhabitable, because it lies between the Tropics of Cancer and Capricorn, nonetheless based their argument on such a plausible foundation that, though today we are seeing and discovering the contrary of what they affirmed, almost everyone still holds this to be doubtful.

ALVIANO   I don't see what doubt there can be about something so tried and true.

BRANDÔNIO   I don't claim that there can be any; but I am saying that the reasons which the ancients gave were so plausible that even today, when we know the contrary of them to be true, they have great weight with all who examine them with interest. For we know now that the sun does not go beyond the tropics, and that each of the tropics is little more or less than 24 degrees removed from the equinoctial line. This comes to 48 degrees from the beginning of one tropic to the end of the other, and is the path that the sun takes in the course of a year, passing twice through the so-called torrid zone. Now that being so (which no one doubts), it was thought that a region so continually exposed to and visited by the direct rays of the sun must be extremely hot, especially since it had been observed that the temperate zones, even though not so close to the sun and not visited twice a year by its direct rays, were so hot in summer that they brought much suffering to their inhabitants, on account of their great heat. Now that being so (and no one doubts it), what did the ancients[10] do wrong, or how did they err, in declaring that this region, so continually exposed to the sun's rays, must be extremely hot, and, as such, incapable of being inhabited?

ALVIANO   Well, then, what *was* the reason for the error of these philosophers?

BRANDÔNIO   Nothing else than this: since they lacked any acquaintance with this zone, they did not know about the cool winds that ordinarily blow within it, except in a small stretch of what we call the Guinea Coast. These winds cool the air powerfully and cause a climate so singularly suited to humankind that I hold it beyond question that this zone is more healthful and temperate than the others. For the heat that the sun causes therein during the day is tempered by the moisture of the night; and also Saturn and Diana, cold planets by nature, have greater influence over these regions—for here they have more direct lines of connection. Thus says Junctinus,[11] basing his teaching on the testimony of Sacrobosco's *Sphere;*[12] and Avicenna[13] does not shrink from believing that it is temperate enough for human habitation. Indeed, there are even authors who claim that the Terrestrial Paradise is situated in these parts.[14] They support their reasoning by saying that the equinoctial line divides the day in two, dividing the 365 circles that we call the day, leaving 182 and a half to each of the parts, whence perforce it follows that the days must be equal to the nights. Thus the inhabitants of this zone can see with the naked eye any of the stars that rise or set at either pole. And also, because the sun passes through this zone twice a year, those authors maintained that its coming caused two winters and two summers, in which they were mistaken also, for we know there is no more than one. For when the sun moves toward the region north of the line, winter comes to the southern part. And when the sun returns to this part, it causes the summer, for it appears that the equinoctial line serves the sun as a divider of the seasons. And thus the inhabitants of this zone come to have five shadows during the year; for, when the sun is right on the equinoctial line, at its rising it casts shadows toward the west, and in the afternoon toward the east, and at noon beneath one's feet. And when the same sun moves into the northern signs [of the zodiac], it casts, oppositely, shadows toward the austral regions.[15]

ALVIANO Then it seems safe to conclude that the ancients erred in saying this zone is uninhabitable, but that their error was reasonable; and that even today, when we have discovered the contrary of what they maintained, we must excuse them, for their mistake arose from nothing else than lack of acquaintance with this coast, every bit of which we, in more recent times, have so thoroughly gone over.[16] Hence, they could have had no knowledge of the winds that ordinarily prevail along it sufficiently to cool the air, which by nature ought to be excessively hot. But it seems to me you have said that the equinoctial line serves as a divider between the world's[17] poles. Now if, according to that, the equinoctial line does divide one thing from another, it perforce must have some body that we do not see, with which it can effect such a division.

BRANDÔNIO I did not say that the equinoctial line divides the world's poles by virtue of having a body to effect such a division, but I said that it appears to divide them. For the equinoctial line is nothing more than a circle imagined by the astrologers to be within the eighth sphere, dividing it into two equal parts, being itself equidistant from the north and south [celestial] poles.[18] It is called equinoctial because when the sun moves along it—which is twice a year, in the beginning of Aries, on March 21, and in the beginning of Libra, on September 23—the equinoxes occur. This is nothing else than that the artificial days[19] are as long as the nights. And this should be understood as occurring only where there is variation in the days of 24 hours, for those lands that lie directly beneath the poles have days six months long and nights just as long again.

This equinoctial line is called also an equalizer of day and night, because wherever it runs it makes the days equal. In the same manner, it divides the first movement, for the first movement—as the philosophers say—must be divided by the action of the mover. Hence the equinoctial line was imagined, in the material sphere, as being able to measure and regulate the movements of the heavenly bodies. And thus this line divides in half the so-called torrid zone, which is situated between the two tropics and has a width of almost 824 leagues, half of which (412 leagues) lies toward the Tropic of Cancer and the other half toward the Tropic of Capricorn. And along the eastern side of all this zone runs the African coast called Guinea, inhabited by black people. On this other, or western, side lie the Indies coast and this Brazil coast, inhabited by brown people.

ALVIANO   I have already heard some learned men discuss the reason why on that African coast called Guinea and Ethiopia,[20] all of the inhabitants—natives of the land—are black and have kinky hair, similar color and hair not being found in any other people the world around. And although they offered reasons to explain this, I confess to you that these were too obscure to satisfy me.

BRANDÔNIO   And what reasons did you hear given to explain the strange fact that those people are different from everybody else in their color and hair?

ALVIANO   It was said that the heat of the sun, which ordinarily visits that zone twice a year with its direct rays, was the cause of the difference in the color and hair of those people; but there is so much to be said against this that I can in no way persuade myself to think that it is the cause. Others declared also that the influences of the heavens, conjoined with the peculiar quality of the land, were the true cause, although it does not appear so to me. And among those men I found others who said that some men, after the universal deluge of waters, must have had such color and hair, either as an inherited characteristic or as a natural tendency, and would have communicated them to their children and grandchildren, who dwell along the African coast. But of all these reasons that I heard from men with a reputation for learning, I tell you that not one of them satisfied me; so I shall appreciate knowing your opinion on this matter.

BRANDÔNIO   I do not think that, in attempting to answer the question that you raised, we are forgetting the purpose of our conversation, which is to discuss only the great things of Brazil. For a new Guinea has been created in this Brazil, what with the great multitude of slaves found here who have come from over there. So true is this that in some of the captaincies there are more of them than there are natives of this land.[21] And all the men who live here have put nearly all their capital into such merchandise. Therefore, since there are so many people in Brazil with this black color and kinky hair, we shall not be getting off our subject if we discuss them.

ALVIANO   Of course not; and this matter should not be passed over in silence, for all the inhabitants of Brazil live, traffic, and carry on their work by means of these people who have come from Guinea.[22] Therefore you may take up this subject, which interests me, and I assure you that such a proposal will not displease anyone if we give the proper explanation.

BRANDÔNIO   As for saying that these innumerable heathen, who are black and have kinky hair, must have been produced by black parents, I consider that ridiculous. For if those first parents were of necessity sons of Adam and, later on, descendants of Noah—of which there can be no doubt—they could hardly take on a skin color and a kind of hair that they had not inherited from them. For up to the present day nowhere in the world have we seen that black children are produced by white parents.

ALVIANO   The contrary is what I have heard, read, and seen with my own eyes; namely, that many white parents have black children. This is told of a lady who, being in the act of love with her husband, happened to look at the moment of conception at the figure of a black man in a tapestry hanging near them; the mental image of what she saw right then was so powerful that the child she conceived from that coupling turned out to be black, just as if it had been engendered by black parents.[23] And I have read of similar cases occurring in the world. A few years ago, in the Kingdom of Angola, a black woman had, by her black husband, twins. One of them was the color of his parents, that is, black, and the other as white and blond as if he had been born in Germany, the son of a German. And I have even seen with my own eyes in this very Brazil, in the town of Olinda in the year 600 [i.e., 1600],[24] a little girl whose father and mother were natives of this very land—and, therefore, brown skinned—but who was as blond and white as ever nature could make her. Her flesh was so delicate and soft that their putting her to bed on a mat was enough for her to rise from it with her body covered with sores. I learned afterwards that she did not live long.

BRANDÔNIO   It is true that very often black children have been born of white parents and, by the same token, white children of black parents. But no one has seen, or found it written, that the children of those who were thus born black or white [of parents of the opposite color] had descendants who were likewise of the same color. For if nature by some chance altered the color of those persons, it was never strong enough to make the new color prevail from generation to generation. Rather, the children of those who were born black, or white, at once recovered the natural color of their grandparents. Henceforth that color persists in the children of the next generation. Therefore, granted that those white parents had some black children, by some chance as I have said—of necessity these [black children] must have been descendants of Adam, and, later on, of Noah, who were white skinned— their children and grandchildren must at once have recovered the white skin of their ancestors, and therefore one should not attach any importance to such cases.[25]

ALVIANO   Can we, then, believe that the influences of the heavens and the peculiar quality of the land may have combined to produce such an effect?

BRANDÔNIO   I hold that false also, for the influence of the heavens and the peculiar quality of the land together may be powerful enough to render the place where they prevail more or less healthful for human habitation, and also to be the cause of few or many sicknesses. But that they have outright power to make people change their color, which by nature was white, to black, is not possible, nor can such a thing be conceived.

ALVIANO   Well, there is no doubt some reason why the countless heathen who dwell along the coast we call Guinea have black skin and kinky hair; and—if you know the reason—I beg you to tell me what it is.

BRANDÔNIO   The truest cause that can be given of that color and that hair is the effect produced by the sun, visiting its direct rays twice a year on the inhabitants of that African coast. The sun's direct rays in that region have more of an effect on its inhabitants than in other regions where they strike slantwise and obliquely. Thus, that is the true cause of the black color and of the kinky hair that we see in all the inhabitants of that coast.

ALVIANO   What you are telling me now certainly strikes me as being more misguided than anything we have yet considered, for if the sun's rays cause a change in skin color and in hair in one region, it follows that our Portuguese who have been living there for many years would have the same color. Likewise, the blacks who are taken from that coast to Spain and to other parts of the world, where they have been living now for many years, would, on the contrary, have to have changed their black color to white, especially their children who are born there. But we do not see this, for, rather, the blacks who live there, they and their children, are as black as the others who have never left their homeland. And likewise the Portuguese who have been living in Africa for many years, and their children, have not ceased being white. By which it appears that the sun's rays do not cause the effect that you have indicated.

BRANDÔNIO   The fact that blacks born in Guinea do not turn white after being transported to our Spain is not a strong enough argument to refute what we have said. For, in the few years that it has been the custom to carry them off to Spain, it would not be possible for them to change the color that throughout so many centuries had been acquired by their ancestors, inhabitants of that zone. Furthermore, if the blacks who live there [in Spain], who were all taken together from those parts [Guinea], continued to reproduce among themselves, and if reproduction continued among their own children, grandchildren, and great-grandchildren, I hold it beyond doubt that they would already have shown a color somewhat less black. But the opposite happens, for the children of those who were carried off first are coupled later on with men or women who had been recently transported, and in this way they continually refresh the black color acquired from their forebears in so long a course of time. And so true is this that our Portuguese who dwell all along that coast, although they may be by quality and nature white and blond, in a short time take on a browner color, so that, in our Lusitania, any man who has spent some time along the Guinea Coast is known merely by the altered color of his face. And the children of those Portuguese who are born in Guinea rapidly take on a darker color, and so in turn their grandchildren, so that if, in the course of the slightly more than a hundred years that the Portuguese have been plying the Guinea trade, so much difference is noticed in the color of those who engage in it, why is it surprising that the natives of that coast should have a black color after all the centuries that their people have lived there?[26]

ALVIANO   So, you still maintain that the sun's rays are the cause of the color that we see in those people?

BRANDÔNIO   Not only do I say that the sun's rays are the cause of such a color, but I also say that they are the cause of their having kinky hair. For surely you must know that, after the universal deluge of waters, the children and grandchildren of Noah began to spread around the earth, each one making his home in that part or region which most pleased him. Whereupon, the descendants of the wicked Ham and his son Canaan[27] came to settle on the African coast in this so-called torrid zone. Finding it so temperate and suited to human habitation, they established their dwelling in the seaside places, for those first settlers always sought out the sea to live along its shores because of the many advantages that resulted therefrom. That coast having been settled thus by those people so many centuries ago, is it too much to think that the sun's rays, which visit them directly twice a year, following them so closely, should turn their white color, which they had inherited originally from their fathers and grandfathers, into that black which we see on them now? For it is certain that anything, although it be white, becomes black if it is burned.

And in the same way I say that that same sun was, and is, the cause of their having kinky hair, for we know by experience that any hair that is touched by the heat of fire curls up at once and becomes kinky. Now, that being so—and there is no doubt of it—it should not be surprising that the hair of those peoples, scorched for so long a time by the sun's rays, became frizzly. Thus I consider it beyond doubt that the black color and the kinky hair that we see in the natives of that coast—why, the rays of the sun were powerful enough to work that change in them.

ALVIANO   If that happened in the way that you suggest, the same effect that you say the sun produces in those inhabitants of the African coast would have to be produced in all the other inhabitants of the same parallel, and underneath the same zenith. But we see quite the contrary. For in the very heart of this torrid zone, where the equinoctial line runs, lie most of the West Indies and this great Brazil coast, both of which are inhabited by brown-skinned people. If it were the sun's rays that worked that change in those other people, as you said it was, those rays ought also to have the same effect on the people here, for they live under the same parallel. Yet we see that the contrary happens.

BRANDÔNIO   You are right to wonder at it, and I admit that that would happen if two important causes—which support my contention—did not prevent it. And thus I tell you that all the inhabitants of this Brazil coast and the Indies would have the same black color and kinky hair that the inhabitants of the opposite African coast have, if it were not for the fresh winds which ordinarily wash this entire coast, and by which the air and land are cooled so that they do not leave room for the sun and its rays to work here the effect they work on the other, the Guinea Coast.

ALVIANO   So then you want me to believe that there are no winds on the Guinea Coast, or that, if there are any, they are not enough to cool the air and land as they do in this Brazil? Yet I know, for reliable persons have told me so, that in many parts of the African coast there is generally a cool wind.

BRANDÔNIO   It is true that the wind does not fail entirely along much of that coast, but all the wind it does get comes from overland. Since the winds in this zone are regularly from the east, those that come to this Brazil coast, where we dwell, come from over the sea, and they are therefore very cold and fresh, while those on the Guinea Coast come from overland, and thus carry with them the noxious vapors and the heat of the same land. Thus it happens that those regions are so sickly and so unfit for habitation by those who live there. Now, on the contrary, the Brazil coast is very healthful and suitable for humankind, the true cause of which is the cool winds that regularly blow in from the sea. And, similarly, we have found that the land breezes, which usually spring up at dawn all along this great American coast, are so prejudicial to the health of men that for this reason they are accustomed to build their houses so that they are not exposed to them. And the only reason for these winds being unhealthy is that they blow from overland. Therefore, there is no doubt that this is one of the causes that the native inhabitants of this Brazil have a brown skin, and not a black one, as the people of Guinea have.

ALVIANO   I approve of your explanation and find it very probable. But, to be better informed on this subject, I beg you to tell me the second reason that you said supports your contention.

BRANDÔNIO   The second cause is that the inhabitants of this Brazil coast are not such ancient settlers as are the blacks of the opposite Guinea Coast. Of the latter we know, by authentic Scriptures,[28] that, after the sons of Ham—from whom they descend—came to settle those regions, they continued right up to the present to dwell in the same land, without misfortune or anything whatever happening to drive them from it. Instead, they continued to propagate, for many centuries cohabiting with women of their own nation. This was not the case with the inhabitants of this Brazil, who are peoples who wandered to it much later. For this reason, and for the other that I have already given you—the cool off-shore winds prevailing all along this coast—the inhabitants escape being black and having kinky hair.

ALVIANO   And what reason can you give me for thinking that the inhabitants of Brazil and of the Indies are more recent settlers in these lands than those people who live on the African coast?

BRANDÔNIO   In the case of the inhabitants of the African coast we have knowledge, from Scriptures worthy of belief, of the very ancient times in which they came to pitch their tents in those parts. But we have no report we can heed of the period during which the peoples of this Brazil coast began to settle here. Now all of them being, as they are, sons of Adam and, subsequently, descendants of Noah, we know that they went out in throngs to inhabit and people the three parts of the world, to wit, Asia, Africa, and Europe. It is not known what paths were followed by the first people who came to settle in these great unknown lands of Brazil and the Indies, which were neither known nor heard of by men for so many centuries. For we have no trace whatever in the Scriptures from which to infer whether they came by sea or by land. And even today, when so much has been discovered, we cannot trace any route by which they might have passed over to this New World.

ALVIANO   I remember having read in Aristotle, in the book in which he wrote of the things that are found hidden in nature, that the Phoenicians, chancing to veer off their course in the Ocean Sea in a ship, sailed four days without sighting land. At the end of that time they came to an unknown land that was ever shifting with the motion of the sea, whose waters would cover and then uncover it, leaving stranded a great quantity of tunny, larger than the usual ones.[29]

In this same book the author himself says that some Carthaginian merchants from the Island of Cales,[30] the farthest point and boundary of the Pillars of Hercules, after many days' sailing came upon some islands far off the mainland [of Spain], which they found uninhabited, for no one lived on them although they abounded with all that was needful for human existence. Now those islands—and in my own mind there's no doubt about it—must have been those that lie nearby [the West Indies], for it would take that many days' sailing to reach the coast of the Indies.[31] Then, after they were peopled, their inhabitants left them, passing over to make their homes on this great unknown mainland [America]—whence the origin of its first settlers.

I have also heard that one Velpócio Américo [sic],[32] a native of Carthage, sailing a ship on the Ocean Sea, driven on by strong winds that did not let him reach land, at last made a landfall on this great Brazil coast, which from his name was called America. Thus I do not see how one can fail to think that from some of those peoples the population of the New World took its start.

BRANDÔNIO   True it is that Aristotle discusses that [the Carthaginian merchant story] in the book referred to; but as to those Phoenicians who he declares found the island that was covered and then uncovered by the waters, leaving many tunny stranded, and who spent four days sailing until they came upon it, I believe without doubt that that must have been some spit of land, which then joined on to a little island off the coast of the Algarve,[33] which we call Ilheta de Pessegueiro [Peachtree Island]. Many tunny are caught right around there even today, for they are accustomed to linger there after spawning. The ebb and flow of the tide must have caused the covering and uncovering by the waters, and the recurrence of storms and earthquakes over so many years sent the spit of land to the bottom of the sea, just as has happened in many other places, leaving visible only what is called Peachtree Island, for it was higher land. Since the Phoenicians who landed there were coming from the Strait of Gibraltar, they would really need those four days to sail that far, especially since they were so little experienced in seafaring.[34]

ALVIANO   That doesn't sound unreasonable to me, and thus I conclude that the Phoenicians did not extend their voyages beyond that island. But what do you say of that other voyage, of the Carthaginians,[35] which took them so many days?

BRANDÔNIO   Those islands which Aristotle says the Carthaginians discovered,[36] abounding in everything needful for human life, are nothing else than the Canary Islands. Before the Castilians discovered them, they had been settled by a people whom they call Guanches, who must have been descendants of those first Carthaginians who discovered the islands.[37] And the days Aristotle says they had spent sailing, before they reached them, were not too long a time for men so little skilled in the art of navigation as they were then. For there is no doubt that, fearful of the winds and seas, they made their voyage longer by not raising as much sail as was needed, and by lowering it at night so that in the darkness they might not strike a shoal where they would have perished. Because of all this, there is no doubt in my mind that it was the Carthaginians who began to settle all the islands called the Canaries.

ALVIANO   And what can you tell me about this Américo who, they say, landed on this Brazil coast and from whom the whole province took its name, being called America?

BRANDÔNIO   Even if everything written about him is true, there is no certain proof that we must accept that this Américo landed on the coast of Brazil any more than on the coast of Africa. For since the ancients lacked our modern navigational instruments, which give us our latitude and position,[38] this Américo's crew could very well have landed on any part of the African coast without realizing that it was the same coast they had set out from. And since the moderns were unaware of this possibility, after the Land of Holy Cross was discovered by Pedrálvares Cabral they insisted on thinking that this was the land which, they said, Américo had discovered; therefore they gave it his name. And it is quite possible that Américo did not know where he was, for in our own times, just a few years ago, a ship leaving Rio de Janeiro for Angola, after sailing many days, made a landfall. Thinking it must be Angola, their destination, they entered the mouth of the Paraíba River, which is on this same Brazil coast.

ALVIANO   And how is it possible that those sailors could have been so grossly mistaken?

BRANDÔNIO   After sailing many days on a straight course, their ship must have come about; and on the next day, seeing the prow pointing west, they ran on in that direction thinking it was east, without noticing where the sun rose and set. Thus, thinking they were in Angola, they found themselves in Brazil, in the mouth of the Paraíba, which lies in the same latitude {6 degrees south}.

ALVIANO   Well, then, Américo's error wasn't so bad after all, considering that these other men made their mistake at a time when we have such great knowledge of navigation.[39] But now, to get back to our subject, I beg you to tell me what opinion you hold on the settlement of this New World.[40]

BRANDÔNIO   Now that you want to draw me out on this subject, which I should much prefer not to become involved in, I shall have to go back a little way to get a good start, in order to present my opinion clearly.

The holy prophet King David, wishing to show his gratitude for the many mercies and blessings he had received from God, planned to raise in his honor a great temple that would be famous for its sumptuousness, wherein his holy name would be magnified and praised by the people. But he was forbidden by the Lord to do this, because of having bloodied his hands killing many enemies in the wars that he waged during his reign. Or, it may be that the unworthy death he gave Uriah, motivated by the unworthy love he bore Bathsheba, was enough for him to be judged "bloodthirsty" by God. Now David, faced with the prohibition God had laid upon him, restraining him from carrying out his great desire, devoted himself to accumulating materials for the construction of the temple. He left these to his son Solomon, charging him to have a care to its beginning and completion, since he had been unable to do it himself.

The wise king, who had inherited from his father the same desire, resolved to make an alliance with Hiram, King of Tyre, in order to collect much gold and silver, ivory and ebony, which he knew would be the very nerve and substance of the work, and absolutely necessary if he were to give it the grandeur he desired. They were to send out every year from Ezion-geber,[41] a port situated on the Red Sea, a fleet of ships which, issuing from that same strait, should seek the desired materials in the region of Tarshish.[42] Once started, this commerce was carried on a long time, the Scriptures stating that these ships went to the port of Ophir,[43] whence they brought back a great quantity of gold, silver, ebony, and ivory, and some parrots and monkeys, spending three years[44] on the round-trip voyage. Well, in view of all that—which cannot be doubted—it is a matter of knowing now just where this Ophir was, which Scripture mentions as being in the region of Tarshish. Now this name of Tarshish in the Greek means Africa, and on that coast ought to be the port of Ophir. Therefore Vatablo Parisiense[45] erred greatly in saying that Ophir was an island situated in the South Sea, off the coast of Peru, discovered by Cristóvão Coloma [sic], and called Hispaniola.[46]

ALVIANO   I cannot bear that any man should commit so great an error to writing, for it was impossible that people still so little expert in the art of navigation should seek the Molucca Islands[47] and from there, by the so-called South Sea, go looking for that island which Vatablo mentions, for that was a sea route unknown to the world until the Spaniards discovered it.

Now, if they had laid their course through these other seas, they would have had to round the Cape of Good Hope and after that go through the Strait of Magellan.[48] I hold this to be impossible, for in recent times, because we have explored this strait so thoroughly, we know that it is not a real strait,[49] but only has that appearance because of the cluster of many islands that are found there along the southern side of it, and that it can scarcely ever be successfully navigated, as was learned by the fleet of Diogo Flôres de Valdez[50] and others, who turned back from its mouth because of the tempestuous winds that ordinarily blow thereabouts.

BRANDÔNIO   At that rate, by neither route could they have made such a voyage, and what you say confirms me in thinking so. Therefore we should seek some place on the African coast where there might be found the things which that fleet carried, which were gold, silver, ivory, rosewood, and some parrots, which Scripture mentions. Many persons believe that this Ophir must be the region which today we call Sofala,[51] which our Portuguese discovered.

ALVIANO   That does not sound very likely to me either, for the Kingdom of Sofala is so close to the Red Sea and to its strait [Bab el Mandeb] that the trip from one to the other can be made in less than thirty days. Thus it is not convincing to say that so short a voyage would have taken Solomon's fleet so long. Even less can one believe that it would have stopped over so long after reaching port, for the delay would be too great for such small items, which are so easy to contract for. And thus it behooves you to seek another port along the African coast, which would require a longer voyage.

BRANDÔNIO   I am convinced—and this opinion is shared by many learned men—that the port which that fleet sought was the [African] coast which today our people call Mina, where the city of São Jorge [St. George][52] is located. For to sail to that coast one would have to round the Cape of Good Hope. Thus, on so long a voyage those sailors would

Map of Brazil and Africa in 1618. Courtesy of the
Bibliothèque Nationale, Paris.

have had to spend as much time as the Scriptures declare they spent on the round trip, since they were little experienced in the art of navigation. And in that region one finds an abundance of those things with which the fleet returned laden. For these reasons, and because many learned men are of the same opinion, I am convinced that Mina was the true Ophir to which those people sailed. Now, if things happened that way, who can doubt that some of the ships of the fleet perforce on their return, because of currents and the weather, must have reached that cape which is called St. Augustine, and that they ended up on the coast of this land of Brazil, and that from survivors of those ships has sprung the population of so great a world?

ALVIANO   I believe rather that this population had its start from Chinese, who, by the so-called South Sea off the Peru coast, managed—in some way or other—to reach a harbor on this great land.[53] For we know beyond all doubt that the Chinese have been seafarers from antiquity, and that most of the East Indies were settled by them. Many traces of them are found there, whence they withdrew to their own kingdoms and provinces, thinking they would be more secure there.

BRANDÔNIO   I do not doubt that the Chinese were mariners in ancient times, or that the Peru coast could very well have had its start with them, or that they might very well have reached some harbor along it, coming from over the South Sea. Still, no trace is found in the speech, or in the customs, or in any other thing whatsoever, of those people's having descended from the Chinese. And if they had descended from them, one could not believe that the heathen of Brazil could have had the same origin, for in speech, customs, and other charac-teristics they are very unlike the heathen of Peru. The latter are exceedingly weak by nature and little inclined to war,[54] whereas the former, who live on this coast, are exceedingly bellicose and spend their lives in wars and raids. Sufficient proof of this is that the heathen of this Brazil coast have never had any contact with those of the Peru coast; neither is there any indication that there ever was any such contact. That was what the Castilians found out when they discovered those regions; for to go from Brazil to Peru a thousand difficulties rise up between: great deserts, dense forests, lofty mountain ranges, and, above all, little or no water. For these reasons, to this very day no one among the natives or among our own people has ventured to cross so great a stretch of land.

ALVIANO   The solution you have given to both problems[55] does not displease me, but I cannot persuade myself that such barbarous heathen as those who inhabit all this Brazil coast are descendants of the Israelites; for, if that were true, surely some of the civilization of their ancestors would have been handed down to them—yet we see none of this in them.

BRANDÔNIO   I admit that the first parents must have shown and taught their children and grandchildren the skills and civilization which they had. But, since these had to be taught by word of mouth alone, they could not be remembered throughout so many generations by folk who lacked written texts, and who had no other means of preserving those skills and that civilization in such remote and unknown lands as those wherein they dwelt.

And thus, with the passage of time, what their ancestors had shown them was gradually swept from their memory, and they ended up in the condition we see them in today. But just the same, we find among them even today many words and proper names pronounced as they are in the Hebrew language, and likewise some customs, such as their taking their nieces to wife. Now, neither of these things would they be doing if they hadn't picked them up from people who practiced them. And, despite all their barbarity, they know the stars in the heavens which we know, although they give them different names. Because of all this, I consider it beyond question that these native inhabitants of Brazil are descendants of those Israelites who first sailed these seas.[56]

ALVIANO   Let us not dispute over this subject any longer, for because of it we have strayed far from the subject of our discussion, in which we were to consider the kindly heavens, the healthful climate, and the good qualities which this Brazil coast enjoys.

BRANDÔNIO   I do not think that we have strayed so far from our subject matter, for everything that we have said was necessary to get over the obstacle that could be raised about the mild climate of this whole Brazil coast—its being situated in the heart of the torrid zone, which the ancients thought was too hot to be habitable, but which, on the contrary, we have experienced to be most suitable for human habitation. As proof of this, even if we had no other, that furnished by the native heathen themselves would be enough. Going about uncovered, and with their flesh naked to the rays of the sun and the fury of the wind and the cuts of the rain, they have no other protection day or night than a little fire, by whose heat they warm themselves. Although they commit such great excesses in eating and drinking inordinately, as is their wont, nonetheless they generally enjoy perfect health and have robust limbs and great strength, which could not be the case unless the good air and climate of the land gave them great help and nourishment.

ALVIANO   There is no one who will question that, for some days ago when I was going by some native villages I noticed some men who appeared to be of an extreme old age.[57]

BRANDÔNIO   There are many Indians all along this Brazil coast who are more than one hundred years old. I know some of them who still have every tooth in their heads, and who retain the utmost vigor, having three and four wives, of whom they have carnal knowledge, and they told me they had never once in their lives been sick. Almost all of these heathen are, thus, in very good health, the cause of all this being the auspicious skies and the good climate of this land.

ALVIANO   I have seen some of the native heathen of this land taken to our Portugal, where they do poorly and most of them die very soon, but I never knew the reason for it.

BRANDÔNIO   The fact that the heathen of this Brazil don't fare very well in Portugal substantiates my argument for Brazil's good climate. Since they leave a most healthful country and one with good, pure air[58] for another which is inferior to the first in a great many ways, their nature, accustomed as it is to the excellent dwelling place and climate that they have in the land of Brazil from which they are taken, does not bear up under the injury caused by the weather in our Spain with its heat and cold. For that reason they cannot do well there, and soon lose their lives.[59] This does not happen to the heathen who are taken there from the Kingdom of Angola and from all of Guinea. Since they leave behind them a sickly land unfit to live in, their nature is content to enjoy the climate of our Spain, which surpasses theirs in every respect of healthfulness. The same thing happens with the heathen who are taken there from the East Indies. But it is just the reverse with Brazil. For any people, of whatever nation they may be, generally live here in perfect health, and those who arrive sick get better very quickly.[60] And the reason for this is that these lands of Brazil are more salubrious and have a better climate than all others.

ALVIANO   Why, I always thought that the reason for the heathen's not flourishing in Spain was nothing else than that they went from a hot climate to a cold one, which cut into them right away and put them in danger of their lives.

BRANDÔNIO   The heathen of Guinea and of the island of São Tomé come from a much hotter land, and yet they do well in Spain, without the cold doing them any hurt. Likewise the cold does not harm those who are brought from India; so the cause is not that, but rather just what I said.

ALVIANO   I concede that I am vanquished, for from the reasons you have given me I recognize this climate of Brazil to be the best in the world in that region where it is not cut by the equinoctial line, for there it must perforce have a bad climate, as does every part of the world where that line passes.[61]

BRANDÔNIO   There, too, you are mistaken, inasmuch as the lands of Brazil where the equinoctial line passes have the same climate as others that are far distant from it. We have very clear proof of this in Pará, recently settled, known by another name as River of the Amazons. The line cuts right through the middle of the area of its port and settlement. It is no less temperate and healthful because of that, and is marvelously suited to human habitation. Indeed, the whole land of Brazil has such favoring heavens and good air that none of the things that ordinarily are harmful in other regions are so here, nor can they build up strength enough to be harmful.

ALVIANO   Being a native of the Kingdom and a newcomer to this land[62] has made me ignorant of many things that are obvious to the old settlers. Therefore, do not be surprised if I ask you some things that are very well known, for they are not so to me, for the reason I just mentioned. For instance, I see no reason why this State of Brazil should be without sickness, as you have claimed it is, when there is so much of it everywhere else in the world. Right here where we are, in only the short time that I have resided here, I have heard complaints from many men of particular infirmities that they suffer from.

BRANDÔNIO   I did not say that there was absolutely no sickness in Brazil, for that would be going against the truth. But what I meant is that the illnesses found here are so light and so easily cured that they almost cannot be reckoned such. Why, just see how many heathen live all along this coast, with their brutish way of life, committing such great excesses in eating and drinking during their drunken bouts[63] (and only one of the many nights that they spend in them would be enough to kill a thousand Europeans), and this still does not do them any harm, and they live healthy and happy. It is true that sometimes a little fever comes over them, but it does not amount to much, and they get over it easily just by bathing in the nearest river they can find.[64]

ALVIANO That's a fine way to get cured! If I were that sick and so much as stuck my foot in the water, it would be enough to put an end to me.

BRANDÔNIO Well, for them to get into the water acts as medicine. And, when they have headaches, they get better just by shaving their heads. It also happens that they have some trouble with their bowels, and for this they take some medicine, in their own fashion, and they cure themselves of it. They often get sick also from an illness called *mal do bicho*,[65] which is the most common indisposition here. This is nothing else than a burning sensation that occurs inside the anus. It is enough to make all the limbs terribly weak and to cause fever and headaches. It is easily cured just by washing that region three or four times with lukewarm water. But, if one does not use such simple medication, that burning sensation will infect the entire intestine and kill the patient. And I have seen that happen to many people.

ALVIANO I never heard tell of a sickness like that in Spain or anywhere else; so I think it must exist only in this state [of Brazil].

BRANDÔNIO I think, rather, that it is very widespread through the whole world, and that a great multitude of people die from it without the doctors' knowing what it is. In Portugal, I knew two or three sick persons who had been bled many times, and the doctors were determined to wear them out with more bleedings. I advised that they wash themselves with lukewarm water, because they might easily be suffering from the *bicho*. When, following my suggestion, they washed themselves only three or four times, they recovered their health perfectly.

ALVIANO Well, what else can a man do to know if he is sick from that *bicho* or something else?

BRANDÔNIO What they do in this country is very simple: they take a little bit of tobacco[66] (also called *erva santa* [sacred herb])—if they haven't got another herb which they call *pajamarióba*[67]—and they put a small amount of this, crushed and mixed with lemon juice, inside the anus of the patient. If he is ill with the *bicho* this will cause a great burning. But in the contrary case he feels nothing, or almost nothing. And this herb, crushed up with lemon juice, also cures this sickness most effectively.[68]

ALVIANO   I am glad that you have let me know such a secret, for at the slightest little twinge of fever or headache I'm ready to give up the ghost, what with the experience I've had with household remedies. If these heathen don't suffer from any other sicknesses than those you have mentioned, they can consider themselves free from illness.

BRANDÔNIO   Oh, they suffer from a few others, for they are attacked too by measles and smallpox, from which a great many people die. But these diseases, especially smallpox, are foreign diseases which generally are communicated to them from the Kingdom of the Congo and from Arda[69] by the blacks brought from there. They kill ever so many of the heathen of this land and from Guinea. In '16 and '17 [1616 and 1617] many rich men in this State of Brazil became poor, because of the high mortality among their slaves.[70] But the curious thing is that this smallpox is not catching except among the heathen natives of this land and those from Guinea, and among persons who are children of white men and natives, who are called *mamelucos,* and, further, among all those born in this country, even though of white parents. But those who come out from Portugal and were born there of either Portuguese or some other European parentage never catch the disease[71]—although I have seen perhaps two or three of them die from it. But "one swallow does not make a summer" among such a great multitude as die of it among the other groups.

ALVIANO   That is an extraordinary circumstance,[72] which some hidden secret influence unknown to us must cause. And now I should like to know how the smallpox is cured.

BRANDÔNIO   Up to the present time, neither those who have much experience in this country nor the doctors who live in it have found any way or regimen to cure such a disease. Considering that it brings on a burning fever, they order the patient bled, and he dies; when they do not order him bled, he dies just the same. And contrariwise, if they bleed him, he lives; and if they don't bleed him, he lives just the same.

But people almost never recover if they catch a certain kind of smallpox, which they call *pele de lixa* [dogfish skin][73] because it makes the patient's skin look like the skin of that fish. The skin peels off the body as if it had been burned in a fire, leaving all the raw flesh exposed. I saw a sick man, and all the skin on one of his legs had come loose and hung from it like a trouser leg. Many people die that way without any preserving remedy being found for such a terrible disease, which is given by one person to another, like the plague.

ALVIANO   The way you describe the smallpox being spread and killing people makes it seem to me no less dangerous than the plague, which must also exist in this state.

BRANDÔNIO   On the contrary, it does not, for the air here is so rarefied and the heavens so benign that they do not permit such a pernicious disease as the plague to be found anywhere along this Brazil coast, the way it is generally found throughout Europe, Asia, and Africa. For in the memory of man there is no recollection of such a disease ever having been found in these parts. The climate is so much against it that many people, coming out from our Portugal at a time when the plague was raging there, infected with and still suffering from the same sickness, began to recover soon after crossing the equinoctial line into the southern zone.[74] The pestilential airs which the ship carried are attenuated and dissipated. And if a little trace of it [the plague] lingers on, it is totally extinguished and over with once the ship touches land on this coast. There can't be any better climate on earth than that!

ALVIANO   That a disease so contagious in other parts of the world should here diminish and taper off is proof enough of the salubrious skies enjoyed by this New World.

BRANDÔNIO   Well, the wholesome atmosphere of the land gives rise to all these wondrous things, and—excepting only the diseases I have named—there are no others, save some abscesses and sores, which the afflicted persons cure easily enough by applying ordinary medication, and some leaves and herb juices that the people know about.[75] There is never any need to have surgeons, barbers, or bleedings.

ALVIANO   It is not so easy to cure abscesses and sores in Portugal, for they take a long time to heal.

BRANDÔNIO   Well, in this Brazil they are easily cured, as I have said. In this connection, I can tell you something that I saw with my own eyes. I would never dare to tell this anywhere that I did not have the witnesses whom I have here.

It happened that one of my slaves, a black from Guinea named Gonçalo, suffered a total closure of the regular channels we have to evacuate the bowels and to urinate. A hole opened up in his belly, and through this he performed his necessities for many days. Then this hole closed up by itself and another hole of the same size opened up in his right side. Through this he likewise performed his necessities for more than six months.[76] At the end of that time, without any treatment or any medicine, he got better again. Once again the regular channels opened up in him and he voided through them as he had before. He was restored to perfect health and lived a long time.

ALVIANO   That is a strange thing that you tell me, and you are wise not to tell it except here, where you offer to back up your statement with witnesses; although for me they would never be more convincing than the fact that it was you who told it. But now I should like to know how the sick are physicked in this country.

BRANDÔNIO   With cathartic medicines that are brought out from the Kingdom and sold in apothecary shops.[77] The land is always well supplied with these, although out here one also finds excellent purgatives which most of the people use, such as the potato[78] (this is greatly esteemed in Portugal also) and pine nuts that are picked from trees the fields are full of.[79]

ALVIANO   Of those pine nuts I have heard a thousand bad reports. They tell me that a purge made of them is ever so terrible, because of the many vomiting spasms that it provokes.

BRANDÔNIO   It used to be so, but nowadays the purge is taken differently, and does not cause those accidents and vomitings.

ALVIANO   I should like to know the way they take the pine nuts nowadays.

BRANDÔNIO   Many people prepare them, after they are shelled, by removing the little skin they have on the outside, and another one underneath, to do which the nut must be opened. They close it right up again and put it inside a fruit called guava. If they don't have a guava, they put it inside one they call araçá,[80] and they put both of them—the pine nut and the fruit—on the embers to roast. When the fruit is roasted, they take the pine nuts out. With the heat of the fire, the pine nuts discharge into the fruit the malignity they had. The fruit is thrown away and the pine nuts are crushed in a mortar with a little white sugar to give them body. When this material has the proper consistency, they make a little ball of it which they again roast on a pot lid on the coals, until it gets to be like marzipan paste. I must warn you that one should use only five pine nuts for a physic, which the patient should take one hour before dawn, and with that he will have a prodigious movement of the bowels, until he is given a chicken broth, which will restrict his stool.

ALVIANO   That is a very easy way to take a physic, and I shall be very glad, whenever I find it needful, to make use of it.

BRANDÔNIO   It also happens in this Brazil, with our Portuguese as well as with the natives, that they have an accident with their bowels, the rectum turning inside out. This lasts for the space of 24 hours, more or less. Although in India this illness, which they call *mordexim*,[81] is fatal, here it is not, for, when the period of the accident is over, the patient gets well without any kind of medicine.

ALVIANO   And when these heathen happen to be wounded in the wars, to which you tell me they are much inclined, how do they go about healing their wounds?

BRANDÔNIO   Nature has provided them with an oil that is taken from a tree called copaiva,[82] and with this they heal their wounds, for it has a wondrous power and in a short time they are recovered. Now when such a wound is a deep one, because it was made with an arrow, and the hole is so small that they cannot make use of the oil, their remedy is to make a hollow in the ground. Into this they throw glowing coals and on top of them they put a board with a little hole in the middle. They get the wounded spot right over this, stretching the patient out on the ground for this purpose. Then, with the heat from the fire, which comes through the hole, the wound discharges all the infected blood and poison into it, and the flesh heals in such a fashion that, without any other treatment, the patient gets better.

ALVIANO   In Portugal I have also heard very good reports of a balsam for use on wounds, which is shipped there from the captaincies in the south.[83]

BRANDÔNIO   That balsam is an excellent remedy for wounds, but it is not found except in the captaincies that export it, which are those in the south. The northern captaincies lack it, and for that reason people there use the oil which I mentioned.

ALVIANO   I have heard a neighbor of mine complain many times about a sore he has on his foot, which will not heal.

BRANDÔNIO   Everybody in this Brazil who has sores or wounds on the head cures them very easily. But those on the feet and legs are more extensive, and the little care the patients are accustomed to take with them makes them slower to heal.

ALVIANO   And our Portuguese who live in these parts, do they use these same copaiva oil and balsam remedies?

BRANDÔNIO   Yes, they do, for they have experimented and found them to be excellent remedies for wounds. But for other sicknesses they follow a different style of treatment, being looked after by Portuguese doctors, barbers, and surgeons.

ALVIANO   And what are the most common diseases among the Portuguese?

BRANDÔNIO   After the Portuguese come here from the Kingdom the land usually tests them out with a fever and chills, which don't amount to much, for with two or three bloodlettings they get over them. And the longer the climate delays in testing them out, the harder the fever and chills strike them, but never to the extent of becoming a real illness. Also, those who have been in this country a long time get the same malaria, tertian and even quartan ague.[84] These are harder on some than others, according to the nature and constitution of each one, but very few people die of such sickness, which the doctors cure with physic and bleedings.

ALVIANO   Despite all the good qualities of the land, I have seen many men here who lacked noses and who had patches of their faces missing, and others half paralyzed, a clear proof of their having been touched by the bubonic humor.[85] It seems to me that this disease is found here to a great degree.

BRANDÔNIO   It is true that through the heat of the land this disease is communicated to many men who lead an intemperate life and who chase after women; but it is easily cured. With a little bit of sarsaparilla, and by obeying the necessary regimen in taking it, the sick recover perfect health. They also recover by doing exercises, taking walks, and doing other things to make the body sweat. In some, who have the disease harder, mercury extinguishes and dissipates it completely. In Brazil this is taken easily and with little risk. As for the men you say you have seen with deformities in their faces, their disordered life is the cause of that, for if they led well-ordered lives they would regain their health like other people.

ALVIANO   Nevertheless, I believe that the Spaniards are not wrong when they say that that disease spread to Europe from these parts.

BRANDÔNIO   The Indians will not agree to that. Rather, they insist that they never had it before the Portuguese came to settle this New World, and that they caught it from them.

ALVIANO   Let us not argue over that, for it matters little to us; but what I do know is that, whether the disease originated here or some place else, it is a terrible thing for those who have it. They also tell me that in this Brazil of yours there are some bugs (*bichos*) that work themselves into your feet.[86] In Portugal they really frightened me about these.

BRANDÔNIO They had no right to give you a scare like that, for lots of people look on these bugs' getting into their feet and having to be taken out as a kind of recreation, because of a pleasant sort of itching which they make.

ALVIANO And what are these bugs like?

BRANDÔNIO Much smaller in size than the fleas in our Portugal, as long as they live in ordinary soil. In sandy soil they are larger, and from the ground they work into the foot, where they grow larger still. When one is careless about taking them out, they get to be the size of a cranberry and are the same color. But when they work into the foot, the itching they cause promptly warns you of their presence. They are easily taken out with a pin or the point of a knife, without any trouble. One can put up with the discomfort caused by these insects (though many people don't consider it discomfort) because of the absence in this country of the other vermin that plague us in Portugal.

ALVIANO And what are these vermin that you say this country lacks?

BRANDÔNIO Lice—which just won't stay here for any reason—and also fleas and bedbugs, which you don't find here.[87]

ALVIANO Just to enjoy being free of those things a man might leave Portugal, where they are such a nuisance, and come to live in Brazil.

BRANDÔNIO It seems that the quality of the land upsets the life of those bugs so that they cannot survive here.

ALVIANO Yet I do not find the land so hot that it would be too much for them.

BRANDÔNIO The temperate heat of the land is what does it, for though the sun often shines on our heads, it nonetheless does little or no harm to the inhabitants, for the fresh breezes that blow most of the time cool its rays so that they give a most tempered heat. Thus, although men go around in little clothing, the sun's rays do not burn them; neither do the winds pierce them. It is true that the moon is considered less healthful, and therefore they protect themselves from it.[88] Still, it is not so harmful that it is bound to addle those who expose themselves to the moonlight.

ALVIANO I have already experienced this good climate, and I look on it as the best that can be, for in midsummer as in winter the land has the same even climate all the time, so that the same summer clothing does for the winter, without its being necessary to double one's wardrobe.

BRANDÔNIO   That's exactly right, and I have also noticed another very curious thing. This is that there is no recollection within the memory of man of there ever having been an earthquake in this province, such as we often have in our Spain.[89]

ALVIANO   That is a thing of no small moment, whence I should think that the land of this Brazil must be heavy and solid, without caverns, caves, or hollows underneath, where the air can collect, which is what generally causes these tremors. It may also be that this is the reason for its good climate, which you have told me so much about; so I should be pleased now if we might go on to discuss its richness and fertility.

BRANDÔNIO   It is already late, and the subject matter is extensive. Therefore it seems wise to me to reserve it for tomorrow, and I shall await you in this place.

ALVIANO   So be it, for I do not wish in anything at all to go against your pleasure.

Notes to Dialogue II

1 · Many contemporary writers both learned and popular pointed out the error of those ancients who thought the torrid zone was uninhabitable; for example, André Thevet, *Les singularitez de la France Antarctique, autrement nommée Amérique*, chap. 19; Louis Richeone, *Trois discours pour la religion catholique* (1597), chap. xxiii, pp. 100–101, quoted in François de Dainville, *La géographie des humanistes*, p. 33; and various academic commentaries on the works of Aristotle, e.g., the one known as the *Conimbricenses* or *Conimbrés*, written by and for professors at the University of Coimbra at the order of the Father General of the Jesuit Order. Dainville, op. cit., pp. 25–27.

2 · In raising near the beginning of his treatise such a question as the habitability of the equatorial regions, Brandão is following a standard practice of his time. Thus Garcilaso de la Vega [El Inca] introduced his *Comentarios reales de los Incas* (1609) as follows: "Having to treat of the New World . . . it seems proper to follow the usual custom of writers and discuss here at the beginning whether there is only one world or many, whether it is flat or round, and also whether the sky is round or flat, whether it is all habitable or only the temperate zones, whether there is a way from

one temperate zone to the other, whether there are antipodes and what they are like, and similar matters which the old philosophers treated very fully and carefully and the moderns do not fail to debate and discuss, each following the opinion that pleases him best." *Comentarios reales de los Incas,* 1:61–62.

3 · The last sentence of Alviano's speech is inconsistent with the context: Alviano is not affirming the wisdom of the ancients, but finding excuses for their mistakes. He should have omitted the *not.* Perhaps the author became confused and thought *not* was required by the sense; it would not be the only instance of Brandão's getting lost in his own sentence structure. Or perhaps it was the copyist who erred: the manuscript shows some uncertainty or revision in the writing of this word. One possibility is that the original word was *nos* [us] rather than *não* [not]. In that case the original reading would have been "The knowledge that we have today of those things has shown *us* that everything is contrary to what the ancients thought."

4 · Claudius Ptolemaeus was a celebrated Greek astronomer, mathematician, and geographer of the second century. He set forth in his *Almagest* his view of the cosmos, which taught among other things that the earth was fixed in the center of the universe and that all the celestial bodies revolved daily and yearly around it. The Ptolemaic concept was generally accepted until Galileo's theory of a heliocentric universe superseded it in the eighteenth century. See David Watkin Waters, *The Art of Navigation in England in Elizabethan and Early Stuart Times,* pp. 41–43.

Brandônio is mistaken in thinking that Ptolemy considered the torrid zone to be uninhabitable. "The equator may be habitable," Ptolemy said, "as the sun does not stay long at the zenith there, but whether it is actually inhabited is not yet known from credible reports." Ptolemy, *Almagest* (Heidelberg), ii. 13, p. 188, cited in James Oliver Thomson, *History of Ancient Geography,* p. 335. Brandão may be thinking of Sacrobosco rather than of Ptolemy; but see below, n. 12.

5 · Marcus Annaeus Lucanus (39–65 A.D.) was a Latin poet, the author of an epic, *Pharsalia* or *Bellum Civile,* which contains digressions on geography that made Lucan a leading authority on this subject along with Virgil and Ovid. With respect to Lucan too Brandônio is in error: Lucan believed the torrid zone to be habitable, on the ground that the cold of the arctic regions offsets the excessive heat produced by the constellations. *Pharsalia,* v. 11. 105–120.

6 · Averroës (1126–1198) was a famous Arabic philosopher, astronomer, and physician, born in Córdoba, Spain. He introduced Aristotle to the Western World and was the first to translate Ptolemy's *Almagest* from the Greek (see above, n. 4). Brandônio is correct in saying Averroës believed the

torrid zone to be uninhabitable. Gasparo Contarini, *Gasparis Contareni Cardinalis ampliss. philosophi sua aetate praeseantissimi de elementis et eorum mixtionibus libri quinque,* fols. 40ᵛ–41ᵛ (hereafter cited as *De elementis*).

7 · Peter of Padua, or of Abano (1250–1316), was an Italian physician and philosopher who dabbled in astrology. His works excited a good deal of enthusiasm in their day, but now seem obscure, argumentative, and laced with contradictions. As Brandônio says, Peter taught that the torrid zone is habitable. Sante Ferrare, *I tempi, la vita, le dottrine di Pietro d'Abano, saggio storico-filosofico,* p. 278.

8 · Albertus Magnus (1193–1280), the eminent German scholastic philosopher and theologian, was a member of the Dominican Order and professor at the University of Paris. His greatest achievement was to make available to Europeans the Aristotelian knowledge of natural science, enriched by additions made by the Arabs and by his own observations in all areas of nature. After carefully reviewing all the reasons against the habitability of the torrid zone and of the lands south of the equator, Albertus concluded (in agreement, he says, with Ptolemy and Avicenna) that those lands are in fact habitable and even agreeable all the year round. Jean Paul Tilmann, *An Appraisal of the Geographical Works of Albertus Magnus and His Contribution to Geographical Thought,* pp. 155–156.

9 · Avicenna, or ibn-Sina (980–1037), was a distinguished Moslem philosopher and physician, whose works were used for centuries as textbooks in Asiatic and European schools. Avicenna taught in his *Canon of Medicine* (bk. 1) and his *Animals* (bk. 10) that the tropics are habitable, though regions near the tropics of Cancer and Capricorn are not. Pierre d'Ailly, *Imago mundi, de Pierre d'Ailly,* 3:646–647; Sérgio Buarque de Holanda, *Visão do paraíso; os motivos edênicos no descobrimento e colonização do Brasil,* p. 184, n. 30; Contarini, *De elementis,* fols. 40ᵛ–41ᵛ.

10 · To Brandônio, apparently, almost anyone who lived earlier than his own age was an ancient. His list of "philosophers" who discussed the equatorial regions includes names from the second to the fourteenth century.

11 · Francesco Giuntini (1523–1590), also known as Junctinus or Juntino, was an Italian theologian and astronomer, author of a commentary on the *Sphaera* of Sacrobosco: *Commentaria in Sphaeram Ioannis de Sacro Bosco accuratissima* (Lyons: Tinghium, 1578). As to the habitability of the equatorial regions, Junctinus hedges. In one place he says he will not take a position for or against it. But in another place he admits that the Portuguese have discovered lands there. *Commentaria,* pp. 178, 330. On the influence of the planets, Brandônio may have in mind a principle stated by Robertus Anglicus: "The influence [of a planet] is stronger when the star [i.e., planet] is in the lower part of its orbit because then the radius [of its orbit] is shorter." "The Commentary of Robertus Anglicus," in

Lynn Thorndike, *The Sphere of Sacrobosco and Its Commentators*, pp. 162, 215.

12 · Johannes de Sacrobosco (John of Holywood), an English monk of the thirteenth century, was the author of a Latin treatise, *Tractatus de Sphaera* (1472), the first work on astronomy disseminated in the Western World after the fall of the Roman Empire. It set forth the cosmogony of Ptolemy (see above, n. 4), and provided the background for all the important works on astronomy, cosmography, and navigation from the thirteenth to the seventeenth century. In addition, it served every navigator as a basic textbook. Waters, *Art of Navigation,* pp. 41–43. Sacrobosco's work was available to the Portuguese as early as 1537 through a translation by Pedro Nunes, with which Brandão may well have been familiar.

Contrary to Brandônio's implication, Sacrobosco states that the torrid zone "is said to be uninhabitable because of the fervor of the sun, which ever courses above it." Thorndike, *Sphere of Sacrobosco,* pp. 94, 129. Of the many commentators on Sacrobosco's *Sphaera,* some agreed with their master that the tropics were uninhabitable; others took the opposite view. Several of the commentaries, including that of Robertus Anglicus but not that of Junctinus, are in Thorndike, *Sphere of Sacrobosco.*

13 · See above, n. 9.

14 · D'Ailly cites several theologians who, following the teachings of Avicenna, concluded that the Earthly Paradise must lie in the torrid zone; see *Imago Mundi,* 3:646–647 and n. 645. After the discovery of America some writers (Columbus among them) theorized that Paradise might be situated in the equatorial regions of the new land, but by the seventeenth century this idea had largely vanished from serious thinking. The theory left traces, however, in the literary imagery of the time, as a number of passages in the *Dialogues* illustrate. Buarque de Holanda, *Visão do paraíso,* pp. 316–317.

15 · This passage is evidently derived from Sacrobosco or one of his imitators or commentators, but these authorities all say there are four, not five, shadows cast in the torrid zone. Here is Sacrobosco (numerals added):

[1] "When the sun is in either equinoctial point their [the inhabitants'] shadow in the morning falls toward the west, in the evening in the opposite direction." [2] "At noon their shadow is perpendicular, when the sun is overhead." [3] "When the sun is in the northern signs, their shadow lies toward the south"; [4] "but when the sun is in the southern signs, then their shadow falls toward the north." Thorndike, *Sphere of Sacrobosco,* pp. 105, 135.

Brandônio leaves it to the reader to include the shadow cast when the sun is in the southern signs. By counting the shadows somewhat differently from his predecessors, he arrives at a total of five shadows.

The ultimate source, Ptolemy himself, mentions only the shadows cast at noon: ". . . for those living under [the equator] the sun is twice at the zenith, at the intersections of the equator and the ecliptic, so that at those times only are the gnomons shadowless at noon. And when the sun passes through the northern hemisphere the gnomons' shadows fall to the south, and when it passes through the southern, to the north." *The Almagest,* bk. II, sec. 6.

16 · Educated men of Brandão's time had been forced by experience to admit that the authority of the ancients must be rejected in many areas, but they still respected these men who had so long been their masters, and found excuses for their errors. Cf. Garcia d'Orta: "Dioscorides must be pardoned, for he wrote with faulty information and from far away, and the sea hadn't been navigated as it has been now; and in this he imitated Pliny and Galen and Isidore [of Seville] and Avicenna and all the Arabs. . . ." *Colóquios dos simples e drogas e cousas medicinais da Índia* (1563; facsim. ed., 1963), coloq. 46, fol. 172.

Brandônio has cited eight philosophers who pronounced on the habitability of the equatorial regions. He stated the views of five of these philosophers correctly: Averroës, Peter of Padua (of Abano), Albertus Magnus, Avicenna, and Junctinus. He stated the views of the other three incorrectly: Ptolemy, Lucan, and Sacrobosco. Thus his show of scholarship rests on but a shaky foundation. Besides, if he had had any real learning, he would certainly have mentioned Aristotle, the ultimate authority for those writers who supported the uninhabitability of the equatorial regions; see Contarini, *De elementis,* fol. 40^r.

17 · Universe's.

18 · Here Brandônio launches into an explanation of some elements of the Ptolemaic cosmology as set forth by Sacrobosco and his commentators.

19 · The artificial day is from sunrise to sunset; the natural day is of twenty-four hours. It was a moot question whether the latter began at sunrise or at sunset.

20 · Van Linschoten defined the Guinea Coast as the area from 9 degrees north to the equator. John [Jan] Huyghen van Linschoten, *The Voyage of John Huyghen van Linschoten to the East Indies,* 1:15.

Early travelers imagined Ethiopia, or Abyssinia, to be in many different parts of Africa or Asia. Brandônio's notion of Ethiopia, however, is evidently that of the sixteenth-century Iberians who "carried their missionary zeal . . . along the coast of what they termed 'Ethiopia' (the modern 'Africa south of the Sahara')." Francis M. Rogers, *The Travels of the Infante Dom Pedro of Portugal,* p. 111. Many of the early maps picture the "Ethiopian Sea" off the west coast of this region. Cf. João dos Santos, *Ethiópia Oriental, e vária história de cousas notáveis do Oriente,* fols. 3^v–5^r.

21 · See I, n. 35. It is not possible to calculate accurately how many Africans were in Brazil in 1618. Kiemen estimates that the number in 1600 was roughly 20,000. Mathias C. Kiemen, "The Indian Policy of Portugal in America," in Lewis Hanke, ed., *History of Latin American Civilization: Sources and Interpretations,* vol. 1, *The Colonial Experience,* p. 254. Some 560,000 blacks were transported to Portuguese America during the seventeenth century, according to Curtin; for the entire colonial period the figure reached 3,647,000. Philip D. Curtin, *The Atlantic Slave Trade: A Census,* pp. 87, 119. As to the white population, there were approximately 50,000 settlers of European origin in Brazil in 1615. Nearly half of these were residents of Pernambuco. Charles R. Boxer, *Salvador de Sá and the Struggle for Brazil and Angola, 1602–1686,* p. 17.

22 · Cf. p. 306: "The farmers live on what the slaves raise," and many other passages that express Brandônio's awareness that the Brazilian economy was totally dependent on slaves. As João de Moura observed, "It is not the style for the white people of these parts, or of any other of our colonies, to do more than command their slaves to work and tell them what to do." Charles R. Boxer, *The Golden Age of Brazil, 1695–1750,* p. 1.

23 · This story reflects a widespread folk belief that goes back at least to classical times. For example, Quintilian (first century A.D.) defended a white woman who had given birth to a black child, explaining that at the time of conception a picture of an Ethiopian was hanging in her room. Simão de Vasconcellos, *Notícias antecedentes, curiosas, e necessárias das cousas do Brasil,* in *Chrônica da Companhia de Jesu do Estado do Brasil,* p. lxxi.

24 · According to this passage, Alviano has been acquainted with Brazil for at least eighteen years. Yet on p. 24 he said he was a newcomer, a statement he will reiterate on p. 105. One might suppose he must have been a trader, making infrequent visits to Brazil, except that he has "resided" there. Perhaps it is a temporary residence, for he expects to return to Portugal with Brazilian curiosities (p. 262). On the whole, it must be concluded that Alviano's status is equivocal. Perhaps Brandão changed his mind about him in the course of composing the *Dialogues.* Certainly, Alviano's prejudices and misconceptions about Brazil are better suited to a new arrival than to an established resident.

25 · Brandônio's theories would not have appeared absurd to his contemporaries, since the laws of heredity were yet to be discovered. Ideas similar or identical to Brandônio's appear in many of the early chronicles.

26 · Vasconcellos (1663) gives a more explicit statement of this theory: "That first man who in Brazil began to be tanned by the warmth of the sun . . . in the course of the long years of his life kept acquiring an intrinsic natural temperament, warmer than he had before: . . . with this he afterwards engendered a son; and the son, living in the same way as his

father, added another degree of warmth and temperament, and the grandson another; until little by little one of these came to have that intensity of warmth and temperament philosophically necessary for a different kind of color; and that was red, which was the highest degree of color which the warmth and temperament of the climate could reach. And this temperament came to be converted into nature [*natureza*]; and thus was necessarily transfused into the seminal power in the male and in the female and by this means passed to all the descendants." Simão de Vasconcellos, *Notícias*, p. lxxii. The theory lasted into modern times: as late as 1803 James Stanier Clarke reported that it was said that the Portuguese who have lived in Angola for some three centuries "are become absolute negroes." *The Progress of Maritime Discovery, from the Earliest Period to the Close of the Eighteenth Century*, 1:237, n. 6.

27 · According to the Book of Genesis, Ham [MS Cham] was the second son of Noah. Because Ham had looked upon his father's nakedness, God cursed Ham's son Canaan [MS Chanaã], saying, "A slave of slaves he shall be to his brothers" (Genesis 9). The Bible relates (Genesis 10) that after the Flood, Ham and his family wandered abroad, reportedly settling for a time in a land that was named for Canaan. According to varying traditions, the Canaanites became ancestors of peoples of Asia and West Africa. Over many years the "sin of Ham" and the Lord's curse on his posterity were cited as a justification for black slavery.

28 · Brandão's contemporaries ordinarily did not distinguish between the Bible itself and the traditional interpretations of commentators, especially those printed as marginal glosses in the various editions of the Bible. It is to such commentaries that Brandônio refers here. See Lee Eldridge Huddleston, *Origins of the American Indians: European Concepts, 1492–1729*, p. 11.

29 · Most of Brandão's contemporaries did not distinguish the Phoenician theory, which Brandônio is presenting here, from the Carthaginian theory, which comes next. One who, like Brandônio, did differentiate between them was the Spaniard Gregorio García, whose *Origen de los indios de el Nuevo Mundo e Indias Occidentales* was published in 1607, only a few years before the *Dialogues* were written. García concluded that the island was either Madeira or one of the Azores (pp. 475–476).

30 · "It is told," said the *De Mirabilibus Auscultationibus* attributed to Aristotle, that people of Carthaginian origin living in "Gades" [Cadiz, occupied by the Carthaginians from 501 B.C.] sailed forth to seek a western land. They did find a rich and fertile island lying beyond the Pillars of Hercules, but further exploration was foiled by the Sargasso Sea. The Carthaginian story was current in the Renaissance only in translation, but it was common knowledge among the educated classes on the Iberian Peninsula. A Spanish

version was given by Oviedo y Valdés in his *Historia general* (1535); another was published by Columbus's son Fernando in his biography of his father. Brandão could have known, or known about, either of these accounts. The Carthaginian was the most persistent of all the theories centering on a transatlantic origin of the Indians. Gustavo Barroso, *O Brasil na lenda e na cartografia antiga*, pp. 25–26; Huddleston, *Origins*, p. 17; Gonzalo Fernández de Oviedo y Valdés, *La historia general delas Indias*, bk. 2, chap. 3; Fernando Colón, *La historia de el Almirante D. Christóval Colón*, in *Historiadores primitivos de las Indias Occidentales*, ed. Andrés González de Barcia Carballido y Zúñiga, 1:7.

31 · According to Oviedo, it is 1,300 leagues in a direct line from Spain to the city of Santo Domingo, on the island of Hispaniola, though the route followed by ships was more than 1,500 leagues in length. The trip from Spain to Hispaniola required from thirty-five to forty days; that from Santo Domingo to *terra firma* [the Isthmus of Panama] from five to seven days. Gonzalo Fernández de Oviedo y Valdés, *Oviedo dela natural historia delas Indias*, chap. 1.

32 · It is hard to see how our author became so confused about Amerigo Vespucci. Not only does he misspell the explorer's name (a mistake that perhaps points to an oral source), but he apparently thinks Vespucci was an ancient Carthaginian. Yet Brandão's faulty information about Vespucci may not be so surprising as it seems at first. Vespucci, after enjoying a great reputation during his lifetime, had become generally discredited as the supposed fabricator of accounts of voyages he had not actually made. By Brandão's time his fame was in fairly complete eclipse, even though as a result of Waldseemüller's map (1507) his name had stuck to the continent he claimed to have discovered. For a summary account of the controversy about Vespucci's supposed fabrications, see Samuel Eliot Morison, *The European Discovery of America: The Southern Voyages* A.D. *1492–1616*, pp. 306–312.

33 · A province on the southern coast of Portugal.

34 · See p. 96, and above, n. 29. Brandão's knowledge of the classics was obviously not very deep, since he seems unaware that the Phoenicians were a seafaring people, who in ancient times had a very great reputation for skill in navigation. He is, of course, thinking of the notable advances in navigation, and especially in the use of navigational instruments, that had been made by the Portuguese and others in recent times.

35 · See p. 97, and above, n. 30. The names Carthaginian and Phoenician were often used interchangeably by the chroniclers, as they had been by the ancients, the Carthaginians being regarded as descendants of the Phoenicians. It is notable that Brandônio distinguished between the two peoples.

36 · See pp. 96–97.

37 · The Guanches were the native residents of the Canary Islands, especially the western islands. They may have come from northern Africa, and ultimately from central and southern Europe. In the fifteenth century many of them were enslaved by the Portuguese and transported to the Madeira Islands, which lacked a native population, to work on the sugar plantations. They had blue or gray eyes and light-colored hair, and perhaps this is why they were thought to have been outlanders.

38 · The Portuguese did not invent the major navigational instruments of the Age of Discovery (compass, astrolabe, quadrant), but they pioneered in using them for navigation on the open seas. As a result, the Portuguese became for the fifteenth and sixteenth centuries the masters of all Europe in the science and art of ocean navigation. George H. T. Kimble, *Geography in the Middle Ages,* pp. 222–240; John Horace Parry, *The Age of Reconnaissance,* pp. 91–95; Waters, *Art of Navigation,* pp. 43–62.

39 · "The great scientific achievement of the Portuguese pioneers was that they brought together and systematized navigational lore; and it was upon this approach to a scientific system of navigation that their discoveries depended." Waters, *Art of Navigation,* p. 43. Cf. above, n. 38.

40 · The designation New World was applied to the recently discovered lands of the western hemisphere as early as Pietro Martire d'Anghiera [Peter Martyr], first chronicler of the West Indies, who used the term in the title of his work *Décadas del Nuevo Mundo* (1504–1511). About the same time the phrase was used as the title of the letter *Mundus Novus,* reputedly written by Amerigo Vespucci, and published in 1504.

41 · Ezion-geber (modern Tell el-Kheleifeh) is on the northern tip of the Gulf of Elath (modern Aqaba) at the northern end of the Red Sea. From this port in biblical times Palestine carried on trade with other countries. The Bible names Ezion-geber as the starting point of King Hiram's expedition to Ophir to obtain gold and other treasure for the building of Solomon's temple. 1 Kings 9:26–28, 1 Kings 10:11 and 22, and 2 Chron. 9:10 (Revised Standard Version).

42 · Some have identified Tarshish with Tartessus, at the mouth of the Guadalquivir River in southern Spain, which was a center of the metal trade down to 500 B.C., but this identification is considered doubtful. The Phoenician word *tarshish* seems to have meant "metal refinery," and hence the name may have been used of various metal-manufacturing centers on the Mediterranean coasts. Therefore "ship of Tarshish" may have denoted originally a cargo ship serving such centers, and later, by extension, any heavy freighter. L. H. Grollenberg, *Atlas of the Bible,* s.v. "Tarshish." There seems to be no authority for Brandônio's assertion that Tarshish means Africa.

43 · Gold from Ophir did in biblical times actually exist in Palestine, as is

proved by an inscription there, but no modern person knows where Ophir was. There are many theories about the place: it was an island in the Red Sea; the west or southwest coast of Arabia; a location in Armenia, South Africa, the West Indies, Peru, the coast of India, Spain, Ceylon. Huddleston, *Origins,* pp. 4, 7, 23, 65; and see *Encyclopaedia Judaica* and *Jewish Encyclopedia,* s.v. "Ophir." The Bible gives Ophir not only as the name of a city but also as the name of a man, the great-great-great-grandson of Noah (Gen. 10:29). The man Ophir was traditionally supposed to have settled in the Far East. Some writers thought his descendants had populated Peru and the rest of America; others connected him in one way or another with the biblical city Ophir. Some modern authorities show considerable confusion on this subject, referring to the "Ophirian theory" without saying whether they are thinking of the man or the city; or citing biblical references to one that really apply to the other.

44 · Writers of the period understood that Hiram's voyage lasted three years, but the biblical text actually says "once every three years" (1 Kings 5), and this not in reference to the voyage but to the sacrifices in the temple that were associated with it. See Huddleston, *Origins,* p. 41.

45 · Correctly, Parisiensis. Franciscus Vatablo, or François Vatable, was a noted hebraist and hellenist who taught at the University of Paris and who initiated Hebrew studies in France. His commentary on the Bible appeared in a polyglot edition of the Bible published in 1545 under the name of Robert Étienne. Vatablo says in his gloss on the third book of Kings, chapter 9 (1 Kings 9:26–28 in the Revised Standard Version): "Ophir is an island very remote from the Ellanitic Strait [Bab el Mandeb, at the southern end of the Red Sea, through which Hiram's fleet passed into the Indian Ocean when it sailed forth to bring gold and other riches for Solomon's temple]. Today it is called Spagniola [Hispaniola], so named by Christopher Columbus. It is in the West, in the land newly discovered. For the gold there is highly esteemed." Franciscus Vatablo, *Biblia Sacra, cum duplici translatione et scholiis Francisci Vatabli* (Salamanca, 1584). Three other biblical passages are concerned with the Ophir story: 1 Kings 10:11 and 2 Chron. 8:18 and 9:10 (Revised Standard Version).

46 · "South Sea" usually referred to the southern reaches of the Pacific Ocean, so named because when Balboa first viewed the Pacific from the coast of Panama he was looking south. Georg Friederici, *Der Charakter der Entdeckung und Eroberung Amerikas durch die Europäer* (3 vols. Stuttgart-Gotha: F. A. Porthese, 1935–1936), 1:40. Apparently Brandão is under the impression that Hispaniola is in the Pacific. This is Brandão's mistake and not Vatablo's: Brandão misquotes his source in saying that Vatablo places Hispaniola in the South Sea. See above, n. 45. Cf. p. 102, where

Alviano supposes that the Chinese reached South America by the "so-called South Sea off the coast of Peru."

47 · Molucca Islands. The manuscript has Ilhas de Maluquo, one of several contemporary spellings for the Molucca or Spice Islands. Vatablo in his commentary does not mention the Moluccas; yet Brandônio seems to assume that Hiram's fleet touched there. The Moluccas played a major role in the Portuguese enterprise in the East. The Portuguese had frequented the islands as traders since 1512; in Brandão's time the Moluccas were under virtually complete Portuguese control. Perhaps Brandão thought they would necessarily be a port of call for any fleet in that area.

48 · The first route envisaged by Brandônio would have taken the voyagers east from Indonesia across the Pacific to the west coast of South America. They would next have had to cross the Isthmus of Panama and then sail east to Hispaniola. This course, though arduous, is a logical one. Not so the second route, which would have led south from Ezion-geber through the Indian Ocean, around the Cape of Good Hope, through the Strait of Magellan, and then north along the Pacific coast of South America. As with the first route, it would then have been necessary to cross the Isthmus. There would have been no point in following this roundabout course: the ships could much better have avoided the Strait of Magellan and sailed north along the Atlantic coast of South America directly to the island of Hispaniola. The conclusion seems inescapable that Brandão thought Hispaniola lay in the Pacific instead of in the Atlantic Ocean. Cf. above, n. 46.

49 · Brandônio is technically correct in saying that the Strait of Magellan is not a real strait: it is bounded on one side by the Archipelago of Tierra del Fuego instead of by solid land. He is also correct in stating that the passage of this strait is one of the most difficult navigational challenges in the New World.

50 · Diego Flores Valdés (to use the Spanish form of his name) was the commander of a fleet sent by the Crown in 1581 to establish forts and settlements on the Strait, but he abandoned the expedition when the fleet reached São Vicente. His second in command, Pedro Sarmiento de Gamboa, reached the Strait with five ships and managed to establish two settlements, but in May 1584, while Sarmiento was anchoring off one of the settlements, Nombre de Dios, a strong gale blew his ship out to sea and he was forced to proceed to Brazil for repairs. For several years this loyal and intrepid man, in spite of every sort of hardship and misfortune, endeavored to relieve the settlements, but the Crown steadfastly turned a deaf ear to his proposals, and Sarmiento was never able to return to the Strait or to deliver the desperately needed supplies and reenforcements. Morison, *Southern Voyages*, pp. 700–707.

In the meantime, an encounter took place off the port of Santos, São Vicente, between Valdés and Edward Fenton, the famous English pirate. Fenton had set out from England in 1582 to reach India by way of the Strait of Magellan, and had put into Santos for supplies. Though Fenton sank one of the Spanish ships, he suffered such severe damage in the encounter that he retired to England.

Don Diego sailed to Bahia and from there to Paraíba, where he aided the Portuguese against the French and Indians. See I, n. 102. Sérgio Buarque de Holanda, ed., *História geral da civilização brasileira*, tomo 1, vol. 1, p. 173; J. F. de Almeida Prado, *A conquista da Paraíba (séculos XVI a XVIII)*, pp. 175–179.

51 · Sofala is on the southeast coast of Africa, south of Mozambique. On Pedro Álvares Cabral's return trip from India, the place was visited by one of his ships, and inquiries were made about its legendary gold trade. "Letter from King Manuel to Ferdinand and Isabella," July 29, 1501, in William Brooks Greenlee, *The Voyage of Pedro Álvares Cabral to Brazil and India from Contemporary Documents and Narratives*, p. 43.

52 · Situated in present-day Ghana (formerly the Gold Coast), São Jorge, or São Jorge da Mina, or El Mina, was a fortified trading post built in 1482 by Diogo d'Azambuja. It is near what is today Cape Coast, about 1 degree west. The fort was erected to protect Portuguese traders from incursions by the Spanish, French, and English. El Mina was an important site for the procurement of gold, ivory, and slaves, as well as a base for exploratory expeditions into the unknown South. Edgar Prestage, *The Portuguese Pioneers*, pp. 199–204; Bailey W. Diffie and George D. Winus, *Foundations of the Portuguese Empire, 1415–1580*, p. 154.

53 · As early as 1555 it was asserted by António Galvão, governor of a Portuguese island in the Moluccas, that the Indians of the New World were of Chinese origin. Galvão suggested that voyagers from China had settled for a time in the New World and that the continent was now populated by their descendants. In support of this view, he pointed out that the Chinese and the Indians had similar fashions and customs and that they resembled each other in certain physical characteristics; for example, small eyes and flat noses. António Galvão, *The Discoveries of the World, from Their First Original unto the Year of Our Lord 1555*, pp. 19–20.

54 · Cf. Brandônio's slur upon the "weak and timorous people" of the Spanish possessions in the New World, p. 20 and I, n. 16.

55 · The two problems are the location of Ophir and the origin of the Brazilian Indians (pp. 99–100).

56 · Through the mouth of Alviano, Brandão has presented several of the current theories about the origin of the Brazilian Indians, and through that of Brandônio refuted each one. These theories referred to (1) the

Phoenicians, (2) Carthaginian merchants, (3) crewmen of "Velpócio Américo," (4) the Chinese. Brandônio himself thinks that Brazil was discovered by Israelites in ships of King Solomon on their return trip from Ophir, and that from the survivors sprang the population of Brazil.

Brandônio's list of theories is by no means exhaustive. Simão de Vasconcellos offered as many as seven hypotheses for the ancestry of the Brazilian Indians: the candidates included Trojans, Carthaginians, Phoenicians, and a number of Hebrew claimants. Simão de Vasconcellos, *Notícias*, pp. lxii–lxx. Gregorio García, in his *Origen de los indios*, reviewed some eleven major hypotheses. All the contemporary theories were limited by the fact that they had to conform to the Christian and Judaic theologies, both of which taught that there had been only one creation. Nobody knew for sure just where this event took place, but most people thought it was not in America. Hence the Brazilians could not have originated in the New World but must have got there from somewhere else. For a modern review of all the theories, see Huddleston, *Origins*.

57 · The chroniclers often mention the unusual longevity of the Indians— sometimes claiming for them a life of as much as 180 years; women were said to have suckled children at the age of 80 or 100. See, for example, *Tidings out of Brazil*, p. 34, and Fernão Cardim, *Tratados da terra e gente do Brasil*, p. 31. There is little evidence to support such claims. Buarque de Holanda says the idea that the Indians lived long is connected with the ancient myth of the Earthly Paradise, which came to be localized in Brazil. *Visão do paraíso*, pp. 272–273.

58 · See I, n. 26.

59 · Prado does not agree that the peninsular climate was the cause of the Brazilian Indians' decline. He thinks rather that in Spain and Portugal the Indians were inadequately provided with food and comforts. In France, he says, where they were treated well, they remained healthy. J. F. de Almeida Prado, *Pernambuco e as capitanias do norte do Brasil (1530–1630)*, 4:215–216.

60 · Most of the chroniclers agree with Brandônio that the natives of Brazil were unusually healthy, but this claim, as Stetson suggests, is likely to be mere propaganda put out by writers who wanted to induce people to settle in Brazil. Certainly the early Jesuit fathers suffered a great deal from hardships due to illness, as their letters testify. Some travelers from countries other than Portugal were anything but complimentary to Brazil's climate. Thus Thevet observed that the natives "are subject to the same ailments as we are. . . . People in that country who live near the sea are subject to putrefying diseases, such as fevers, catarrh, and others." John B. Stetson, Jr., in Pero de Magalhães de Gandavo, *The Histories of Brazil*, 2:204–205, n. 17; Thevet, *Singularitez*, fols. 88ᵛ–89ʳ.

61 · Cf. pp. 87–89.

62 · Cf. above, n. 24.

63 · See p. 318 and VI, n. 52.

64 · Candido Mendes de Almeida, writing in 1759, still thought the water in Brazil was so healthful that though elsewhere water worsened disease, in that country fevers and other ailments were effectively treated simply by washing with it. *Memórias para a história do extincto Estado do Maranhão,* 2:20.

65 · Disease of the worm (*doença de bicho, bicho de cu, máculo, mal del culo*) was a diarrhea caused by worms, prevalent not only among the Indians but among slaves newly brought over from Africa. In both Brazil and Angola the names "disease of the worm" and "chronic *bicho*" were given to yellow fever because a large percentage of the victims were infested with whipworm (*Trichuris trichiura* L.). Yellow fever was described under the name disease of the worm as early as 1623 by the physician Aleixo de Abreu. He said it was a disease primarily of Africa but also occurring in Brazil and in Lisbon. Francisco Guerra, "Aleixo de Abreu (1568–1630), Author of the Earliest Book on Tropical Medicine . . . ," *Journal of Tropical Medicine and Hygiene* 71 (March 1968):64–65. The confusion of names and the similarity of some of the symptoms of *mal do bicho* and yellow fever may be responsible for Brandônio's statement that some patients suffering from *bicho* are easily cured while others have high fever and die.

66 · When tobacco was introduced into Portugal (probably under João III), the people, like the Indians Brandônio describes, used the drug primarily as a medicine. "I have heard it said," wrote Antonil, "that pipe tobacco, smoked in moderate amount in the morning before breakfast, moistens the humidity of the stomach, aids digestion as well as regular evacuation, soothes the chest attacked by asthmatic flux, and reduces intolerable toothaches." André João Antonil [João António Andreoni], *Cultura e opulência do Brasil por suas drogas e minas,* p. 318.

67 · Also *payemannióba* and *manjerióba.* MS *pajemarieba.* Coffee senna (*Cassia occidentalis* L.). The plant has medicinal properties. Rodolfo Garcia, ed., *Diálogos das grandezas do Brasil,* II, n. 4.

68 · Piso recommended washing with cold or tepid sea water mixed with the juice of a fresh lemon. Guilherme Piso, *História natural do Brasil ilustrada,* chap. 16 and n. 166. Other contemporary remedies for the *bicho* included filling the "fundament" with gunpowder, sweat, or wax from the ears. A particularly drastic treatment was to flush out the rectum with cotton wads soaked in a mixture of lemon, pepper, whiskey, and gunpowder. "And there were those who survived this cure," remarks Garcia, ed., *Diálogos,* II, n. 3.

69 · The Ardras, Ardas, or Adras were a group of Gêges or Dahomeys who in

the twelfth or thirteenth century broke with the parent aggregation to form a separate kingdom of Arda (Ardrah, Ardra, Arder, Ardes, Ardas). The new state was situated on the east-west coast of Africa in the region that is now Togo and Dahomey. In the sixteenth century Europeans used Arda as a source of slaves for the Northeast of Brazil. *The Cambridge History of Africa*, 4:224, 616.

70 · A similar epidemic in 1597 had halted Feliciano Coelho de Carvalho and his men as they marched to rescue Rio Grande do Norte from the French and their Indian allies. Brandão did not experience that epidemic because he was in Portugal in that year; see I, n. 83, and p. 133.

71 · Anchieta reports that in the epidemic of 1562 as many as 30,000 blacks and Indians died, but he mentions no deaths of Portuguese. Joseph [José] de Anchieta, *Cartas, informações, fragmentos históricos e sermões (1554–1594)*, p. 356.

72 · MS *constolação*. Some earlier editors thought this was a mistake for *consolação* [consolation], but consolation makes no sense in the context. The word is certainly not a mistake but is an alternative spelling for *constelação;* an almost identical spelling, *costolação*, is recorded in 1527 (José Pedro Machado, *Dicionário etimológico da língua portuguesa*, s.v. "constelação"). In modern usage the word means "constellation," but earlier it also had other meanings, one of which was "climate" and another "combination of circumstances or events." "Constellation" is clearly inappropriate here, since Brandônio has not been discussing the stars. In fact, he apparently did not believe in astrology: on p. 25 he declared that "We should not take any stock in those things." In the present passage either "climate" or "combination of circumstances" would make sense. Brandônio may well have been thinking of the climate, or certain characteristics of it. He often attributes the favorable conditions of life in Brazil to the climate; thus he asserts on p. 92 that "the influence of the heavens and the peculiar quality of the land together may be powerful enough to render the place where they prevail more or less healthful for human habitation, and also to be the cause of few or many sicknesses." But since Brandônio's reference appears to be intentionally vague, the rendering "circumstance" has been chosen.

73 · A malignant form of smallpox, named for one of its symptoms. (The skin of the dogfish was used like sandpaper to smooth wood.) In 1695 the disease killed 5,000 white persons in Maranhão and Pará, and caused a loss in slaves whose cost was disastrous. Serafim Leite, *Suma histórica da Companhia de Jesus no Brasil, 1549–1760*, p. 170.

74 · Many stories are told about the fortunate changes that supposedly occurred on ships when they crossed a particular latitude, usually the equator. Thus Bartolomé de las Casas describes how at a certain point in the voyage across the ocean the innumberable lice that infested the ship disappeared,

only to return when the vessel reached the same latitude on the return trip. *Apologética historia sumaria,* 1:92. Similar claims are made by Oviedo, *Natural historia,* chap. 42, and by Jean Baptiste Labat, *Nouveau voyage aux isles de l'Amérique,* 3:315, 444. In *Don Quixote,* when the Don and Sancho Panza are voyaging in the enchanted bark, Don Quixote bids Sancho "search himself for vermin, to ascertain whether they have passed the Equator" (pt. 2, bk. 3, chap. 29).

75 · Métraux points out that, though the early writers on Brazil list many medicinal herbs, they rarely indicate whether the Indians used them for medicinal purposes or whether it was the Europeans who discovered their virtues. Alfred Métraux, "The Tupinambá," in Julian H. Steward, ed., *Handbook of South American Indians* (hereafter cited as *HSAI*), 3:130–131.

76 · According to Garcia (*Diálogos,* II, n. 6), Gonçalo was probably suffering from a suppurated appendix.

77 · Purgatives were an important part of the seventeenth-century *materia medica.* Along with bloodletting, they were the standard treatment for almost every ailment.

78 · MS *batata.* Brandônio is certainly referring to the Brazilian *Operculina convolvulus Manse,* a wild climbing plant that grows from Maranhão to São Paulo. Its tuber is filled with a milky juice and a resinous purgative. The Tupis called the plant *jeticucu.* Personal communication from Donald Simpson, formerly Assistant Curator of Botany, Field Museum of Natural History, Chicago.

79 · The tree is called *pinhão de purga* [purge pine] or *pinheiro do inferno* [infernal pine]: *Jatropha curcus.* The nuts are an emetic and a drastic laxative. The oil, which is extracted from the nuts, is still sold in pharmacies. Garcia, ed., *Diálogos,* II, n. 7.

Europeans early showed an interest in Indian medicinal plants, as the present discussion illustrates. As early as the mid-sixteenth century, they began to devise prescriptions of their own, using Brazilian flora. Leite, *Suma,* p. 166. See above, n. 75.

80 · Perhaps the *araçá da praia* (*Psidium variabile* Berg), a small fruit similar to a loquat. F. C. Hoehne, *Botânica e agricultura no Brasil no século XVI,* p. 237. See Gabriel Soares de Sousa, *Notícia do Brasil* (1945), 2:21, n. 12.

81 · Brandônio appears to be describing a mild form of cholera that is distinct from the usually fatal Asiatic cholera. Garcia d'Orta says the East Indians called the disease *morxi* and the Portuguese corrupted this word to *mordexim.* Pyrard de Laval describes *mordexim* as an ailment that attacks suddenly and "is accompanied by severe headache and vomiting, and they cry aloud a great deal, and usually they die of it." According to Dellon (1698), the disease was treated by burning the feet with an iron. Garcia

d'Orta, *Colóquios* (facsim. 1963), fol. 74ᵛ; François Pyrard de Laval, *Voyage de François Pyrard, de Laval,* pt. 2, p. 15; Gabriel Dellon, *Nouvelle relation d'un voyage fait aux Indes Orientales,* p. 301.

82 · Copaiva balsam or oil is produced by all the South American species of *Copaifera.* The oil is extracted from the tree by tapping. Samuel J. Record and Robert W. Hess, *Timbers of the New World,* p. 248. Various chroniclers mention the copaiva tree, notably Magalhães de Gandavo, who describes the extraction of the oil as he observed it in the sixteenth century. Pero de Magalhães de Gandavo, *História da Província Sancta Cruz,* in his *Histories of Brazil,* vol. 1, fols. 18ᵛ–19ʳ.

83 · This balsam is derived from the *cabureíba* or *cabriúva* tree (*Myrocarpus fastigiatus* Fr. Allem), which is found in the southern captaincies, especially Espírito Santo. Cardim tells how the balsam was extracted: "The bark is pierced, and a little cotton put on the cuts, and at regular intervals they go and collect the oil that is distilled from them." Cardim, *Tratados,* p. 54. Simão de Vasconcellos describes at some length both the *cabriúva* (*cabureigba*) balsam and the copaiva (*copaigba*) balsam mentioned in n. 82. *Chrônica,* bk. 1, p. 59.

84 · In tertian fever, or ague, paroxysms recur every forty-eight hours; in quartan fever, every seventy-two hours.

85 · Brandônio seems to be describing a form of syphilis rather than the bubonic plague—reflecting a common confusion, since many of the symptoms are similar. The description here applies rather well to syphilitic rupia, a pustular eruption with extensive destruction of tissue, usually on the face and causing death. Contemporary writers were quick to blame the "intemperate life," as Brandônio does, for syphilis and similar diseases. Thus Thevet says of syphilis (*pians*): "It evidently comes from some malversation, such as too much carnal frequentation between man and woman, since these people are very luxurious, carnal, and more than brutal, especially the women. . . . This sickness is nothing else than the pox today so common in our Europe." Thevet, *Singularitez,* chap. 4.

86 · This is *bicho de pé* (*Tunga* [ex-*Sarcopsilla*] *penetrans*), a parasite observed in the West Indies by Oviedo as early as 1547 and still common in Brazil. Richard Flecknoe, an English traveler writing in 1654, described the condition with unsurpassed vividness: "But that which molested me most of all, was a certain kind of animated dust, which insensibly ingenders to worms in your feet as big as Magots in a cheese . . . ; at their first ingendering in my feet, [I was] assaulted with so fierce an itch as 'twas the greatest pleasure in the world to scratch it, which presently was succeeded by so intollerable a pain, as I never remember to have felt the like." *A Relation of Ten Years Travells in Europe, Asia, Affrique, and America,* p. 75. Cf. Oviedo, *Natural historia,* chap. 81.

87 · Many contemporaries echo this baseless claim, which is often related to the crossing of a particular latitude, especially the equator, by ship. Cf. above, n. 74.

88 · "The moon is very prejudicial to health and corrupts things very much," Anchieta wrote in 1585. *Cartas*, p. 424. He and Brandônio are not totally wrong. Night is an unhealthful season in the tropics: after sunset there is greater activity by mosquitoes in propagation of tropical diseases—an association totally unsuspected at the time of the *Dialogues*. Prado, *Pernambuco*, 4:229.

89 · There is some truth to this statement: Brazil, unlike Brandão's native Iberian Peninsula, is not in a seismic region.

Dialogue III

In Which Is Discussed the Trade in Sugar,

Brazilwood, Cotton, and Timber

There are six ways to get rich in Brazil, according to Brandônio. Dialogue III describes four of these ways. Before he is fairly launched on a description of the first of them (the sugar industry), Brandônio digresses to generalize about the relative potentials of Brazil and India as sources of wealth. The Dialogue considers the profitable industries of Brazil—varying somewhat from the title—as (1) sugar, (2) trade, (3) brazilwood, (4) cotton, and (5) timber. One additional means of making money is crowded in—the gathering of ambergris. If the colonists would properly utilize the resources of their land, Brandônio asserts, it would bring in far more revenue than India.

   This discussion of economic factors and of the India trade shows the author's knowledgeability as a financier and practical economist, familiar with large-scale business operations both colonial and peninsular. He moves with ease from the oriental trade in spices and other "drugs" to smuggling operations in Peru, methods of exporting brazilwood, or the cause of the decline in the price of cotton. He is full of aggressive plans for increasing the profit from the new land, but like many of his modern confrères *he complains that the government is slow to move. Brandônio's realistic account of the sugar industry reminds the reader that the author was himself a sugar mill owner. He must have experienced at first hand the luxurious living he describes as characteristic of the wealthy class in the Northeast.*

   As a businessman Brandônio is interested in every natural resource of his adopted country, but his interest is not purely an economic one. For instance, in his catalogue of the available timber he names an astonishing number of trees, evaluating them not only for their commercial uses but also for their grandeur as an element in the rural scene. Obviously this was a businessman who delighted to spend his leisure hours exploring the new land, observing as minutely as he could, taking careful notes, and, no doubt, extolling the virtues of the country to anyone who was willing to listen to him.

Perhaps Brandão feared that the financial data and the long lists of products would seem dull to some readers. As a relief, he has inserted several odd and interesting anecdotes, apparently from his own experience. The significance of these is often carefully underscored by the comments of Alviano, that useful interlocutor, always on hand to make sure the reader does not miss the point or take the wrong side of the argument.

BRANDÔNIO   So as not to be thought negligent, I have been waiting for you quite a while already, enjoying the cool breeze that blows in here from the sea.

ALVIANO   An unexpected caller made me incur the guilt of being late, but it is not too late for us to begin our conversation, in which we had decided to discuss the richness, fertility, and bounty of this Brazil. I beg you, therefore, tell me whatever you know of these things, for here I am, eager to hear what you have to say.

BRANDÔNIO   The riches of this New World, and likewise its fertility and bounty, are so great that I do not know with which of them to make a start. But, since all of them deserve consideration, I shall make a salad[1] of them, as attractive and tasty as I can. Now to begin, I will say that the wealth of Brazil consists of six things, from which its settlers grow rich,[2] and these are: first, the production of sugar; second, trade; third, the wood they call brazil [brazilwood]; fourth, cotton and timber; fifth, the growing of food crops; sixth and last, cattle raising. Of all these things, the principal nerve and substance of the wealth of the land is the production of sugar.[3]

ALVIANO   That wealth which comes only from making sugar cannot be of much importance, for we see that the inhabitants of our eastern India grow rich from many different things, such as a great quantity of most useful drugs, very fine cloth, gold, silver,[4] pearls, diamonds, rubies and topazes,[5] musk,[6] ambergris,[7] silks,[8] indigo,[9] and other goods with which every year the ships come back to Spain heavily laden.[10]

BRANDÔNIO   It is true enough that all those things, and still others, are brought back from those parts; but, just the same, I shall endeavor to prove that taking nothing more than sugar out of Brazil is a greater thing, and brings in more profit to His Majesty's Treasury, than all those East Indies.

ALVIANO   You are bold to venture so far, and to attempt such a thing seems an act of madness, for it is as far from being demonstrable as are the heavens from the earth. I beg you, therefore, not to let anyone hear such a proposition from you, for most men would think it ridiculous.

BRANDÔNIO   I shall not be moved to retract what I have said by all those dark looks you are giving me. Rather, I intend to prove clearly what I am stating—just as I did on another occasion in the Kingdom, before their Lordships the Governors,[11] in the year '97 [1597]. For you are not going to deny to me that every year three, four, and sometimes five ships go from the Kingdom out to India, and come back from there laden with merchandise.[12]

ALVIANO   That is right.

BRANDÔNIO   Likewise you will not doubt that each one of these ships, from the time its keel is laid until it is under sail, costs His Majesty's Treasury around forty thousand cruzados.[13]

ALVIANO   Nor do I deny that.

BRANDÔNIO   And that likewise every year His Majesty sends out in them about two hundred thousand cruzados in cash—reales of eight and four[14]—for the purchase of India pepper.[15]

ALVIANO   And very often more.

BRANDÔNIO   And likewise, in wages to the soldiers and seamen who enlist to go out to India, in housing allowances for his officials, in bonuses to gentlemen and other individuals, he pays out a great deal of money.

ALVIANO   There is no doubt of that.

BRANDÔNIO   You must also be aware that every one of those ships, after it has returned safely from India laden with merchandise, brings His Majesty—aside from the pepper it carries—from forty-five to fifty *contos de reis* [45:000$000–50:000$000][16] (and the ships are let publicly at about that sum to persons who bid for them[17]). At the present time, this amount is considerably less, so that His Majesty gains little from it, because of discounts that are made at the India House.[18] Add to this fact that often no more than one or two of the ships get back to the Kingdom safely.[19]

ALVIANO   That can be granted; but beyond that money which, as you have said, His Majesty gets from the ship contracts, his ministers collect freight charges for his Treasury on those same ships. That must amount to quite a sum.

BRANDÔNIO   The freight charges from each ship bring His Majesty's Treasury some three *contos de reis* [3:000$000], and it was at that price that a friend of mine contracted for them in '601 [1601]. Out of those three contos, the viceroy in India grants so many exemptions[20] from freight charges to private persons that almost all the profit is eaten up by those and similar things, whence it follows that His Majesty pockets very little money from the freight charges.

ALVIANO   But how can it be that ships of such great tonnage[21] bring in so little from freight?

BRANDÔNIO   The cause of this is the many stowage privileges that His Majesty grants on them. The captain has his own cabin and storeroom and other accommodations that are always reserved for him. Likewise with the pilot, the mate, the boatswain, the boatswain's mate, and the sailors, for all these have quarters assigned to them, and even the ship's boy and the cabin boy have their own. Thus, the quarters that are distributed in this way, and the stowage privileges that His Majesty grants, take up all the available space in which it would have been possible to stow goods that would pay freight charges.[22] There you have the reason that His Majesty's Treasury has but little income from the ships.

ALVIANO   I understand that matter well enough, but not the overall calculation you are making.

BRANDÔNIO   I am making that calculation to prove my contention that Brazil is richer, and is a source of greater profit to His Majesty's Exchequer, than all of India. Surely you will not deny that for the ships to come back laden as they are with goods, the whole Orient must needs be gutted—what with collecting pepper from Malabar[23] and cinnamon from Ceylon,[24] cloves from Molucca,[25] ambergris and nutmeg from Banda,[26] musk,[27] benzoin,[28] porcelains[29] and silks[30] from China, cotton cloth[31] and indigo[32] from Cambay and Bengal, precious stones[33] from Baiagate[34] and Bisnaga[35] and Ceylon. All those things from all those places must be gathered together[36] if the ships that come back to the Kingdom are to come laden with them; and, if they were not collected thus, the ships would not have a cargo.

ALVIANO   That is clearly the case, as everyone knows.

BRANDÔNIO   Not the whole of Brazil but only three captaincies, Pernambuco, Itamaracá, and Paraíba—and of them only the inhabited parts—account for fifty or sixty leagues of coast, more or less. The inhabitants of these captaincies have not spread even ten leagues back into the bush. In just that strip of land, without the help of a foreign nation or help of any other kind,[37] the Portuguese, by their own labor and industry, cultivate and take from the bowels of the earth enough sugar every year to lade one hundred and thirty or one hundred and forty ships, many of which are of very great tonnage.[38] For the establishment and maintenance of all that, His Majesty does not spend from his own Treasury a single penny. All those cargoes of sugar are carried to the Kingdom and enter his customhouses, where they pay the tolls due His Majesty. Now if the cargo these ships carry were to be transported in ships the size of those that make the India voyage,[39] twenty great ships of that tonnage would not be enough to accommodate it all.

ALVIANO   Although I cannot deny that that is so, still the duty paid on the sugar cargoes is of much less value to His Majesty's Treasury than the duties levied on the goods and drugs that come from India.

BRANDÔNIO   You are mistaken, for the ships that service the three northern captaincies I have named, without taking into account the southern captaincies, must carry somewhat more than five hundred thousand arrobas of sugar.[40] (I would say that about one hundred thousand arrobas of this sugar is of the kind they call *panelas*.[41]) All of these different qualities of sugar pay duty at the customhouse in Lisbon: the white and the brown pay 250 reis per arroba, and the *panelas* pay 150 reis per arroba. This is in addition to the consulage.[42] All this, added up, amounts to more than three hundred thousand cruzados for His Majesty's Treasury. And he does not have to spend a single real from his own purse on the maintenance of this state [Brazil], for the income from the tithes that are collected from this land is enough to support it.

Now, in this connection, figure out the income he has from the other captaincies, to the south, among which is Bahia de Todos os Santos, the capital of this whole state. After making that calculation, set up an account of credit and debit, the way a shopkeeper does, and on one side write down what His Majesty spends each year on the ships that he sends to India—wages of soldiers and seamen, housing allowances for his officials, and bonuses to private individuals—and add the cash that he sends out to buy pepper. Now put down on the other side what India renders His Majesty, and also the price at which he lets the contract for the ships that come from there. And note carefully how much you will have to add to make that equal the income that he collects from Brazil, from only the three captaincies I mentioned,[43] and you will see how much this latter exceeds the income from India.[44] Thus I do not need any other proof to demonstrate the truth of what I claimed.

ALVIANO   That income which you are crediting to Brazil appears excessive, for not all sugar pays the full duty. We know, for instance, that some sugar pays no duty at all, because of the exemption that His Majesty has granted to persons who set up new sugar mills.

BRANDÔNIO   That's true; but the exemption that His Majesty grants on new sugar mills does not last more than ten years, and when these are over it expires.[45] Granted that those mill owners and small planters who export sugar on their own account always pay less duty,[46] still there are only a few who do that.[47] And it cannot be claimed that [the loss] amounts to very much. Furthermore, in my reckoning, I purposely did not include in my total the income from the brazilwood that the same three captaincies export to the Kingdom; this amounts to more than forty thousand cruzados a year. That is what His Majesty's ministers collect in the Kingdom from the brazilwood contractors. Similarly, I have excluded from the income of the customhouses of the state [Brazil] the duties paid on cotton and timber in the customhouses of the Kingdom, which amount to a very large sum. Balancing one thing against the other, you will find that the income from these sources is greater than the loss from the exemptions you pointed out.

ALVIANO   As a matter of fact, I was so convinced of the opposite of what you have so clearly shown and proved that my mind is still reeling, and what you have said seems a dream to me. Nonetheless, I know for a fact that in Portugal I have seen mansions built by men with large incomes from fortunes they made in India, and I found none—or almost none—who have similar houses and enjoy incomes from wealth brought back from Brazil.

BRANDÔNIO   But that is the greatest proof of their wealth! For the men from India, when they leave there to return to the Kingdom, carry with them all the property they own, for none of them own any real estate in India worth mentioning. All their capital is invested in movables, which they take aboard ship with them. With the money from the sale of these goods in the Kingdom, they acquire the incomes and build the mansions you spoke of. But the settlers in Brazil have all their wealth invested in real estate, which they cannot take back to the Kingdom! And when somebody does go back there his land must needs stay behind. You must have known many such men in Portugal. It is not possible for them to retain great holdings here and buy more property there, and they prefer to have it in Brazil, where they derive a great income from it. To sum it up, you will come across many men in this country who are worth fifty, one hundred, and even two hundred thousand cruzados, and very few such in India. And if the people who live in Brazil were more enterprising, they could avail themselves of still more things that would make them rich and increase His Majesty's revenue from Brazil.

ALVIANO   I should very much like to have you tell me just what things would give so great a return.

BRANDÔNIO   I was understating the case when I said that Brazil could be richer and yield more revenue for His Majesty's Treasury if the King or the gentlemen of his Council[48] would only turn their eyes toward it. For if they would, then Brazil could make the Dutch and other foreigners[49] who send ships to India cease their shipping and their trade, without His Majesty's having to draw his sword against them or to spend a single real to bring it about.

ALVIANO   That will have to be done by magic, for I do not see how ordinary measures can achieve it.

BRANDÔNIO   It can be achieved without magic, if only His Majesty and the gentlemen of his Council make up their minds to it.

ALVIANO   Then tell me how it can be done.

BRANDÔNIO   It is well known that the Dutch do not send their ships to India at the expense of the States [General], but rather that the merchants themselves pay the costs and expenses of fitting out the ships that sail there.[50] The capital to build the ships and buy the goods they carry is subscribed by many persons who wish to invest in this. Some put in more, others less, according to the amount of cash they have on hand. An account is drawn up and the contribution of each man is represented by a certain number of shares. When the voyage is over and the ships have come back safely, the cargo is sold, and expenses are paid from the gross returns. From what is left they calculate the percentage of profit and make good accordingly to each one of the subscribers, who gets back the capital he invested plus that percentage.[51]

ALVIANO   You are quite right, for a good friend of mine who spent a long time in Flanders told me that that is the way they do it. But what has that got to do with Brazil's being able to make those nations give up their trade?

BRANDÔNIO   It has a lot to do with it. We already know that the largest and most valuable cargo that their ships seek in India is pepper. The cloves, amber, nutmeg, chinaware, benzoin,[52] and other things that they bring back are merely accessories, and not the mainstay of their trade. For a very little of each one of those is enough to glut the northern markets, and those foreigners cannot bring back cinnamon,[53] cloth,[54] or indigo[55] because these items are not found in the parts of India where they trade. And so it is pepper that they want, pepper that they go to fetch, and pepper that gives them a profit from their overseas trade.[56]

ALVIANO   What are you getting at?

BRANDÔNIO   I say that His Majesty ought to do just what King Dom Manuel, of glorious memory, did to stop the trade in pepper that was brought overland, by way of Cairo, to Venice, whence it was distributed and sold over all of Europe.

ALVIANO   And what did the King do?

BRANDÔNIO   After the seaway to India had been discovered, and wishing that the pepper should pass through the hands of the Portuguese alone, and that only their ships should bring it to Europe, the King determined to close off all that trade through Venice, and he did it in this way: he sent trustworthy men to that city to find out exactly how much a quintal[57] of pepper cost there and the price at which it had to be sold if the dealers there were to make a profit on it.

After he was well informed on all this, he sent his pepper to Flanders with some Portuguese agents to sell it at such a low price that, if the Venetian pepper had been sold at the same price, those merchants who dealt in it would have ended up losing much money. Thus everyone who had to have pepper hastened to buy the King's, because it was cheaper. Now since the Venetians could not let their pepper go at such a price without taking a great loss, because it had cost them so dearly, they gave up their trade in it.[58]

ALVIANO   Come, out with it now, whatever you have in mind!

BRANDÔNIO   I tell you that all the land in this Brazil is so disposed to growing pepper that great quantities of different kinds of it grow wild in the fields without being cultivated at all. It is not the same kind as that which comes from India, which doesn't grow here because there are no proper seeds for it. But, if we had the right kind of seeds, that quality of pepper would grow profusely.

ALVIANO   That I do not doubt, for I myself know that the land here is well disposed for growing pepper. When the birds eat it, the pepper grows wherever they leave their droppings, even on the trunks of trees. But you must finish clarifying the point you are getting at with all these arguments.

BRANDÔNIO   These arguments lead up to what I have in mind. And this is that His Majesty should send a ship to India for the sole purpose of bringing back pepper seed in casks, or in something else in which it could travel safely. Now this caravel[59] should run along the coast of Brazil and deliver the seed to all the captaincies. The captains major should parcel it out amongst the settlers, obliging them to plant and process it. In this way more pepper could be obtained from Brazil than from the Malabar Coast.

ALVIANO   But couldn't the pepper that the India ships ordinarily bring be used for planting?

BRANDÔNIO   No, because that pepper—so they say—has had lye passed through it,[60] which keeps it from germinating. So, now, if there were a great deal of pepper in this Brazil it would end up costing His Majesty little or no trouble, and even less money, to transport it to Portugal. Imitating King Manuel, he could send it to market at such a price that the Dutch would wind up losing a great deal of money if they tried to sell theirs, which they had to go to India to get. Therefore, since they would derive no profit from their commerce, the Dutch would have no reason to persist in it, and that would put an end, without expense and without bloodshed, to a struggle that has cost Portugal so much. And His Majesty, although sending his pepper to be sold more cheaply, would lose little, if he did not actually make money, because it would cost him less to transport it to the Kingdom and to buy it in Brazil.[61]

ALVIANO   The reasoning behind your proposal is so convincing that surely no one can doubt that the results would be what you predict. Indeed, I wonder that you do not at once take ship for the Kingdom and lay the proposal before His Majesty, for so much great good would come of it for all the State of India.[62]

BRANDÔNIO   I have already discussed it with a minister who held a high position in His Majesty's Treasury. Although he thought it a marvelous idea, his answer was that the present procedure in the pepper trade is so firmly established in Portugal that it would be very hard to replace it with another system. And since I realized that such an attitude is an ancient evil in our Portugal,[63] beyond all remedy, I brought the conversation to an end, as I shall right now, leaving the job to those whose duty it is to correct such things, if they have a mind to.

ALVIANO   You are right! To try to set the world straight is an error on the part of people like us who have so small a station in it;[64] so let us get back to our subject. If I remember correctly, you were going to tell me what constitutes the riches of Brazil, the chief source being, you said, the production of sugar.

BRANDÔNIO   And that is right, for sugar is Brazil's chief distinction and source of wealth.[65] In its cultivation, the system followed up to the present time has been this: the captains major, who are tenants of His Majesty, each one in his own captaincy, divided—and even now still do divide—the land among the settlers, giving to each one as much as he has the means to cultivate. Then the persons to whom these lands are given build sugar mills on them, if they have the capital to do so. If they lack capital, they sell the land to persons who *are* able to build. One must have great resources and capital to get a sugar mill into operation. For a mill powered by water, like most of those that have been built so far, or even one of those that are called *trapiches* and are turned by oxen,[66] costs pretty close to ten thousand cruzados {4:000$000} by the time it is all built.

ALVIANO   You seem to be saying that there are other kinds of sugar mill than those that are powered by water and the *trapiches* that are turned by oxen.

BRANDÔNIO   That's right. The water-powered mills, you see, are built on fast-flowing rivers. In addition, tanks are put up to hold back the water so that the mill can grind with even greater power.[67] In these mills the sugar cane is ground between two large rollers that are turned by a wheel on which the water strikes with great force;[68] then the bagasse[69] is pressed beneath heavy timbers, called *gangorras*.[70] Oxen are used to make them press tight together; this releases and expels from the bagasse all the juice the cane holds. The juice is collected in a tank and then turned into great copper cauldrons, which are placed on top of furnaces in which fires are lighted. By the heat of these the sugar is cleansed, boiled, and purified. To refine and fortify it further, they have to stir in some lye, made from ashes.

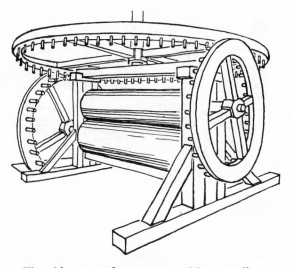

The older type of cane press, with two rollers placed horizontally. Hamilton Fernandes, *Açúcar e álcool ontem e hoje* (Rio de Janeiro: Instituto de Açúcar e de Álcool, 1971), p. 27. *Courtesy of the Edward E. Ayer Collection, The Newberry Library, Chicago.*

There are other mills that do not use water, and these are the *trapiches* I spoke of. They grind the cane with a contrivance of wheels that is set up for this purpose, turned by oxen, but in the rest of the sugar making the same process I have described is followed.

But a newly invented press, which they call *palitos*,[71] has recently been introduced. This does not require such a big setup, and likewise uses either water power or animal traction. This invention is considered so fine that I think all the old-style mills will be scrapped and only this new device will be used.

ALVIANO   One must always prefer what can be done with less labor and expense, and since this new contrivance of the *palitos* achieves exactly that, I am sure everyone will adopt it. But I would like to know how they make a loaf of that fine white sugar which is sent to Portugal and which we see out here.

BRANDÔNIO   The process is this: after the sugar-cane juice is cleansed and thickened in the cauldrons, it is transferred to boilers that are also made of copper. Here it is heated until it reaches the point of

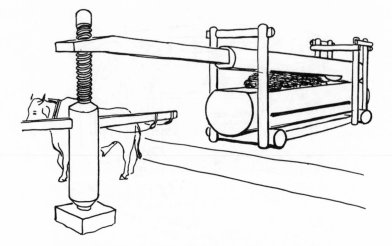

The *gangorra* described by Brandônio presses out the residue of
juice from the cane. Hamilton Fernandes, *Açúcar e álcool ontem e
hoje* (Rio de Janeiro: Instituto de Açúcar e de Álcool, 1971),
p. 25. *Courtesy of the Edward E. Ayer Collection,
The Newberry Library, Chicago.*

coagulation and takes on body. From there they put it into earthenware
molds,[72] inside of which it gains consistency and hardens. After it has
cooled, they take it to a large building called the clarifying house,[73]
which is outfitted just for this purpose. Here the molds are set into
holes cut in a plank. Then they pull out the plug in the bottom of
the mold, and through it the treacle drains off into gutters of the
same planking, which they place underneath to catch it. The treacle
that drains off from the molds in this way runs into a big tank, and
from it they later make the molasses, and still another quality of sugar
that they call *batidos*.[74] And when the molds have stopped draining,
they pour over the sugar some water that has particles of clay suspended
in it. That is what makes it white, the way we see it.

ALVIANO   It is hard for me to understand how the clay, which seemingly
ought to soil the sugar and turn it black, can whiten it instead.

BRANDÔNIO   The first sugar makers did not know about that for many
years either, and they used to spoil it the way they made it. At last
a chicken disclosed the secret: it happened to fly up onto a mold of
sugar with its feet covered with clay. All around that part where its

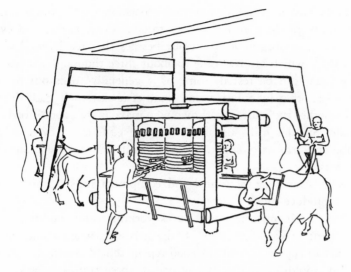

The newer type of cane press, with three vertical rollers
(*palitos*). It could be powered either by water or by oxen
(*trapiche*). Hamilton Fernandes, *Açúcar e álcool ontem e hoje*
(Rio de Janeiro: Instituto de Açúcar e de Álcool, 1971),
p. 31. *Courtesy of the Edward E. Ayer Collection,
The Newberry Library, Chicago.*

footprints were impressed, the sugar turned white. That was how they
learned the secret power of the clay to turn things white, and they
put it to use.[75]

ALVIANO   The chicken was not a bad teacher, to reveal in that fashion
how they could correct the dark color of the sugar, for there is such
a great difference in value between the white and the dark sugars.
And, if a mill produces a great quantity of the good quality, it cannot
fail to bring the owner a profit.

BRANDÔNIO   There is a vast difference between the good sugar mills
and the bad ones. Assuming that their owners can afford the necessary
personnel and equipment, good mills can become supremely valuable
if they have three other things; namely, plenty of good land to plant
cane on, enough water so that the press will never have to stop,[76] and
a quantity of wood in thick stands of timber.[77] Neither the cane nor
the wood should be far from the mill, but rather so located that both
things can be transported easily. Now when sugar mills are of this

quality and have all the necessary personnel and equipment, they generally produce every year up to six, seven, eight, and even ten thousand arrobas of *macho* sugar, besides the treacle, molasses, and syrups,[78] which always come to about three thousand arrobas. When the sugar can be tested, some of it generally turns out to be very good, another lot inferior, and some of it extremely bad, depending on whether the master workmen who make it are good or bad at their trade. Smaller mills usually produce five, four, or even only three thousand arrobas of sugar, and such mills are of little profit to their owners.

ALVIANO   And what personnel and equipment must a mill have if it is to produce much sugar?

BRANDÔNIO   It must have fifty slaves working—and good ones;[79] fifteen to twenty yoke of oxen, with the necessary wagons and harnesses; plenty of copper utensils in good repair; reliable foremen; ample firewood, molds, and lye. If any one of these things is lacking, then right away the production of sugar falls off because of it.

ALVIANO   Now tell me if all the sugar that is produced belongs to the mill owner.

BRANDÔNIO   If all the cane from which it is made belongs to the mill owner, then all the sugar is his too. But this is seldom the case, because of the large capital and great equipment needed to plant cane fields and run a mill.[80] Thus, most of the owners generally parcel out their cane fields in *partidos* [tracts],[81] which they do in this manner: the mill owner contributes the land and even some assistance beyond that.[82] The smallholder on his side undertakes to plant the cane and afterwards to cultivate and cut it and carry it to the mill, all according to the terms of their agreement. When the cane has been pressed and the sugar refined, the tithe on it is paid first of all from the gross product. After that is paid, a division is made on the basis of thirds, fifths, or even halves. Division by thirds means that two-thirds of the sugar goes to the mill owner and one-third to the smallholder. Division by fifths means that three-fifths goes to the mill owner and two-fifths to the smallholder. Division by halves means that each party gets the same amount; but division by halves—being of scant profit for the mill owner—is rarely met with, except in the case of a person to whom a favor is owed or who plants the cane on his own land. But whatever type of contract exists, there is no division of the treacle—the molasses and syrups—for all these belong freely and *in solido* [wholly] to the mill owner, who has no obligation to share them beyond paying on them the tithe that is due to God.

ALVIANO   And when the division is made that way,[83] how much sugar would the mill owner receive?

BRANDÔNIO   He would always get from four thousand to four thousand five hundred arrobas of *macho* sugar, besides the treacle and syrups, which will amount to from two thousand five hundred to three thousand arrobas.[84]

ALVIANO   How much does it cost a mill owner to produce enough sugar each year so that his own share will be the amount you mention?

BRANDÔNIO   One of these mills—I mean one of the really good ones—will always have expenses of three thousand five hundred to four thousand cruzados. If any of its slaves die, so that others have to be bought, expenses will be even higher.[85]

ALVIANO   That is a lot of money, and if that much has to be put out, the profit a sugar mill brings its owner cannot be so great as people have told me it is.

BRANDÔNIO   But it is still a good profit. It often comes to five or six thousand cruzados, free and clear.[86] And if the owner ships his sugar to the Kingdom himself, his profit will be much greater. Not only does he get a higher price for it in Portugal,[87] but he can avail himself of the right of exemption. This means that if his mill is a new one he has ten years during which he does not have to pay any duty at all in the customhouses. When that time is up, he nonetheless enjoys in perpetuity a half exemption. This means that he pays the customhouse only half the regular duty, just as if his sugar were sent over by a smallholder, for smallholders have that exemption.

Some of the mills enjoy greater exemptions than others. Those that are situated in a proprietary captaincy pay the proprietor a yearly water tax of three to four percent of all the sugar they make, and that amounts to a lot. But mills in the captaincies owned by the Crown are exempt from paying His Majesty such a tax—which is no small privilege!

ALVIANO   Nonetheless, the mills situated in Potosí,[88] which press the earth from which silver is taken, must have quite a different income from that of the mills you have been boasting of to me, which produce sugar. At least I would rather have the income from one of the former.

BRANDÔNIO   You are mistaken there, for I have seen figures on that, worked out by men who were well acquainted with both operations.

They found that the income from sugar mills was ever so much greater. Proof enough of that is that we see very many exceedingly rich owners of sugar mills, whereas most of the men who own silver mills are very poor and in debt.

ALVIANO   That cannot be the fault of the silver mills, but must be the result of the excessive expenditure which those men are accustomed to incur for themselves and their houses. I have been told that they are tremendously extravagant.

BRANDÔNIO   In that respect the sugar mill owners of Brazil are not one whit behind them, for many of them also go to the greatest expense, with many richly caparisoned horses and liveries,[89] and with the costly clothing that they and their children ordinarily wear. For in this state every four days there are bullfights, jousts with staves, tilting at the ring, and similar sports,[90] on which both organizers and participants spend a vast amount of money. They are, furthermore, very liberal in giving expensive presents. And I have heard men who have had much experience at the Court in Madrid say that even there they do not dress better than do the mill owners, their wives and daughters, other rich men, and the merchants of Brazil.[91] I will give only one very strong proof of this wealth: in the Captaincy of Pernambuco there is a House of Mercy[92] that every year spends thirteen or fourteen thousand cruzados, more or less, to discharge its obligations. All of this is given in alms by the inhabitants of that captaincy, for the hospital does not have any income of its own to speak of.[93] Indeed, its superintendents [*provedores*]—a different one is appointed every year—spend more than three thousand cruzados out of their own pockets. All the other captaincies have charity hospitals that spend much money, but the one in Pernambuco spends more than the others.

ALVIANO   That is a strong argument in support of your claim for the great wealth of Brazil. And since you have said enough about the first source [sugar] of that wealth which you attributed to the entire province, let us go on to the second source, which you say is trade.

BRANDÔNIO   Many men in Brazil have acquired a great amount of wealth in cash and property through trade, though the most successful are merchants who have come out from the Kingdom for that purpose. This trade is conducted in two ways. The first way is that they come out with a round-trip passage, sell their goods, invest their profits in sugar, cotton, and even very fine ambergris, and then return to the Kingdom, sometimes in the very same ships they came in.

The second way is for merchants to live in this country and keep retail shops. Their stores are filled with expensive goods, including all kinds of the best linens, the richest silks, the finest fabrics, and marvelous brocades.[94] There is a lavish use of all these out here, which brings great profits to the merchants who sell them.

ALVIANO   Now the merchants who live here and keep shop, do they perhaps order their stock from the Kingdom, or do they buy it from persons who bring it out from there?

BRANDÔNIO   Many of them do order their stock sent out from the Kingdom, but most of them buy from other traders who bring goods out. They pay forty or fifty percent of the purchase price in advance, depending on the kind and quality of goods and whether they are scarce or plentiful out here. And on these merchants depend yet others who operate on a smaller scale.

ALVIANO   And what type are they?

BRANDÔNIO   There are many persons who make their living and become very rich just by buying goods from the merchants in towns or cities and carrying them back to sell on the sugar plantations and farms that lie far out. They often make more than one hundred percent on them.

In the Captaincy of Pernambuco I once saw a certain trader make a deal that I did not approve of and considered illicit. He went out and bought a shipment of Guinea slaves for quite a sum of money, paying cash for them. Then, the very same instant, without actually having received the slaves, he turned around and sold them to a farmer, on credit over a certain period, which was less than a year, at more than 85 percent over the price he paid for them.

ALVIANO   Now where I come from that is called, in good Portuguese, *usury!*[95] It is a curious thing, withal, that one could make so much money right on the spot, from one minute to the next, without taking any risk.

BRANDÔNIO   Well, it can be done. And it happens so often that many traders of that sort and many of the storekeepers here are owners of great property in sugar mills and farms. Many of them live on their estates, and some of them are married.[96]

ALVIANO   Men who can prosper so in a foreign land must have great abilities.

BRANDÔNIO   You must realize that Brazil is a crossroads of the world. I mean no offense to any other kingdom or city when I call it that.

At the same time, it is a public academy in which one may easily learn every manner of civility, polite discourse, courteous behavior, how to make a good business deal, and other accomplishments of similar importance.

ALVIANO   It ought rather to be just the contrary, for we know that Brazil was settled first of all by persons of evil ways and men who had been banished from Portugal for their crimes, and therefore persons of scant civility. Their not being of gentle birth surely was enough for them to lack all refinement.[97]

BRANDÔNIO   There is no doubt of that. But you must realize that the first settlers who came to Brazil had many opportunities to get rich in a hurry on account of the liberality of the land. As they prospered, they promptly shed their evil nature, which the necessity and poverty they had suffered in the Kingdom had brought out. And the children of those men, having those riches and enthroned as rulers of the land, sloughed off their old skin just the way a snake does, and adopted in everything the most polished manners. I must add that later on many gentlemen and persons of noble birth came out to this state. They married here and became attached to the colonists by family ties. Thus there was developed among them all a mixture of fairly gentle blood. Furthermore, all kinds of people come from all parts of the world to do business in Brazil, and they transact this business with the residents of the country.[98] Now the latter are usually very shrewd, either because of the highly favorable climate or because of the auspicious heavens. So they pick up from the foreigners whatever they think useful. They carefully preserve this knowledge and put it to use in their own good time.

ALVIANO   To be able to imitate and to steal abilities from those who have great ones, why, that is to wrest the club from the hands of Hercules!

BRANDÔNIO   That's just what the people in Brazil do, to the point that the sons of Lisbon and those of other parts of the Kingdom come here to learn fine manners and with them make themselves new men, thanks to the refinement that formerly they lacked.

But it appears to me that long ago we lost the thread of our discussion, in which we were considering the profit that trade brings to those who engage in it in this Brazil.

ALVIANO   But this other discussion, by which we were briefly distracted, should not displease those who may hear of it,[99] especially the Brazilians. But, leaving that aside, you have yet to tell me if Brazil has any commerce beyond that with the Kingdom.

BRANDÔNIO   Oh, yes. Brazil does a great trade with Angola and the Rio de la Plata. Ships with all kinds of goods are sent to Angola and come back carrying slaves to be sold here, and the men who deal in slaves make a big profit. Further, the ships bound for Angola from the Kingdom put in at the Captaincy of Rio de Janeiro, where they take aboard cargoes of manioc flour, the chief foodstuff of the land, which is cheaper there. Carrying it to Angola, they exchange it for slaves[100] and ivory, which they bring back in great quantities.

ALVIANO   All that concerns Angola. But I wish you would tell me about the business that is done with the Rio de la Plata.

BRANDÔNIO   Many *peruleiros*[101] come up regularly from the Rio de la Plata in carracks and in caravels[102] of small tonnage. They bring a vast sum of *patacas* of four and eight reales,[103] and worked and unworked silver in cones and in bars, both gold dust and grain gold and some wrought into chains. They take these things to Rio de Janeiro, Bahia de Todos os Santos, and Pernambuco and exchange them for the different kinds of goods they need. Leaving all their silver and gold behind them here, they stow their goods aboard and make the return trip to the Rio de la Plata. And even our local merchants have an interest in this trade, for it is of no small profit to them. A few of these *peruleiros* settle down in Brazil, and use their money to make loans on notes, or to loan money at interest, or to buy sugar; or they take it with them to Portugal.

ALVIANO   That is not a bad business, when you pick gold and silver as its fruit! But all of the trade which you have discussed, and from which so much profit is derived, seems to end up in the hands of foreigners, and the profit goes to them and not to the settlers.

BRANDÔNIO   For the most part that is so, because the people of this country are busy looking after their sugar mills and improving their farms, and they don't want to get involved in trade. The few who do so are satisfied just with sending their sugar to the Kingdom and ordering sent out from there whatever they need for their farms. But in everything else they leave the door wide open to the merchants, who carry on their business most profitably. As an excellent illustration of this, I can tell you of a case which I myself witnessed.

In the year '92 [1592] a small businessman came straight to Pernambuco from the Algarve, his ship laden with wines from Alvor,[104] a little olive oil, a lot of raisins and figs, and many other things that are always brought out from there. He had invested a capital of 730$000, according to his bill of lading, which I saw. This man stayed out here six months, sold his stock for cash, and made close to seven thousand cruzados [2:800$000] on it. He invested this in the finest white sugar, paying 650 reis per arroba. Now, because he bought that sugar so cheaply, he must surely have doubled his money once again when he sold it back in Portugal.[105]

ALVIANO   I admit that a country where businessmen can make a profit like that must be very bountiful.

BRANDÔNIO   You can see how bountiful it is from just one thing that I shall tell you. There is a private citizen of good standing, a settler in the Captaincy of Paraíba in this Brazil, who—though owning no more than a single sugar mill—boldly promised to give everyone who would build a house in the city [Filipéia], which then was just being laid out, 20$ [20$000] for each house of stone and mortar more than one story high, and 10$ [10$000] for a house of one story. And he kept his word over a long period, during which many houses were put up, without there being any profit to him other than the gratification of his desire to see the city grow. And now, to complete this story, I will tell you that he undertook, further, to build the city's House of Mercy, a thing of vast expense because of the size and grandeur of its church, which now is almost finished.[106] Having given you that one example, I want to go on to a discussion of the third commodity on which the settlers of this state make money[107]—and a good deal of it—which is brazilwood.[108]

ALVIANO   I beg you to do so.

BRANDÔNIO   Brazilwood, from which this whole province takes its name, as I have already explained, yields a red dyestuff, which is excellent for dyeing wood and silk, and for making paints and other things. Though it is found throughout all the state, the best and most valuable brazilwood is cut in the captaincies of Pernambuco, Itamaracá, and Paraíba, for it far surpasses in coloring strength the wood found elsewhere.[109] Thus only the wood from the three captaincies mentioned is considered good enough to be sent to the Kingdom. There it sells for four and sometimes five milreis per quintal, depending on how abundant the supply is.

ALVIANO   Tell me now, how do the settlers in this Brazil make money on the wood, and how much does it bring His Majesty's Treasury?

BRANDÔNIO   Brazilwood is His Majesty's own drug and, as such, is protected so that no one may deal in it except the King himself or those who have received his license under contract. A long time ago anyone was permitted to trade in it, paying His Majesty's Exchequer one cruzado on every quintal he cut. But since the feeling was that there were many abuses under that system, the order establishing it was revoked so that the trade should be handled only under contract, as is the case today. About forty thousand cruzados are paid to His Majesty's Treasury for a contract,[110] which is let in the Kingdom. It is specified that in any one year the contractors may not take out from this state, especially from the three captaincies I have mentioned, more than ten thousand quintals of the wood, although if they cut less in one year they may make it up in the next.

ALVIANO   I had no idea that brazilwood was the source of so much revenue for the Exchequer without His Majesty's having to spend a single real for it, whereas he must spend so many cruzados in India to purchase other drugs.

BRANDÔNIO   All Brazil[111] is a source of revenue for His Majesty's Exchequer, without entailing any expense—a fact that ought to be very much appreciated!

ALVIANO   And what profit do the settlers make on the wood?

BRANDÔNIO   A great deal, for many settlers make their living simply by going into the forest and hauling the wood out with oxen to a waterway, where they sell it to persons who have a license to ship it.[112]

ALVIANO   Now tell me how they cut this wood.

BRANDÔNIO   Well, it's like this: they go some twelve, fifteen, and even twenty leagues out from the Captaincy of Pernambuco in search of the greatest stands of it, for it cannot be found any closer at hand, since the demand has been so great.[113] There, amidst great forests, they find it. The tree has a smallish leaf, and thorns along the trunk. The men who engage in this occupation take many slaves from Guinea[114] with axes. After the tree is on the ground, they remove all the outer layers, for the brazil is in the heartwood. In this way a tree of tremendous girth supplies a piece of wood no larger than your leg. After it is trimmed, they pile it up. From there they cart it in wagons, five or six logs being tied together, until they get it to storage sheds, where barges can come alongside to take it aboard.[115]

ALVIANO   It must be a hard job to cut timber that way. Unless the yield is great, the merchandise will end up being very expensive.

BRANDÔNIO   Oh yes, the yield is great. Many of these men cut one to two thouand quintals of brazil every year and haul it out with their ox teams. After they have got it to the storage sheds, they sell it for seven to eight tostons[116] per quintal, and sometimes for more than that. They make a lot of money on it, and many men have made their fortunes that way.

ALVIANO   If that's the way it happens, we can say that God gives the settlers in Brazil gold and silver in their fields, and that from something they have neither planted nor tended they pick the fruit.

BRANDÔNIO   You know how true that is, but I can tell you that they find other things of even greater value that cost them neither work nor effort.

ALVIANO   Now how can that be?

BRANDÔNIO   It's like this: many men in this Brazil get rich from the quantity of ambergris they find on the beaches, in varying amounts.[117] There was a certain settler who came upon such an abundance of it that he didn't think what he had found could be real ambergris. Deciding that it must be tar or pitch, he set to work using it to caulk a boat that he had pulled onto the ways for this purpose. He went on with the job until some of his cronies who saw him working at it showed him his mistake. And even though he had by then used up much of the ambergris, he still had a great deal left.

ALVIANO   That sounds like one of the tales of Trancoso;[118] so I find it hard to believe!

BRANDÔNIO   It is the absolute truth, and it happened just the way I've told you. But so we won't have to go begging for such stories at other people's houses, I'll tell you one about something that happened to me, and if you doubt this I can still find you some trustworthy witnesses to vouch for me. Now this happened in the year '83 [1583], when I was in the Captaincy of Pernambuco, in the town of Olinda, at the time that a fleet was making ready to sail for the Kingdom. I was kept pretty busy, what with having to write letters for over there. An employee of mine arrived, a man whom I delegated to collect the sugar tithes, which I was in charge of at the time. Comilão [Glutton] was his nickname.[119] He told me, in the greatest secrecy, after we were in a room by ourselves, that the day before, when he was on his way to take some fish out of a trap he had in the Extremo River,[120] he had found a great quantity of some substance on the beach. He then handed me a big ball of the stuff he said he had found. It must have weighed about six to seven *arráteis* [pounds]. He told me that there was so much of this on the beach, close to the water, that he and two blacks he had taken with him spent more than three hours carrying it in an old sugar mold and two calabashes, until they had it all out of the path along the beach and hidden away among some mangroves, making altogether a fair-sized mound.

I was then a newcomer in the land and had not yet seen any ambergris out here. In Portugal some had come into my hands, but that was ambergris from India, and it was white and had a marvelously good smell. But what the fellow had found was black and slimy, and smelled like fish oil. I felt such a revulsion from touching it that I threw the ball of it out of the window into some thick foliage, keeping in my fingers only three to four ounces of it that stuck to a little piece of paper I had used to take hold of it. To get rid of the paper, I tossed it into the drawer of a writing desk that I had opened.

I dismissed the young man, telling him he shouldn't make so much of what he had found, for it must be some kind of filth that had been cast up on the beach. With this the poor chap went away, unaware of the fortune that was slipping through his hands. Three years went by, and during this time a relative of mine to whom I was under great obligation came out here from the Kingdom. When he decided to go back home, I had to give him an important document to take with him. I could not find it; so I searched through all the desk drawers for a long time, and in one of them I came across the scrap of paper with that stuff sticking to it, which I had tossed in there. Now, with time it had lost the bad smell of fish oil and taken on another, a very good smell; so it was clear to me that it was ambergris. Finding it there I was confused, for I could not recall when or how I had put it in that drawer or where it had come from. At last, searching my memory, I hit on what had happened, with no small regret! Imagining that I still might remedy what was really beyond repair, I sent for the fellow who had found it. He was married by this time, and when I told him what had happened he was almost ready to hang himself. Just the same, we both got on our horses and went to the place where he had found the ambergris. He now had trouble locating the spot, and in the end we found nothing and decided that the crabs, birds, and other filthy creatures must have eaten it.

ALVIANO   That was a strange thing indeed, and the loss of so great a possession is surely to be regretted. I would never have believed that it happened that way if you had not told it to me in all truth. But how could that ambergris be black? I thought that ambergris was always white or gray.

BRANDÔNIO   In this Brazil of ours there are two kinds of ambergris: one is found along the coast of Jaguaribe, and being white or gray sells for 4$000 [ten cruzados] per ounce and sometimes more; the other is found from Pernambuco down to Bahia and is black, although some white ambergris does turn up there occasionally. The black is worth three to four cruzados an ounce.

ALVIANO   I am so distressed by the story of what happened to you that I don't want to hear any more talk about ambergris. Let us go on to consider the fourth source of wealth, according to the order you have been following.

BRANDÔNIO   Just the same, before I discuss that, I want to tell you a funny story about the discovery of some ambergris just a few days ago in this state.[121] A certain man who was going out fishing went in the direction of the Captaincy of Rio Grande, to a cove that the coast forms there. He wanted to take his jangada[122] out but did not have a stone to make an anchor. Casting his eyes over the beach, he saw one that seemed just about the right size for that; so he took it, tied his line to it, and shoved off in the jangada to go fishing. When he reached the place where he wanted to fish, the jangada kept drifting with the wind; so he dropped his anchor, but it floated on the water as if it were made of cork. Now, seeing that the trouble he had taken with that anchor availed him nothing, since it floated, he came back to shore. Just then a friend of his was coming down to the beach to go out fishing in another jangada. He told him about the trouble he had had with the anchor that floated. His friend, who must have been a cunning fellow, told him not to worry about that, for he was not feeling very well himself and had made up his mind not to go fishing, and said he had his anchor there and the man could use it. The first fellow accepted the offer of the anchor and went off to fish, leaving the floating stone in the hands of the new arrival, who had recognized it at first sight as ambergris. Hoisting it onto his shoulders, he disappeared with it and realized a great profit from it, for it weighed almost a full arroba [thirty-two pounds].

A Brazilian jangada. Kaspar van Baerle, *Rerum per octennium in Brasilia . . . Historia* (1647). Illus. no. 35, following p. 136. *Courtesy of the Edward E. Ayer Collection, The Newberry Library, Chicago.*

ALVIANO   That was a real stroke of luck! And since the distribution of wealth among men is pretty much a matter of luck, if I may say so, you need a great deal of it to discover something as valuable as ambergris. But since I am still distressed by what you have told me, I beg you take up the thread of your story again.

BRANDÔNIO   As I recall, I said that the fourth way for the settlers in Brazil to make money is in cotton and timber. Cotton used to be more highly valued than it is today, and it brought more profit to those who dealt in it. [123] So I shall discuss it first.

ALVIANO   What has caused it to decline in value?

BRANDÔNIO   The fact that there is too much of it in Venice and in other places, so that what is exported from Brazil loses its value. But the land is ideally suited to growing cotton; so the crop is always large everywhere here. It is planted from seed and in a short time matures and is picked. After it is removed from the ball in which it grows they bale it, and in this condition it is known as dirty cotton. When the seeds are separated it is called clean.

To separate the seeds they use a contrivance of two revolving axles. When the cotton is put through them the seeds drop out on the side where it was inserted, and the cotton comes out on the other side from between the two axles.[124] They used to sell it here for two milreis the arroba, and that left a large profit for the planters, since it cost them very little to grow it. It would sell in the Kingdom for four milreis the arroba, but now it brings much less, in both countries, for the reason I have explained.

ALVIANO   And how is this cotton carried to the Kingdom?

BRANDÔNIO   They carry it inside large bags that are made just for this purpose out of burlap. It is pounded down so that the bag is firm and hard. Since it is so tightly packed, it doesn't hurt to carry it to the Kingdom on the open decks of the ships, for the rain does no damage to it. Now I think that's enough about cotton, although I might add that much very good strong work cloth is made from it in this Brazil.

ALVIANO   Well, let us get on to a discussion of the timber,[125] which must be a thing of greater importance.

BRANDÔNIO   I certainly would have been glad not to become involved in such a task, for there is so much to say on that subject. No matter where I look, I see leafy trees, thick forests, tangled woods, and pleasant fields. A soft, sweet springtime seems to pervade the whole, for all year long the trees enjoy the freshest verdure and are as green in summer as they are in winter [sic]. They never shed all their leaves as they do in our Spain, but rather as soon as one falls another is born. Beauteous landscapes like these so delight the eye that even the avenues of poplars and other such trees, which in Madrid, Valladolid, and other towns and places in Castile are planted and tended with such eager care for the delight and recreation of the people, are greatly inferior and cannot be compared to these. For here the forest and woods are natural and not artificial. They are studded with groves of such tall trees—whose great crowns and fresh foliage prevent the sun's rays from visiting the earth in which they thrive—that an arrow sent from taut bow by brawny arm is unable to surpass their height. There are so many kinds of similar plants and trees that the eye cannot contemplate them all and is satisfied only to give thanks to God for having created them as they are. Whence I most certainly believe that if there were some good herbalists in this Brazil they could—from the species and nature of the plants and trees—compile many volumes of books bigger than those of Dioscorides,[126] for they enjoy and contain within themselves the greatest powers and secret qualities. Their richness in this respect can be gauged by even just the few of them that we make use of.

ALVIANO   To hear you talk, we have in Brazil so many new Thessalonian fields.[127] You have praised them so eloquently, depicting so many great things and such superb qualities in them, that the desire has come over me to transform myself into a rustic shepherd just to be able to enjoy their freshness.[128]

BRANDÔNIO   It would not be a bad thing for you if you did, for all I have said falls far short of what I might have told you.

ALVIANO   I admit that the fields may have the charm that you proclaim, but I never heard it said that the plants they produce enjoy such medicinal virtues as, you hold, abound in them.

BRANDÔNIO   I do not wish to be distracted by showing you the truth of what I say, contrary to your opinion, for there would be no end to that. I shall only tell you of two cases that I know of and saw with my own eyes, and from them you will understand how much more I could tell you.

Now the first of these is that there was living in my house a little mulatto girl of tender age, who was born there and whom I loved dearly, for I had reared her. A slave of mine, with diabolic intent, spurred on to this by the girl's having told me of a theft he had committed, gave her poison, so that in a very short time she was all swollen up, had turned black, and was breathing heavily, frothing at the mouth, with her teeth clenched and her eyes all white. By these and other things she showed all the signs of being at death's door. Seeing the girl in such a state, not only was I extremely sorrowful, but I had a firm suspicion that poison had brought this about and that the guilty person must have been the very slave who had, in fact, given it to her, for he had among his fellows the reputation of being a sorcerer and herbalist. Hence I had him seized, assuring him that he would live no longer than the girl did, because I knew for a certainty that he had given her the poison. I said some other things to him and even showed him what I intended to do, which was to run him through the cane press;[129] therefore, he should try quickly to find a remedy for the evil he had done. Fear of these threats worked so powerfully on him that he undertook to cure the sick girl on condition that he might have leave to go to the woods to pick some herbs for this purpose. I consented to what he asked of me, but I had him shackled to another house slave,[130] whom I secretly charged to note carefully the herb that was picked so that we might recognize it later. But the first slave was so crafty that, to keep from revealing it, he picked many different herbs, among which was the one he had need of, but in such a way that the slave who was shackled to him could not tell which one was the herb he was going to use.

They both came back to where I was waiting for them, and the herbalist brought his drug, which he had already crushed in his hands and chewed up with his teeth. On arriving he did nothing more than go up to the poisoned girl and force the herb's juice inside her mouth, which he opened with a spoon, and then into her ears and nostrils, rubbing her briskly with it on the wrists and the body joints. Then— oh, marvelous thing!—in a trice the girl opened her eyes and mouth and began to void a vast lot both above and below, after which the swelling of her body began to go down, and within one day she was as sound as she had been before.

I was most woefully upset because I did not know what the herb was, but I was never able to get that slave, either by threatening him or by offering him presents, to show me what it was. All I was able to tell, from a little piece of it that I took from his hands, was that it was a fuzzy herb.

ALVIANO   I would have forced him to it with tortures, for an antidote so preservative and of such power ought to be known to the world.

BRANDÔNIO   Nothing would work with that slave. The other case was that of a slave of little value, one of those from Angola.[131] I have seen him pick up the most poisonous snakes and wrap them around himself. Although they bit him in many places, their bites did him no harm. Yet with other people the bites of those same snakes would be fatal within twenty-four hours. I marveled at this, and thought that it must be the work of magic words or the power of some kind of spell. But in the end I found out that it wasn't either one.

When I had won the black's good will by means of presents, he finally showed me some roots and another herb, telling me that whoever rubbed his joints with the juice of that root, after chewing it well in his mouth, could in all safety pick up as many snakes as he wanted to, without fear of their bites' doing him harm, no matter how poisonous the snakes might be. I tried it myself and had experiments made, and it is still used by my slaves today.

The herb he gave me at that time was one that would cure any kind of snake bite, and not the special antidote I mentioned. When the bite was generously coated and rubbed vigorously with the herb and its juice, and when the slave had taken other measures, such as doing some more massaging, the bite healed. Ever so many men who had been so bitten by those poisonous creatures were cured, and as easily as if they had only been stung by a bee. That black is dead now, but some other slaves of mine make good use of that same herb.

ALVIANO   Well, you must do me the favor of ordering your slaves to give me a little piece of that root and herb, which I shall always carry about with me, for whatever may happen. But I should like to know if the root and herb are good for anything else than as an antidote for snake poison.

BRANDÔNIO   I have not experimented with it yet, because of my own negligence. But just as this Brazil has antidotes against poison, so also it has many trees and plants that yield most subtle poisons. They are much used by the Guinea blacks, who kill many of their fellows by this means.[132]

ALVIANO   And who revealed the secret of the poison to the slaves?

BRANDÔNIO   They knew all about it in their own country before they came over, and in this land they do great damage to the settlers by killing their slaves.

But it appears to me that we are getting off the subject of our conversation, for we were going to consider how the inhabitants of this Brazil have become rich men by dealing in lumber. They saw up a great deal of it to make crates in which they pack their sugar, and they also produce much fine planking, which they export to the Kingdom. And there are excellent woods for building houses and for making furniture such as writing desks, sideboards, beds, and the like.

ALVIANO   And do the settlers themselves cut the timber and finish it?

BRANDÔNIO   No, for the people in Brazil lord it more than you can imagine. Instead, they have their slaves saw it up. There are some men who every year have from one to two thousand sugar chests made up, which they sell to mill owners, small planters, and merchants at 450 to 500 reis apiece, depending on how big the supply is. That will give you an idea of how much timber there is. Although this state has been settled a long time and a large number of boards have been cut for chests every year, the forests never fail to supply enough wood for many more.

ALVIANO   And what wood are these chests made of?

BRANDÔNIO   The chests are made from soft woods such as the *munguba*,[133] *ibirarema*,[134] nitta, strangler fig, *camaçarim*,[135] and one called garlic pear and another called whitewood,[136] and there are different varieties of each one of these. For sugar chests they always try to get soft wood, since it is easier to saw.

ALVIANO   What lumber do they use for houses and other construction, and for the planks that you say are shipped to the Kingdom?

BRANDÔNIO   Many excellent kinds, the best in the world. And there are so many of them that there isn't a man who could know them all or name one out of twenty of them, even if that man were a woodcutter whose job is nothing other than to chop them down in the forests.

ALVIANO   Just the same, I wish you would tell me what some of them are like.

BRANDÔNIO   If you wish, I shall try to tell you something about the few whose names I know. The woods that I have heard about and whose properties I can recall are these: *açabengita*,[137] a very hard, yellow wood that yields a dye of the same color; the beautiful red *jatobá*;[138] the *piquiá*,[139] very hard and yellow; another kind that is golden in color called yellowwood,[140] excellent for boards; the golden *jatobá*; the *maçaranduba*[141] and the *cabaraíba*,[142] both of which are reddish in color and make fine furniture, especially chairs; the jacaranda,[143] which in our Spain is so highly prized for making beds and other furniture; the *conduru*,[144] a very strong wood that makes good beams. The *sapupira*,[145] too, is used for planking, but also to make ox carts and keels for ship frames; the *camaçarim*[146] is suitable for boards. Another is called bow-wood,[147] for they make good stout bows of it; the sapucaya[148] is very good for mill axles and for foundation supports; the canafistula,[149] which is dark in color; the *camará*,[150] which is highly valued because it is a very sturdy wood; ironwood [*pau-ferro*], so named because it is equal to that metal in strength; another called holy wood [lignum vitae], so highly valued and known everywhere; the *buraquií*,[151] which can be used for many things; angelim,[152] which in the East Indies they consider a capital wood; and the incorruptible cedar, which the Scriptures praise; and then the *burapiroca*,[153] a blond wood which they use for house frames; *buraem*,[154] which almost never rots and which they use for planking ships; copaiva,[155] which is a very beautiful black; *urundeúva*,[156] of a bright red color, as is *guanandim*.[157] Both of these grow only in the salt water marshes and swamps. Another wood is called *quiri*,[158] and it is so hard that it cuts through iron. Its white outer layer can be substituted for ivory in fine furniture; its inner pith shows the water and coloring of a very beautiful jasper. There is another wood very similar to it, which comes from Jaguaribe. These few come to my mind from among the many that I might have mentioned, all of which grow in the captaincies north of Cape St. Augustine. I have little information on the different kinds of wood in the South, since I have never traveled in those parts.[159]

ALVIANO   A few days ago I saw an old man carrying a stick as big around as an arm band, which he used as a staff. Since it looked big to me I thought that it must be too heavy to be used that way. I picked it up and found that it was so light I could hardly feel it in my hands, for it weighed less than a skein of cotton.

BRANDÔNIO   That wood, or—more accurately—that stalk, comes from a thick reed called *tabua* [cattail], which they use for making mats. When it is very old it looks like the staff you saw. There is also another wood, which they call *jangada*[160] because out of it they make jangadas to go to sea in. It, too, is very light, and for that reason they use it to make the poles for the litters in which, as I shall explain later, the women are accustomed to ride.[161]

ALVIANO   I don't know where else in the world could be found so many different kinds of useful woods as you have mentioned. I am surprised that His Majesty does not make use of them for carracks and galleons, and he could have those built right here.

BRANDÔNIO   When I was in the Kingdom in '607 [1607], the *Conde Merinho-Mor,* comptroller of His Majesty's Exchequer,[162] asked for my opinion on two matters: first, whether ships could be built in this state, and second, whether it would be possible to manufacture pikes[163] here—for he said that it was a great bother to order them from outside the Kingdom. I told him that there was no possibility of building any sizable ships in this state, for the timber was too far away, since the sugar mills had used up what stood nearby, and that it would be very expensive to haul timber out to the waterways. I also observed that it would be very hard to get the needed workmen and to keep them on the job. Even though they were sent out from the Kingdom on salaries, they would quickly disappear into the country, where they could not be found.

But today I have changed my mind, because with the recent settlements in Maranhão and in Pará, which is the River of the Amazons, His Majesty could have many ships built up there, for there are vast stands of timber along the water's edge that could be used easily and cheaply. And the workmen sent out from the Kingdom for the purpose would not be able to run away, for as yet there are no plantations and settlements in the back country up there where they might hide out.[164]

ALVIANO   That is not a bad suggestion for His Majesty to adopt, and I think he ought to put it into execution right away. But as for the pikes, what answer did you give the Minister?

BRANDÔNIO   I told him that any number of good ones could be made in this country out of a wood called pole wood (*pau d'hástea*), which is excellent for the purpose. So that he might test the truth of what I told him, I promised to send him some pikes made over here—I was on my way back here at the time. As soon as I arrived I did what I had promised, but I never had any further word about the matter.

ALVIANO   I am amazed to hear you name so many kinds of wood. From the different names you give them, I take it that they all vary in appearance and qualities.

BRANDÔNIO   Yes, they do; so much so that rarely does one tree resemble another, in either its foliage or its trunk. And I must not forget to mention two very remarkable specimens that I came across, both of them in the Captaincy of Paraíba. One of these was a strangler fig tree of great girth. Even though its trunk was hollow, the tree was not dead, for its leaves were green and perfect. But inside its hollow trunk another tree had grown, a mangrove whose own trunk was seven palms around. Now this tree had penetrated the cavity in the other tree so that the mangrove's boughs, which were quite large, were growing all tangled up at the top with those of the fig. They had grown in such disordered fashion that they appeared to be just one tree, and only by the difference in their leaves could one tell which was which. Thus the two trees had grown from separate roots and different trunks, but one inside the other.

The other strange thing I saw was in the Copaoba Mountains: a very tall tree had grown astride a rock that stood more than twelve palms high above the ground. On both sides of the rock the tree's roots came down to the earth, seeking nourishment for its trunk and branches. I could never understand how such a plant could grow astride that rock without having any soil in between to sustain it.

ALVIANO   You have told me of so many marvels that this one does not surprise me, although it is a very strange thing indeed. But since you have spoken about mangroves, tell me if it is true that their roots grow down from the top. I am so absentminded that I have not yet noticed whether that is so.

BRANDÔNIO   The mangroves grow mostly on the tidal flats in the salt marshes that lie between rivers subject to the ebb and flow of the tides. There are two kinds of mangrove, the red and the white. The red is sturdier and grows better on the tidal flats. The white mangrove is a soft wood and prefers firmer soil somewhat removed from the salt marshes. Both of them thrust their roots down from the top,[165] but the red mangrove has many more roots than the white has. Now with that, let us end our conversation for today. I will admit that I for one just can't take any more!

ALVIANO   I shall always bow to your pleasure, but on the condition that tomorrow we meet again in this spot, at our customary time, to carry on our discussion.

Notes to Dialogue III

1 · The term *salad* was sometimes used to describe a literary work of diverse subject matter. Antoine de la Sale had this meaning in mind in his punning title, *La salade nouvellement imprimée à Paris* (1527; facsim. rpt. Boston: Massachusetts Historical Society, no. 113, 1924). La Sale further justified his title by the fact that the book "contained" a number of herbs. Both these explanations apply equally to Brandônio's "salad."

2 · Brandônio's candid avowal that profit was the prime motive in settling Brazil would not have surprised a contemporary. Profit making was central not only to individual enterprise but to governmental policy and practice where Portugal's possessions overseas were concerned. João de Barros, commenting on the voyage of Pedro Álvares Cabral to India (1500–1501), declared that "all other motives were subordinated to that of profit, which always prevailed in every decision." *Da Ásia de João de Barros e de Diogo do Couto,* decade 1, bk. 6, chap. 1, p. 7. Barros's frankness is unusual. More commonly it was asserted that the chief goal of the conquests was the conversion of the heathen: "The principal end which the Kings of Portugal had from the beginning, and have today, in conquering new lands," said Luís Figueira, S. J. (1637), "is not so

much in expanding their empire as in communicating the Faith and the Gospel to the Infidels." "Memorial sobre as terras e gente do Maranhão," *Revista do Instituto Histórico e Geográfico Brasileiro*, tomo 94, volume 148 (1923):430. This pious sentiment was repeated in many a royal decree. Thus there was a solid basis in fact for both Barros's and Figueira's views.

3 · Sugar was still a luxury, being sold to the individual consumer like spices, by its pharmaceutical weight. It brought fifty times the price of honey, which remained the ordinary sweetener as it had been for centuries. See Noel Deerr, *The History of Sugar*, 1:100–114; Vitorino Magalhães Godinho, *Os descobrimentos e a economia mundial*, 2:458–464; Frédéric Mauro, *Le Portugal et l'Atlantique au XVIIe siècle (1570–1670)*, pp. 192–211. On the consumption of sugar in Europe see Edmund Oskar von Lippmann, *História do açúcar desde a época mais remota até o começo da fabricação do açúcar de beterraba*, 2:155–238. The most detailed description of the Colonial Brazilian sugar industry in all its aspects is Andrée Mansuy's edition of André João Antonil [João António Andreoni], *Cultura e opulência do Brasil por suas drogas e minas*, pp. 74–289; this edition includes a French translation and copious notes. A new study of Brazil's colonial sugar industry, by Stuart B. Schwartz, is to be published soon.

4 · Brandônio may give a wrong impression when he includes gold and silver in his list of exports from India. Most of the trade in raw gold and raw silver, as well as in coins, went in the opposite direction—from the mines of the New World to the East, though some gold from Malacca and some silver coins were sent to Europe from Ormuz by way of Goa. Perhaps Brandônio is thinking here of the splendid ornaments and art objects, both religious and secular, which were made in India for sale in Europe. Such objects were available in Lisbon as early as the beginning of the sixteenth century. João Lúcio d'Azevedo, *Elementos para a história econômica de Portugal (séculos XII a XVII)*, p. 104; Fernand Braudel, *La Méditerranée et le monde méditerranéen à l'époque de Philippe II*, 1:422–423; Donald Frederick Lach, *Asia in the Making of Europe*, 2:10, 113, 119.

5 · Various parts of India and Indonesia were sources of emeralds, rubies, amethysts, diamonds, topazes, sapphires, and semi-precious stones. All the sixteenth-century chroniclers of India describe the fabulous jewels found there. See especially Duarte Barbosa, *The Book of Duarte Barbosa*, 1:226, n. 2, and 2:217–226; John [Jan] Huyghen van Linschoten, *The Voyage of John Huyghen van Linschoten to the East Indies, from the Old English Translation of 1598*, 2:136–158; Tomé Pires, *The Suma Oriental of Tomé Pires*, 1:86; Ludovico di Varthema, *The Travels of Ludovico di Varthema*, pp. 101, 190; cf. Lach, *Asia*, 1:826. Glamorous as these gems appear

to the imagination, the products of Indian agriculture were and are much more valuable, especially spices.

6 · Musk is made from secretions of an accessory male gland of the Asiatic deer, *Moschus moschiferus*, an animal found in the central part of Asia towards China and towards India. The Chinese have exported musk since the sixth century, but the best quality was considered to come from Burma and Bengal. Linschoten, *Voyage*, 2:94–95; Isaac H. Burkill, *A Dictionary of the Economic Products of the Malay Peninsula*, s.v. "deer," 1: 787.

7 · The South Arabian coasts have been especially fruitful in ambergris, and it was the Arabs who developed trade in the substance. Ambergris is likewise found in other Asian waters, including those of Sumatra, Malaysia, the Maldives, and the Cape of Comorin. Cabral took some ambergris back to Portugal from India, though the product was already gathered on the coasts of Portugal. Burkill, *Economic Products of the Malay Peninsula*, s.v. "ambergris."

8 · In Brandão's time Portuguese ships brought back much silk cloth, mostly from China and Persia. Raw silk, which came from Persia and Syria, had to be sent by caravan to the Mediterranean and thence transported to Europe. It was only a few years after the *Dialogues* were written that most of these sources were closed to the Portuguese through military and economic setbacks at the hands of the English, Persians, and Japanese. See Charles R. Boxer, *The Great Ship from Amacon: Annals of Macao and the Old Japan Trade, 1555–1640*, pp. 158, 170; and Niels Steensgaard, *Carracks, Caravans and Companies: The Structural Crisis in the European-Asian Trade in the Early 17th Century*, p. 158.

9 · Indigo belongs to a large genus of herbs, the *Indigofera*, which are found throughout the tropics. Most of the indigo at this time came from the north of India, but a small amount, generally considered to be of inferior quality, was produced on the Coromandel Coast (southeast India). Peter Mundy and Jean Baptiste Tavernier give interesting descriptions of the preparation of indigo by hand.

Portugal imported indigo from India from 1516 on, at first in small amounts, but by the first quarter of the seventeenth century in quantity, because indigo was replacing traditional dyes such as woad and logwood. The Portuguese monopoly on indigo was short-lived: by Brandônio's day the English were already drying some indigo in Surat [Gujarat], and a few years later the Dutch were to develop their own trade in the drug.

See Peter Mundy, *The Travels of Peter Mundy in Europe and Asia, 1608–1667*, 2:221–223; Jean Baptiste Tavernier, *Travels in India*, 2:8–12; Magalhães Godinho, *Descobrimentos*, 2:110; Burkill, *Economic Products of the Malay Peninsula*, s.v. *Indigofera;* Chandra Richard de Silva, "The

Portuguese East India Company 1628–1633," *Luso-Brazilian Review* 11 (1974):188–189.

10 · The ships were laden above all with the "useful drugs"—pepper, cloves, mace, nutmeg, cinnamon, and ginger. As is well known, spices were the most wanted of Asiatic products; in fact, the traffic in spices was the first in importance of all world traffics. Braudel, *Méditerrannée,* 1:500. Thomas Mun, writing in 1621, estimated the average annual European consumption of several Asian products as follows:

Pepper	6,000,000 lbs.
Cloves	450,000 lbs.
Mace	150,000 lbs.
Nutmeg	400,000 lbs.
Indigo	350,000 lbs.
Persian raw silk	1,000,000 lbs.

A Discourse of Trade, from England unto the East-Indies, p. 11. It is evident from this list that of all the spices pepper was in greatest demand.

11 · The "governors" were the five members of the Council of Portugal; see I, n. 159. The governors serving in 1597, the year in which Brandônio presented his views to the Council, were the following: Miguel de Castro, archbishop of Lisbon, who presided; João de Silva, count of Portalegre; Francisco Mascarenhas, count of Santa Cruz; Duarte de Castelbranco, count of Sabugal; and Miguel de Moura, secretary in charge of documents. The council led an erratic existence, being replaced from time to time by a viceroy and then restored. João Pedro Ribeiro, *Dissertações chrono-lógicas e críticas sobre a história e jurisprudência ecclesiástica e civil de Portugal,* 2:196.

12 · Steensgaard estimates that each ship returning to Lisbon between 1571 and 1610 brought an average of 6,270 quintals (about 414 tons) of pepper, spices, and other drugs. *Carracks,* p. 168.

13 · Brandônio's figure may be too high. His contemporary Figueiredo Falcão itemizes the cost of two ships constructed in 1615 and 1616, for totals of 25:500$000 and 25:000$000 respectively. These amounts included such necessities as seamen's pay, furnishings, and equipment. Luiz de Figueiredo Falcão, *Livro em que se contém toda a fazenda e real património dos reinos de Portugal, Índia e ilhas adjacentes,* p. 205.

14 · Reales of eight are, more correctly, "pieces of eight reales," and these are the "pieces of eight" beloved of romantic fiction. In addition to the pieces of eight and of four that Brandônio mentions, there were pieces of one, two, sixteen, and thirty-two. The Portuguese cruzado was nor-mally regarded as equivalent to ten Spanish pieces of eight (Magalhães Godinho, *Descobrimentos,* 1:283). It is impossible to place a modern value on colonial coins because the rate of exchange has varied over time. These

silver coins were ultimately derived from the rich Spanish mines of Mexico and Peru, and they were greatly coveted by the English and Dutch East India companies for their Eastern trade. The fact that Portugal, at this time united with Spain, could draw upon these vast resources of silver gave it an immense economic advantage over England, the Netherlands, and other commercial rivals. William Foster, ed., *The Voyage of Nicholas Downton to the East Indies, 1614–15,* p. xii, n. 2; De Silva, "Portuguese East India Company," pp. 181–182.

15 · The Portuguese Crown bought pepper in the East, transported it to Lisbon, and sold it at fixed prices through the India House (see below, n. 18) to purchasers in northern Europe. Two hundred thousand cruzados was a normal figure for the annual purchase of pepper by Portugal from India at this time. The best original source on the pepper trade is Francisco da Costa's *Relatório sobre o trato da pimenta,* written in the early seventeenth century and published in *Documentação ultramarina portuguêsa,* 3:293–379. See also João Lúcio d'Azevedo, *História econômica,* pp. 150–151; Hermann Kellenbenz, "Der Pfeffermarkt um die Hansastädte," *Hansische Geschichtsblätter* 74 (1956):32; Lach, *Asia,* 1:143–147; Magalhães Godinho, *Descobrimentos,* 1:283.

16 · The standard conto [*conto de reis*], like the conto of gold [*conto de ouro*], was a unit of accounting. The *conto de reis* was equivalent to 1,000,000 reis [1:000$000], the *conto de ouro* to 400,000,000 reis [400:000 $000], or 1,000,000 cruzados.

17 · Luiz Mendes de Vasconcellos is in close agreement with Brandônio. He says that just the duties for each ship carrying goods from the Orient, exclusive of pepper, brought the King forty-five contos. *Diálogos do sítio de Lisboa* (1608), in *Antologia dos economistas portugueses,* p. 132. To this amount the freight charges should be added. Formerly separate contracts had been let for collecting freight and customs duties, but at this time they were usually let together. In 1614 Cosme Dias obtained a contract for collecting freight and customs duties on the ship Nossa Senhora do Cabo for the sum of 52,300,000 reis. Magalhães Godinho, *Descobrimentos,* 2:98. If the three contos Brandônio mentions below as the freight charge in 1601 is added to his figure of forty-five to fifty contos, the total of forty-eight to fifty-three contos, or 48,000,000 to 53,000,000 reis, agrees well enough with the sum paid to Dias.

18 · The India House [*Casa da Índia*], in Lisbon, was the headquarters for trade between Portugal and her possessions overseas. It was a huge establishment that regulated the unloading and distribution of goods, collected duties, inspected imports, and even supplied and equipped Portuguese merchant fleets. Its thousands of employees, dispersed throughout the far-flung Portuguese Empire, included legal and judicial

personnel, administrators, and clerical and manual workers of almost every description. See Charles E. Nowell, *A History of Portugal,* p. 88; Nicolau de Oliveira, *Livro das grandezas de Lisboa,* pp. 302–305; De Silva, "Portuguese East India Company," pp. 152–205.

19 · Between the years 1500 and 1635, about 11 percent of the Portuguese ships that set out to India from Lisbon were lost en route to the East, and about 15 percent on the return trip. The losses varied greatly at different periods. During the years from 1580 to 1612—thus shortly before the *Dialogues*—only 37 percent of the ships got back safely. Magalhães Godinho, *Descobrimentos,* 2:77; Lach, *Asia,* 1:40. De Silva discusses the causes of shipwrecks on the return trip from India in his "Portuguese East India Company," pp. 175–179. Much of his analysis applies to Brazilian as well as to Indian voyages.

20 · One of Brandônio's heavy-handed puns: the word for exemptions, *descontos,* is balanced against the word for the monetary units, *contos.*

21 · The "ships of great tonnage" were carracks, or *naus,* the vessels most commonly associated with the India trade; see I, n. 30.

22 · All officers and crewmen were allotted liberty chests [*caixas de liberdade, quintalados*], a name for stowage space in their cabins and on deck in which they could bring home certain goods wholly or partially duty free, to sell on their own account. The right of stowage space was badly abused, especially on the trip home, when crates and packages belonging to the crew members were often piled so high on the decks that to make one's way from prow to poop one had to climb over mounds of baggage and merchandise. This crowding was not only inconvenient but also extremely hazardous. No doubt it was the principal reason that more ships were lost on the way back to Portugal than en route to India. Charles R. Boxer, *The Tragic History of the Sea, 1589–1622,* pp. 17–18; idem, "Admiral João Pereira Corte-Real and the Construction of Portuguese East-Indiamen in the Early 17th Century," *The Mariner's Mirror* 26 (1940):392; Magalhães Godinho, *Descobrimentos,* 2:88–90; Diogo do Couto, *O soldado prático,* p. 6.

23 · Malabar was the source of most of the pepper imported to Europe. In the early sixteenth century, Malabar pepper had been preferred by consumers over the Indonesian varieties, but by Brandônio's time public taste had changed in favor of pepper from Sumatra and Java. Later on the Portuguese made strenuous efforts to break into the Indonesian pepper trade, but they were prevented from doing so by the Dutch commercial and naval power in the East. De Silva, "Portuguese East India Company," p. 184.

24 · The cinnamon tree, from whose inner bark the spice is produced, is found in all of Malaysia, but the best cinnamon was *Cinnamon zeylanicum,*

from Ceylon. Since the Portuguese controlled the western and south-western coasts of Ceylon, where the spice grew, they were able to prevent their rivals from obtaining it in any great quantity. Besides serving as a condiment, cinnamon was thought to be good for the stomach and nerves and for sweetening the breath. By the early seventeenth century it was a favorite drug for sailors to store in their liberty chests. See Garcia d'Orta, *Colóquios dos simples e drogas e cousas medicinais da Índia* (1563; facsim. ed., 1963), coloq. 15, fol. 64; Linschoten, *Voyage,* 2:76–78. For the production and marketing of the cinnamon of Ceylon, see Tikiri Abeyasinghe, *Portuguese Rule in Ceylon, 1594–1612,* pp. 135–140, and Chandra Richard de Silva, "Trade in Ceylon Cinnamon in the Sixteenth Century," *Ceylon Journal of Historical and Social Studies,* n.s., 3, no. 2 (1973):14–27.

25 · Cloves are the small, unopened flowers or buds of a tropical tree, *Eugenia caryophyllata*. Five clove-producing islands in the Moluccas were in 1521 the only place in the world where cloves grew. Lach, *Asia,* 1:595.

26 · Nutmeg is the kernel of the seed of *Myristica fragrans,* an evergreen tree that grows wild in the Molucca and Banda islands. The seed has a fibrous covering from which another spice, mace, is made. Mace was in greater demand than nutmeg, and hence mace sold for seven times as much, usually in a "package" with nutmeg to assure sale of the latter spice.

The Bandas are a group of small volcanic islands, variously numbered from three to six, in the East Indies, the largest island having the name Banda. "This place supplies the whole world with [nutmeg and mace], for they grow nowhere else, save some trees that are planted out of curiosity, as I have seen at Goa and other places. On this account many foreign merchants from all parts resort thither," says Pyrard de Laval, *Voyage de François Pyrard, de Laval,* pt. 2, pp. 175–176. Herbert Jacobs in the Introduction to his *Documenta Malucensia* gives a good account of the Moluccas, the Banda Islands, and the spice trade. For contemporary descriptions see Pires, *The Suma Oriental,* 1:205–209, and Linschoten, *Voyage,* 1:115–116 and 2:84–86.

27 · See above, n. 6.

28 · Benzoin, or benjamin, is the resin of the tree *Styrax benzoin,* of Sumatra, and of other species found in Thailand [Siam]. It was used in medicines, ointments, and perfumes. Henry Yule and A. C. Burnell, *Hobson-Jobson, A Glossary of Colloquial Anglo-Indian Words and Phrases,* s.v. "benjamin."

29 · Even in the earliest times each Portuguese vessel returning from the Orient brought 40,000 to 60,000 pieces of china. The porcelain was exported to Europe from Indian entrepôts and therefore was known as India porcelain [louça da Índia]. Van Leur estimates the total Chinese porcelain in the India trade at about 120,000 to 140,000 pieces a year.

Magalhães Godinho, *Descobrimentos,* 2:110; Jacob Cornelis van Leur, *Indonesian Trade and Society: Essays in Asian Social and Economic History,* p. 126.

30 · See above, n. 8.

31 · Literally, linen [*linho*]. There were in South Asia three major centers of production of cotton cloth for export, of which the most important was the Sultanate of Gujarat (called Cambaia by the Portuguese). Cloth produced there came in a great variety of styles, qualities, colors, and patterns, and was considered the best in Asia. The other two centers were the Coromandel Coast and Bengal, the latter being famous for its fine white cottons. See Linschoten, *Voyage,* 1:91; Barbosa, *Book,* 2: 145–146; Magalhães Godinho, *Descobrimentos,* 2:109.

32 · See above, n. 9.

33 · See above, n. 5.

34 · Baiagate or Baiajate ["Land beyond the (western) Ghats"] is the Deccan plateau region in southern India.

35 · The great Hindu Empire of Vijayanagar in South India was known to contemporary Portuguese as Bisnaga. By the late sixteenth century the empire had collapsed in the face of repeated Muslim incursions, but the Portuguese continued to use the old name till well into the seventeenth century.

36 · The products were gathered together in several storage centers in India. At first the principal entrepôt was Cochim, but after the Portuguese captured Goa, that city became the capital of Portuguese India and its commercial and shipping center as well, collecting and shipping wares from secondary centers such as Ormuz to the north and Malacca to the southeast, as well as from Mozambique on the opposite shore of the Indian Ocean. In addition to the products catalogued by the author here and on p. 132, the ships brought back medicinal plants, metals for use in industry, lacquer ware, Arabian horses, rice, opium, wax, slaves, ebony, and ivory. The city of Lisbon, where these precious wares were on display throughout the century, resembled a vast and splendid emporium. Lach, *Asia,* 2:10. See also João Lúcio d'Azevedo, *História econômica,* pp. 103–104. From Lisbon goods were sent to stock the retail shops of Brazil, as described by Brandônio on pp. 146–147.

37 · For once, Brandônio has something favorable to say about the settlers. Usually he sees their tarrying on the seashore as yet another example of their reprehensible lack of enterprise. Perhaps his favorable judgment in this passage owes something to the fact that he was himself a sugar planter.

38 · In 1618 the usual cargo of sugar was 360 chests or crates [*caixas*]. Mauro, *Portugal et Atlantique,* pp. 210, 227. Assuming that an average chest of

sugar weighed 20 arrobas (see I, n. 155), the cargo of a typical sugar ship was something like 7,200 arrobas, or about 115 tons.

39 · See I, n. 30.

40 · According to Campos Moreno (1612), between 500,000 and 600,000 arrobas of sugar were exported from Brazil each year. This approximates Brandônio's figure of 500,000 arrobas (8,000 tons) in 1618 for the three northern captaincies (Pernambuco, Itamaracá, and Paraíba), which furnished the bulk of the sugar. Cardim reported that in 1584 there were only 40 ships engaged in this operation. Brandônio's figure of 130 to 140 ships in 1618 reflects the tremendous increase in the production of sugar in only thirty-four years. Diogo de Campos Moreno, *Livro que dá razão do Estado do Brasil—1612*, p. 116; Fernão Cardim, *Tratados da terra e gente do Brasil*, p. 295.

41 · *Panelas* were inferior sugars made from the liquid drained off the molds in which the sugar was clarified.

42 · The consulage [*consulado*] was a tax imposed by the government on all imports into Portugal. It was originally intended to defray the cost of fleets for coastal defense and for convoying merchant ships, but the proceeds soon came to be largely diverted to other uses. Charles R. Boxer, *The Dutch in Brazil, 1624–1654*, p. 43, n. 1. In addition to the *dízimo* or tenth of the harvest mentioned by Brandônio, the Crown received, in Brazil, a storage fee for the use of the warehouse or dock, freight charges, and miscellaneous fees imposed at various times. In Lisbon, besides the consulage, there was the *sisa*, a sales tax. In 1614 these charges on sugar yielded in Lisbon alone 280 reis per arroba to the Crown. Mauro, *Portugal et Atlantique*, pp. 224–225.

43 · Figures given by Campos Moreno for the period 1610 to 1612 show that the average annual receipts for Brazil, excluding the three southern captaincies (at that time a separate administrative unit), were 43:036$000 and the expense 36:024$790, for a profit of almost 20 percent. The three northern captaincies—Paraíba, Pernambuco, and Itamaracá—together produced an amazing profit of 86 percent. See the table compiled by Hélio Vianna in his edition of Diogo de Campos Moreno's *Livro que dá razão*, p. 217.

44 · Brandônio's contemporary, Luiz Mendes de Vasconcellos, concurs: "From these lands [Brazil and the Atlantic islands] we receive the benefits that the conquest of India denies us," he declares; and again, "It would have been better not to try to conquer India." Modern historians agree. "The colony [Brazil] as a whole yielded more money to the home government than it cost in administrative and defense expenditure, whereas the Asian possessions were a heavy financial liability to the crown," says Boxer. Mendes de Vasconcellos, *Diálogos do sítio de Lisboa*, p. 88; Charles R.

Boxer, *Salvador de Sá and the Struggle for Brazil and Angola, 1602–1686,* p. 17. Cf. João Lúcio d'Azevedo, *História econômica,* pp. 120, 148; Michael Naylor Pearson, *Commerce and Compulsion: Gujarati Merchants and the Portuguese System in Western India, 1500–1600,* p. 136.

45 · The ten-year exemption for new sugar mills went back to the time of Tomé de Sousa, first governor of Brazil (1549–1553). The privilege was abused by some mill owners, who at the end of the ten years let their mills go to ruin and later rebuilt them, thus becoming exempt for another ten years. Besides the exemption for new mill owners, permanent exemptions were enjoyed by mill owners who were ecclesiastics and by certain other favored persons. Garcia, ed., *Diálogos,* III, n. 4; Mauro, *Portugal et Atlantique,* pp. 221, 229.

46 · Brandônio says later that smallholders paid half duty (p. 145). Full duty was paid by middlemen who bought sugar from the mill owners and shipped it to Portugal as a speculation.

47 · That is, export sugar on their own account.

48 · A number of councils, many of them short-lived or with overlapping functions, were created by the government during these years. Presumably this is the Council of Portugal, to which Brandônio had already expressed his views on this subject (see p. 133, and above, n. 11). But it might be the Treasury Council [Conselho da Fazenda], which supervised the royal income and property both in Portugal and abroad, and had the duty of collecting and paying accounts for the Crown. Oliveira, *Grandezas de Lisboa,* pp. 292–294; Stuart B. Schwartz, "Magistracy and Society in Colonial Brazil," *Hispanic American Review* 50 (1970):717.

49 · The English were the first to make serious inroads on the Portuguese oriental trade. As early as 1602–1603 James Lancaster had made a highly successful voyage to the Orient to obtain pepper. But the ruin of the Portuguese sea power was primarily accomplished by the Dutch, who by 1609 had broken the Portuguese monopoly of the oriental spice trade. "As Portugal's eastern empire crumbled away," says Symcox, "its Brazilian and African colonies became correspondingly more important; in fact the rise of a 'second Portuguese empire' in the South Atlantic [in the early seventeenth century] more than compensated for losses in the Indian Ocean." De Silva, "Portuguese East India Company," p. 152; Geoffrey W. Symcox, "The Battle of the Atlantic, 1500–1700," in Fredi Chiapelli, ed., *First Images of America: The Impact of the New World on the Old* (hereafter cited as *First Images*), 1:272.

50 · The States-General was the central executive body of the Netherlands government. Meilink-Roelofsz observes that the Dutch enjoyed a considerable advantage over the Portuguese in that their overseas enterprises were carried on by merchants, whereas in Portugal foreign trade was a

government concern—in fact, largely the personal business of the King. The Dutch merchants had a centuries-old tradition of foreign trade behind them, whereas the Portuguese maritime officials of higher rank were members of the nobility, with its traditional contempt for commerce and for physical labor. Marie Antoinette Petronella Meilink-Roelofsz, *Asian Trade and European Influence in the Indonesian Archipelago Between 1500 and About 1630,* p. 178.

51 · A widespread agency for carrying on trade in the northern Netherlands was the *rederij,* a highly flexible type of cooperative enterprise in which a group of people would join together to buy, own, build, charter, or freight a ship and its cargo. The individual investors would contribute capital in varying proportions, and they might range from wealthy merchants on shore with substantial quotas to deckhands with their mites. Later this developed into a more advanced form of commercial enterprise, the joint-stock company. A still more highly developed organization, the Dutch East India Company, was formed in 1602 and legally enjoyed a monopoly of the India trade, but the earlier forms of cooperative enterprise persisted well past Brandônio's time. Charles R. Boxer, *The Dutch Seaborne Empire: 1600–1800,* p. 6. Brandônio's apparent ignorance of the Dutch East India Company's existence may be due to the fact that in 1610 the King had revoked the New Christians' right to trade with the colonies. Arnold Wiznitzer, *Jews in Colonial Brazil,* p. 50. Hence the author's knowledge of the subject may go back to an earlier period during which he or his friends may have been involved in more primitive cooperative trade enterprises.

52 · See above, n. 28.

53 · See above, n. 24.

54 · The major centers for the production of cotton cloth in India (see above, n. 3) were, as Brandônio realizes, somewhat distant from the Dutch centers of power in the East Indies. Nevertheless, even as Brandão was writing, the Dutch—like the English before them—were successfully breaking into the cotton cloth trade.

55 · See p. 132, and above, n. 9.

56 · Brandônio was quite correct: pepper was the most wanted of all the Asiatic drugs. "Among the spices," says Magalhães Godinho, "pepper always played a preponderant role because, contrary to the others, it brings about mass commerce; only ginger is cheaper, but production and trade in the latter bring about strikingly inferior volume, while pepper, all by itself, exceeds in quantity all the other spices together." See Magalhães Godinho, *Descobrimentos,* 1:492, 514; Simonsen, *História econômica,* p. 38; Kristof Glamann, *Dutch-Asiatic Trade 1620–1740,* p. 73; Braudel, *Méditerrannée,* 1:422, 500; and n. 10 above.

Portugal fully shared the general eagerness for pepper. The original aim of Portuguese exploration in the East had been to find a sea route to India in order to obtain pepper and cinnamon. "First for the *Portingal*," wrote John Wheeler in 1601, "we know that like a good simple man, he sayled everie year full hungerly (God wot) about 3 parts of the Earth almost for spices, and when he had brought them home, the great rich purses of the Antwerpians, subjects of the King of Spaine, ingrossed them all into their own hands." John Wheeler, *A Treatise of Commerce*, p. 36. Francisco da Costa, writing in the early seventeenth century, called the pepper trade the most notable rarity in the crown of Portugal. *Relatório*, p. 349. See Charles R. Boxer, *The Portuguese Seaborne Empire*, *1415–1825*, p. 60.

We should not assume that European traders carried off the bulk of Asian drugs. For pepper, the total production in Asia at this time was probably close to 1,000,000 quintals (65,000 tons). Less than one-tenth of this amount went to Europe, the remainder being consumed within Asia. Pearson, *Commerce and Compulsion,* pp. 111–112.

57 · A quintal is equal to 4 arrobas, about 132 pounds.

58 · Brandônio's explanation of how Dom Manuel stopped the Venetian trade in pepper is unacceptable to modern historians. Political and economic crises faced by Venice at the beginning of the sixteenth century interfered far more seriously with the Venetian pepper trade than did any machinations of the Portuguese monarch. It is true that a little later in the century Afonso de Albuquerque, viceroy of India, instituted a plan to gain control of the Indian Ocean and blockade the Red Sea by force of arms. The Portuguese prohibited the transport of pepper to the Red Sea and thence to Europe, and all vessels sailing in the Indian Ocean had to have Portuguese licenses on pain of having their goods confiscated and all aboard enslaved. But the attempted monopoly never operated with full effectiveness, though the Portuguese did manage to regulate maritime trade in the Indian Ocean to an appreciable extent during most of the sixteenth century.

Boxer, *Portuguese Seaborne Empire*, p. 48; Lach, *Asia,* 1:98–103; Magalhães Godinho, *Descobrimentos,* 1:509–510; Meilink-Roelofsz, *Asian Trade*, pp. 116–117; Frederic Chapin Lane, "Venetian Shipping During the Commercial Revolution," *American Historical Review* 38 (Jan. 1933): 219–239. For a detailed analysis of the relation between demand and price in the pepper trade, see Lach, *Asia,* 1:143–147.

59 · See I, n. 30.

60 · In India some merchants, when they took the pepper to be weighed, poured water on it and then spread over it sifted ashes, which got into the wrinkles of the husks and thus increased the weight. In 1597 at

Malacca a large quantity of pepper was spoiled in this way en route to Portugal. Francisco da Costa, *Relatório,* p. 352. When ashes are combined with water, lye is formed; so Brandônio is probably referring here to some such procedure, though he does not say whether the purpose was to adulterate the pepper, to preserve it, or to prevent it from germinating.

61 · An example of Brandônio's habit of saying first what happened last—techically, the rhetorical error of *hysteron proteron,* "putting the cart before the horse."

62 · "State of India" was the Portuguese designation for the Portuguese discoveries and conquests in the East. It included scattered areas between the Cape of Good Hope and the Persian Gulf on one side of Asia, and Japan and Timor on the other. Charles R. Boxer, "The Portuguese in the East 1500–1800," in Harold C. Livermore, ed., *Portugal and Brazil: An Introduction,* p. 186. Perhaps Brandão meant to write "State of Brazil" rather than "State of India." But it is not impossible that he meant exactly what he said. The carrying out of his plan would in fact benefit Portuguese India by undercutting the Dutch trade in the East.

63 · The traditionalism deplored by Brandônio was one of the principal obstacles to the development of profitable commerce not only in India but also in Brazil. J. F. de Almeida Prado, *Pernambuco e as capitanias do norte do Brasil (1530–1630),* 4:154. Though Portugal was rapidly losing ground in the East, she was reluctant to give up traditional policies like this one. "It was . . . an index of the lack of commercial initiative of the Portuguese," says De Silva, "that they did not successfully diversify their trade once the profits from pepper had declined. The problem was partly that the Iberian ruling class still thought in sixteenth-century terms—of enforcing a monopoly of the sea route and driving the Dutch and the Engish out of Asia—rather than of competing with them on a commercial basis." "Portuguese East India Company," p. 192.

Only a few years after the *Dialogues* were written—in the middle years of the seventeenth century—Portugal's power in India virtually came to an end. The government then began, belatedly, to encourage the cultivation of Asiatic spices in Brazil, just as Brandônio had urged. See José Roberto do Amaral Lapa, *O Brasil e as drogas do Oriente,* pp. 9–10.

64 · This is surely false humility, for Brandão-Brandônio hardly occupied a "small station" in life. He was a wealthy sugar producer and landowner who had the ear of powerful and aristocratic officials in both Portugal and Brazil. "To be a master of a sugar mill is a title to which many aspire," Antonil declares, "for it carries with it the privilege of being waited upon, obeyed, and respected by many. If he is—as he ought to be—a man of great capital and a good administrator, to be a sugar mill

owner may well be esteemed in Brazil as titles are esteemed by nobles of the Kingdom." Antonil, *Cultura e opulência*, p. 84.

65 · In 1612, eight of eleven captaincies (excluding the three most southerly) had 170 mills, with annual export production of between 500,000 and 600,000 arrobas. By 1627–1628 the number of mills had risen to 230. Boxer, *Salvador de Sá*, pp. 179–180.

66 · To turn the wheels of a trapiche a mill owner needed sixty oxen, which were worked in five shifts of twelve oxen each. Mules were sometimes used instead of oxen. Magalhães Godinho, *Descobrimentos*, 2:465–466.

67 · In some mills the wheel was turned by the current directly. In others the water was held in a raised tank, from which it was directed downward into cups fastened to the circumference of the wheel; the pressure thus created turned the wheel. Ibid., 2:465.

68 · What Brandônio actually says is "two large rollers that turn a wheel on which the water strikes"—another example of *hysteron proteron*. Of course it is the wheel that turns the rollers, and not vice versa.

69 · The bagasse is the pulp left after the juice of the sugar cane has been extracted.

70 · Monteiro explained that the *gangorras* of a sugar mill corresponded to the beams that press the juice from the grapes in a grape press, except that the former were much larger. After the cane had been ground in the mill, it was placed in round wooden boxes three palms high. Here the heavy wooden *gangorras,* powered by oxen, pressed out the last of the juice. Jácome Monteiro, *Relação da Província do Brasil, 1610,* in Serafim Leite, *História da Companhia de Jesus no Brasil*, 8:404.

71 · The new press was introduced into Brazil about 1612. It consisted of three wooden rollers in a vertical position, the central roller being connected to the other two by gears. The central roller was turned by means of a water wheel or by oxen or horses. The cane was passed through twice so that all the juice was extracted without the necessity for *gangorras* (see p. 140).

72 · The mold, or form, was a conical vessel of baked clay, its top shaped like the mouth of a bell, with an orifice at the bottom by which the treacle ran out just as Brandônio describes. The cone-shaped deposit of crystallized sugar that was left was the "loaf of that fine white sugar" that Alviano inquired about. Antonil stated in 1711 that a sugar mill could produce 4,000 loaves of sugar in the normal eight-month milling cycle. His editor, Andrée Mansuy, says this was the average output, and adds that a loaf of sugar normally weighed three to four arrobas. For shipping abroad the sugar was broken up into powder or very fine particles and then packed into crates. Antonil, *Cultura e opulência*, p. 84 and n. 2; p. 256, nn. 8 and 11; Simonsen, *História econômica*, p. 122, s.v. *forma*.

73 · A century later, Antonil described a first-class clarifying house with its equipment in the Sergipe do Conde, a model sugar plantation near Salvador. *Cultura e opulência*, pp. 234–253.

74 · See below, n. 78.

75 · The "secret" was known to Dioscorides, Galen, and the Arabs, at least so far as it applied to the clarification of wine, fruit juice, rosewater, and other liquids. Lippmann, *História do açúcar*, 1:295. The clay used to purge the sugar was taken from an *apicu* or *coroa:* a beach in the salt marshes that is inundated by the tide and is covered with light-colored sand mixed with clay. *Glossary of Brazilian-Amazonian Terms*, comp. Donald Farquhar, Helen Macmillan, and Bernard Siegel, quoted in James L. Taylor, *Portuguese-English Dictionary* (hereafter cited as *Taylor*), s.v. "coroa"; *Pequeno dicionário brasileira da língua portuguesa*, 7th ed., s.v. "apicum"; Antonil, *Cultura e opulência*, p. 151 and n. 11, p. 242 and n. 1.

76 · In the Pernambuco region the harvest season for sugar was the spring and summer months, corresponding roughly to the time from July or August through January or February, as these months are somewhat less rainy than those of the fall and winter. The freshly cut cane had to be processed while it was still moist to keep it from turning sour. Antonil, *Cultura e opulência*, pp. 160–161, nn. 1 and 3.

77 · The timber was needed both for construction and for fueling the furnaces of the mill. Similar lists of requirements for sugar mills are given by other chroniclers; e.g., Cardim, *Tratados*, pp. 283–284; Campos Moreno, *Livro que dá razão*, p. 112; Antonil, *Cultura e opulência*, bk. 1, passim. Stuart B. Schwartz in his "Free Labor in a Slave Economy" (Dauril Alden, ed., *Colonial Roots of Modern Brazil*, pp. 147–197) lists the principal equipment and expenses of a sugar grower in 1620. Brandônio's production figures are generally in agreement with those of his contemporaries. Cf. Magalhães Godinho, *Descobrimentos*, 2:464–465.

78 · "This drug [sugar] has its nobility, its common sort, and its mixtures," said Antonil. *Cultura e opulência*, p. 264. *Macho* sugar is that of the highest quality, white and fine and usually taken from the tops of the sugar forms. Several syrups are run off in the various stages of the refining process; from one of these syrups the *branco batido* [mixed white] is made after the syrup has been recooked and stirred again. For a detailed description of the refining process, see ibid., pp. 264–270.

79 · "The slaves are the hands and feet of the mill owner because in Brazil it is not possible without them to acquire, conserve, and increase wealth or to keep the mill going," said Antonil in a famous statement. Ibid., p. 120. There were strong opinions as to which regions of Africa produced the best slaves. Many of these opinions were in conflict, partly because

the nomenclature applied to the various groups was often vague. See Charles R. Boxer, *Salvador de Sá,* pp. 233–235.

80 · The production of sugar required not only money but time. The growth cycle was from twelve to fourteen months in length; another eighteen months was required to manufacture the sugar, pack it in chests, and ship it to Europe. Magalhães Godinho, *Descobrimentos,* 2:470.

81 · A detailed description of the *partido* system is given in Schwartz, "Free Labor," pp. 153–167.

82 · The independent grower could often negotiate with the mill owner to obtain such advantages as the loan of slaves and oxen or a preferred place in the grinding schedule. Ibid., p. 154.

83 · "That way" presumably means division by thirds or by fifths, the most common methods.

84 · Brandônio is thinking of a medium-sized to large mill, one producing from 6,000 to 10,000 arrobas (see pp. 143–144). If the production was in the lower range of these amounts—say, between 6,000 and 7,000 arrobas—two-thirds or three-fifths of the total yield would be in the neighborhood of 4,000 to 4,500 arrobas, the figures Brandônio gives.

85 · See I, n. 36.

86 · Brandônio stated on p. 140 that a mill might cost about 10,000 cruzados. Thus, on Brandônio's own showing, the mill owner could recover his investment in two years after production began.

87 · According to Magalhães Godinho, the value of sugar at least doubled, or even tripled, on its voyage from Brazil to Portugal. *Descobrimentos,* 2: 472.

88 · Potosí, in what is now Bolivia but was then High (or Upper) Peru, was the center of the Peruvian silver industry. With its population of about 150,000, Potosí was by far the largest city in the New World. Lewis Hanke, *The Imperial City of Potosí,* pp. 28–29; Gwendolin B. Cobb, "Supply and Transportation for the Potosí Mines, 1545–1646," *Hispanic American Historical Review* 29 (1949):25–45.

In early Colonial times the Peruvian silver was smelted, but in 1571 the amalgamation, or patio, process was introduced, and this became the standard method of reducing silver ore. In this process the ore was put through an arrastra (crushing mill) and then treated with mercury, which collected the silver in the form of an amalgam. John Lloyd Mecham, *Francisco de Ibarra and Nueva Vizcaya,* pp. 216–218 and n. 30. For illustrations and a detailed description of the patio process see Henry G. Ward, *Mexico in 1827* (London: Colburn, 1828), 2:434–439 (cited in Mecham, loc. cit.).

89 · Cf. p. 40. Cardim relates that "the men are so high-spirited that they

buy jennets at 200 and 300 cruzados, and some own three or four high-priced horses." *Tratados,* pp. 295–296.

90 · Cf. ibid., pp. 92, 295.

91 · Several other chroniclers give similar descriptions of luxurious living, especially in Pernambuco and Bahia. Cardim vividly describes the habits of the upper classes in Pernambuco: "They dress, and clothe their wives and children, with all kinds of velvets, damasks, and other silks, and they go to great excesses in this. The women are very much the lady, and not very devout. . . . They are much given to festivals. When an honorable girl marries . . . her relatives and friends are dressed in velvet, some in crimson and some in green, and others in damask and other silks of various colors; the banners and saddles of the horses are of the same silks in which their masters are dressed." Similarly, Calado reported as early as 1584 that the women of Olinda dressed in taffeta, camlet, velvet, and other silks and rich brocades, and wore so many jewels that it seemed as if pearls, rubies, emeralds, and diamonds had rained on their hands. Cardim, *Tratados,* pp. 295–296; Manuel Calado, *O valeroso Lucideno e triunfo da liberdade,* 1:39–40; Gilberto Freyre, *Casa-Grande e senzala,* 1:359–360 and n. 146.

92 · The Holy House of Mercy [*Santa Casa da Misericórdia*] is a lay charitable brotherhood, founded in Lisbon in 1498 and transplanted to all the Portuguese possessions overseas. Pernambuco disputes with São Vicente the honor of being the site of the first House of Mercy. Olinda and Ilhéus had Houses of Mercy as early as the 1560s; today they exist in many Brazilian cities. At first the institutions were dedicated to the task of interring the dead, but their activities came to be extended to various other charitable services. Of these the most important everywhere was ministering to the sick, the function for which Brandônio cites them. See A. J. R. Russell-Wood, *Fidalgos and Philanthropists: The Santa Casa da Misericórdia of Bahia, 1550–1755,* pp. 40, 350–351.

93 · Cf. Silveira's donations to the House of Mercy in Paraíba, p. 150, and below, n. 106.

94 · Cf. p. 39, and above, n. 36.

95 · There is no indication who the tricky tradesman was. Usury was common in Brandão's time and place. A noted practitioner of the art, João Nunes, lived in Pernambuco, and Brandônio must have known him personally; in fact, the two men served together in the conquest of Paraíba. Nunes amassed a fortune of 200,000 cruzados—immense for the time. He was brought before the Inquisition on charges of usury and other offenses. Garcia, ed., *Diálogos,* III, n. 8. See Sônia Aparecida Siquiera, "O comerciante João Nunes," *Anais do Simpósio Nacional dos Professores Universitários de História* (Campinas, 1971), pp. 231–247.

96 · According to Prado, Brandônio mentions the married condition of some traders because it was unusual. Traders within Brazil often remained bachelors or else left their families in Portugal; in this way they could carry on their commercial activities most advantageously, moving rapidly to any place where money was to be made. J. F. de Almeida Prado, *A conquista da Paraíba (séculos XVI a XVIII)*, p. 287. Cf. António Cardoso de Barros's remark in a letter to João III of Portugal: "One married man is worth ten bachelors here; for where the single men only try to get away, the married men strive only to develop the land and live on it." Idem, *A Bahia e as capitanias do centro do Brasil (1530–1626)*, 1:102.

97 · Pyrard de Laval similarly disparaged the Brazilian settlers. "Most of the Portuguese there are exiles, bankrupts, or criminals," he observed in his *Voyage*, pt. 2, p. 333. Adriaen van der Dussen wrote that the King of Spain sent criminals to populate Brazil and thus "gave origin to a race that now makes no distinction between right and wrong." *Relatório sobre as capitanias conquistadas no Brasil pelos holandeses (1639): Suas condições econômicas e sociais*, translated and edited by José Antonio Gonsalves de Mello (Rio de Janeiro: Instituto do Açúcar e do Álcool, 1947), p. 84.

Degredados [exiled criminals] had been a part of Brazil's history ever since the discovery of the land. Cabral had left behind him in 1500 two such unfortunates, who managed to survive and later acted as interpreters. As the country was explored and settled, *degredados* were regularly transported there. Many of the persons transported were political or religious dissenters, or were guilty of very minor offenses. Gabriel Soares de Sousa, *Notícia do Brasil* (1945), 1:245; *Documentos para a história do açúcar*, 1:31.

In the light of these facts, the unfavorable views of Brazil just cited are not surprising. They are, however, grossly unfair to Brazil, as Brandônio shows in his following speech. The disreputable persons to whom Alviano refers constituted only a small part of the population; and there was a good supply of aristocrats and wealthy people in certain regions, such as Pernambuco and Bahia. "The nobility, the soul of all this great body [i.e., the political state of Pernambuco] is innumerable and illustrious, since it is derived from the greatest houses of Portugal, Castile, France, Italy, and Germany, who going at different times to Pernambuco, left numerous descendants," says Domingos do Loreto Couto in his eulogy of Pernambuco, *Desaggravos do Brasil e glórias de Pernambuco*, p. 222. Brandônio observed on p. 45 that the Bahians were "of aristocratic stock and wealthy people." In addition to the disreputable and the aristocratic extreme, there was the vast majority of poor people who migrated to Brazil in search of a better life. See Charles R. Boxer, *The Golden Age of*

Brazil, 1695–1750, p. 10; and Hélio Vianna, *Estudos de história colonial*, pp. 43–55.

98 · *Natural da terra* is defined by dictionaries as "native," but Brandônio often uses the phrase to mean "permanent resident of the country," whether born there or not. Here *naturais da terra* seems to mean "European residents," or "settlers." Other examples are on pp. 149 and 272.

99 · Perhaps an indication that Brandão expected that his manuscript would be published or at least circulated.

100 · In the early seventeenth century some 15,000 slaves were exported each year from the Congo and Angola to Portuguese and Spanish America. Of these, 4,400 were sent to Pernambuco, 4,000 to Bahia and Rio de Janeiro, and the remainder to Spanish outlets. As Brandônio indicates, the profits of the slave trade were immense. Boxer, *Salvador de Sá*, p. 225. For detailed accounts of the traffic in slaves, see Magalhães Godinho, *Descobrimentos*, 2:520–587, and Mauro, *Portugal et Atlantique*, pp. 147–181.

101 · In the original meaning of the word, a *peruleiro* was a wealthy Spaniard from Peru (see p. 27 and I, n. 60), but in the most common seventeenth-century sense a *peruleiro* was a smuggler—a trader who purchased goods in Brazil and transported them to Peru to be exchanged for silver, a traffic forbidden by law in both colonies. The illegal trader might enter Brazil at Rio de Janeiro and there purchase articles to be sold in the silver country, especially in Potosí (see above, n. 88), center of the silver trade. The city, built on a barren mountainside, depended for its very existence upon imports of food and agricultural products from outside. The goods packed by a *peruleiro* consisted mainly of cloth and hardware, originally from northern Europe, since there was little industry in Portugal. He might also transport a supply of slaves for sale.

The illegal traffic between Brazil and Peru was highly profitable: "The employment of 100 ducats in Spain, being brought hither [to Rio de Janeiro], will yield 1,200 and 1,500 ducats profit," wrote Francisco Soares to his brother Diogo in 1596. Boxer, *Salvador de Sá*, p. 76 and n. 16. In spite of its illegality, smuggling apparently did not involve any social stigma. In fact, the *peruleiro* attained such standing and vogue that even today the popular language preserves the word to describe a man of opulent and refined appearance.

The standard work on the *peruleiros* of the Rio de la Plata is Alice Piffer Canabrava, *O comércio português no Rio da Prata (1580–1640)*; see especially pp. 96–102, 126–131. See also Boxer, *Salvador de Sá*, chap. 3.

102 · See I, n. 30.

103 · A Spanish real of silver was equal in value to 40 Portuguese reis. Hence

a *pataca* [coin] of 4 [reales] equaled 160 reis, and a *pataca* of 8 ["piece of eight"] equaled 320 reis. *Taylor*, s.v. "pataca."

104 · Alvor is a small town in the province of Algarve, in the south of Portugal and on the Atlantic coast. It is still important for its exports of wine, olive oil, and dried fruit, especially figs.

105 · Cf. above, n. 87.

106 · The generous citizen was Duarte Gomes da Silveira. Twenty years after the *Dialogues* Elias Herckmans confirmed the account of Silveira's philanthropies in his "Descrição geral da Capitania da Paraíba," *Revista do Instituto Arqueológico, Histórico, e Geográfico Pernambucano* 5 (Oct. 1886): 246, quoted in Garcia, ed., *Diálogos*, III, n. 11. Silveira's holdings in Paraíba made him the neighbor of Ambrósio Fernandes Brandão, their mills served by the same waters. It is a mystery why Brandão did not identify this fellow citizen by name here, as he did on p. 150.

Silveira was to outlive Brandão by many years. At the end of 1634 he took part in the battle with the Dutch for the city of Filipéia, after the surrender of the city suffering severe persecution for refusing to cooperate with the Dutch officials. He was still living in Paraíba, an active old man, in 1644. Garcia, ed., *Diálogos*, III, n. 11.

Brandônio's remark that the church of the House of Mercy was almost finished in his time establishes a date by which it had been started—a date that would otherwise be unknown, since the church records were lost during the Dutch invasion. Irineu Ferreira Pinto, *Datas e notas para a história da Parahyba*, 1:37–38.

107 · The first two avenues to wealth—sugar and trade—were discussed earlier in this dialogue.

108 · See I, n. 48.

109 · Pernambuco's brazilwood was the best of all. Monteiro, *Relação*, p. 405. Campos Moreno remarked that Paraíba was the most profitable place in which to cut brazilwood, because here the investor did not have to pay the *redízimo*, as he would in the proprietary captaincies. *Livro que dá razão*, p. 204.

110 · Figueiredo Falcão gives the figure for the ten years beginning with 1602 of 21:000$000, or 52,500 cruzados. *Livro em que se contém toda a fazenda*, p. 29. (The figure is incorrectly cited as 24:000$000 in Campos Moreno, *Livro que dá razão*, p. 116, n. 36.) If Brandônio's figure of 40,000 cruzados for 1618 is right, the price of a contract for brazilwood fell about 20 percent between 1612 and 1618. One reason for the drop may have been the decreasing accessibility of brazilwood stands as more and more of the trees were taken out—a fact that will be mentioned by Brandônio below, on the same page.

111 · Perhaps a pun, glancing at both the country and the wood, for both of

which Brandônio has made this claim. Brandão and his contemporaries often used *brasil* as a short form for *pau-brasil*, brazilwood. The manuscript in this place capitalizes the initial letter, but Brandão sometimes does this for the name of the wood as well as for the name of the country. A claim similar to that made here for "brazil" was offered for sugar on p. 135.

112 · Some of the sugar planters profited by the dead season, when the mills were at rest, to cut and transport the wood. Mauro, *Portugal et Atlantique*, p. 121.

113 · Brazilwood was already becoming scarce because of excessive exploitation. "Without question, it is one of the most flagrant cases in the world of near-extinction of a vegetable species by the destructive economic behavior of man," says Bernardino José de Souza, *O pau-brasil na história nacional*, p. 241.

114 · See I, n. 35.

115 · The cutting and loading procedure is described in detail by Alexander Marchant, *From Barter to Slavery: The Economic Relations of Portuguese and Indians in the Settlement of Brazil, 1500–1580*, pp. 28–47.

116 · A toston [Portuguese *tostão*] was worth 100 reis.

117 · See I, n. 82.

118 · Gonçalo Fernandes Trancoso was a Portuguese teacher of the humanities. His *Contos e histórias de proveito e exemplo* appeared in Lisbon from 1585 to 1596, the first book of novelas to be published in Portugal. Of the thirty-nine tales, some are derived from popular tradition and some imitated from Boccaccio and other authors. The work long enjoyed great popular favor, and even today in the North of Brazil fantastic tales are known as stories of Trancoso. Garcia, ed., *Diálogos*, III, n. 16. There is an edition of the *Contos e histórias* in the *Antologia portuguesa*, edited by Agostinho de Campos (Paris and Lisbon: Aillaud e Bertrand, 1921).

119 · Brandão was indeed in Pernambuco in 1583, occupied with his duties as an employee of the tax farmer Bento Dias de Santiago. The worker's name is a realistic detail that seems more likely to have been recollected than invented.

120 · This river, which runs just south of Recife, is now called the Jaboatão. *Primeira visitação do Santo Ofício às partes do Brasil: Confissões de Pernambuco 1594–1595*, ed. José Antonio Gonsalves de Mello, p. 15.

121 · The "funny" story that follows is really just as tragic as the preceding anecdote that made Alviano feel so sad. In both incidents the finder of ambergris loses an opportunity to make a great profit. The differences are that (1) the first calamity happened to a dependent, the second, presumably, to an unknown; and (2) the first calamity was the result of an accident, the second of trickery, which the speakers appear to find

both amusing and admirable. These reactions throw an interesting side-light on the characters of Brandônio and Alviano and by implication on business attitudes of their time.

122 · The word "jangada" is Kanarese (from Kanara, on the west coast of India). In that region the word refers to a log catamaran. The Brazilian jangada, however, is native to America, the name having evidently been attached to it on account of a supposed similarity to the Indian craft. It is a three-person raft that is used in both fresh and salt water, especially on the northeast coast, for fishing and transportation. In Brandônio's day the Indians used it for battle as well. It is usually constructed of three pieces of wood, each twelve to fifteen feet long, held together by two transverse planks. In one of the latter a hole has been drilled, in which the mast is fixed. The other transverse plank supports a small bench, on which the pilot hunches to find some shelter from the waves that wash over the raft. From the mast the Indians hung the sail and also a sack of manioc and a calabash of sweet water. These craft sail with remarkable swiftness, sometimes as much as ten miles an hour. It is not uncommon to see them as far as forty miles out at sea. When the wind tips the raft to one side, the sailors right it by transferring their weight to the opposite side. If it overturns, as often happens, the sailors, who are expert swim-mers as a matter of course, simply pull out the mast, fix it on what is now the top side of the boat, and continue to navigate as if nothing had gone amiss. As might be expected, jangadas ordinarily carry only goods that cannot be damaged by water. John Horace Parry, *The Discovery of the Sea*, p. 4.

123 · Cotton was known to the natives before the discovery of Brazil, and there are many references to the plant throughout the early history of the colony. "According to Watt, the plant in question is the *Gossypium brasiliense* Macf., called kidney cotton from the shape of the seeds. It is indigenous to South America, more especially Brazil and Guiana. It is not to be confused with the so-called tree cotton (*G. arboreum*). *G. brasiliense* is a sub-arboreous bush with very large leaves. As a shrub it reaches between 4 and 5 feet in height, but occasionally becomes a small tree." Marchant, *From Barter to Slavery*, p. 61, n. 40, citing Sir George Watt, *The Wild and Cultivated Cotton Plants of the World: A Revision of the Genus Gossypium* . . . (London, 1907), pp. 17, 295–315.

Cotton grew in Brazil in both the wild and the cultivated state. The Indians used it to make threads on which to hang the ornaments they wore around their necks, and ropes for weaving hammocks or binding prisoners. Hans Staden watched the Indians plant the seeds, and Jean de Léry described how the women prepared and spun the cotton.

From the beginning of the period of colonization, cotton was cultivated by Europeans on a modest scale, especially in Maranhão, chiefly to supply local needs such as garments for slaves and poor whites. The cultivation of cotton was already diminishing in Brandão's time. A century later it is not even mentioned by Antonil in a list of products he includes in *Cultura e opulência*, pp. 488–493. Cotton began to recover its importance in the early nineteenth century, when, because of a series of droughts, the production of sugar began to diminish, and increased amounts of cotton were needed for the European textile industry.

Hans Staden, *Warhafftiger kurtzer bericht aller von mir erfarnen håndel und sitten der Tuppin Indas*, in *Warhaftige Historia und beschreibung einer Landtschafft der wilden, nacketen Grimmigen Menschfresser Leuthen in der Newenwelt America gelegen*, chap. 38; Jean de Léry, *Histoire d'un voyage faict en la terre du Brésil*, 2:19–20, chap. 13; Jonathan D. Sauer, "Changing Perception and Exploitation of New World Plants in Europe, 1492–1800," in *First Images*, 2:829, n. 46; Burkill, *Economic Products of the Malay Peninsula*, s.v. *"Gossypium"*; F. C. Hoehne, *Botânica e agricultura no Brasil no século XVI*, pp. 76–77, 125, 139, 152; Carl Ortwin Sauer, "Cultivated Plants of South and Central America," in Julian H. Steward, ed., *Handbook of South American Indians* (hereafter cited as *HSAI*), 6: 533–538; Mauro, *Portugal et Atlantique*, pp. 369–370.

124 · Brandônio is describing a primitive form of cotton gin, something like the *churka*, an ancient device that has been used in India and China up to modern times. Labat saw similar machines in the West Indies in the eighteenth century. A comparable contrivance was still used in Brazil in 1809, when Henry Koster observed it there. Such a machine produces about five pounds of lint a day. *Encyclopaedia Britannica*, 11th edition, s.v. "cotton"; Jean Baptiste Labat, *Nouveau voyage aux isles de l'Amérique*, 2:401–403; Henry Koster, *Travels in Brazil*, 2:170–171.

125 · The Brazilian forest extended over the entire eastern coastal zone from Cabo São Roque, in Rio Grande do Norte, to Cabo Frio, just north of Rio de Janeiro. Mauro, *Portugal et Atlantique*, p. 117. Brandônio's following lyrical outburst in praise of Brazil's forests is surely one of the most delightful passages in the *Dialogues*. It shows that this hard-headed businessman had a sincere appreciation of the esthetic features of his adopted land.

126 · Pedanius Dioscorides (fl. about A.D. 50) was the Greek author of a treatise on medicinal plants and medicinal animal products, the *De Materia Medica*, for sixteen centuries the leading text on pharmacology. It was published in 1478 in Latin and in 1499 in Greek. According to Miguel Colmeiro y Penido (*La botánica y los botánicos de la península hispano-lusitana*, p. 2), a Spanish translation of the work, by Andrés Laguna, appeared in 1555. It went through a number of editions before 1618,

and so it is no surprise that Brandão was familiar with the reputation of the book; he shows no acquaintance with its contents.

127 · Thessaly, in northern Greece, was the site of a beautiful and romantic valley called Tempe. In classical times its scenery was celebrated by the poets, and it was considered to be one of the favorite haunts of Apollo. Cf. John Keats, "Ode on a Grecian Urn," which praises "Tempe or the dales of Arcady." Sebastião da Rocha Pitta makes an observation similar to Alviano's: the scenery in Bahia brings to his mind "Tempe of Thessaly . . . and the Gardens of the Hesperides . . . because this land in continuous spring is the garden of the world . . . the Terrestrial Paradise . . . the Elysian Fields." *História da América portuguesa*, p. 60.

128 · Usually the author assigned passages of the rhapsodical tenor of this one to Brandônio, apologist extraordinary for Brazil (e.g., Brandônio's preceding speech). But here it is Alviano who celebrates in a classical image the pastoral beauties of the land.

129 · This sadistic method of punishment, or more properly of execution, was only too much of a reality. Labat, writing about the West Indies in 1696, attributed it to the English, who were said to inflict it on blacks and Indians who had committed grave crimes or raided the property of whites. Labat, *Nouveau voyage*, 3:208–209.

130 · The word used for house slave is *ladino*, which meant a slave who had been in the country long enough to have become christianized and "Brazilianized" and who had been trained to do labor requiring a low order of skill, especially domestic work. The *ladino* stood in contrast to the *bossal*, or new arrival, who was inclined to be stubborn and resistant. See Freyre, *Casa-Grande e senzala*, 2:492, and Antonil, *Cultura e opulência*, p. 123, n. 9.

131 · Though Brandônio is not well disposed toward this particular slave from Angola, the Bantus from that area were the most highly desired of all blacks in Brazil. Along with the natives of the Congo, they were considered quicker to learn mechanical operations, stronger, more competent, and more easily adaptable to the conditions of slave existence than were members of other tribes. Kaspar van Baerle, *Rerum per Octennium in Brasilia et Alibi Gestarum, sub Praefectura Illustrissimi Comitis I. Mauritii Nassaviae . . . Historia*, p. 215 (misnumbered 115); Boxer, *Salvador de Sá*, p. 233; Jean Baptiste Dutertre, *Histoire générale des Antilles habitées par les Français* (4 vols. in 3. Paris: Thomas Iolly, 1667–1671), 2:496.

132 · Africans were expert in the use of poisons and also in the cure of their effects. Poison was a commonly used instrument of revenge among the blacks of Brazil. In their religious procedures, too, poisons played a prominent role. See Prado, *Pernambuco*, 3:117–120.

133 · See I, n. 2.

134 · MS *burarema*. *Gallesia integrifolia* (Spreng.) Harms. Brandônio has inadvertently included in his list the Portuguese name of this tree, *pau d'alho* (garlic pear). This wood is still used for rough construction. Samuel J. Record and Robert W. Hess, *Timbers of the New World*, s.v. *"Gallesia,"* pp. 424–425.

135 · MS *camasarim*. *Terminalia pagifolia* Mart. and Zucc. Garcia, ed., *Diálogos*, III, n. 20.

136 · *Piptadenia moniliformis*. MS *pau branco* [whitewood]. The plant is also known by the Tupi name *catanduba*, "very thin forest." Aurélio Buarque de Holanda Ferreira, *Novo dicionário da língua portuguesa* (hereafter cited as *Aurélio*), s.v. "catanduba."

137 · Not identified.

138 · Also *jutahy*. MS *jatauba*. *Hymenaea courbaril* L. Like the golden *jatobá* mentioned just below, the red *jatobá* is excellent for construction of all kinds, including boatbuilding, as well as for cabinet work. From the resin a high-quality varnish is made. The Indians use the bark for making canoes. Record and Hess, *Timbers*, p. 281, s.v. "Hymenaea."

139 · Also *pequiá marfim*. MS *piquia*. Brandônio's description, "hard and yellow," makes it practically certain that this is *Aspidosperma centrale*, a wood used today for heavy construction. Ibid., p. 59, s.v. "Araracanga group."

140 · Probably the *vinhático*, *Plathymenia reticulata* Benth. Henrique de Beaurepaire Rohan, "Chorographia da Província da Parahyba do Norte," *Revista do Instituto Histórico e Geográfico Parahibano* 3 (1911):213, s.v. "Amarello." The wood has many uses from cabinet work to general construction, and the Indians sought out the finest specimens for making dugout canoes. Record and Hess, *Timbers*, pp. 309–310, s.v. *"Plathymenia."*

141 · Also *massaranduba*. MS *masaranduba*. Any of several milk or cow trees of the family Sapotaceae, especially *Mimusops*, here probably *M. huberi* Ducke. A reddish hardwood, very durable and strong. Record and Hess, *Timbers*, p. 502, s.v. *"Manilkara or Mimusops."* For the fruit, see IV, n. 139.

142 · Also *cabreuva, cabrué, cabureíba*. This name is used for both *Myrocarpus fastigiatus* Fr. Allem and *M. frondosus* Fr. Allem. Record and Hess, *Timbers*, p. 297, s.v. "Myrocarpus"; *Aurélio*, s.v. "cabriúva."

143 · A name given to several woods, notably Brazilian rosewood, *Dalbergia nigra* Fr. Allem, long considered the most beautiful of Brazilian woods, which has been used for fine furniture in Brazil and in the United States. Record and Hess, *Timbers*, p. 252, s.v. "Dalbergia."

144 · MS *comduru*. *Brosimum paraense* Huber. Record and Hess, *Timbers*, p. 380, s.v. *"Brosimum."* The red inner core of this tree was used for fine furniture, and the young trees for braces in the sugar mills, according to Soares de Sousa, *Notícia do Brasil* (1945), 2:65.

145 · Also *sebipira, sepepira, sucupira*. A name applied to two or more species

of the genus *Bowdichia*. This highly durable wood was used extensively in the colonial period for construction exposed to water, such as boat hulls and water wheels. Record and Hess, *Timbers*, p. 236, s.v. *"Bowdichia"*; Antonil, *Cultura e opulência*, pp. 188–193 and nn. 2 and 24.

146 · See above, n. 135.

147 · Probably *Tecoma conspicua*, the wood most commonly used for constructing bows. Claude Lévi-Strauss, "The Use of Wild Plants in Tropical South America," in *HSAI*, 6:474.

148 · Almost any species of the genus *Lecythis*. The sapucayas are members of the widespread group of monkey-pot trees. Brandônio will list the uses of the bark on p. 208; see also IV, n. 84. He will describe the fruit on p. 217; see also IV, n. 143. Record and Hess, *Timbers*, p. 226, s.v. *"Lecythis."*

149 · Probably *Cassia grandis* L.f. When found in the open, this is usually a spreading tree of medium height, but in the forest it grows as tall as 100 feet. The wood is used for construction. Ibid., p. 240, s.v. *"Cassia."*

150 · MS *camara*. Common designation for various plants of the verbena and nightshade families. Antônio Geraldo da Cunha, *Dicionário histórico das palavras portuguesas de origem tupi*, s.v. *camará*.

151 · Antônio Geraldo da Cunha thinks this is the *ibiracuí* mentioned by Jerônimo Rodrigues as used for building a canoe (*A Missão dos Carijós, Relação do P. Jerônimo Rodrigues*, in Serafim Leite, *Novas cartas jesuíticas* [*de Nóbrega a Viera*], p. 206). Cunha, *Dicionário tupi*, s.v. "ibiracui."

152 · The angelim of the East Indies is *Artocarpus hirsuta*. In Brandão's time this wood was highly valued on the west coast of India for shipbuilding. In Brazil the name angelim is applied to the genus *Hymenolobium* as well as to some species of *Andira* and *Vataireopsis*. Linschoten, *Voyage*, 2:56; Record and Hess, *Timbers*, p. 282, s.v. *"Hymenolobium."*

153 · MS *burapiroqua*. Antônio Geraldo da Cunha identifies this as a plant of the myrtle family. *Dicionário tupi*, s.v. "ibirapiroca."

154 · Also *buranhém*. This name is applied to several species of the genus *Pradosia*. The wood is used today for the frames of vehicles, farming implements, oars, and heavy interior construction. Thevet mentions this tree under the name *Hyvourahé*; he says the Indians made a remedy for certain diseases by boiling the bark. Record and Hess, *Timbers*, pp. 505–506, s.v. *"Pradosia"*; André Thevet, *Singularidades da França Antárctica, a que outros chamam de América*, p. 275 and n. 1, p. 302 and n. 1, p. 303.

155 · This name, of Tupi origin, perhaps designates *Copahyfera officinalis* L. The wood is excellent for ships' yards and masts. Francisco Augusto Pereira da Costa, *Anais pernambucanos*, vol. 2, *1591–1634*, p. 365.

156 · Also *uriunduba*. MS *uremdeuba*. *Astronium urundeuva*. Strongly resistant to decay, the *urundeúva* is used for woodwork exposed to the weather. *Aurélio*.

157 · Also *guanandi, olandi, lanti*. MS *guoanadim*. Brazil beautyleaf (*Calophyllum brasiliense* Camb.), a strong, useful wood. Another name for this tree is *jacareúba*. Antonil mentions it under the name *landim carvalho*, adding to the Tupi the Portuguese word for oak. Record and Hess, *Timbers*, p. 179, s.v. "Calophyllum"; Antonil, *Cultura e opulência*, p. 192 and n. 23; James L. Taylor, *A Portuguese-English Dictionary* (hereafter cited as *Taylor*), s.v. "guanandi."

158 · MS *query*. Presumably the *quiripiranga* (*piranga* = red) (*Caesalpinia ferrea*). *Taylor*, s.v. "quiripiranga." Like other ironwoods, it is hard to cut, but Brandônio is certainly exaggerating when he says it will cut through iron.

159 · See p. 15.

160 · A small or medium-sized tree of the genus *Apeiba*, most likely *A. tibourbou*. Its wood, light and soft, has little use except for the fishing craft of the same name (see p. 154 and n. 122 above). Record and Hess, *Timbers*, p. 530, s.v. "*Apeiba.*"

161 · See p. 306 and VI, n. 8.

162 · This was Duarte de Castelbranco, count of Sabugal. Ribeiro, *Dissertações*, 2:196.

163 · In the early seventeenth century pikes were still an indispensable weapon of the common soldier.

164 · It was a matter of controversy at this time and indeed well into the eighteenth century whether it was most efficient to build ships in Portugal, in India, or in Brazil. The arguments against Brazil echo those presented by Brandônio: there was a lack of dependable labor; timber was scarce, since the sugar planters wanted to keep the available timber for their own use; many of the materials would have to be sent from Portugal, and of course this would greatly increase the cost. In the very year in which Brandão was writing, a Jesuit father reported on the possibility of building galleons in Brazil, and concluded that it would cost at least twice as much to construct such a vessel in Brazil as in Portugal. The Crown, however, made determined efforts to develop shipbuilding in Brazil, and royal shipbuilding yards were established later in the century at Rio de Janeiro, Belém, and especially Bahia. These turned out some excellent ships as well as some that were severely criticized. Boxer, *Portuguese Seaborne Empire*, p. 211.

165 · The mangroves that grow in the swampy ground along the seashore include various species, the most common being the *Rhizophorsa mangle* L., popularly known as the red mangrove. This is the one that sends out long roots from its branches.

Cardim, like Brandônio, was struck by the unusual appearance of the mangrove plant: "One kind of mangrove casts down from above some shoots sometimes as long as a lance till they reach the water . . . and these remain fixed in the earth: While these branches are young they are tender, and because they are hollow inside excellent flutes are made of them." Cardim, *Tratados,* p. 83, and see the note, ibid., p. 123, by Rodolfo Garcia.

Dialogue IV

Foodstuffs, Dyestuffs, Potherbs,

Fruits, Fibers, Vegetables

য়

In Dialogue IV Brandônio describes the food and utility crops of the Northeast of Brazil, the fifth of the six sources of wealth he listed at the beginning of Dialogue III. Brandão's knowledge of Brazilian crops is wide if not often deep, and his observations clearly reflect many years of on-the-spot observation, inquiry, and experimentation. He is full of practical ideas for the commercial development of the crops, and several of his suggestions anticipate practices and uses not developed until long after the writer's time. And his survey of Brazilian agricultural techniques gives him a number of opportunities to reprimand the settlers for their failure to exploit the possibilities of their land.

As always, Brandônio's interests are not limited to the purely commercial. The final section of the dialogue pictures an imaginary vegetable and flower garden, the contents of which are chosen no less for beauty than for utility. Here Brandônio reaches lyric heights unmatched in any other portion of the Dialogues. *If these passages are occasionally pretentious and marred by trite classical allusions, they nevertheless show us a man who deeply values his adopted country and who celebrates not only its material gifts but also its aesthetic offerings.*

ALVIANO   All yesterday afternoon I waited for you in this same place, but since you didn't come, I went home sooner than I had planned to.

BRANDÔNIO   Something came up that prevented me from keeping my promise to you. But, if the truth must be known, I wanted to step back a few paces to get a running start on what we must discuss today, for the subject matter is so rich that it requires much study if one is to know how best to proceed to an accurate description of the riches and great things of Brazil. You realize that most of what I intend to discuss pertains to the northern captaincies, for of those to the south I know but little; as I told you on another occasion, I have never traveled in those parts. But there is so much to say about the subjects that I do intend to discuss that I don't know where to begin!

ALVIANO   Give me a general account of things, as best you can, so that you can do what you have in mind—show me just what the wealth of this state consists of.

BRANDÔNIO   I could give you an idea of it in a few words by demonstrating only one thing, which is—and don't think I am joking, for I shall attempt to prove it—that if the three captaincies of Pernambuco, Itamaracá, and Paraíba all belonged to one lord, who enjoyed sovereign jurisdiction and was exempt from paying the tribute of a vassal, they would bring him in each year more than a conto of gold.[1]

ALVIANO   I'm here to tell you that the entire Kingdom of Portugal doesn't bring in as much as that to His Majesty, and you want to prove that those three captaincies can produce that many cruzados!

BRANDÔNIO   That is no foolish fancy or mad pretension, but rather a fact of which I will soon prove the truth, as I have already done in several other cases. And thus I repeat that, if the three captaincies belonged to one sovereign lord, his revenue from them every year would amount to the figure I named. For I have already shown you how I reckon that the sugar that is sent to the Kingdom from these three captaincies alone brings His Majesty's Exchequer, in the duties paid at the customhouses, more than three hundred thousand cruzados.[2] Now a sovereign lord could collect just as much in export duties if he allowed the sugar to be shipped wherever people wanted to send it.[3] He could also collect some sixty thousand cruzados more, which the tithe on it amounts to; ten or twelve thousand in land rents, which are paid to the proprietary captains but which would be paid to him, who would himself be the proprietor; likewise, forty thousand cruzados' revenue from the brazilwood; in the same manner, import duties of 21 percent on goods and merchandise shipped to the three captaincies from any part of the world; and this, according to my estimate, ought to amount to around one hundred and fifty thousand cruzados. Now all this is very well known and there can be no doubt about it. But what is not known, and has not yet been tried, is that great revenue also could be derived from the following: India pepper, which could be planted and harvested in the way I have already suggested,[4] and many other kinds of pepper that are excellent and are much prized by foreigners; malaguetta [red pepper],[5] a great abundance of which is picked growing wild in the woods without even being tended; ginger,[6] which one could cause to be cultivated, for the land is most suited to it, and this would bring much profit if it were shipped to Flanders and other foreign lands; indigo, a vast amount of which could be manufactured, for the herb from which it is made (and which in India and in the [West] Indies is planted and tended with care and diligence) grows here in the open fields in great quantity, without any cultivation; a great amount of the drug could be made from it.[7] So if all those things were developed, together with those that already are being exploited, they ought to bring such a sovereign lord, if they were handled as I have explained, an income of much more than that conto of gold that you so marveled at.

ALVIANO I do not doubt that, if all those things came to pass. But, since they are not being developed, there is no reason for us to dwell on them. So I beg you, let us go on with our conversation, which, I believe, is today supposed to be on how the settlers of this state grow rich by farming.

BRANDÔNIO I will do so, but I felt obliged to put your doubts to rest as conclusively as possible. Now, coming to what we are interested in, in order to pick up the thread of what we shall have to say about farming it behooves us to begin first of all with food crops.

ALVIANO It seems reasonable to me that you should do so, for it is with them that all farming has its beginning, and on them that so much care and diligence are lavished.

BRANDÔNIO The foodstuffs with which the inhabitants of Brazil—white men, Indians, and Guinea slaves—sustain themselves are several, some very good and others not so much so. Of these the chief and best are three, and among them manioc[8] occupies first place. This is the root of a stalk that is planted by sticking it into the ground. Within a year it is fully grown and can be eaten. Since this foodstuff is made from a woody root, in Portugal they call it "wood meal."

ALVIANO That is so, and when people want to heap scorn upon Brazil, the main thing they bring up against it is that there they eat meal made from wood.

BRANDÔNIO Well, that meal is an excellent food and is so good that it deserves to be put in second place, right after wheat, for it surpasses all the other foods that are used throughout the world.

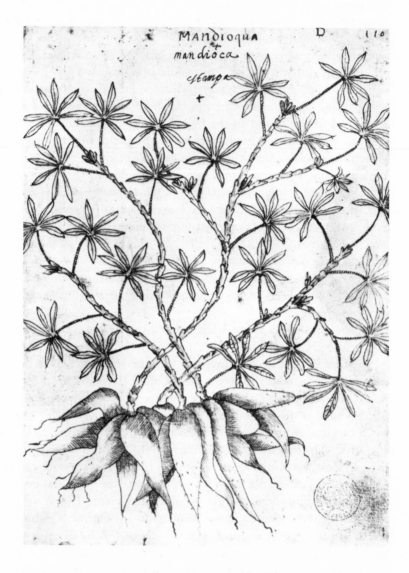

Manioc plant, with tubers. Cristóvão de Lisboa, *História dos animais e árvores do Maranhão* (1624; facsim. Lisbon: Arquivo Histórico Ultramarino e Centro de Estudos Históricos Ultramarinos, 1967), fol. 110. *Courtesy of the Edward E. Ayer Collection, The Newberry Library, Chicago.*

Manioc grating wheel. *Courtesy of the Edward E. Ayer Collection, The Newberry Library, Chicago.*

ALVIANO   So tell me what steps are taken to bring this food to perfection so that it can be eaten.

BRANDÔNIO   It is done like this: after it has ripened, the root is pulled out of the ground. It is about as thick as your arm, and sometimes longer. After its outside skin has been peeled off, it is grated on a wheel that they make for this purpose, the rim of which is covered with copper like a grater.[9] Afterwards, they are most careful to squeeze out all the juice in a press made for this very purpose.[10] When they take the manioc out of the press they set it aside, shaped into balls, which they break apart when they roast it at a low heat in ovens resembling the boiling pans for sugar—and made for this purpose out of clay.[11] That is the way it is made into meal. But to make it really good they have to add tapioca to it, and the more tapioca they put in, the better the meal is. The meal that is made this way is called "war meal,"[12] for it lasts a great length of time without spoiling, and they even take it with them to eat when they are out at sea.

ALVIANO   And what is that tapioca, which you say they add to the meal?

BRANDÔNIO   It is made from the water or juice that was pressed out of that same manioc. After it has stood in a bowl, a very white sediment forms on the bottom, like the flour in Alentejo.[13] After the water on top has been thrown away, what is left is called tapioca, and it is this that I said they mix with the manioc meal. And for starched neck ruffs and other such things it is better than any starch they make in Portugal.

But there is a remarkable thing about this: the water or juice that is thrown away after the tapioca has [formed][14] is a very powerful poison. If any man or beast eats or drinks it, he dies without hope of cure.[15] Even after it has been thrown on the ground, some worms are created by that moisture. If these are dried and powdered, they make the strongest and most perfect poison you can imagine.

ALVIANO   I don't think the food from which so powerful a poison comes can be very healthful.

BRANDÔNIO   Well, I'll tell you something more. Even the root, before it is treated the way I have told you, is poisonous and kills anyone who eats it—except for one variety of this root, which they call *macaxera;*[16] this one is eaten roasted or boiled and has the flavor of the chestnuts of our country.[17] Nonetheless, if the other kind, although so poisonous, is prepared the way I described, it becomes a most healthful food and is well suited to human consumption, and it has never been known to do anyone any harm.

ALVIANO   But if one kind of manioc is poisonous by nature, as you say, and another kind is not, why don't they use the non-poisonous one instead?

BRANDÔNIO   They don't do so because the one that is harmless can be eaten without any prior treatment, and therefore it is often stolen. Since it is a food crop that is always in the fields, people go out and pull it when they want something to eat. Thus it is a great attraction to thieves, who are inclined to steal the kind that they can eat right away without treating it. There is still another way, beyond the one I have already explained to you, to make the meal more appetizing. Well-born and refined persons have it done this way, because it is so delicious.

ALVIANO   Well, tell me that way of preparing it.

BRANDÔNIO   They take the manioc after it has been dug up and put it to soak in running water until it rots, for that is a better way. When it has rotted, they peel off the skin and break it up in their hands. After it is all broken up, they put it in the oven to cook, as I have already explained. When it is cooked they eat it right away. The hotter it is, the better, and it is so good that many people turn down the finest white bread for it.

They also use the freshly grated manioc to make a kind of wafer, which they call *beiju*[18] or, to use another name, tapioca. These are served at table in place of bread and will keep for many days.

ALVIANO   You go on transforming this manioc in so many different ways that it will end up having more colors than the green lizard![19]

BRANDÔNIO   But there are still other ways that they transform it. One way is this: after the manioc has rotted in the water, the way I told you (and when prepared this way it is called manioc mash [*mandioca puba*]), they peel it and cure it in a smoky corner over an open fire.[20] After it is cured and dried, they call it *carimã*. They make an excellent flour[21] from it that they use for mush made with chicken broth or fish broth, and sometimes with sugar.[22] Both of these dishes have a marvelous flavor and are very nourishing. They also give a similar kind of mush to sick people, for whom it is very good; and they call that *mingau*.

ALVIANO   Now tell me what they charge for an *alqueire*[23] of ordinary meal, and how much of it is needed to sustain a man.

BRANDÔNIO   The *alqueires* in these captaincies are two and a half times as large as those of Portugal; so an *alqueire* out here is equal to two and a half in Portugal. Now one of these *alqueires* is enough to sustain a man for the space of a month and is worth 250 to 300 reis.[24] Sometimes it is cheaper, depending on whether it is scarce or plentiful.

ALVIANO   Since you have given the first place for usefulness, among the foodstuffs of Brazil, to manioc, tell me now what is the second one in the settlers' preference.

BRANDÔNIO   The food that holds second place (though in many parts of the world it holds first place) is rice.[25] In this province it is produced in great abundance, at the cost of little labor. But the inhabitants, on account of the manioc, which I have discussed, plant very little rice, considering it to be almost a fruit and not a staple, since they think manioc is more nourishing.

ALVIANO   But that cannot be true, for rice is an excellent food, and, because it is, the greater part of Asia lives on it.

BRANDÔNIO   That is so, but the inhabitants of this land make more use of manioc—even though this means more work for them, for rice is easily grown anywhere; on the marshlands, which are good for nothing else, it grows best of all. It is true that, because it is not replanted, as it is in India, it does not all ripen at the same time, and because of that, harvesting it is more work. But, from another point of view, that makes it easier, since the rice can be harvested two or three years and still produce just as many new shoots; for the stubble that is left, if it is not trodden under and destroyed by beasts, turns green again at the beginning of the following winter and produces perfect fruit.

ALVIANO   Let us go on now to discuss the third kind of food crop that you said was prized for its goodness.

BRANDÔNIO   The third one is maize, which in our Portugal is called *zaburro*[26] and in the West Indies *maís* and by the Indian natives of this land *abati*.[27] It is a most useful food for the sustenance of the Guinea slaves and the Indians. It is eaten roasted and boiled. After it has been made into meal they make cakes of it, which are very tasty when eaten while they are hot. It is very important as fodder for horses and feed for fowls.

ALVIANO   At least in the [West] Indies it is so considered, and they use it widely.

BRANDÔNIO   Well, in this land it may be had for very little effort, indeed with great ease, so much so that every year they have two harvests of it.

ALVIANO   I don't see how that can be, unless you wish to say that this province has two winter seasons.

BRANDÔNIO   No, there is only one, as I have said, but the two crops are harvested this way: at the time of the first rains, which come more or less at the beginning of February—the opening of winter—the maize is planted. When the month of May comes it is picked, for it is already fully grown. Then right away they plant it again in the same ground, and for the second time it bears fruit, which is picked in August.

ALVIANO   How very fertile the land must be that gives two harvests during the year!

BRANDÔNIO   It is so fertile that with some plants there are three, as I shall explain later.[28] And those are the three principal food crops that are used in Brazil.

ALVIANO   I don't see that you make any mention of wheat, rye, and barley, or of millet, foodstuffs that are so esteemed in our Spain and throughout all Europe and, in general, throughout most of the world; so it looks to me as if the land does not produce them.

BRANDÔNIO   I was trying not to talk about those foodstuffs, so as not to shame myself and the other inhabitants of this state. The land does not produce them, not through any fault of its own, but rather because of the little interest and less industry of those who live in it. I have already planted wheat, two or three times, in the Captaincy of Pernambuco. The right time to plant this ought to be around St. Peter's Feast,[29] toward the end of June, more or less, for the weather then would be pretty much like that in Portugal at planting time. Now, of this wheat, I let one part grow just as it had been planted; the second part I cut with a scythe to hold it back; and the third part I mowed twice that same way. All of that wheat grew to maturity, though that which had been mowed gave better heads, and of this I harvested close to an *alqueire*, for there was not enough seed to give more. And every single stalk sprouted five to six ears; it is true that some of them were chaffy. But the trouble with this kind of sowing is that not all of the wheat matures at the same time. Rather, when some of the ears are perfectly ripe others are still soft and milky, and yet others are just starting to beard out. So it was necessary to cut the firm, ripe ears and leave the others, which makes a lot of work.[30]

ALVIANO   And could not some way be found to correct that?

BRANDÔNIO   I think it could, for in the year '99 [1599] in Portugal, when I was discussing the subject with an elderly Asturian nobleman, he happened to tell me that in the country where he lived there was a large meadow that was never cultivated—despite its great fertility— because the wheat grew that way in it. But for a few years back they had been using an excellent remedy, so that it then gave perfect wheat that all ripened at the same time so that it could be harvested. Now the remedy was that, after the wheat had been sown and was about a span above ground, they put the plow to the field to pull up the wheat and cut it into pieces, diminishing somewhat the vigor of the soil, and in this way it came to bear fruit again like other wheat. After this, when I had come back here, I was eager to try what the Asturian had suggested. I replanted some grains of wheat, which I had sowed in fertile soil,[31] and they all began to ripen in the same way and started to bear fruit at the same time. But the crop did not reach maturity because in a single day, before sundown, the birds ate it all up.

ALVIANO   Well, why didn't you try the experiment a second time?

BRANDÔNIO   Because the inhabitants of this land have infected me with their malady of negligence. But I have a feeling that if wheat were planted on the high plains [*campinas*], which have a rather sandy soil, it would reach maturity without any further care,[32] though I did not try that. All my experiments so far have been in low-lying *massapê*[33] lands, of great fertility, where the wheat grew too luxuriantly. This would not be the case on the high plains, because that is poorer soil.

ALVIANO It is truly pathetic to see how little interest the inhabitants of this province have, when they can't work up enough spirit to try out something so important and from which such great benefits would result for everybody. But what can you tell me about rye, barley, and millet?

BRANDÔNIO With rye and barley I have not yet experimented, but I have with millet. Now that grows better and more abundantly than it does in Portugal.[34] Yet it is not used, for the people in this land are satisfied with just what their ancestors made use of. They have no wish to add anything new, even though they understand clearly that they would derive much benefit from it. In this they show themselves to be so many stepfathers to Brazil, while for them she is a very kind mother!

ALVIANO I don't know what to say in the face of such carelessness and negligence, except that they are all ungrateful to God when they haven't the wit to take advantage of the benefits he gives them and holds out for them in this state, although I believe, too, that eventually someone will come along who will exploit them.

But now, it seems to me you said that beyond those three foodstuffs whose quality and nature you have described, there are still others.

BRANDÔNIO Yes, there are, and people fall back on them when harvests are poor, though that rarely happens in this country. Now these foodstuffs are: first, the root of the *gravatá*,[35] which grows wild in the fields without cultivation and from which they make a meal that is very nourishing. The second is the leaves of the manioc, boiled, which they call *maniçoba*.[36] These, too, are excellent in time of famine, and even at other times many people eat them. The third is the fruit of a large tree called *umari*,[37] which likewise serves for food. The fourth, some little coconuts, the local name for which is *aquê*.[38] These, after they are ripe, are picked from the small palms on which they grow in clusters. When they are peeled and split open, a deliciously sweet substance is extracted from the meat by pressing it between the hands under water. After cooking this over the fire, they make various porridges of it, and eat these along with the meat of the little coconuts. A great many of the savages of the land and of the Guinea blacks live on that. The fifth is the root of the *cipó,* which they call *macunã*.[39] They reduce this to meal and eat it after it is boiled.

ALVIANO   You say that the foodstuffs you have told me about are useful in time of famine, but I don't see how that can be. When barrenness is general, it extends to all seed plants, fruits as well as vegetables.

BRANDÔNIO   It is true that in Spain it happens that way, but not here in Brazil. All these things grow in the fields without being cultivated; since they are wild, they are always to be found in great abundance, no matter that the weather is like.

ALVIANO   That way there must never be any fear of famine in this state.

BRANDÔNIO   When there is famine, people never die from it, for they have recourse to such substitutes as those. And with that, let us press forward, though I will confess to you that I see before me so many things I must discuss that I dread to enter so vast a maze. But since I have taken it upon me to speak of the great things of Brazil, I shall first of all show you the immense fertility of its fields, and next I shall conjure up a refreshing [vegetable] garden abounding with a diversity of things, and after that I shall lay out an orchard supplied with various trees bearing superb pomes, and likewise a flower garden with countless flowers and daisies in it.[40] And then you shall judge whether one can call Brazil a worthless land, as you wished to at the beginning.

ALVIANO   I see already that I was mistaken, and so that I may be totally disabused, I beg you to follow out that order, for it strikes me as wonderful.

BRANDÔNIO   I wish to give first place among the vegetables of this land to the lima beans,[41] for they are extremely good; and both in size and in flavor they are much better than those in Portugal. But the plant is different, too, both in its leaves and in its manner of growth, being here a climber, like ivy. They can be picked either green or ripe, and both ways they are excellent.

ALVIANO   Portuguese lima beans must not grow here, for no one uses them.

BRANDÔNIO   Yes, they do grow here, but the settlers in this Brazil prefer these others, because they are native here and are grown with less trouble and are more productive.

Another vegetable, which is also very good, is a bean like those of Portugal.[42] These grow in great quantities and are used both fresh and dried.

They also harvest lots of peas in this country, which they use just the way they do in Portugal. Then there is another kind of bean, the *guandu*,[43] which was brought here from Angola. It grows on low trees and has an excellent flavor, and it is considered a superb vegetable.

ALVIANO I never heard of beans growing on trees.

BRANDÔNIO Well, these are a different variety and therefore grow on trees. Likewise there is found another kind of bean, called *sapotaia*,[44] which grows in a pod. There is also a kind of grain, similar to what they call *naxenim*[45] in India, but I think, rather, it is the same as that brought from Angola. The slaves call it *masa*.[46] Sesame grows so readily that from a small sowing of it one reaps a large harvest. There is another kind of vegetable that they call *amendoim* [peanut].[47] These are like little acorns, and inside each shell are two nuts that are marvelously nourishing and tasty. They are eaten roasted, boiled, and even raw without any preparation. And a canelike one called *piçandó*,[48] which is considered a vegetable. And, further, there is a root that is harvested by digging it out of the earth, called *tamoatarana*,[49] very tasty, and yet another to which they give the name *taioba* and another called *taiá*,[50] all very nourishing roots.

ALVIANO You are producing so many vegetables that I am already thinking that those of Spain must be inferior to them.

BRANDÔNIO Well, I still have a lot to tell you about them. Now there is something that looks like what in the Kingdom they call the Guinea squash; but I think, rather, it is indigenous. There are two kinds of them, one called *jerimu*[51] and the other *jerimu pacova*.[52] Many people depend mainly on these for food, because they are so nourishing. Each is eaten roasted or boiled, and when you add a little oil and vinegar it can be a dainty on the tables of the grand folk, for whom it is also prepared with sugar. These are much esteemed and will keep for many days without spoiling.

ALVIANO In Portugal, too, those squashes that you call *jerimus* will keep a long time without spoiling.

BRANDÔNIO Well, here in Brazil they grow much better. There are also lots of squashes called calabashes.[53] Some of them are enormous, but there are some smaller ones which they eat. I have seen some of the big ones that would hold two and a half *alqueires*[54] of meal, the equivalent of five Portuguese *alqueires*.

ALVIANO Where there are gourds like that you can do without sacks, for the sacks will hold little more [than the calabashes].

BRANDÔNIO Why, yes; and I'll show you some if you want to see them, so that you won't have any hesitation in believing it. Many excellent potatoes[55] are also grown in the earth, much better than those that are sent to Portugal.[56] People use these to make tidbits, wonderful sweets, and panfuls of a potato dessert like marmalade. They also eat them baked or boiled. In addition, they produce many good *inhames* and also *carás,* which are of the same species but much bigger.[57]

Now all these vegetables—for that is what they really are—can be kept in the house many days without spoiling. And, above all, the very best vegetable of them all is a nut called cashew, delicious and very nourishing. These will keep for a long time and are eaten roasted. People use them for everything, in place of almonds.

ALVIANO   You have named so many different kinds of vegetable that one would need a primer to learn their names. But I would like to know why people don't also make use of the seeds—chickpeas, lentils, and lupines of our Portugal—and I suppose the reason is that they won't grow here.

BRANDÔNIO   Oh, they'll grow here, for I planted some of them, though not a large quantity, and they turned out well. I can think of no other reason for their not being used than the general slackness in Brazil, which I have already mentioned.

ALVIANO   The more you tell me of that the better opinion I have of the land and the worse opinion I have of its settlers.

BRANDÔNIO   You can say anything you want to on that subject, for the general guilt is so great that anyone who tried to defend the settlers would be making a mistake.

But, now that we are getting on with our discussion of the fruits the fields produce, I wish to show you that the Brazilian fields are such that those of Elysium—so celebrated by the poets in their fancies—are much inferior to them, as is also the vile Mohammed's[58] fabled paradise, which owed its bliss, they say, to the rivers of honey and butter that flowed through it. For these fields of ours, real fields and not dreams spun by the mind, will be found to enjoy those things which, with their studied imagery, the poets depicted. For in these fields of ours you will find rivers of the most excellent honey and the most marvelous butter,[59] which the inhabitants make use of with little effort.

ALVIANO   I don't know how that can be.

BRANDÔNIO   Well, believe me, it is true. For the fields abound with many honey trees, and innumerable bees build their honeycombs in holes in them, and in holes in the ground too,[60] and in such quantity that to harvest the honey nothing is needed except an axe—with a few blows of which the tree is opened—and a bowl to catch the honey as it pours out. There is such a great quantity of it that on honey alone, and no other food, many persons sustain themselves, as I shall explain later on when I discuss the customs of the heathen.[61] And besides the honey that is collected in this way, there is a wild fruit called *piquiá,*[62] somewhat like an orange, which has inside it a delicious substance like clarified honey, which you eat with a spoon. Now these one can truly call rivers of honey and not the fabled Mohammedan ones.

Then, if you want to look for rivers of butter, I can give you a great quantity of it in the abundant milk taken from cows, goats, and sheep. Marvelous butter is compounded from it, and a lot of another quality is made from the hogs, of which there are a great many in this state, both domesticated and wild.[63]

ALVIANO   No one can deny that, for I see clearly that it is so and that we have at hand the true Elysian Fields of which the poets sang.

BRANDÔNIO   That's not the end of it, for there are many other things in our fields that I still must show you. I think the first should be the great number of wines that are found in its forests. These are not like our Portuguese wine, which is made of grapes (not because the land here would not produce a very good wine, but because of the negligence of the inhabitants, as I shall explain later on), but consist of other kinds that are found in great quantity, such as the wine that is made from the juice of the sugar cane, which the heathen of this land and the Guinea slaves think is wonderful.[64] And there is another made from sugar and spices, quite a bit like mead, which the whites consider something very fine. Also, a wine is made from bees' honey mixed with water, which is delicious and most beneficial to the health of those who drink it regularly. Another wine is made from a fruit called cashew, which is found everywhere in the fields. Many white people drink it. Then there is palm wine, of the kind made in the country of the Kaffirs,[65] of which a vast amount could be made because the land abounds with these plants. Also there is the wine made from the sap of the coconut tree, so popular in India, which the inhabitants of this land do not make use of because of the general failing I have pointed out.

ALVIANO   Having so many kinds of wine, one could easily get along without those that are brought from the Canaries and the Island of

Madeira, especially since there is the one that you said is like mead, which I am very fond of.

BRANDÔNIO Well, those I have mentioned exist in great abundance. And, now that they have been considered, I want to show you the great quantity of oils that are obtained from the fields without any cultivation. First of all a very good-tasting oil, and not a little of it, is taken from the fruit of a tree called *batiputá*,[66] which grows wild in these fields. And from the fruit called *inhanduroba*,[67] the size of a peach, which has some beanlike seeds inside, they make a great amount of oil that is marvelous for lighting. It has another excellent quality that is not to be minimized: the birds and animals will positively not eat it. Also from some pine nuts,[68] which have laxative properties, a great deal of oil is taken, and it has the same advantage. From the jimson weed, with which the land abounds, much oil is also made, especially from one kind, of a distinct variety, that has kernels the size of hazelnuts. When these are removed and pressed, they give an oil without leaving any bagasse. Then, without any other processing, it can be used instead of tallow for whatever application one wishes, and as an ointment and a curative of wounds it is considered very good. This little fruit has so much oil inside it that if you put it on the end of a stick it will burn like a torch as long as the oil lasts, which is a great while.

You can also make coconut oil, such as they use in India, because there are so many coconut palms here; but the lame spirit of the Brazilians, which I have so often pointed out, keeps them from making use of this benefit.[69]

ALVIANO A country with so much oil surely can never suffer from lack of it.

BRANDÔNIO One could very well do without the oil that comes from the Kingdom—and likewise many other imports, as you will be seeing in the course of our conversation. The chief of these would be linen and other kinds of cloth, for a great deal of it might be made right here in this country.

ALVIANO And how so?

BRANDÔNIO I have already told you about the large amount of cotton[70] that is harvested here. Now, since in India so much cloth is made from it, is there any reason why it cannot be made here too, when the inhabitants shall be so disposed? Besides cotton there are found in the fields some leaves of a tree called tucuma.[71] From this is made a very good yarn, very fine and strong. This is the plant that is used in the [West] Indies to produce the pita[72] fiber that is so much prized in Spain. Although it grows better here, and in greater quantities, they do not make use of it.

There is also found a wild plant, called *gravatá*,[73] which gives a great supply of fine and useful fiber. And thus from the many things that grow in the fields all sorts of cloth can be made.

ALVIANO   Though all that may be very good, our textiles [those of Spain and Portugal] are of an excellent quality and are esteemed the world over for that reason.

BRANDÔNIO   No one can deny the truth of that, but cloth could also be produced in this province in great quantities, so that it could be shipped to Spain to sell, especially that made of hemp,[74] though people here make no use of it.

ALVIANO   They ought not to neglect it, for these fibers, being so important, should be prized everywhere.

BRANDÔNIO   There seems to be no remedy for such negligence, as I have said before. And so that you may see more clearly how rich this land is, I will show you in the fields the finest wool, which could be used for woolen cloth, linings for garments, and stuffing for mattresses, pillows, and cushions.

ALVIANO   Well, if ewes and rams graze in the fields, who doubts that one can take that wool from them?

BRANDÔNIO   It is true that those rams and ewes can supply it abundantly. But that is not the sort of wool I am discussing, but another variety, produced by the tree called *munguba*.[75] This is the fluff that gave rise to our conversation. Beyond any doubt it will make very good cloth and hats. There is also another tree, whose name I do not know, which gives a quadrangular fruit about the size of a pine cone, inside which there is a kind of wool that I think is the same thing that in India they call *paina*,[76] which is wonderful for everything that requires stuffing—beds, clothing, or other things. And besides this kapok, which abounds in the fields, many white people have pretty good mattresses made of the cattail, a reed that grows in the marshlands. Because this has lots of body and is quite thick, it is good to lie upon and is very warm. And there are many other kinds of reed from which very fine mats can be made.

ALVIANO   You have already shown me in these American fields enough foodstuffs and vegetables to sustain many people, and likewise honey, butter, wine, oil, linen and woolen fabrics, and soft beds to rest on. Now I expect nothing else than that you give me houses to live in!

BRANDÔNIO   And what would you think if I were to give them to you?

ALVIANO   That is impossible, unless you were to get Urganda[77] to build them for you by magic.

BRANDÔNIO   Well, you must not think it impossible; for without the labor of stonemasons, or carpenter's dividers, or the ironsmith's maul, or the help of brickmakers, very good houses are put up in this state out of things that you gather in the fields.

ALVIANO   Well, tell me how this is done, and don't keep me any longer in suspense.

BRANDÔNIO   I have already told you about the many kinds of wood that there are in this country. People have it cut by their slaves and build houses with pitched roofs. Instead of nails one uses two kinds of rope, with which the timbers are tied and made fast. One of these is called *cipó* and the other *timbó*.[78] They are so strong and so good for this purpose that there is a common adage which says that if it were not for the *cipó* Brazil could not have been settled, so many different things is it used for. A house put up this way is just as easy to cover, for from the same fields they pick a plant called sape grass,[79] which takes the place of tiles, and has the good feature of being warmer than tiles. And also from a tree like a palm, which is called pindova,[80] a very good roof can be made. And in the countryside many inhabitants of this state live in houses built in this manner, though there are also some very well-built houses of stone and mortar.[81]

ALVIANO   Though I know full well that what you tell me is the pure truth, nonetheless these things seem fantastic to me because of their extraordinary nature. But you mentioned that ropes are made from the *cipó* and the *timbó*. I would like to know if they could be used in shipbuilding.

BRANDÔNIO   In no case can they be used for that, but only for the things I mentioned or similar things. But ship's tackle is made from the bark of a tree called *embira*,[82] from which they make excellent ropes, strong and durable. They could also make ropes from coir [coconut fiber],[83] like those they make in India, because there are so many coconut palms in this country (and there would be still more if they would plant them), from which they could get a great deal of coir for this purpose. For that matter, in Paraíba there is a palm, and the coconuts it yields, instead of having edible meat inside, are all filled up with coir, something I never saw anywhere else. But they make no use of it.

Further, from the bark of another tree, called sapucaya,[84] is made a marvelous oakum for caulking ships, which is better and more durable than what is used at present. There grows in the fields also a kind of rattan, like that of India, which they call *titarimbó* [?].[85] This is marvelous for making hampers and baskets. And likewise there are some canes, which they call Bengalese walking sticks,[86] as good as those of India. And so that I won't forget it, I shall speak of two things that the fields are thick with, one very good and the other pretty bad although worthy of some consideration.

ALVIANO   And what are they?

BRANDÔNIO   The good thing is hearts of palm,[87] excellent to eat, much better than those of Portugal. They are taken from certain palm trees, lofty and beautiful. And the bad thing is an herb called sensitive plant.[88] It so much dislikes to be touched that it wilts and dries up when a person touches it with his hand. It stays that way for a while until, little by little, it turns green again. And though people have worked to discover the theory for the cause of this, they have not as yet been able to ascertain it. And the root of this herb is a most subtle poison, which kills beyond hope of cure whoever eats it.

ALVIANO   A marvelous thing and worthy of study is that, and with it, so it seems to me, you must now have finished with the miraculous things which you declared abound in these fields. Therefore it would be a good idea for us to begin to discuss some others.

BRANDÔNIO   I have not finished, but am only now getting started, for there are also to be found in those fields marvelous drugs, such as peppers of all kinds and varieties, large and small, and still others that have a sweet flavor. The land produces ginger[89] abundantly when it is planted, better in size and everything else than that which is brought from India. Another fruit is picked from a tree called *embira;*[90] lots of people use it, and rightly everybody ought to use it, for it is an excellent drug, producing all the effects of pepper, cloves, and cinnamon; and it dyes like saffron, a thing that no one will believe until he tries it; and it has a very good smell. A great quantity of malaguetta pepper[91] is also found growing wild in the woods and fields. It is only a short time back that it was discovered, and it may be that I was the first person to discover it, so little curiosity dwells in these parts. And one cannot overlook the herb from which indigo is made. In India this is planted and tended with much care and diligence, while here it grows without anyone's bothering, and with very little work one could make a great supply of indigo from it. I have already experimented with it and made a little, and it was so fine and good that one would not prefer that which is made in the Indies.[92]

ALVIANO   All those drugs would be of great value if they were put to use and shipped to foreign parts, especially that *embira* which you praise so highly.

BRANDÔNIO   The people in this country take no interest in anything. Now, besides drugs, there are many dyestuffs that could be used.[93] And without mentioning the wood called brazil,[94] for that is so well known, there is another dye as good as the one which that gives, if not even better, called *urucu*,[95] of a marvelous red color. The fruit grows in bunches and is similar to a plum, and the tree looks like a small banana plant. This fruit makes an excellent dye, with more changes than a chameleon, for it can be made to give different colors, and when the dye is set it lasts a very long time and preserves its color strength perfectly. And there's another dark wood—I don't know its name—which has an effect quite like gall, for when you put some splinters of it in water and add a little bit of vitriol, the wood and water at once become as black as ink. I had some experiments made with this wood in the Kingdom, and the dyemasters thought this dye was a good one with which to make the first dyeing, the one that all the others are laid over. Also a very fine yellow dye is made from a wood called *tatajuba*.[96] And from the fruit of a tree, genipap[97] by name, a black dye is made. Though the juice of this fruit is white, if anyone rubs himself with it the part he rubs turns black, and nothing will take the black away for the space of several days, no matter how often he washes.

ALVIANO   I heard someone tell of a practical joke that was played in Spain. Some of that juice was thrown into the holy water font on a holy day of obligation, and everyone who took water from the font got black spots. This caused great consternation, especially among the women, for the spots remained on them until enough days went by for the color to fade.

BRANDÔNIO   There is also another wood that comes from a small tree called *arariba*,[98] which gives an excellent red dye, much finer and brighter in color than brazilwood. The women use it on their faces.

There are found also some deposits of very fine red ochre, and another variety of it that is white, which they call *tabatinga*.[99] They use this instead of lime to whitewash the houses, and it makes them very white and clean.

ALVIANO   But why don't they rather use lime?

BRANDÔNIO   They do make a lot of it here, but in many places they use the *tabatinga* because it is more readily available. Likewise the fields abound in a great quantity of marvelous tree gums, such as a very fine resin; and another, from the cashew tree, which is excellent for gluing paper; and yet another from a tree[100] that yields a yellow dye, and they use it as wax for sealing letters. To bring this to an end, there are so many kinds of gum that I do not venture to name them all; I shall only say that a lot of wax is taken from the trees where the bees make their honey, as well as a great quantity of aromatic resin that is dug out.[101]

ALVIANO   I have already seen many people use that aromatic resin for headaches, and with great success.

BRANDÔNIO   Well, here they don't use it even for that, and still less do they take advantage of the power of many medicinal roots and herbs, which are useful alike as physics and for healing wounds. They think those that come from Portugal, even though they arrive rotten, are better, because they cost money. I don't know what more to tell you, except for two things, and with them I shall cease my roaming through the fields and forests: even soap for washing clothes can be found there, and if you wish to trap birds, I can give you an excellent birdlime produced by the nitta tree.[102] And with this we shall go on to lay out the vegetable garden that we have promised.

ALVIANO   You have told me so much about the wild fields and forests that I don't see what more can be expected from this garden. Now since it is a cultivated thing, it ought to exceed them greatly in its production, and I don't see any place left where you can put it.

BRANDÔNIO   Oh, we can find somewhere to fit it in without putting it at a disadvantage in comparison with other gardens.[103]

ALVIANO   Don't forget that, to be complete, a garden must have water wheels, ponds, and reservoirs to water it, and I know that they don't have those in Brazil.[104]

BRANDÔNIO   One really can't say that a thing doesn't exist when it very well could exist; for Portugal itself was not before it was! I mean that before the gardens, reservoirs, and water jets that we see today in such numbers were invented, Portugal lacked them, for nothing is made by itself. By which I mean that if this land at present lacks all those things, the fault is not its own but that of those people who don't make them for it. For here are the finest waters in the world, from the most torrential rivers to smaller ones, and more brooks and springs than you can count, from which could be made those delightful fountains, reservoirs, and jets, at very little cost. And thus one cannot say that there is a lack of what exists!

ALVIANO   I have heard that in the Captaincy of Paraíba, in addition to the water being excellent, there are some springs so health-giving that those who drink regularly of them do not suffer from the stone or from colic. [105]

BRANDÔNIO   Many experiments have shown that to be so, and for that reason governors, bishops, and powerful persons order such water to be taken to Pernambuco for them to drink.

And because we have much to talk about and it is already growing late, since we know that there is no lack of water, let us get started on our vegetable garden, which can have many good kinds of lettuce, a great quantity of turnips, an infinity of kale, all planted and picked with little effort.

ALVIANO   How now? Is there, by chance, some other way of planting and picking than is used in Portugal?

BRANDÔNIO   Yes, there is, especially with the kale. They let some of it grow until it sprouts; then they pick the sprigs that have seed sprouts on them and stick them into the earth, and they take root right away, and in a short time they become beautiful big heads of kale.

ALVIANO   This must be because the vegetables grown in this soil do not produce seeds, as I have already heard it said.

BRANDÔNIO   They produce seeds all right, and it is a bad habit to send to Portugal for them, especially for lettuce, which produces an infinity of seeds. Our garden must also have very fine chicory, chard, borage, coriander, mint, parsley, fennel, cumin, and amaranths of various kinds and colors—for all these things are found in abundance here.

ALVIANO   The gardens of Spain do not produce a greater number of vegetables.

BRANDÔNIO   It can also have water parsnips, watercress, common purslaine, and a superb variety of mustard, the leaves of which are eaten raw or boiled, and some large leaves that they call *inhambus*, [106] which are very good to eat, for after they are boiled they have a delicious piquancy; and, likewise, another kind of leaf, the *taioba*,[107] which is somewhat like kale, and is much esteemed.

ALVIANO   He who has those things will not go hungry.

BRANDÔNIO   And carrots, wild artichokes, eggplants, cucumbers, watermelons, all the common squashes, tender and delicious, and some other smaller ones which they call *taqueira* [small, flat pumpkins], tobacco, which in Portugal they call the sacred herb,[108] and above all melons beyond counting, all of them so extremely good that only with difficulty can you find a bad one in the lot; and with all these things in abundance you be the judge of whether I can have a good garden.

ALVIANO   Rather do I wonder at the general neglect to make more gardens.

BRANDÔNIO   Well, there is not a soul who has a complete one or who is willing to spend time to make it so, and nothing could be more unfortunate.[109] Now if this way one can make the vegetable garden good, the flower garden will be no worse, because of the many varieties of flowers with which it can be populated and adorned. So many and so different are they and of such strange varieties that it is impossible that anyone should be able to discover all of them or to know their names. So I shall mention only a few of them that are most commonly grown, such as the orange flower, which grows abundantly; stocks of many different kinds and colors; yellow, red, and white carnations; jasmines, honeysuckles, garden balsam, night jasmine; and *alfavaca* and *manjericão* [both basils], which the fields are full of.

Another kind of flower they call *camará-açu;*[110] and another, *maracujá*,[111] worthy of esteem and consideration for its beauty, the various colors of which it is composed, its beautiful radiating corona, and other particularities worthy of note. In conclusion, the flowers native to this land are so many that I do not dare to venture into such deep water as to try to discuss them all. To make figures, designs, and other ornaments, there are so many kinds of liana that are marvelous for this, because of the way they stretch, that the myrtles of Portugal are far behind them.

ALVIANO   I am astonished to hear it, for I did not imagine Brazil to be like this.

BRANDÔNIO   Now if arbors are required to adorn this vegetable and flower garden, I can give you many [climbing plants], such as one that gives good shade and pleasant greenery, and produces a fruit called *curuá*,[112] the size of an ordinary squash. When it is picked and put in a box for some days, it acquires such a sweet smell that it is enough to spread great fragrance all through the house, and it will keep many days without spoiling.

Other arbors are made with the *maracujá*, whose blossom I have already described, which gives a fruit the size of a pine cone, very delicious, and the flesh of which, similar to that of the squash, you suck or eat with a spoon; it has much flavor and a marvelous smell. There are four varieties of these: one called *maracujá-açu* because it is big; the second, *maracujá-peroba*, which is excellent for preserves; the third, *maracujá-mexira*; the fourth, *maracujá-mirim* because it is small; and all of them make good arbors and give equal shade.[113]

ALVIANO   It seems to me that you are forgetting our grape trellises, for I have seen some of them in this country.

BRANDÔNIO   No, I was not forgetting them, but deliberately avoided mentioning them so as not to throw shame once again on the settlers of this state.[114] Now you must know that any sort of vine will grow here luxuriantly, but the people here use only the trellised ones. These give many dark grapes and some marvelous white ones, and they produce this fruit two and three times a year.

ALVIANO   That is impossible.

BRANDÔNIO   Though it may seem so, it is not. For that has been my experience many times—I mean their giving fruit three times a year; there is no need to talk of their producing twice a year, for that is very well known.

ALVIANO   Well, tell me how that happens.

BRANDÔNIO   By doing nothing more than pruning the vines as soon as you have picked the fruit, for then they mature again and in four months' time they have perfect fruit once more. I have even seen some men who, in order to have fruit at the time of parties they planned to give, pruned the grapevines four months ahead of time, and they produced grapes, without fail, at the time resolved upon.

ALVIANO   Well, if grapes grow so easily and in so short a time, why don't they make wine of them?

BRANDÔNIO   Not to be obliged to discuss the reason for that, as I have said, I was endeavoring not to get involved in this subject, for in many parts of this Brazil they could make more wine than in Portugal because those regions are free from ants, which are what harm the

The *maracujá,* a kind of passion flower, with its fruit. Cristóvão de
Lisboa, *História dos animais e árvores do Maranhão* (1624; facsim.
Lisbon: Arquivo Histórico Ultramarino e Centro de Estudos Históricos
Ultramarinos, 1967), fol. 137. *Courtesy of the Edward E. Ayer Collection,
The Newberry Library, Chicago.*

vines. I know of one place especially, the Copaoba Mountains,[115] which are a matter of fifteen to eighteen leagues distant from the captaincies of Pernambuco and Paraíba, that would produce wine beyond measure, for this is well-watered land,[116] cool and without a single ant.[117]

ALVIANO   It hurts me to hear you say things like that, and I wish it were in my power to correct them.

BRANDÔNIO   Time will cure this disability, as it usually does. And now that I have laid out for you the vegetable and flower gardens, and the arbors with their fountains, reservoirs, and water jets, as I promised, I wish to organize the orchard that is lacking. With this we shall put an end to our conversation for today.

Now I shall divide this orchard into two parts, not because there *are* any like that, but because there *could* be, when the desire for development shall stimulate those of us who live here and who don't know how to use what is right at hand. I shall first lay out a grove of citrus fruit trees[118] and then go on to the orchard proper, separating in my discussion the fruits that are already in use and under cultivation from those which negligence has so far allowed to remain wild.

This grove can be populated with beautiful, bushy green orange trees, all covered over with the whitest flowers, whose delicate fragrance will lift the spirits of those who enjoy them. They are weighed down with delicious, bright oranges, in such great number that often there are more oranges than leaves, some so sweet that in comparison with them sugar and honey lose their value;[119] beaked ones so good to eat that one can never get enough of them; also some sour ones, which are marvelous for the use to which they are put because they have so much juice.

To go along with the orange grove there will be beautiful, tall lemon trees, with such a burden of fruit that men will marvel that they can bear up under it, and they will have that fruit the year round, so that when one tree is in bloom another is beginning to bear fruit and yet another is ready for picking. To these lemon trees will be added a great many sweet lime trees, with their well-shaped fruits, excellent in taste and in flavor, which are produced in this land in much greater number than in Portugal. And likewise another variety of citrus fruit that is called Adam's apple,[120] considered very good. Dominating all the rest, making this garden beautiful, will be some great French lime trees,[121] whose cheerful yellow gladdens the eye. The modern grapefruit[122] also will not be lacking, for these grow in quantities. Running along the edges almost like a wall will be the thorny citron trees, loaded down with beautiful fruits, bigger than an oil jar, which are much valued for preserves, and these ripen all through the year.

ALVIANO   If that's the way things are and groves can be made like that, then I must admit that the groves tended and cultivated in Portugal with such great labor are inferior to these, for I do not see in them more varieties of citrus fruit tree than you have pointed out.

BRANDÔNIO   And even the other fruit trees have a certain indescribable quality of greenness and freshness that makes beautiful landscapes. And because the sun is already sinking, I want to get on with the discussion of the promised orchard, in which I want the first fruit to be figs, for I have always been very fond of them. These grow in such quantity, not only the red *berjaçotes*,[123] but also the white, the black, and other varieties, that the very dunghills are covered with these fig trees. They bear fruit twice a year, and in such profusion that it would startle you. Let us right away lay out an avenue of pomegranate trees, with their crested fruits, which enclose within themselves superb rubies,[124] and which flourish in this land. The twisted quince trees will keep them company with their fragrant, golden pomes, which grow abundantly in some of the captaincies of this state. A delightful shade will be cast by great banana trees, whose fruit is known by the same name, though in India, on the contrary, they call them figs.[125] Some are large, some are smaller, of different varieties and types, delicious to eat and good to smell, and there is an infinitude of them. A native fruit of this country will keep them company—the guava, the size of a melocotone peach.[126] It grows on medium-sized trees, close to the trunk; there will also be rising up, with its tiny leaves suitable for making a tasty sauce, the tamarind,[127] of medicinal value and prized for that reason throughout the world. In the shady places, growing low like a cardoon, will be the much-praised and beautiful pineapple,[128] which resembles a pine cone and gives out a sweet smell that imparts to it the savor of all the best-tasting things there are. And with this I have concluded the plants and trees that up to now are in use and are cultivated in this Brazil.

ALVIANO   Even if there were no others, those would be enough to make it famous for an abundance of fruits.

BRANDÔNIO   Well, those that up to now are still wild, for lack of people to cultivate them, are infinite in number. And since it is not possible to recall them all, I shall proceed to discuss only those that occur to me. And let us, therefore, give the first place—for the beauty of the plant—to the *cajá* [American hog-plum], which in India is called *ambare,* and which they use there for so many purposes and here for nothing except to eat it when it's ripe, and then it has a tart flavor and leaves a strong smell on your hands. Another fruit, called *oiticoró,*[129] of the size of a large pine cone, has so much flavor that I think without doubt it is better than pear preserves or marmalade, which the world esteems so highly, and this is produced on a very large tree. The *araticu,*[130] similar to the jackfruit[131] of India, is not a bad fruit. Another kind of *araticu,* called *apê,*[132] is small in size but great in taste. These are so flavorful that there isn't anybody who can get enough of them (and a friend of mine made fritters of them that were marvelous). The *mangaba*[133] can be said to be one of the best fruits in the world, and is rather like the fruit of the service tree of Portugal. The bountiful cashew tree,[134] proud of being different from the other trees, bears its fruit the opposite of the way all others do, for the nuts that other fruits hide within themselves these cashews flaunt on the outside, so that they put a finishing touch on the fruit at its base in such fashion as to show anyone not familiar with them that this is where the fruit had its start.[135] It is a beautiful and delicious pome that many people live on as long as it is in season. The good qualities of its cashew nuts I pass over in silence, for I have already discussed them.[136] The *jamacaru,*[137] whose plant is like the cardoon, gives a most delicious red fruit; the *pitomba*[138] is similar to a plum; the *maçaranduba*[139] looks like a cherry; the *guabiroba*[140] looks rather like an olive, and is sweet; the *oiti*[141] is the size of an egg; the *gravatá*[142] is a long white fruit that you eat by sucking it, and it has a fine taste; the sapucaya[143] is a big tree that produces a cone with nuts inside that are good to eat; *uvaias*[144] look like the fingers of your hand and taste like figs; the *ingá*[145] is similar to a carob pod, and is sweet tasting; the *macujé*[146] is an excellent fruit, like pears; the jambul[147] is like a white plum; the *peiti*[148] resembles a date and is very delicious; the canafistula[149] grows in the woods, its great pods filled with pulp.

ALVIANO Well, for heaven's sake! Why don't they take it to Portugal and use it there?

BRANDÔNIO Not even in its native land do they take advantage of such a fruit. The truth is that, since the plant is wild, the fruit itself looks a little wild; but, if it were cultivated, I have no doubt that it would

Gathering cashews. Some of the Indians are squeezing the fruits to make
a drink. The nut can be seen growing at the end of the fruit. André
Thevet, *Les singularitez de la France Antarctique . . .* (Paris: Héritiers de
Maurice de la Porte, 1558), fol. 120ᵛ. *Courtesy of the Edward E. Ayer
Collection, The Newberry Library, Chicago.*

Sapucaya tree and fruit. Gulielmi Pisonis, . . . *De Indiae utriusque re naturali et medica* . . . (Amsterdam: Ludovicum et Danielem Elzevirios, 1658), p. 135. *Courtesy of the Edward E. Ayer Collection, The Newberry Library, Chicago.*

be as good as what they use in Portugal. And leaving aside this canafistula, let us get on with our orchard, for I still have a lot of plants to set out in it. Of these, let the first one be a fruit they call *piquiá*, which I have already discussed,[150] the fruit of which is something like clarified sugar, very delicious; the *cambucá*[151] is another fruit, red, similar to the morello cherry; the *ibá-mirim*[152] is like a lemon; the *uti*[153] is a long fruit, delicious to eat; the *bacupari*[154] is like a peach; the *comixá*[155] is a tiny fruit like a myrtle berry; the *grexiuruba*[156] is another one like the Adam's apple;[157] the *eicajeru* [icaco plum] is like our early plum; the *ambu*[158] is like a white plum; the *guapuronga*[159] is like the bastard grape; the *piquiá*[160] has the appearance of a loquat; the *pitanga*[161] is like a morello cherry; the *tatajuba*[162] is like a mulberry; the *hicambu*[163] is similar to a peach, and its root if eaten will kill any thirst no matter how great; the *murici*[164] is rather like a myrtle berry; the okra is a pod-shaped fruit like an eggplant;[165] the papaya is a pome the size of a quince, very sweet; the *araçá*,[166] of the size of an apricot, is very tasty—good marmalade is made from it; another kind of *araçá* is surnamed *"açu"* because it is big,[167] and it is most esteemed for eating. These are the fruits that have occurred to me at the moment, though there are still infinite others to be named which I cannot remember, and which the inhabitants of Brazil so far have carelessly allowed to remain wild, scattered through the forests. If they were cultivated, they would increase in nourishment and flavor.

ALVIANO   Certainly you have kept me in suspense with such a variety of fruits as you have named. Of these you could make not only one orchard, but a hundred thousand orchards. And therefore I am most repentant of having held Brazil in different repute than it merits.[168]

BRANDÔNIO   I am glad that you make that retraction, and so that you will not envy the poplars and aspens of our Portugal, with which similar orchards and gardens are so greatly enhanced, I wish to give you in their place the great, lofty coconut palms, which make no less a murmur when their leaves are whipped by the wind.[169] And with them let us put an end for today to our conversation, for it is already getting to be time for us to go home.

ALVIANO   As you wish, on condition that tomorrow you come at the usual time to this same place.

Notes to Dialogue IV

1 · A conto of gold = 400,000,000 reis (400:000$000). See III, n. 16.
2 · See p. 135.

3 · Brandônio is advocating free trade—a bold suggestion for his time, when nations took it as a matter of course that their colonies were to be exploited for the benefit of the metropole. During the period of Spanish domination (1580–1640) the Spanish government restricted the Brazil trade to Portuguese merchants and Portuguese markets; even Spanish merchants were excluded. Not until the separation of Portugal from Spain was Portugal at liberty to negotiate treaties of commerce, alliance, and peace with France, Holland, and England. Roberto C. Simonsen, *História econômica do Brasil (1500–1820)*, p. 353.

4 · On pp. 138–139.

5 · See below, n. 91.

6 · Introduced during the sixteenth century from Africa, ginger thrived in Brazil until 1578, when the King created a monopoly on the spice and forbade its export from Africa and Brazil because it posed a threat to the India ginger trade. In Bahia, at least, this order was largely ignored. Stuart B. Schwartz, *Sovereignty and Society in Colonial Brazil*, pp. 158–159; Frédéric Mauro, *Le Portugal et l'Atlantique au XVIIe siècle*, p. 368.

7 · Indigo had been cultivated for some time in Spanish America (in Mexico, Guatemala, El Salvador, and—in smaller amounts—in Panama and the West Indies). When the plant was discovered in Brazil, its extraction was at first prohibited by the Crown, lest the markets for East Indian indigo and for woad from the Azores should be damaged. (For the production of indigo in India, see p. 132, and III, n. 9.)

Brandônio's observations are confirmed by Gedeon Morris de Jonge, a Dutchman who during the first half of the seventeenth century traveled though Maranhão, Pará, and Amazonas looking for products that might be of commercial advantage to the Dutch West India Company. During the Dutch occupation of the Northeast of Brazil (1630–1654), the invaders conducted highly successful experiments in the cultivation of West Indian varieties of indigo, but because of the troubled conditions of the period just before their expulsion, the Dutch did not undertake to exploit commercially either the native or the imported product. By the time Portugal regained control of her colony, the oriental spice trade had been lost to the Dutch and English, and the Portuguese Crown authorized the cultivation of indigo in Brazil. Still it did not actively support the industry, and only in the eighteenth century, under the leadership of the viceroy, Luís de Almeida, marquess of Lavradio, was action taken to promote the production and exportation of native indigo. The result was the development of a flourishing industry during the 1780s and 1790s in Rio de Janeiro. But Brazilian indigo was never able to compete successfully with that grown in other parts of the world, and by 1818 indigo had become a negligible item in Brazil's national production. José Hygino, "Relatórios e cartas de Gedeon Morris de Jonge," *Revista do Instituto Histórico e Geográfico Brasileiro* 58, pt. 1 (1895):241; Joan Nieuhof, *Memorável viagem marítima e terrestre ao Brasil,* p. 294; Dauril Alden, "The Growth and Decline of Indigo Production in Colonial Brazil," *Journal of Economic History* 25 (March 1965):35–60; idem, *Royal Government in Colonial Brazil,* pp. 372–376.

8 · Also *mani, mandioca. Mani* [manioc] + *coba* [leaf]. Antônio Geraldo da Cunha, *Dicionário histórico das palavras portuguesas de origem tupi,* s.v. "maniçoba." The tuber exists in many varieties, some of which are toxic. Manioc does not have the nutritive qualities of wheat because of a lack of albuminous materials, such as gluten, but it was the basis of alimentation in the colonial period and is still so today in large areas of Brazil. Magalhães de Gandavo describes the cultivation of manioc in somewhat more detail than Brandônio. Pero de Magalhães de Gandavo, *História da Província Sancta Cruz,* in his *Histories of Brazil,* vol. 1, fol. 16ʳ; see also Simonsen, *História econômica,* pp. 370–371.

9 · Brandônio is thinking of a type of grater introduced into Brazil by the colonists. This grater was in the shape of a large wheel and was operated like a grindstone; there is a picture of it in Guilherme Piso, *História natural do Brasil ilustrada,* p. 62. Similar graters are still in use in the Brazilian backlands, but some of these are now motor driven.

Before the arrival of the colonists the Indians used an even more primitive type of grater. It was made of wood and set with animal teeth, bones, stones, or spines, which might come from the *catizal* (*Ireartes ventricosa*), a species of the *papaxiuba* (*pashiuba*) palm. Charles Wagley and Eduardo Galvão, *The Tenetehara Indians of Brazil,* p. 40. For illustrations see Julian H. Steward, ed., *Handbook of South American Indians* (hereafter referred to as *HSAI*), vol. 3, plates 89 and 90.

10 · The manioc press was an elastic tube made of the fibers of the *jacitará* palm (*Desmonchus*), having a loop at each end. The Indian woman packed the grated manioc, which was in the form of a moist paste, into this tube, and hung it by one of the loops to a branch of a tree. She passed a pole through the other loop and into a hole in the tree trunk, sat down on the end of the pole, and used it as a lever, drawing out the tube to its full length by the pressure of her weight. This expressed the juice, which flowed into a bowl placed under the tube. Louis Agassiz and Elizabeth Cabot Agassiz, *A Journey in Brazil,* p. 176; Alfred Métraux, "The Tupinambá," in *HSAI,* 3:102, and see plate 90.

11 · The contorted structure of this sentence is typical of Brandônio's often formless style.

The pot, a conical earthen vessel, was set in a smoke hole, a fire started in the hole, and the contents of the pot stirred with a stick until dry. After the Portuguese came, the *farinha* oven was sometimes made of copper rather than of clay. Jorge W. Marcgrave, *História natural do Brasil*, p. 67.

12 · This coarse meal, or flour, could be stored for months and even years. Brandônio calls it war meal [*farinha de guerra*] because the Indians took it along for rations on military expeditions. The Tupi word is *uí-antã* (*uí* [flour] + *antã* [hard]). Milliet notes in his edition of Jean de Léry (*Viagem à terra do Brasil*, p. 113, n. 208) that *uí* was one of the first Tupi words encountered by Europeans, since it appeared in António Pigafetta's *Relazione del primo viaggio intorno al mondo* (1520) (Rome: Ministero della Pubblica Istruzione, 1894), p. 26. See Gabriel Soares de Sousa, *Notícia do Brasil* (1945), 1:325–326.

13 · Alentejo, "the granary of Portugal," is in the southeastern part of the country. Luiz Mendes de Vasconcellos speaks of "the wheat of Alentejo, the best we know of." *Diálogos do sítio de Lisboa* (1608), in *Antologia dos economistas portugueses*, p. 114.

14 · What Brandônio actually says is "after the tapioca has been removed." Obviously, he misspoke, for it is the water that is removed (by being thrown away), as Brandônio himself describes. The sediment, which is the tapioca, is left in the container. Even today in Brazil one can see tapioca made by hand in this way.

15 · The juice contains prussic acid. Soares de Sousa describes similarly the poisonous properties of manioc juice. "Neither men nor animals can resist this terrible poison," his editor notes. Soares de Sousa, *Notícia do Brasil* (1945), 1:320. Cf. Magalhães de Gandavo, *Sancta Cruz*, chap. 5, fol. 16.

16 · MS *macaxeira*. This is the term used in the North of Brazil for sweet manioc, which is known in the South and elsewhere as *aipim*.

17 · Despite Brandão's enthusiasm for Brazil and some twenty-five years of residence there, Portugal is still "our country."

18 · Manioc flour is as coarse in appearance as gunpowder, says Gabriel Dellon. It is "always heavy and almost insipid, and it causes obstructions in those who are unaccustomed to it. Little cakes are made out of this flour, which are called *Bejous*. These are more appetizing, but of no better quality." Soares de Sousa describes *beijus* as thin, dry, toasted wafers. He says that they were invented by Portuguese women and were not used by the Indians. Nevertheless, the word is Tupi-Guarani in origin: *mbe-jú* [rolled up]. Gabriel Dellon, *Nouvelle relation d'un voyage fait aux Indes Orientales*, p. 255; Plínio Ayrosa, "Glossário," in Marcgrave, *História natural*, p. xci, s.v. "beiu"; Soares de Sousa, *Notícia do Brasil* (1945), 1: 319 and n. 2.

19 · *Lacerta viridis*, a large lizard, common throughout western and southern Europe.

20 · The process of curing the manioc is described in detail by Soares de Sousa, *Notícia do Brasil* (1945), 1:325. Many other cured foods, especially meats and fish, were standard fare among the Indians, partly because they could be preserved in times of plenty to tide the people over periods of scarcity, and partly because they could be carried along on hunting and war-making expeditions. See Hans Staden, *Warhafftiger kurtzer bericht aller von mir erfarnen håndel und sitten der Tuppin Indas derer gefangner ich gewesen bin,* chap. 11; Luís da Camara Cascudo, *História da alimentação no Brasil,* pp. 88–89.

21 · Manioc flour or meal was made by pounding the *carimã* in a wooden mortar. To Brazilians of the manioc-growing regions, "flour" means manioc flour unless some qualification is added, e.g., "wheat flour." Alexander Marchant, *From Barter to Slavery: The Economic Relations of Portuguese and Indians in the Settlement of Brazil, 1500–1580,* p. 64, n. 50.

22 · The manioc flour was boiled in water, being stirred until all the lumps were dissolved; then other foods were added. Prado says this mush is "the aboriginal mingau." From ancient times the Brazilian Indians had mixed *carimã* with other foods, forming it into small balls called *bolotas*. The Portuguese women quickly imitated them and learned to combine *carimã* with egg yolks and milk to make bread, cakes, fruit-filled dainties, and many other delicacies. Soares de Sousa, *Notícia do Brasil* (1945), 1: 325–326; Marcgrave, *História natural,* p. 67; Maximilian Alexander von Wied-Neuwied, *Travels in Brazil, in the Years 1815, 1816, 1817, Part 1,* p. 66; J. F. de Almeida Prado, *A Bahia e as capitanias do centro do Brasil (1530–1626),* 3:203–204; Alfred Métraux, "The Guaraní," in *HSAI,* 3:102; Cascudo, *História da alimentação no Brasil,* pp. 107–111.

23 · The *alqueire* varied in volume from time to time and from place to place. Brandônio's (Brazilian) *alqueire* probably equaled about $3\frac{1}{5}$ pecks. See Charles R. Boxer, *The Golden Age of Brazil, 1695–1750,* p. 356.

24 · This is about one-sixteenth of the cost of a cow, according to Brandônio's figures on p. 265.

25 · Vicente do Salvador corroborates Brandônio's statement. Much rice grew in Brazil, he says, along with maize and potatoes. But this was not true rice (*Oryza sativa* L.). Rather, it was certain aquatic or semi-aquatic grasses, native to the Americas, which resemble rice in appearance and have been called by various names, such as "wild rice" and "Indian rice." Examples are *Luziola longivulvula* Doelle, which grows near Salvador, and *Streptochaeta spicata* Schrad., found in the mountains of Rio de Janeiro. The "wild rice" grew in lagoons and was harvested by the Indians working from canoes. In the eighteenth century the native rice, which was red, was replaced by white rice (Asiatic in origin), introduced from the Carolinas. Information furnished by Donald Simpson, formerly Assistant

Curator of Botany, Field Museum of Natural History, Chicago. Vicente do Salvador, *História do Brasil 1500–1627*, p. 73; Simonsen, *História econômica*, p. 371; Soares de Sousa, *Notícia do Brasil* (1945), 1:309 and n. 2; Mauro, *Portugal et Atlantique*, p. 371.

Prado casts some doubt on Brandônio's statement that rice held second place among the foodstuffs of Brazil, suggesting that Brandão as a Portuguese and a merchant may well have been misled by his knowledge of India and other Eastern lands where rice is the principal cereal. It is a fact that rice seldom occurs in the lists of Brazilian food crops given by the chroniclers or by naturalists writing about the period. Apparently, after some initial success rice was not much used as a food in Brazil during the colonial period but was replaced by manioc. J. F. de Almeida Prado, *Pernambuco e as capitanias do norte do Brasil (1530–1630)*, 3:206.

26 · The New World variety of corn or maize, *Zea mays*, was called *milho zaburro* by the Portuguese, probably because it was (wrongly) identified with the Old World *zaburro* [sorghum], which in its early stage of development it resembles. This is an example of the European practice of endowing plants and animals in new lands with names of familiar species which they were thought to resemble. Other instances of borrowed nomenclature in the *Dialogues* are Brandônio's use of *onça* [ounce] and *tigre* [tiger] for jaguar; see p. 278 and V, n. 189. See Edward F. Tuttle, "Borrowing Versus Semantic Shift: New World Nomenclature in European Languages," in Fredi Chiapelli, ed., *First Images of America: The Impact of the New World on the Old* (hereafter cited as *First Images*), 2: 597; Yakov Malkiel, "Changes in the European Languages Under a New Set of Sociolinguistic Circumstances," in *First Images*, 2:589– 590; and Bernard I. Cohen, "La découverte du Nouveau Monde et la transformation de l'idée de la nature," in Union Internationale d'Histoire et de Philosophie des Sciences, *La Science au seizième siècle* (Paris: Hermann, 1960), p. 195. Gerbi notes that Oviedo was possibly the first to point out the mistakes in naming animals and plants by writers in their desire to find similarities between the Old World and the New. As Buffon put it, "The names had confused the things." Antonello Gerbi, *The Dispute of the New World*, p. 28.

In Brazil maize was often referred to as Guinea corn [*milho de Guiné*]. Soares de Sousa used the latter term in 1587, noting that Guinea corn was given to the Guinea slaves to eat, but that they didn't like it, preferring a similar cereal of their own country. Soares de Sousa, *Notícia do Brasil* (1945), 1:331. Nowadays, the Portuguese word *zaburro* means both sorghum and a certain variety of maize.

27 · *Abati* in Tupi-Guarani means "small grain"; the word is used for both maize and rice. More commonly, rice is *abati-mirim*, "very small grain."

28 · On p. 213 Brandônio will tell how grapes are harvested two and three times a year.

29 · The Feast of Saints Peter and Paul, June 29 in the Catholic liturgical calendar.

30 · Fernão Cardim reports a similar problem with the soil: in Rio de Janeiro and Piratininga the settlers did not raise wheat because it required too much work, for the soil was so rank that the grain did not grow at a uniform rate. "One grain yields seventy or eighty heads," he explains, "and some are ripe while others are just starting, and it multiplies almost *ad infinitum.*" *Tratados da terra e gente do Brasil,* pp. 94–95, "Trigo."

31 · Presumably Brandônio's thoroughly confused account was intended to convey that he plowed up the wheat and replanted the field (rather than the grains of wheat). The word here translated "replanted" is used in the same sense on p. 197, where Brandônio tells how in India rice is replanted for the same purpose as Brandônio's wheat.

32 · About twenty years after Brandônio, the problem of soil too fertile for wheat growing was noted by Joan Nieuhof, a Dutchman who traveled in Brazil from 1640 to 1649 and chronicled events in the colony during the Dutch occupation. To counter this problem, Nieuhof says, sand was added to the soil instead of fertilizer. *Memorável viagem,* p. 296.

33 · *Massapê* is the black, clayey soil of the Brazilian northeast coastal region, ideal for growing sugar cane but not good for wheat.

34 · For centuries millet had been extensively grown in humid regions of Portugal. It existed in two varieties—*milho miúdo* and *milho painço.* A. H. de Oliveira Marques, *Daily Life in Portugal in the Late Middle Ages,* pp. 26–27.

35 · Also *caroatá, caraoatá, caroá, caravatá, garuatá, caraguatá,* etc. Brandônio uses this name—in various spellings—for almost any *Bromelia* or *Bromelia*-like plant. Perhaps he is thinking here of the bromeliad *macambira,* which produces a tuber that was scraped to make flour. *Diccionário histórico, geográphico e ethnográphico do Brasil,* 2:465, s.v. "gravatá."

36 · *Mani* [manioc] + *çoba* [leaf]. The manioc leaves were ground in a mortar and boiled for at least twenty-four hours, until they became sufficiently soft to be eaten. Today the leaves are cooked with fish and meat mixtures, such as *mocotó* [feet of calves and oxen], salt tongue, tripe, and pig's head. *Glossary of Brazilian-Amazonian Terms,* comp. Donald Farquhar, Helen Macmillan, and Bernard Siegel, quoted in James L. Taylor, *Portuguese-English Dictionary* (hereafter referred to as *Taylor*), s.v. "maniçoba"; Cunha, *Dicionário tupi,* s.v. "maniçoba."

37 · Also *maré, marí, marinheiro; Geoffroya superba* H. and B., or *G. spinosa.* Plant of the family of the Icacinaceae. The fruit is the size of a large pear and is of a yellowish-green color. It is inedible raw, but is eaten

cooked, accompanied by meat or fish, as a substitute for bread or flour. Martius noted that the seeds constitute a powerful vermifuge. Carlos [Karl] Friedrich Philipp von Martius, *Natureza, doenças, medicina e remédios dos índios brasileiros* (1844), p. 251; Marcgrave, *História natural*, p. 121, and p. xlii, item 287; Cunha, *Dicionário tupi*, s.v. "umari."

38 · *Aquê* may be Plínio Ayrosa's *aqué*, a species of palm tree; Ayrosa notes that the word does not appear in dictionaries. "Glossário," in Marcgrave, *História natural*, p. xci, s.v. "aque." Perhaps *aquê* or *aqué* was the "local name" for some variety of the palm *piçandó* (*Diplothemium maritimum* Mart. or *D. campestrex* Mart.) and its fruit; see below, n. 48.

39 · Also *macuna, mucunã, mucuná.* Any of a number of lianas, or climbing plants of the family Leguminosae. During prolonged droughts the inhabitants of Ceará frequently ate not only the roots, which are similar to manioc roots, but also the beanlike fruits of this liana. Some varieties have seeds that are poisonous, and the people believed that they could eliminate the poison from the fruit by thorough washing, but, according to Pirajá da Silva, the toxic effects of the plant sooner or later manifested themselves in a general swelling, pallor, irrational behavior, and finally total anemia and dropsy. The *macunã* fruits, dried and mashed, were also applied to wounds, for which they were considered a very effective remedy. Soares de Sousa, *Notícia do Brasil* (1945), 2:39 and n. 5. Cf. Adolfo Ducke, "Estudos botânicos no Ceará," *Anáis da Academia Brasileira de Ciências* 31 (June 30, 1959):279–280.

40 · The daisy (*bonina*) was a greatly admired flower; Geoffrey Chaucer had called it "the emperice and flour of floures alle" (Prologue, *Legend of Good Women,* line 185). Some varieties of daisy, however, were considered weeds. John Gerard, *The Herball or Generall Historie of Plantes* (1597), p. 512. But Brandônio often names pairs whose members overlap, and this stylistic habit may well explain his "flowers *and* daisies."

41 · Portuguese *fava* (*Phaseolus lunatus* L.). The Tupi is *comandá-guaçu* [big bean]. Early accounts of New World vegetation often noted that the American species of bean differed in shape and color from the European varieties and had a better taste. Nevertheless, they were similar enough to familiar Portuguese species for the Europeans to call them by the same names. F. C.Hoehne, *Botânica e agricultura no Brasil no século XVI*, p. 158; Jonathan D. Sauer, "Changing Perception and Exploitation of New World Plants in Europe, 1492–1800," in *First Images*, 2:832, n. 92.

42 · The common bean [Portuguese *feijão*], a designation embracing several varieties of *Phaseolus vulgaris* L. The Tupi is *comandaí* or *comandá-mirim*, "little bean." Hoehne, *Botânica*, p. 158. For both *fava* and *feijão* see further John William Purseglove, *Tropical Crops: Dicotyledons*, 1:296–301, 304–310.

43 · The pigeon pea (Angola pea, Congo pea, no-eye pea, etc.; *Cajanus indicus* Spreng.). The word *guandu* may be of Congolese origin. The pigeon pea is one of the oldest cultivated plants in the world, as is proved by its presence in ancient tombs; one of these, in Egypt, dates from the twelfth century B.C. Thought to be native to equatorial Africa, the pigeon pea is now naturalized in the West Indies, tropical America, and India. The shrub was cultivated from early times in Brazil. E. Lewis Sturtevant, *Sturtevant's Notes on Edible Plants,* ed. U. P. Hedrick (Albany, New York: J. B. Lyon Co., 1919), s.v. "*Cajanus indicus* Spreng."; *Enciclopédia brasileira Mérito* (hereafter cited as *Mérito*), s.v. "guandu."

44 · The dog caper or bottle cod (*Capparis cynophalophora* L.), a long, almost cylindrical bean. *Novo Michaelis dicionário ilustrado* (hereafter cited as *Novo Michaelis*); Aurélio Buarque de Holanda Ferreira, *Novo dicionário da língua portuguesa* (hereafter cited as *Aurélio*).

45 · MS *nachenim*. Three-spike goosegrass, parrot-foot grass, Persian grass (*Eleusine tristachya*). Rodolfo Garcia says the East Indian name for this cereal is *nanchni* or *nachini*. The grass is widely disseminated throughout the world and is cultivated on a large scale in Africa and Asia, both as food for human beings and as provender for horses and other animals. The Portuguese brought it to Brazil by way of Angola. *Taylor,* s.v. "capim"; Rodolfo Garcia, ed., *Diálogos das grandezas do Brasil,* IV, n. 6; Robert W. Schery, *Plants for Man,* p. 395.

46 · Perhaps *masa* is *massango* (*Pannisetum typhoideum*), a grain related to millet that was used in Africa for food and was brought to Brazil with the slaves. Cascudo, *História da alimentação no Brasil,* p. 116.

47 · *Arachis hypogaea* L. The Portuguese word *amendoim* is derived from the Tupi *mandubi* influenced by *amêndoa,* almond. The Brazilian peanut was transported to other continents, thriving especially well in Africa, where the natives preferred it to the African variety (*Voandzeia subterranea* Thouars). The Indians cultivated the peanut with strange rituals, celebrating the harvest, in May, with great rejoicing and festivals. Only the women were permitted to cultivate the plant, and it had to be harvested by the same women who had planted it; otherwise it was thought that the crop would spoil.

The Portuguese settlers were quick to make this native crop their own, and in Colonial Brazil the peanut was an important foodstuff. Soares de Sousa describes how the Portuguese women learned to substitute peanuts for almonds in their traditional sweetmeat recipes. *Notícia do Brasil* (1945), 1:335 and n. 1; Prado, *Pernambuco,* 3:202–203 and n. 40; *Aurélio,* s.v. "amendoim."

48 · Also *buri-do-campo, buri-da-praia,* and *ariri.* MS *passendo.* *Diplothemium campestre* Mart., a low wild palm bearing small yellow coconuts. The

fruits have a delicious pulp like that of hazelnuts, and are one of the few food resources for travelers in the backlands. Soares de Sousa, *Notícia do Brasil* (1945), 2:26 and n. 7; *Mérito*, s.v. "buri-da-praia"; Hoehne, *Botânica*, p. 248; *Aurélio*, s.v. "ariri."

49 · Also *tamatarana, tamotarana. Saranthe marcgravii* Pickel. It has a small, edible root about the size of a duck egg, which is cooked like a potato and has an excellent flavor. Marcgrave includes drawings of the plant with his description, *História natural*, pp. 53–54. Cunha, *Dicionário tupi*, s.v. "tamatarana"; Alexandre Rodrigues Ferreira, "Diário da viagem philosóphica pela Capitania de São-José do Rio Negro," *Revista do Instituto Histórico e Geográfico Brasileiro*, tomo 51 (1888):128. See also Cristóvão de Lisboa, *História dos animais e árvores do Maranhão*, fol. 112.

50 · *Taioba* and *taiá* are two names for the same species, *Colocasia antiquorum* Schott. In Tupi *taiá* = piquant and *oba* = leaf. The species exists in two varieties, the names *taioba* and *taiá* being used indiscriminately for both. Both varieties are valued as food, but one is used for its greens and the other for its roots. It is evidently the latter variety that Brandônio is describing here. Hoehne, *Botânica*, p. 209; Soares de Sousa, *Notícia do Brasil* (1945), 1:330 and n. 4.

51 · Also *geremu, gerumu, gerimu, jurumu.* MS *jeremu.* Squash (varieties of *Cucurbita moschata* Duchtr.). According to Pirajá da Silva, *jerimu* means "bottleneck." Soares de Sousa agrees with Brandônio that the squash described here is indigenous to Brazil. The natives boiled or roasted the squashes whole and served them cut up like melons, or cured them in smoke to preserve them for the entire year. Soares de Sousa, *Notícia do Brasil* (1945), 1:333–334 and n. 2; Hoehne, *Botânica*, p. 213. For the different varieties of squash found in Brazil, see Zacharias Wagener, *Zoobiblion: Livro de animais do Brasil,* comment by Bento José Pickel on item 47, p. 373.

52 · *Pacova* means "leaf that rolls up on itself." The term was used of a number of plants that fit this description.

53 · *Lagenaria vulgaris* Ser. The common calabash, as Brandônio implies, was primarily a container, used to store food, as a drinking vessel, or, if small, as a scoop. "These are their tableware," said Soares de Sousa. After smoke-curing the gourds, the Indians colored them black inside with the juice of the genipap and yellow outside with a dye made from the *tatajuba* tree, both of which Brandônio himself will mention on p. 209. See Soares de Sousa, *Notícia do Brasil* (1945), 1:334 and n. 3; Hoehne, *Botânica*, pp. 213–214.

54 · If Brandônio's *alqueire* equaled about $3^1/5$ pecks (see above, n. 23), the large calabashes held some two bushels of meal. Candolle says they sometimes weighed as much as 200 pounds. Alphonse de Candolle, *Origin*

of Cultivated Plants (New York: Appleton, 1902), p. 250, citing *Le Bon Jardinier* (1854), p. 180.

55 · MS *batata*, a name that technically applies to all tubers, including both white and sweet potatoes.

56 · Prado, in quoting this passage, silently changes *a Portugal* [to Portugal] to *de Portugal* [from Portugal], but this emendation seems without justification. *Pernambuco*, 3:234.

57 · That is, both *inhames* and *carás* are larger than the tubers he has just referred to. Both *inhames* and *carás* are varieties of yam, but Brandônio, like many Brazilians even today, thinks of these vegetables as belonging to a category distinct from the potato. *Cará*, the smaller of the two, includes various species of the genus *Dioscorea*, especially *D. heptaneura* Vell.; all these species may be indigenous to Brazil. The *inhame* (*Alocasia indica* Schott. and *A. macrorhiza* Schott.) was brought to Brazil from Cape Verde and São Tomé in the sixteenth century. Hoehne says that today the *inhame* is commonly confused with the *cará*, perhaps because the blacks, familiar with the *inhame* in Africa, applied the same name to the somewhat similar *cará* that they found in Brazil. Today, Brazilians prefer the *cará* for taste. Soares de Sousa, *História do Brasil* (1945), 1: 329; Cascudo, *História da alimentação no Brasil*, pp. 80–82; Hoehne, *Botânica*, pp. 187–188, 332; Garcia, ed., *Diálogos*, IV, n. 6.

58 · "Vile Mohammed" and "vile Mohammedan" were common epithets for the prophet and his followers, having something of the currency "damned Yankee" has enjoyed in some periods and some localities in the United States. See, e.g., Luís de Camões, *Os Lusíadas*, canto xcix.

59 · See pp. 203–204 and I, n. 78.

60 · The bee is indigenous to both the New World and the Old. "They all have their honey in hollow trees, and I have often dug it out with the savages," says Hans Staden, *Kurtzer bericht*, chap. 35.

61 · Brandão neglects to keep this promise. He does say that the Tapuias "subsist on honey . . . as well as on . . . game"(p. 325). He also mentions an animal, the *eiratê*, that he says lives exclusively on honey (p. 275).

62 · Also *pequeá, piqui, pequiá, pequi*. MS *piquia*. Several trees and fruits go by these names. The fruit referred to here is probably *Macoubea guianensis* Aubl. "No one has described this fruit better than Soares [de Sousa]," remarks F. C. Hoehne. Soares de Sousa says it is the size of a quince, full of a white, very sweet juice, which in summer is extremely refreshing. Cardim too noticed this fruit with its delicious pulp "like clear honey, as sweet as sugar." The fruit, a drupe, has a thick skin like that of an orange. It is valued as a food, especially by dwellers in the backlands, who depend on it heavily in the *piquiá* season, February to March. It is eaten boiled or baked, with salt and manioc flour. Both kernel and pulp

can be eaten raw, but the former is enclosed in an endocarp covered with bristles, which easily wound the mouth of the eater; no doubt this is why Brandônio says the fruit is eaten with a spoon. Hoehne, *Botânica,* pp. 231–232; Soares de Sousa, *Notícia do Brasil* (1945), 2:15 and n. 2; see also Cardim, *Tratados,* p. 53. There is a drawing of a *piquiá* (*pekia*) in Marcgrave, *História natural,* p. 293.

63 · No true pigs are indigenous to Brazil. Brandônio's wild pigs must have been peccaries. The domesticated pigs he refers to were imported from Portugal. "Butter made from hogs" is evidently lard [*banha*], still today an important cooking fat in Brazil.

64 · The wine is *cachaça* or *garapa;* the latter name is also given to other drinks, some fermented and others unfermented, made from honey or fruit juices. This "detestable mixture," as Nieuhof called it, is prepared from the scum that forms on the surface of the cane juice during the cooking process and before distillation, as a result of an accumulation of impurities. The drink is sweet when fresh but becomes sour after it has been allowed to ferment for a time. Pyrard de Laval said *garapa* was drunk only by slaves and Indians. A modern variety is still popular in sugar-producing areas such as the Northeast.

Wagener describes the role of *garapa* in the festivals of African slaves. On Sundays, which after an arduous week's work they might be given to use as they pleased, the blacks gathered in certain places and danced to fifes and drums. The dances were of African origin, and often held religious significance. They were carried on in a disorderly fashion, everyone joining in—men and women, children and old people, all fortifying themselves frequently with drafts of the sweet *garapa.* The revelers danced all day, until sometimes they could not recognize each other for the dust and filth that covered them.

Nieuhof, *Memorável viagem,* p. 304; François Pyrard de Laval, *Voyage de François de Pyrard, de Laval,* pt. 2, p. 336; Wagener, *Zoobiblion,* item 105, "Negertanz," pp. 223–224, and the ethnographic comment on this item by Egon Schaden, pp. 390–391; Alberto José de Sampaio, *A alimentação sertaneja e do interior da Amazônia,* p. 259, s.v. "garapa." Cf. André João Antonil [João António Andreoni], *Cultura e opulência do Brasil por suas drogas e minas,* p. 132, n. 41; p. 218; p. 253 and n. 20. Cf. also pp. 318–319 of the present work.

65 · The Kaffirs are a Bantu people. Linschoten defined their territory as including "Mosambique, and all the coast of Ethiopia, and within the land to the Cape de bona Speranza [Cape of Good Hope]." John [Jan] Huyghen van Linschoten, *The Voyage of John Huyghen van Linschoten to the East Indies,* 1:269–270.

On the coast of this area during the colonial period many Portuguese ships were wrecked en route to or from India. The survivors endured almost incredible hardships on their long trek through the Kaffir country to safety. See the contemporary accounts edited by Charles R. Boxer, *The Tragic History of the Sea, 1589–1622.* João dos Santos, a Dominican father, who traveled over parts of this area between 1586 and 1597, reported that the Portuguese in Kaffraria drank palm wine, though the Africans preferred wine made from grain. *Ethiópia Oriental e vária história de cousas notáveis do Oriente,* fol. 9ʳ.

66 · Also *abatupitá; jabutapitá* (*Gomphia parviflora* DC.). The oil extracted from the seeds has medicinal and culinary uses. Garcia, ed., *Diálogos,* IV, n. 8; Cunha, *Dicionário tupi,* s.v. "jabutapitá."

67 · Also *pacapiá; nhandiroba* (Bahia); *fava de São Ignácio falsa* [false St. Ignatius bean] (Minas Gerais); *jabotá* (Pará); *guapeva* (São Paulo). A species of *Fevillea,* probably *F. trilobata* L. According to Le Cointe, the oil and seeds are energetic purgatives. Paul Le Cointe, *Árvores e plantas úteis,* p. 329, s.v. "pacapiá."

68 · See p. 109, and II, n. 79.

69 · Vicente do Salvador similarly points to the Brazilians' failure to make full use of the coconut palm. In India, he says, many useful products were extracted from the tree. There is a solid basis for the criticism voiced by the two chroniclers, for in some regions of the world coconut palms supply almost all the necessaries of life: the nuts provide food and drink, the trunks wood for houses and furniture, the leaves materials for furniture and roof thatching, the shells utensils and ornaments, the sap and flower clusters wine. Vicente do Salvador, *História do Brasil,* p. 69; Dellon, *Nouvelle relation,* pp. 83–87. In fairness to the Brazilians, it should be noted that Brandônio himself mentions several ways in which palm trees were utilized in Brazil: for food (pp. 200, 208), for wine (p. 204), for roofing (p. 207, and see below, n. 80).

70 · See III, n. 123.

71 · Any one of various species of the palm trees *Bactris* and *Astrocaryum.* The leaf contains delicate green threads, which can be twisted into a very strong twine useful for fine fish nets, hammocks, textiles, cordage, and bowstrings. The Pareci tribe (recently extinct) in the southeast corner of Mato Grosso produced from tucuma fiber hammocks so light they could be worn as belts, yet strong enough to sustain the weight of two persons. The plant has never come into commercial use in Brazil. See Claude Lévi-Strauss, "The Use of Wild Plants in Tropical South America," in *HSAI,* 6:472; Wied-Neuwied, *Travels in Brasil,* pp. 238–239; Hoehne, *Botânica,* pp. 159, 307–308; *Aurélio,* s.v. "tucum."

72 · A strong fiber obtained from the common century plant (*Agave americana*) and other species of the genus *Agave,* and not, as Brandônio supposes,

from the tucuma, which has similar fibers. Pita fiber is used for cordage, brushes, rugs, sacking, and hats. Information supplied by the Field Museum of Natural History, Chicago.

73 · MS *caraoata*. For other spellings see above, n. 35. Whereas in Spanish America the agave was the principal source of fiber for ropes and textiles, the Indians of Brazil and Guiana used fibers taken mainly from the tucuma palm tree (see above, n. 71), but also from several Bromeliaceae, especially *B. fastuosa* and *B. serra*, both known as *gravatá*. From the leaves of these plants excellent cloth was made, comparable in quality to linen. Triangular corpuscles on the stalk produce white fibers that rival cotton, though they are less thin and strong than those made from palm fibers. These were used for fishing lines and sewing thread. Cardim, *Tratados*, pp. 67–78; Lévi-Strauss, "Use of Wild Plants," in *HSAI*, 6: 474; Marcgrave, *História natural*, pp. 87–88.

74 · Brandônio uses the Portuguese word for hemp, *cânhamo*, but true hemp is an Asiatic plant. Brandônio probably refers to the *Kenaf hibiscus* (*Hibiscus cannabinus* L.), whose fibers can be substituted for those of the true hemp. *Taylor*, s.v. "cânhamo"; *Aurélio*, s.v. "cânhamo" and "cânhamo-brasileiro."

75 · Also *mungubeira, monguba*. A silk-cotton tree, probably some species of the family Bombaceae belonging to any of several genera. The fibers are produced in the seed pods. The *munguba* is related to the several species, found in southeast and central Asia, from which kapok is derived. Donald R. Simpson, formerly Assistant Curator of Botany, Field Museum of Natural History, Chicago. See I, n. 2.

76 · Also *panha*. This Portuguese word comes from the Malay *pañni*. A synonym is kapok, another word of Malay origin. The material consists of the downy fibers that surround the seeds of various plants, especially those of the families Bombacaceae, Asclepiadaceae, and Tiliaceae. It is now extensively used in industry. *Aurélio*, s.v. "paina."

77 · Urganda was a fairy of folklore and romance, related to such figures as Mélusine, Morgan le Fay, Viviane, and Titania.

78 · The *cipó* and the *timbó* are lianas belonging to numerous botanical families. These vines are long and flexible, sometimes reaching 300 meters in length. Both are most commonly seen twined around trees. The *timbó* group includes thinner varieties of vines (*Serjania* and *Paullinia*), which can be twined or plaited. *Cipó* is derived by Pirajá da Silva from *icipó* = *ib* [tree] + *ci* [stick to] + *pó* [fiber]. *Timbó*, according to Martius, is from *ty* [juice] + *mobi* [bind]. On the other hand, *Aurélio* suggests for *timbó* "something white or gray," or "vapor or exhalation," the latter referring to the narcotic effect of the liana on fish: the *timbós* were crushed and thrown into streams to narcoticize or poison the fish so that they could be picked up by hand. Indians and some whites used them instead of

nails to fasten together the timbers of their houses, and also as materials for ropes and baskets. Carlos [Karl] Friedrich Philipp von Martius, *Beiträge zur Ethnographie und Sprachenkunde Amerika's zumal Brasiliens*, 1: 614; Soares de Sousa, *Notícia do Brasil* (1945), 2:81; Hoehne, *Botânica*, p. 305; *Aurélio*, s.v. "timbó"; Lévi-Strauss, "Use of Wild Plants," in *HSAI*, 6:475.

79 · *Imperata brasiliensis* [Trin.?], a grass much used for the purpose Brandônio mentions. *Aurélio*, s.v. "sapé."

80 · Tupi *pindá* [hook] + *oba* [leaf] = leaf with hooks; or *pindo* [palm tree] + *oba* [leaf]. The tree is in fact a palm; in Brandão's time several species of the genus *Attalea* could be designated by the name pindova.

The leaves used for roofs were taken from the "eye" of the tree. The eye is the young leaves, still curled up, growing at the central point from which rise all the branches of the tree. With these leaves the Indians covered the framework that formed the tops of their houses, thus obtaining an insulation that not only kept the inhabitants warm in winter and cool in summer, but also beautified the interior of the dwelling. Its use was risky, however, because of the many open fires that the Indians maintained inside their houses (see p. 311, and VI, n. 33). Unfortunately, only three or four leaves can be obtained from each tree for the purpose in question, and to do this an entire palm has to be destroyed; in this way thousands of these majestic trees have been lost. Hoehne, traveling in the North of Brazil in 1911 and 1912, found this method of insulation in use on the rivers Juruena and Tapajós. He says the leaves were passed rapidly through a flame and then woven into mats, which were attached to roof and walls. Houses covered with palm leaves are still in use in Brazil today. Soares de Sousa, *Notícia do Brasil* (1945), 2:25–26 and nn. 1 and 2; Hoehne, *Botânica*, p. 246.

81 · See I, n. 97.

82 · *Embira* is the name for various plants of the families of the Anonaceae and the Thymelaeaceae (especially the genus *Daphnopsis*). These plants produce a fiber, likewise called *embira*, that is suitable for caulking and cordage. Cunha, *Dicionário tupi*, s.v. "embira."

83 · Coir is a fiber obtained from husks of the coconut palm (*Cocos nucifera* L.). The husks are softened in water, and then the fibers are separated out either by hand or by machinery. For the use of coir in India in colonial times, especially for caulking, see Garcia d'Orta, *Colóquios dos simples e drogas da Índia* (1891–1895), 1:237, and n. 1, pp. 245–246. India is still a great producer of coir.

84 · Any of several species of *Lecythis*. The material used for caulking is the inner bark, which consists of many thin layers. Samuel J. Record and Robert W. Hess, *Timbers of the New World*, pp. 226–227.

85 · The MS reading is not clear. Garcia thinks this may be *taquarimbó*, a kind of bamboo (*Chusquea ramosissima*). Garcia, ed., *Diálogos*, IV, n. 8.

86 · MS *bengala*. No doubt the *Bambusa vulgaris* Schrad., a bamboo used for walking sticks, fences, lattices, and cages. Le Cointe, *Árvores e plantas úteis*, p. 454, s.v. "taquara."

87 · The palm heart, or palmito, consists of various tender parts of the palm, which are variously enumerated by different authorities. Perhaps the most satisfactory definition is that of Le Cointe: the terminal shoot stripped of the green leaves that surround it and reduced to the white central leaves. The palm Brandônio has in mind here is probably either *Euterpe oleracea* Mart. or *E. edulis* Mart., both of which are found in the Northeast. In order to extract the palmito, the tree must be cut down. Thus the practice was as destructive as that of using the "eye" of the palm tree for roof thatching (see above, n. 80). "He who eats a palmito eats a palm," said Garcia d'Orta. Some palmitos can be eaten raw, but usually they are roasted or boiled. They are a prime delicacy, very tender, with a flavor resembling that of chestnuts. As Lévi-Strauss noted, the palmito was one of the few vegetables in the native diet. There exists today in Brazil an industry devoted to their preparation and export. Cascudo, *História da alimentação no Brasil*, pp. 83–84; Le Cointe, *Árvores e plantas úteis*, p. 333, s.v. "palmeira açaí"; Lévi-Strauss, "Use of Wild Plants," in *HSAI*, 6:470; Theodor Peckolt, *Volksbenennungen der brasilianischen Pflanzen und Produkte derselben in brasilianischen (portugiesischen) und von der Tupisprache adoptirten Namen*, p. 176; Garcia d'Orta, *Colóquios dos simples e drogas e cousas medicinais da Índia* (1563; facsim. ed., 1963), fol. 67ᵛ.

88 · Brandônio uses the Portuguese word *viva*. Perhaps he is referring to Tupi *juquiri* (*Mimosa pudica* L.), of the family Leguminosae, division Papilionacea, which has a poisonous root. M. Pio Corrêa, *Flora do Brasil*, s.v. "juquery," p. 100. Vicente do Salvador describes the sensitive plant and its affiliates in almost the same words as Brandônio, except that he does not say the plant is poisonous. He concludes that this plant must have some occult quality, similar to the lodestone's ability to attract iron. *História do Brasil*, p. 72.

89 · See above, n. 6.

90 · It is impossible to identify with certainty the particular *embira* Brandônio had in mind. It may be *Xylopia frutescens*, which produces clusters of red berries that split open when ripe and are sometimes used for spice. Record and Hess, *Timbers*, p. 56, s.v. "Xylopia."

91 · Malaguetta has been known and used in Europe as a spice and medicament since the beginning of the thirteenth century. In 1486 João Afonso Taveiro explored the coast of Benin, in the delta of the Niger, and brought back

the first pepper that the Portuguese had obtained in Guinea. This consisted of *Afromomum melegueta* and *Afromomum granum-paradisi,* species that have at times been fused under the single name *Amomum granum-paradisi.* In Europe the fruit was known as Guinea pepper, grains of Paradise, Guinea grains, and red pepper. From the Pepper Coast, malaguetta was brought in the slave ships to Brazil, where it was put to the same uses as in Europe.

There also existed a native Brazilian pepper, *quiinha-apûã = quiinha* [pepper] + *apûã* [elongated]. This is *Capsicum conoides,* called by the Portuguese *malagueta da terra* [native pepper]. It is impossible to know whether Brandão in this passage had in mind African or Brazilian pepper, since the former became acclimatized so quickly in Brazil that he may well have assumed it was indigenous.

See Cascudo, *História da alimentação no Brasil,* pp. 126–127, 129; Soares de Sousa, *Notícia do Brasil* (1974), p. 457, note on "malagueta" by Frederico V. Edelweiss; Magalhães Godinho, *Descobrimentos,* 1:475–485.

92 · Brandônio could be referring to either the East or the West Indies, since both produced indigo. Since he has just been discussing the East Indian product, most likely that is what he has in mind here. See above, n. 7.

93 · Brandônio forgets that he has discussed two dyes already, in his preceding speech.

94 · See I, n. 48, and p. 150.

95 · *Urucu* is made from the thin skin that covers the seeds of the annatto (anatto, arnatto), *Bixa orellana* L., a shrub or small tree. The seeds are washed and mashed, and the pigment, which settles to the bottom of the container, is dried, mixed with animal or vegetable oil or gum, and formed into balls or cakes. The Indians colored their bodies and hair with the dye and also used it on cotton thread, implements, weapons, and ceramics. Even today *urucu* is sometimes used to dye rice a deep red. Record and Hess, *Timbers,* p. 89, s.v. *"Bixa";* Lévi-Strauss, "Use of Wild Plants," in *HSAI,* 6:477–478; Benjamin Hunnicutt, *Brazil, World Frontier* (New York: Greenwood Press, 1949), p. 142. Perhaps the purpose of dyeing rice red was originally to make it resemble the native rice, which was replaced in the eighteenth century by white rice from the Carolinas.

96 · Also *tatagiba, tataíba. Maclura xanthoxilon* End. According to Pirajá da Silva, *tatajuba* is *tatá* [fire] + *iba* [tree] = fire tree, because the wood was used to kindle fires by friction. The dye, which was made by boiling the wood, imparts a lively yellowish color. Soares de Sousa, *Notícia do Brasil* (1945), 2:67, n. 1; Marcgrave, *História natural,* p. 119.

97 · *Genipa americana* L. This plant is a close relative of the gardenia. Ac-

cording to Soares de Sousa, the color begins to fade after nine days. The Indians used genipap juice not only for dyeing gourds and painting the body, but also for tatooing and for drying up the pustules of yaws. Soares de Sousa, *Notícia do Brasil* (1945), 1:334 and n. 3, and 2:15–16 and n. 4; P. H. Dorsett, A. D. Shamel, and Wilson Popenoe, *The Navel Orange of Bahia, with Notes on Some Little-Known Brazilian Fruits*, p. 21; Métraux, "The Tupinambá," in *HSAI*, 3:111; Lévi-Strauss, "Use of Wild Plants," in *HSAI*, 6:478.

98 · Probably *Sickingia rubra* Mart., whose bark provides a red dye that was known to the Indians. The wood is used for fine carpentry. Record and Hess, *Timbers*, pp. 470–471, s.v. "Sickingia."

99 · *Tabatinga* is a pasty white clay found in river beds. Garcia, ed., *Diálogos*, IV, n. 11. The word comes from Tupi *taba* [clay] + *tinga* [white].

100 · Perhaps *catinga branca* (*Linharia tinctoria* Arruda, of the family of the Lauraceae), a forest tree found in Paraíba. Its wood is boiled to produce a beautiful yellow dye, which, however, is not fast. Henrique de Beaurepaire Rohan, "Chorographia da Província da Parahyba do Norte," *Revista do Instituto Histórico e Geográfico Paraibano* 3 (1911):226, s.v. "Laurineas?"

101 · The resin now known as South American copal is extracted from a number of trees, notably the *Hymenaea courbaril* L. (see III, n. 138), which may be the tree Brandônio has in mind. The tree is known in Brazil as *jatobá* or *jutahi*. There are several ways of gathering the pale yellow or reddish gum that exudes from the bark. Left to itself, it trickles to the ground, where it hardens into lumps that gradually become buried in the soil and are extracted by digging around the roots of the tree. Another method is to wound the bark and then dig the resin out of the tree; the material thus obtained is softer and less valuable. It is not clear which of the two ways of "digging out" the resin Brandônio refers to here. Copal was not exported from Brazil until 1669. It is now employed in the manufacture of varnish and, to a minor extent, for incense, for medicinal purposes, and as a cement for mending crockery. Record and Hess, *Timbers*, p. 281; Simonsen, *História econômica*, p. 373.

102 · Birdlime is any sticky substance that can be smeared on twigs so that birds landing on them or brushing against them will stick fast. The nitta tree bears pods that exude such gum. The Portuguese name for this tree, *visgueiro*, means sticky tree.

103 · Brandônio's garden combines the best of three worlds, for it brings together a variety of plants of Brazilian, Portuguese, and African origin. Garcia points out, however, that with respect to flowers Brandônio largely limits himself to Portuguese varieties. The only Brazilian flowers included are the *camará-açu*, the *maracujá*, and the *curuá*. Garcia, ed., *Diálogos*, IV, n. 14.

Brandônio's imaginary garden closely resembles contemporary descriptions of the gardens of Jesuit *colégios* in Salvador, Rio de Janeiro, and Olinda; cf. Serafim Leite, *História da Companhia de Jesus no Brasil*, 1: 54, 412–413, 455–456, and Cardim, *Tratados*, pp. 289–290. No doubt these as well as Brandônio's fictive garden were patterned after the gardens of Portugal. Brandão would have a quite recent memory of the latter, since he had returned to Portugal in 1597 for a sojourn of some ten years, and during this time he planned and set out a large garden at his home in Lisbon.

104 · Brandônio seems to agree with Alviano that there were no irrigated gardens in Brazil; he made a similar remark on p. 24. Yet his statements on this subject cannot be taken literally, for he must have known of the elaborate garden at the Jesuit *colégio* in Olinda, which as early as 1584 had arbors, a pomegranate orchard, a well, a fountain, and a reservoir; it is described by Cardim in the passage cited in n. 103 above; and see I, n. 133.

105 · Diogo de Campos Moreno mentions such a spring in Filipéia, which was considered effective against the stone. *Livro que dá razão do Estado do Brasil—1612*, p. 203.

106 · Also *nhambi*. According to Pirajá da Silva, this is *Eryngium foetidum* L., an herb with a leaf resembling coriander, which the Indians ate raw and also used as a seasoning. The Tupi name is derived from *ia* [herb] + *mbi* [edible]. The *inhambu* is still esteemed as an essential ingredient of many Bahian dishes. Soares de Sousa, *Notícia do Brasil* (1945), 2:30 and n. 6.

107 · For the *taioba* plant that has edible roots see above, n. 50.

108 · MS *tabaco*. The name tobacco comes from the West Indies; it means "pipe or tube for smoking." The Tupi word for tobacco is *petim* (*pitim, petum, betun*). The Indians twisted the tobacco leaves and enclosed them in a cigar-shaped tube more than a foot in length made of dry palm leaves, called a *petimbabo*. Through this device they "drank smoke." Tobacco played an important part in Indian ceremonial rites: before making important decisions, the council of warriors drank smoke to clarify their thinking. Certain magical powers were attributed to tobacco: see VI, n. 36. Tobacco use spread early from the Indians to the Portuguese in Brazil and eventually throughout Europe. Both Indians and Portuguese employed tobacco not only for pleasure but as a treatment for the *mal do bicho* and for other medicinal purposes. See pp. 106–107 and II, n. 66. Africans were passionately fond of tobacco and so it became an important medium of exchange in the African slave trade. Soares de Sousa, *Notícia do Brasil* (1945), 2:43 and n. 1; Mauro, *Portugal et Atlantique*, p. 371;

Cardim, *Tratados,* pp. 66–67, "Erva santa"; João Lúcio d'Azevedo, *Elementos para a história econômica de Portugal (séculos XII a XVII)*, p. 100.

109 · See pp. 210–211 and n. 104 above.

110 · Also *cambará-açu. Lantana camara* L. The Tupi word is *caa* [leaf] + *mbará* [painted] + *açu* [big]. The yellow and red flowers resemble carnations. Cardim praised their sweet smell, and noted that they were used to decorate altars. *Tratados,* p. 67, and p. 118, note.

111 · This name is applied to several species of the passionflower (*Passiflora*). The blossoms are shaped rather like small bells, violet at their extremities. They rise from a yellow base, in the middle of which is a pistil somewhat resembling a hammer and studded with three small buttons shaped like nails. It is these buttons that have given the flower its name, with its reference to the Crucifixion or Passion of Christ. Sérgio Buarque de Holanda notes that "after it is called to one's attention" one can see in the flower, in addition to the "nails," other objects associated with the Passion, such as scourges, a crown of thorns, and wounds. Sérgio Buarque de Holanda, *Visão do paraíso; os motivos edênicos no descobrimento e colonização do Brasil,* p. 260. There is an appreciative description of the passionflower, along with an excellent drawing, in Jean Baptiste Labat, *Nouveau voyage aux isles de l'Amérique,* 1:359–360 and illustration after p. 380.

112 · Also *cruá, curubá, crauá, croá.* The casabanana (*Sicana odorifera*). It is used not only as an ornamental plant but also as a popular medication. *Taylor* and *Aurélio,* s.v. "cruá."

113 · The four plants listed by Brandônio all belong to *Passiflora,* but naturalists disagree as to what species each plant represents. *Maracujá peroba* is probably *Passiflora edulis* Sims, a small yellow fruit with a sweet smell and an acid flavor. It is used to prepare ices and other delicacies. *Maracujá mexeira* may be Beaurepaire Rohan's *Passiflora moxilla,* "very sour and used for lemonades." Le Cointe, *Árvores e plantas úteis,* p. 289; Beaurepaire Rohan, "Chorographia," p. 217.

114 · The settlers were hardly so much to blame as Brandônio says: it was ants that in many regions of Brazil made it almost impossible to raise grapes, as Brandônio himself implies just below (pp. 213–214).

The chroniclers agree that ants were the greatest plague known to Brazilians. "There are so many ants here that the Portuguese call them 'the king of Brazil'; they devastate all the crops with incredible speed," said Marcgrave, *História natural,* p. 252. Cf. Soares de Sousa, *Notícia do Brasil* (1945), 1:305, and Joseph [José] de Anchieta, *Cartas, informações, fragmentos históricos e sermões* (1554–1594), p. 122. If it had not been for these pests, Pernambuco's topography and climate would have made it a highly favorable region for grape growing. To this day the farmers of the Northeast are deterred from the cultivation of grapes by this same problem. Prado, *Pernambuco*, 4:37–38; Beaurepaire Rohan, "Chorographia," p. 236, s.v. "Ampolideas." Today grapes for wine are grown successfully in plateau regions of the South, principally in Rio Grande do Sul and Minas Gerais.

115 · Cf. p. 34. Brandônio's praise of the Copaoba region was echoed by Elias Herckmans, a poet and adventurer who traveled through the Copaoba Mountains in 1641 and described the agricultural possibilities of the area. "The air is healthful and very temperate; at night it is colder there than in the lower regions of Brazil, a fact which is certainly due to its height. . . . [These lands] are suitable for sugar cane and other crops as well as for cereals, wine grapes, and various European products, since the said lands are not so subject to ants as the other parts of Brazil. They are watered by various rivers of fresh water." Elias Herckmans, "Descrição geral da Capitania da Paraíba," *Revista do Instituto Arqueológico, Histórico, e Geográfico Pernambucano* 5 (Oct. 1886):265–266, cited by Garcia, ed., *Diálogos*, 1, nn. 18 and 19.

116 · MS *terra fresca*, a designation used in the Northeast for regions of moist soil, usually beside rivers or streams, or at the foot of hills where there is plenty of water. Bernardino José de Souza, *Dicionário da terra e da gente do Brasil*, p. 314.

117 · See above, n. 114.

118 · Literally "thorny trees," formerly the name for citrus trees. Campos Moreno, *Livro que dá razão*, p. 132, n. 6.

119 · Sweet oranges were introduced into Portugal from India early in the sixteenth century. The Portuguese already knew the bitter orange, which was used like a lemon. Donald Frederick Lach, *Asia in the Making of Europe*, 2:12, n. 33, citing Georges Gallesio, *Traité du citrus* (Pisa, 1917), 2:297; and Marques, *Daily Life in Portugal*, p. 25.

120 · The manuscript has the Portuguese *zamboa* (var. *azamboa*). According to Pirajá da Silva, this is the *Citrus medica verrucosa* Brotero, a yellow citrus fruit similar in appearance to an orange but much larger. Unlike Brandônio, Pirajá da Silva considered it insipid. Soares de Sousa, *Notícia do Brasil* (1945), 1:307, n. 6.

121 · *Citrus lumia* Willd., of Asiatic origin, not the fruit now called French lime, which is *C. bigaradia* Risso. Loc. cit.

122 · Brandônio's "modern" grapefruit has been superseded by still more recent varieties, which were introduced into Brazil in the twentieth century.

123 · A tough-skinned fig native to the province of Algarve, in southern Portugal. Pero de Magalhães de Gandavo, *Treatise on the Land of Brazil*, in his *Histories of Brazil*, 2:164 and n. 114.

124 · The glistening crimson seeds.

125 · Bananas originated in southeast Asia, were transported from there to

Africa about the beginning of the Christian era, and later came to Europe. They reached the Americas in 1516 and quickly became so well established that early travelers in those continents thought the banana was an indigenous American plant. Soares de Sousa reported that in India bananas were called figs, a statement confirmed by Brandônio's remarks here. The Tupis called the fruit *pacova* [leaf that rolls up], a term they also applied to other plants with leaves that turn in on themselves. Charles B. Heiser, Jr., *Seed to Civilization: The Story of Man's Food*, pp. 158–159; Soares de Sousa, *Notícia do Brasil* (1945), 2:5–6 and n. 1.

126 · In 1656 John Parkinson described the "melocotone peach" as "a yellow fair Peach, but differing from [other yellow peaches] in that this hath a small crooked end or point for the most part, it is ripe before them, and better relished than any of them." John Parkinson, *Paradisi in Sole: Paradisus Terrestris*, p. 580. In modern usage *melocotão* (*maracotão*) is a peach produced by grafting a certain variety of peach onto a quince. Antônio de Moraes e Silva, *Diccionário da língua portugueza*, s.v. "maracotão."

127 · *Tamarindus indica* L. Burkill regards this tree as a native of Africa south of the Sahara and also of the parts of India towards Africa. It is cultivated through India and Burma for the acid pulp of the pod, which is a laxative and also makes a cooling drink in fever. Isaac H. Burkill, *A Dictionary of the Economic Products of the Malay Peninsula*, s.v. "*Tamarindus*"; Henry Yule and A. C. Burnell, *Hobson-Jobson: A Glossary of Colloquial Anglo-Indian Words and Phrases*, s.v. "tamarind."

128 · Tupi *ananás*. The history of the pineapple (*Ananas comosus* Lindl.) is uncertain. Mexico and Panama, as well as South America, have been suggested as its place of origin. The genus name comes from the Tupi *nanã* [to smell]. The resemblance to a pine cone noted by Brandônio resides in the pineapple's shape and its rugose surface. Soares de Sousa, *Notícia do Brasil* (1945), 2:33, n. 1; Yule and Burnell, *Hobson-Jobson*, s.v. "ananas"; Heiser, *Seed to Civilization*, p. 8.

129 · This is *Couepia rufa* Ducke. Vicente do Salvador called it *giitis coroe*, the word *coroe* [ugly] referring to the rough and knotty appearance of the fruit. It has a delicious smell and taste. *História do Brasil*, p. 69; Hoehne, *Botânica*, pp. 316–317.

130 · Any Brazilian species of the genus *Anona*. Sugar apple, custard apple, sweetsop, soursop, bullock's heart are among the many picturesque names given by English-speaking peoples to these species, all native to tropical and subtropical America. Some species are the size of a pine cone; others weigh as much as two kilograms. The skin is incised with a smooth, delicate pattern; the pulp is firm, white, and juicy, with a sweet smell and a slightly sharp taste. Soares de Sousa, *Notícia do Brasil* (1945), 2:

17 and n. 13; *Aurélio*, s.v. "araticum"; Record and Hess, *Timbers*, p. 53, s.v. "*Anona.*"

131 · MS *jaca*. The jackfruit (*Artocarpus heterophylla* Lam.) is closely allied to the breadfruit. The name is from the Malaysian *chakka*. The fruit was brought to Brazil from the Orient in the colonial period and is very common there today. The seeds are eaten roasted; the fruit too is eaten, though some find it insipid. *Taylor*, s.v. "jaca"; *The American Heritage Dictionary of the English Langauge* (1969).

132 · Beaurepaire Rohan identifies the *araticu-apê* (*apê* = peeling) as *Anona pisonis* M. Less complimentary than Brandônio, he says the flavor is only passable, but would be excellent if the fruit were cultivated. Beaurepaire Rohan, "Chorographia," p. 216, s.v. "Anonaceas"; Cunha, *Dicionário tupi*, s.v. "apé."

133 · *Hancornia especiosa* Gom. "One of the noblest fruits of this America," Father António do Rosário called the *mangaba*. The name comes from Tupi *mangá-ibá*, "sticky tree," the epithet referring to the plant's latex, from which rubber is extracted. The Tupi also called the fruit *temiú-catu*, "good eating." António do Rosário, *Frutas do Brasil numa nova, e ascética monarchia*, p. 132; Soares de Sousa, *Notícia do Brasil* (1945), 2:11 and n. 1.

134 · See pp. 203, 204, 210, and 319.

135 · For a somewhat less mystifying description of the cashew fruit and nut, see Soares de Sousa, *Notícia do Brasil* (1945), 1:343–344 and n. 1; cf. Hoehne, *Botânica*, p. 220.

136 · On p. 203.

137 · Also *jamaracaú, mandacaru, janamacará*. The name is applied to a number of species of the genus *Cereus*, a cardoon. In the manuscript there is written between the lines above this word, in a different hand, *Jamandacarus naçẽ na praia* [*Jamandacarus* grow on the beach]. The unknown annotator was right, for the plant grows in dry (and even in rocky) terrain. *Mérito*, s.v. "mandacaru"; Garcia, ed., *Diálogos*, IV, n. 15; Simão de Vasconcellos, *Notícias antecedentes, curiosas, e necessárias das cousas do Brasil*, in *Chrônica da Companhia de Jesu do Estado do Brasil*, 1:cxxx–cxxxi; *Aurélio*, s.v. "jamacaru."

138 · A myrtle berry, *Eugenia luschnathiana* Berg. The fruit is golden yellow and pleasantly but sharply acid, and has a spicy fragrance. Dorsett, Shamel, and Popenoe, *Navel Orange*, pp. 20–21.

139 · Probably Soares de Sousa's *maçarandiba* (*Mimusops elata* Alemão), a thick-skinned fruit that resembles a strawberry and has two pits. The meat is sweet and delicious, but the juice is extremely sticky. *Notícia do Brasil* (1945), 2:18 and n. 20. For the wood of the *maçaranduba* tree see III, n. 141.

140 · Also *gabiroba, guabiraba. Campomanesia fenzliana caerulea* Berg. The name *guabiroba* is also applied to several other fruits of the same genus. Garcia, ed., *Diálogos,* IV, n. 15. See also Dorsett, Shamel, and Popenoe, *Navel Orange,* pp. 29–30.

141 · Also *guti, güti, utim, uiti.* MS *goti. Moquilea salzmanii* Hook. fil. This fruit is similar in appearance to a pear and grows on a tall tree. It is delicious sliced and dipped in wine, and it makes excellent marmalade. Soares de Sousa, *Notícia do Brasil* (1945), 2:16 and n. 5.

142 · Also *caroatá, caraoatá, caroá, caravatá, garuatá, caraguatá,* etc. MS *garuata.* A Bromelia closely related to the pineapple, perhaps *B. karatás.* Though the taste is delicious as Brandônio says, the skin of the raw fruit blisters the lips. Cardim asserted that if a pregnant woman eats it she is likely to die immediately. The fruit is still not cultivated in Brazil, but occurs wild and is gathered and brought to market by the Indians. The name *gravatá* is commonly applied in Brazil to a number of other bromeliaceous plants as well as to this one. Brandônio has mentioned one variety that produces edible roots (see above, n. 35), and another that supplies fibers for ropes and textiles (see above, n. 73). Cardim, *Tratados,* p. 67; Dorsett, Shamel, and Popenoe, *Navel Orange,* pp. 21–22.

143 · Almost any species of the Brazilian genus *Lecythis.* The fruits, locally known as paradise nuts or creamnuts, are large, dark brown balls having a circular opening with a lid that eventually falls away and releases the seeds. These are about the size of brazilnuts and have a smooth, somewhat wrinkled brown shell and a delicious, creamy kernel. The nuts are not much exported because there is such great local demand for them and because they are hard to collect, the bulk being eaten by monkeys and other forest animals. Record and Hess, *Timbers,* p. 226, s.v. *"Lecythis."* For the bark, see above, n. 84; for the wood, see above, p. 160.

144 · A myrtle berry, *Eugenia uvalha.* The Tupi name is *iba* [fruit] + *ya* [sour]. The fruits are yellow and of the size and shape of a small pear. *Aurélio,* s.v. "uvaia."

145 · Trees or shrubs of the genus *Ingá* (family Leguminosae) are widely distributed over tropical America. In Paraíba, Beaurepaire Rohan heard of the *ingá cabeludo* [hairy *ingá*] and the *ingá tripa* [tripe *ingá*]. The fruit, which is enclosed in a pod, is similar to that of the carob tree of Europe. Beaurepaire Rohan, "Chorographia," p. 219, s.v. "Leguminosas"; Soares de Sousa, *Notícia do Brasil* (1945), 2:11 and n. 2.

146 · Also *mocugê, mucugê;* MS *maquije. Couma rigida* Muell. Arg. Soares de Sousa says this fruit is eaten like a fig and is so delicate that "it is not surpassed by any fruit of Spain or anywhere else; and it has a very good smell." *Notícia do Brasil* (1945), 2:15 and n. 3.

147 · Also *joambo, jambool* (E. Ind.). Rose apple, plum rose (*Eugenia jambos* L.).

Indigenous to India and Malaya, the jambul tree is widely cultivated as a shade and fruit tree throughout tropical America. Dorothy and Bob Hargreaves, *Tropical Trees Found in the Caribbean, South America, Central America, Mexico*, p. 58.

Pyrard de Laval, who saw the tree (he called it *ambou*) in the Maldives, said it resembles a medlar. He reported that the fruit, which is similar to a white plum as Brandônio says, is sweet and well flavored. He added that the stone too has a good taste, but if even a little of it is eaten, it disorders the senses, and too much of it causes a strange sickness that leads to death. Pyrard de Laval, *Traité et description des animaux, arbres, et fruicts des Indes Orientaux observez par l'autheur*, in *Voyage*, pt. 2, p. 392.

148 · Possibly Soares de Sousa's *pati* (*Cocos botriophora* Mart.), a wild palm. Soares de Sousa describes its small palmitos and its cocos "the size of nuts," with edible pulp. *Notícias do Brasil* (1945), 2:26 and n. 5.

149 · A name applied to several varieties of senna, but most commonly to *Cassia fistula* L., which was brought to Brazil from Asia and Africa. Other names for the plant are drumstick tree, goldenshower senna, and purging cassia. There are also native varieties of cassia in Brazil. Vasconcellos reported that in the São Francisco River region the pods, or canes, of the canafistula were so large that a single one provided enough pulp for a vigorous purge. Alviano, the businessman, quickly sees the plant's potential as an article of commerce: it is certainly the purging function of the canafistula that he has in mind when he recommends that it be exported to Portugal. *Taylor;* Soares de Sousa, *Notícia do Brasil* (1945), 2:38 and n. 3; Vasconcellos, *Notícias*, 1:xlvii–xlviii; Pietro Martire d'Anghiera, *Décadas del Nuevo Mundo*, 2:611.

150 · On p. 204, and see above, n. 62.

151 · A myrtle berry, *Myrciaria plicato-costata* Berg. The *cambucá* is quite similar to the grapelike fruit of the *jabuticaba*, the best known of the fruit-bearing species of *Myrciaria* but unknown to Brandônio because it is a native of southern Brazil. The *cambucá*, which is produced directly upon the trunk of the tree, is of an orange yellow. It has a large pit and only a small amount of pulp, but this has a delicious, slightly tart flavor. Soares de Sousa, *Notícia do Brasil* (1945), 2:18 and n. 22; Dorsett, Shamel, and Popenoe, *Navel Orange*, p. 30; Record and Hess, *Timbers*, s.v. "Myrciaria," p. 408.

152 · Not identified. The Tupi means simply small fruit.

153 · Perhaps Brandônio is thinking of the *uchi* (*uxi, uaxua, uxipuçu*) (*Saccoglottis uchi* J. Hubl.), an ovoid fruit that has a delicious flavor and aroma but contains scanty meat surrounding a large seed. It yields an oil that is good for cooking. The wood of the tree is used for construction purposes.

Manoel Pio Corrêa, *Flora do Brasil,* p. 70; Peckolt, *Volksbenennungen,* s.v. "uchi."

154 · MS *ubacropari. Rheedia brasiliensis* Planch. and Triana. This fruit, which grows on a beautiful pyramidal tree that is found near the sea, is about the size of an apricot and is thick skinned like an orange, with a white pulp that has a delicious, slightly acid flavor. It is highly esteemed, especially for sweets and jams. Dorsett, Shamel, and Popenoe, *Navel Orange,* pp. 30–31.

155 · Also *grumixama. Eugenia dombeyi* (Spreng.) Skeels or *E. brasiliensis* Lam. A deep crimson fruit, crowned at the apex by green sepals. It is related to the pitomba and is sometimes called "the cherry of Brazil." The pulp has a mild, pleasant taste. The *comixá* is most common in the south of Brazil. Garcia, ed., *Diálogos,* IV, n. 15; Dorsett, Shamel, and Popenoe, *Navel Orange,* pp. 19–20, s.v. "grumixama."

156 · Not identified.

157 · See p. 215, and above, n. 120.

158 · Also *umbu, imbu. Spondias tuberosa.* When ripe, this fruit makes delicious eating. The tree has great tuberous roots from which people traveling through the backlands obtain drinking water; hence its name, which means "tree that gives to drink." Soares de Sousa, *Notícia do Brasil* (1945), 2:13, n. 1.

159 · Also *guapuronga, guapuranga.* MS *ubaperungua. Marliera tomentosa* Camb., a well-known fruit resembling a cherry. Garcia, ed., *Diálogos,* IV, n. 15; Record and Hess, *Timbers,* p. 407, s.v. "Marlierea."

160 · Brandônio has just referred to a *piquiá* he had described earlier (p. 204); see above, n. 62. The present passage might well apply to the same fruit. He spells the word variously *piquea, piqueâ, piquia, piquiâ.* Not only are the spellings of this word legion, but the name is applied to a number of different fruits. It is impossible, therefore, to be certain whether Brandônio is repeating himself here or whether he is thinking of an altogether different fruit.

161 · The Brazil cherry (*Eugenia uniflora*), or any related fruit. *Taylor. Pitanga* means "red" in Tupi.

162 · *Maclura xanthoxilon* End. This fruit has an excellent, tart flavor and is eaten plain or mixed with sugar and wine. Marcgrave, *História natural,* p. 119 and n. 283; Soares de Sousa, *Notícia do Brasil* (1945), 2:67 and n. 1. The wood of the tree is used to produce a yellow dye; see p. 209, and above, n. 96.

163 · Perhaps an inversion of Tupi *cambuí (Eugenia vellosiana).* This plant has a small yellow fruit of a delicious tart taste. Soares de Sousa, *Notícia do Brasil* (1945), 2:16 and n. 10.

164 · Also *mureci, mborici.* MS *morosi.* The common name of several shrubs and

trees and their fruits belonging to the Malpighia family. Brandônio is probably referring to the cowhage cherry (*Byrsonima verbascifolia* Rich.), which grows on a small tree near the sea. The fruit is yellow, is smaller than a cherry, and has a sweet smell and a delicious flavor recalling that of the sharp cheese of Alentejo, says Soares de Sousa, *Notícia do Brasil* (1945), 2:18 and n. 18. *Appleton* says the name *murici* is also used for the Barbadoes cherry and the Surinam cherry.

165 · All eggplants belong to the same species, *Solanum melongona* L. A number of varieties of eggplant have fruit that is long and narrow—that is, pod shaped.

166 · MS *arasa*. See II, n. 80.

167 · MS *arasa-açu*. *Psidium variabile* Berg. One of the best-liked fruits in South America, having a delicious, tart flavor. The tree, which grows near the salt marshes close to the sea, bears a fruit resembling a loquat. Hoehne, *Botânica*, pp. 237–238; Soares de Sousa, *Notícia do Brasil* (1945), 2:17 and n. 12.

168 · Alviano capitulates—though not finally—to the arguments of Brandônio in favor of Brazil.

169 · Evidently trees were planted to produce sound effects in Portuguese and Brazilian gardens.

Dialogue V

In Which Are Discussed

the Fowls, Fishes, and Land Animals

This dialogue treats of the sixth and last of the sources of wealth Brandônio listed in Dialogue III (p. 131). Though he had defined this source as cattle raising, he extends his discussion to include many other Brazilian animals both domestic and wild.

Brandônio tries to organize the creatures on the basis of the four elements, but quickly realizes that this grouping breaks down with respect to fire. Exploring the other three elements, he describes in turn fowls, fishes, and animals. Like many another observer, he confesses that he is almost overwhelmed by the vast number of animal species that exist in Brazil. Though many of his descriptions are too general to be of great use, there is a considerable residue of information that has practical or scientific value.

This dialogue contains several of the most entertaining of Brandônio's anecdotes.

BRANDÔNIO   I do not want you to thank me for taking up my post earlier than usual; for I wished in this way to exercise my will power, which is as valiant a deed as David's vanquishing the giant.

ALVIANO   And what caused you to make that effort?

BRANDÔNIO   I was alarmed at how shameful it would be not to keep my word, which I had given you, to tell you all the great things of Brazil. I supposed that I had leaped the greatest hurdle when I discussed the abundance of plants and how the settlers of this land were growing rich from them;[1] and I racked my brain to see what else I should tell you. I found that my leap had not taken me far and that I still had ahead of me—as far as the eye could see—the highest and most difficult hurdles, which are those that are at hand today for me to discuss. For there pass before my mind's eye so many fowls of different varieties and types, so many unfamiliar fishes, differing in both their nature and their form and unknown to the world, so many wild beasts of strange appearance and habits, that it would require huge volumes if one were to describe all of them. Those things were making dreadful faces at me, trying to get me to go back on my promise. Yet, seeing that I could not do so without getting a bad reputation, I ventured to press forward with the discussion of the things contained in the elements[2] that envelop the land of Brazil, without, however, considering fire—the loftiest element of all—for I hold it to be absolutely sterile, and the salamander,[3] which they say is engendered by it, to be a thing of fable; surely, if there were salamanders, they ought to be found in the furnaces of Brazil's sugar mills, which always have their fires burning. And since fire's closest consort is air, I would like to begin there with what I have in mind, which will be to discuss the fowls, both domestic and wild, that are found throughout this region.

The domestic fowls are innumerable chickens,[4] some of which are larger than the ordinary ones; many good turkeys,[5] which are raised easily, since the climate is fine for breeding them; and pigeons, ducks, and mallards, which are excellent eating. These are the fowls that are raised at home in this Brazil, and they lay a great multitude of eggs.

ALVIANO   Well, in what part of the world could be found more kinds of domestic fowl than those you have named? At least I never saw more in Spain, though many different kinds of wild fowl are found there, and much prized they are.

BRANDÔNIO   With respect to wild fowls, this whole province far surpasses Spain. If you will give me your attention, and if I can recall their names and characteristics, you will be amazed; though, however much I may tell you, I shall always be stopping short.[6]

ALVIANO   I give you my word not to occupy my thoughts in anything else than listening to you.

BRANDÔNIO   Besides the domestic fowls that I have mentioned, in the woods and fields are found a great many *jacus*,[7] which are like forest hens and are considered just as good, for they are nice and plump. Another fowl of the same type is called *araquã*,[8] and is no less esteemed. Another, the *mutum*,[9] is the size of a large turkey and is no less prized. The jabiru stork,[10] which is much larger than a peacock, is so big that it will feed a company of half a dozen, even if they are starving; and it is a most savory meat. Another fowl that is not unworthy of its good reputation is the *uru*.[11] The *juhuapupe*[12] is similar to the partridge of our Spain, and I don't think I'm going too far if I say that the former is superior. The *inhambu*[13] also resembles the partridge and is of the same size. No larger than a quail is the *nambu*, which in goodness, taste, and flavor is no whit inferior to the pheasant of Europe that is so much appreciated. There is no counting the doves, which are rather fat and are easy to catch; and likewise quails and wood pigeons. All these wild birds are caught with very little effort, and thus they end up, just like the domestic fowl, serving the inhabitants of the land.

ALVIANO   And how do you hunt them?

BRANDÔNIO   They are caught with snares and traps, and also with muskets and arrows, for hunting birds are not used in this Brazil as they are in Portugal, since the men don't want to take the trouble.

There are also found in the fields some birds called anis.[14] These birds are very strange, for, besides the fact that their song resembles weeping, they don't have any blood at all, nor have they ever been found to have any. They are of a dismal black color.

ALVIANO   Such a bird is new to me, for I never heard tell of any other that was totally without blood.

BRANDÔNIO   Well, that's the way it is, for these birds don't have any. Some other birds found up-country are the jandaya parakeets.[15] At the time that the new crops are harvested, especially the various kinds of grain, they come down to the seacoast to feed on them. They are so persistent in this that it is hard work to drive them off, for loud shouts and beating on basins and killing them with sticks won't drive them away from the corn fields. As a matter of fact, I have sometimes seen even men attacked by them.

ALVIANO   The harpies[16] must have been like that.

BRANDÔNIO   If the jandayas had such faces as the poets describe, I would not doubt that they were the very same. There is another bird, called *sabiá*,[17] which looks like the ouzel[18] of Spain, and I think it really is the same, for it sings just like it, not differing by more than a single note. There are also nightingales, though they are not so musical as those in our country, for they lack that sweet quavering trill that they have in Portugal.[19] Indeed, all the birds of Brazil are inferior songsters.[20] The *cujujuba*[21] is a little bird with a hooked beak. When it realizes that it has been caught, it voluntarily closes its anus and voids no more through it, and so it dies.

ALVIANO   It might also die from not eating, for it probably refuses food because it takes its captivity so hard.

BRANDÔNIO   It appears, rather, to choose that way to die, for we know that it does not actually refuse to eat. The *macugagá*[22] got its name from the loud cry that it repeats many times. The toucan[23] is a most beautiful bird with feathers of different colors, contemplation of which delights the eye. The *canindé*[24] is a bird which, though small in body, has a very long tail; *apecu*[25] is a bird that has four spurs like those of a cock; *guarainhete*[26] is a bird with black and yellow feathers; *garateuma*[27] is a yellow bird that is very beautiful; *anacãs* look like parrots but are not of the same species.[28] Another bird, whose local name is *guarainghaetá,*[29] has a curious nature, which I wish to pass over in silence because it would take too long to describe it.

ALVIANO   Oh, but I would rather have you tell me everything you know about it.

BRANDÔNIO   This bird has such great love for its offspring that, to keep them from being stolen, it ordinarily makes its nest near a colony of bees. The bees serve as guardians, so to speak, for the young birds. Since every creature is afraid to get close to the bees because of their sharp sting, the young birds are free from danger. Such love does this bird have for its young that, to get food for them, it goes and throws itself among certain insects, which cling to its flesh. It doesn't dread the bites of the insects, but finds pleasant the pains they cause, which are payment for the assured nourishment obtained in this way for the young birds. The parent feeds the insects to them when they are hungry, and it's only for this reason that the insects are kept so handy. And these birds are feathered in various colors.

ALVIANO   No more is written even of the pelicans[30] to eulogize the love they have for their young.

BRANDÔNIO   There are some other birds, too, which we call woodpeckers, because they give blows with their beaks on the trunks of trees, and such hard blows that anyone hearing them, and not knowing about this type of bird, would certainly think it was an axe chopping wood. Another bird, called *tamatião-açu,*[31] is often found in the fields of this land. It has most beautiful feathers, and always flies very high, uttering cries that seem almost human. And likewise there is another, which is not inferior to it in the beauty of its plumage, called *curicaca.*[32]

They give the name *araçari*[33] to a little bird which, though it is no bigger than an egg, has a bill more than half a span long. Another bird, called *biguá,*[34] is similar to a duck. *Juruvas*[35] are birds that nest in holes in the ground and have feathers sea green in color; and likewise another called *pirariguá.*[36]

A few days ago they brought a bird to show me, which they said was called *japu,*[37] yellow in color and considered quite a prize. The *quirejuabe*[38] is a blue bird prized by the heathen of this land; and there is another one called *tiquaran,*[39] and another, a red one, called *guaxa.*[40] Also there is another kind of bird whose song is like a baby's crying, and its name is *cunhatainape.*[41]

The *tucanaçu*[42] is another type of bird, which has a bill the size of your hand, although its body is not big; and another bird that they call *taraba.*[43] And among them all are found the kingfishers and swallows of our Portugal.

ALVIANO   I always thought that swallows were African birds and that they passed over from there to Spain in the summer to nest. I am surprised that they are found out here.

BRANDÔNIO   Yes, they are found here in great numbers.[44] Another bird, *peitica*[45] by name, is one that the heathen find very worrisome, for it is a bird of ill omen that obliges them to take extreme measures if they come upon it or hear it singing, as I shall explain later[46] when I tell you about the customs of this land. Very large rheas[47] are also found. They are said to eat iron; but I think that is just a fable, for I never saw them do it, and I have seen many. When these rheas run, they lower one wing and raise the other to the wind, so that their wings resemble a lateen sail, and that way they run faster than a horse. There are others of the same type that are called seriemas;[48] they use their feet and wings to run, and this way they move exceedingly swiftly without ever rising from the ground.

ALVIANO   There are many of these in Africa, and I have heard the same things said of them.

BRANDÔNIO   There are a countless number of parrots,[49] which go in flocks the way pigeons do in our country. Wherever they pass by they make a frightful hubbub, and they are good to eat. There are different varieties of them, such as those they call king parrots, which can be distinguished by the elbow of the wing, which is red; these are the best ones to be taught to talk. Another kind, which they call *curicas,*[50] are not so beautiful, but when they take to talking they do it very well. And another, which is considered foreign, is called *suia*.[51] And likewise beautiful big *araras*,[52] which also talk if they are taught. And another kind, almost of the same variety, to which they give the name *tuim* [love bird], is small in body and very beautiful. It repeats reasonably well everything it is taught. Of all these the most prized is the one they call *quaiaquaiai,* and this has dark gray, black, and green feathers.

ALVIANO   In Portugal I saw some parrots that had been taken over from here. Their colors were all different, but so carefully studied that it was plain that they had been done by hand.

BRANDÔNIO   And so they had, for to give the parrots those colors they pluck their feathers. Where they pull them out the skin is covered with blood, and then they place—wherever they wish—the skins of certain frogs, which have the ability to give them those colors.[53]

ALVIANO   I am glad to know this, for I had been given to understand that they were natural. I must say that you have amazed me by the many kinds of birds and fowls you have named for me. They are of such strange and different types that I should think that nowhere in the world could one find a greater number of them. It is wonderful that you are able to remember their names, especially when they are such tongue twisters.

BRANDÔNIO   Well, there are just as many more to be named, but it is not possible for me to retain in my memory such a great diversity of them. And I still have not discussed the many kinds of birds of prey that are found in this land, all of which are of such quality that the finest ones bred in Iceland[54] could never sustain comparison with them. The most esteemed of these birds is a variety they call *garataurana*.[55] It has on its head a crown like a king's, which nature created—rather like a cock's comb. Among all the birds of prey it is the swiftest and most agile hunter. Now, since one comes from the specific to an understanding of the general, I want to tell you something that I saw happen with one of these birds. A man of very noble birth, His Majesty's governor in one of the captaincies of this state, had one of these birds that was tame, for it had been raised in the house. One day, flying up from its perch, it lighted on top of some stones that had been piled up nearby. A big cat caught sight of it and, thinking his prey was as good as captured, stealthily crept up on the bird, intending to pounce on it and carry it off in his claws. But as soon as the hawk sensed the approach of the cat, it raised one foot, standing on the other. For a short while they both stayed that way, each one thinking that it would feast itself on the other. Finally, when the cat raised his head, the hawk, hurling itself on the cat, sank its talons into him. A little bit later the cat relaxed his limbs as if dead, and when they tried to rescue him, they found he really was dead.

ALVIANO   It's a strange thing how ferocious that animal is and how great the strength with which it is endowed.

BRANDÔNIO   Well, I can tell you something more. A few days after that they brought a good-sized suckling pig to that gentleman as a present. When it was turned loose in the house, the hawk pounced on it, and a short while afterward, when they got it loose from the hawk's talons, the pig was dead.

ALVIANO   A bird as daring as that must be of no little use, and I should like to know how they hunt with it in this country.

BRANDÔNIO   They do not use these birds for hunting, and those who could do so, but don't, have something of an excuse, for the land is so covered with forest that it would not be possible to release the hawks without losing them.[56]

Besides these, there are some other falcons or hawks[57]—I don't know what kind—likewise very agile at hunting, but not so big as the one I mentioned. One of these is called *piron*[58] and another *ganhiapiruera*.[59] And another kind they call *eixua*,[60] and another like it is named *taguató*,[61] and there are others—the caracara[62] and also the *guaquaqua*,[63] and likewise the *jacurutu*,[64] which is terribly ugly in appearance. And, in addition to all these, there is a kind called *suindá*,[65] which hunts both by day and by night. All these birds that I have named have hooked beaks and curved talons.

ALVIANO   There certainly are many more birds of prey in this country than in Iceland or in any other part of the world.

BRANDÔNIO   All that I have named are excellent for hunting, for they can carry any fowl in their talons, no matter how large it is, and they overtake the swiftest bird once they set out after it. There are other birds that never show themselves until sunset, when it is almost dark; then large flocks of them appear, chattering loudly. Their name is *burau*,[66] and I would compare them to the martins of our country. *Kacum*[67] is the name of a bird that never sleeps, and turns night into day.

ALVIANO   Are there by chance any nocturnal birds around here?

BRANDÔNIO   Yes, all of that kind that are known in Portugal are found here, and still some others that were never seen there. There are also vultures, which are known here by the name of *urubu* [the common black vulture of Brazil], larger that those of Europe.

Besides the birds that I have discussed, there is an infinitude of others that feed on fish and hunt their food in the rivers and lagoons. All of them are marvelously good to eat; for example, the very beautiful ducks and mallards, and other kinds that are called *irerês,*[68] *paturis,*[69] curlews, *sericóias,*[70] and roseate spoonbills,[71] which have marvelous red and white plumage. Another kind is called the *carão,*[72] and it is like the curlew; and the *gaquara,*[73] a bird that fishes only at night; the *gararina*[74] ordinarily lives only in the water. All of these birds are found in great quantity along all the rivers and lagoons, and they are very easily taken with muskets, arrows, and other means that are devised for this. Now with that I confess I have exhausted all that I had stored up in my memory to tell you about the birds, and there are still many others that I don't know anything about.

ALVIANO   You have spoken of so many of them that I marvel at your having been able to recite their names and characteristics as you have. And now it seems to me that you are obliged, according to your promise, to go on to a discussion of the fishes—inhabitants of the third element, the waters—following the order in which you said you had resolved to carry out your disquisition.

BRANDÔNIO   Since you will hold me to my word, before I plunge into those waters I must not fail to tell you one thing worth your consideration, which I have not mentioned so far. It is not the least of those things that lend beauty to the airy element. Now this is, that in the years of drought there descend into these parts from the bush country countless numbers of butterflies of varied hues, which with their multitude do fairly fill and occupy the lower concave of the firmament. They all inerrantly make their way due north without deflecting from that path for any reason. I have never seen iron touched to lodestone bear more truly towards the north. This is so invariably the case that if, along their way, they should chance to meet with a great fire, they prefer to rise up very high and pass over it, sticking straight to their course, rather than veer off to either side, which would be easier for them. They run on incessantly in this way, in never-ending multitudes, for the space of twelve to fifteen days, until they have all gone by, finishing off their journey by drowning themselves in the waters of the sea.[75]

ALVIANO   A strange thing that is and indeed worthy of reflection. I believe there must be some cause that obliges those little birds [sic] infallibly to seek the north.

BRANDÔNIO   I think so too; but I do not wish to weary myself with speculation about it, lest I fall into a river like Aristotle.[76] Rather, I shall be content to begin with what I have to say about the fishes, which dwell in the third element, the waters.

Among these it is fitting that we give the first place to the delicious *bejupirá* [cobia], for I think that it, among all the meat fish, can carry off the palm from all for quality, and that the highly esteemed plaice of our Spain is much inferior to it; the *carapitanga*,[77] another kind of fish, of medium size, very tasty; the mackerel, of which all that are caught in this state are excellent; the fish called sierra,[78] so esteemed in the East Indies; *camurupim*,[79] a large fish and very good to eat, whose scales are as large as a half quarto of paper. I once saw them do a strange thing which for me was a clear proof that there is love even among those silent swimmers.

ALVIANO   And what did you see them doing that gave you the idea that there is love among them?

BRANDÔNIO   A weir had been made in a certain river for people to catch fish in (in this country they call it a *camboa*[80]). Two fish of that kind came up to it and one of them went inside, leaving its companion on the outside. The gate closing against it, the fish that had gone inside was held captive, and when the tide went out it was caught and killed. Its companion, or to speak more precisely its consort, for such it must have been, which had stayed outside, kept waiting for it as long as the tide made that possible. But when the water began to ebb, the fish left that spot and went away so as not to be left stranded, first giving some great smacks on the water with its tail, as if desiring thereby to show the feelings that moved it. And afterwards it continued to come back and take up the same station for the space of six or seven days, always at the time that the tide came in. It was as if it came to look for its companion in the place where the latter had been lost. There it gave the same slaps on the water as it had done the first time.

ALVIANO   That is no small argument to prove that in every living thing love can be found, although in greater degree in some beings than in others.

BRANDÔNIO   Well, it happened just as I described it. They also catch many dolphins, jewfish, moray eels, hake, striped mullets, sharks, albacores, bonitos, *lavradores,* swordfish, needlefish, common jacks, surmullets, and sardines. All those kinds of fish are meaty and good to eat.

ALVIANO The same kinds are found in Portugal.

BRANDÔNIO But they are found here in greater quantity. And before going on, I want to tell you about a strange fish, if one may call it such. It is known as a sea cow,[81] a name that was given to it because in the face it looks almost like that animal, although it is about twice as big, not in height but in length and breadth. Some of this kind weigh more than two oxen do. This fish is harpooned in the freshwater rivers at the point where they empty into the sea. When eaten it has the same flavor and taste as beef. There is no difference between those two meats; so if they are mixed in a pan it is hard to tell one from the other. Hence this fish can be boiled with greens, and hash and croquettes are made of it, for it is used for everything that beef is used for. I have given it to several persons to eat without telling them what it was, and they assumed that they were eating beef.

ALVIANO I would worry about eating it on fish days,[82] for I would think that I was eating meat.

BRANDÔNIO People were worried about that here, and the question gave rise to great disputes. But the theologians decided that, since that fish (for such it seems to be) lives always in the water and never leaves it to look for food, it is really a fish and should be considered such. The *ubarana*[83] is a good fish, and so is another called *gaibicuaraçu*,[84] and also the *camurim*[85]—and a little fish that they call stonefish[86] because it has a stone in its head rather than brains. It is very wholesome and is considered good for the sick to eat, and great quantities of these are caught.

ALVIANO I never heard tell of beast, fowl, or fish that had a stone in its head in place of brains.

BRANDÔNIO Well, these little fish have one, exactly as I have said. The *curimã*[87] is a fish that resembles the other mullets, but it is bigger and more meaty; the *carapeba*[88] is a fish prized for its meat, found both in the sea and in freshwater rivers; the *curimatá*[89] is thought to be the shad of Portugal, for it has the same appearance and just as many bones; the piranha[90] is a fish little bigger than your hand but with such great fighting spirit that it surpasses sharks in voracity. And although there are many sharks hereabouts they are not feared so much as these piranhas, which have the temper of lions and are found only in the freshwater rivers. They have seven rows of teeth, so sharp and cutting that every one of them could be used as a razor or a lancet. As soon as these fish sense a person in the water, they set upon him like wild beasts. They easily carry off in their mouths the parts they bite, leaving the bone stripped of flesh. They strike most often at the testicles, which they at once cut off and carry away along with the victim's manhood. For this reason one finds many Indians who lack these members.

ALVIANO   I give you my word that so long as I live nothing will induce me to go into the rivers of this land, for even if they had only a palm of water in them I would be thinking that the piranhas were after me to disarm me of that which I prize most.

BRANDÔNIO   You may safely go into [almost] all the rivers without fear, for these piranhas are not found in all of them. Indeed, I have only heard of their being found in the São Francisco River[91] and in the Una,[92] and in others like them which are well known to be infested with piranhas. They are good to eat and can be caught with a fishhook, although many hooks are lost because they bite them off.

There is another type of fish called cockfish,[93] because it carries its dorsal fin very erect. The *salé*[94] is another kind and is also very good to eat. The *saaçu*[95] is a fish with great big eyes and is most delicious to eat; the *saúna*[96] is similar to the *curimã*.[97] The *mandi*[98] is like a sole. There are grunts,[99] *corcovados*,[100] and *baiacus*,[101] the last having a frightening quality in that they are poisonous.

ALVIANO   And how poisonous are they?

BRANDÔNIO   This fish, which is not very big, resembles a toad. Its gall is so pure a poison that anybody who eats it or anything that has touched it cannot escape death, for it is the most potent venom of all that are found in Brazil. However, if one removes the gall from this fish without breaking or spilling it or letting it touch any part of the meat, one may eat the fish roasted or boiled without any danger.

ALVIANO   No matter how it was prepared, I would never eat it, for I would always think that it had some of the gall in it.

BRANDÔNIO   Well, there's still another thing about this fish. If you rub its belly after it is dead, it swells up like a toad. The *tamoatá*[102] also has a means of protection, and when it is on the defensive its scales are like blades. *Arares*[103] defend themselves in the same way and have a head larger than their body. The *jacundá*[104] is a freshwater fish and is an excellent food for sick people, as are the *piaba*[105] and the *sarapó*.[106]

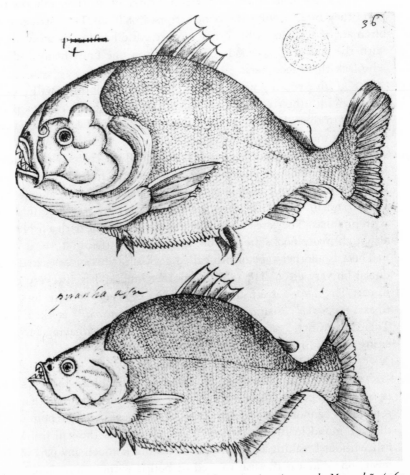

Piranhas. Cristóvão de Lisboa, *História dos animais e árvores do Maranhão* (1624; facsim. Lisbon: Arquivo Histórico Ultramarino e Centro de Estudos Históricos Ultramarinos, 1967), fol. 36. *Courtesy of the Edward E. Ayer Collection, The Newberry Library, Chicago.*

The *traíra*[107] is a fish with many bones, which hatches some worms inside its head. There are also lots of sea turtles, which, though they are marine animals, come ashore to lay the eggs from which their young come forth.

ALVIANO   Although I have often heard people talk about those turtles, no one ever mentioned that habit of theirs.

BRANDÔNIO   Well, that's the way they do, just as I've told you. There are also many shrimps in the sea and the lagoons inland, of extraordinary size, and also freshwater turtles.

ALVIANO   Don't go any further, for you have discussed so many varieties of fish, of different qualities and kinds, that just thinking about their names and characteristics is confusing.

BRANDÔNIO   Well, I can still tell you that this land of Brazil is so fertile in producing fish that, in the wintertime, when ponds form in fields where there never were any fish, some are very soon found in there. They call them *muçus,*[108] and they look like eels. A vast number of shrimps also appear. So everybody up in the bush country lives on them. They have wicker fish traps, with bait inside them, set out at night in the ponds, and at dawn, when they have them brought in, they are full of those kinds of fish.

ALVIANO   If they are caught as easily as that, the settlers in this land surely never suffer for lack of them.

BRANDÔNIO   Of the kinds that are caught in traps, there is a great abundance.

ALVIANO   But the other kinds of fish—how do they catch them here?

BRANDÔNIO   With trammels[109] and nets, and in traps that they make with stakes.[110] Lots of fish enter these with the incoming tide, and once they are inside, the gate is closed on them. As the waters recede, the fish are left almost on dry land and are picked up without any trouble. But most of the settlers in this state get nearly all the fish they consume by sending their blacks out on their jangadas.[111] The slaves sail these out to the open sea, and with a hook and line they take beautiful big fish. They catch a lot of fish this way, and at sunset they bring their jangadas back to shore.

ALVIANO   And why do they not use boats to go out to sea to fish, like the little trawlers of our Portugal?

BRANDÔNIO   Because it is not the custom. A few persons who started to do that soon gave it up. Along the lagoons and rivers lives an animal named capybara.[112] It lives in the water but feeds on land. It resembles the otter in its habits, though not in its appearance. And it is good to eat.

ALVIANO   And is this animal considered fish or meat?

BRANDÔNIO   It is considered meat, because its flesh is very wholesome and delicious.[113] Furthermore, it is only logical that it be considered meat, for it feeds on land, which is the point that should be decisive in resolving such doubts.[114]

    Besides these capybaras, some very big lizards are found in the same rivers and lagoons. The natives of the land call them *jacarés* [alligators], but they are not so carnivorous as those of India. These lizards lay eggs rather like duck eggs but not so round, for they are somewhat flat, and they incubate them in the water. They have only to look at them, for their glance is sufficient to produce the young inside them, as birds do with the warmth of their feathers. And in time little lizards are hatched from them.

ALVIANO   That sounds like a story one can't believe.[115]

BRANDÔNIO   Don't think that it's a fable, for they brought me some of those eggs that had been found in the water. When they were broken, out of each one of them came two little lizards already alive that squirmed all around. Now with that you must excuse me from saying any more about the fishes, and give me leave to pass on to the shellfish, of which there are a great many of different kinds in this province.

ALVIANO   I noticed that you didn't mention whales, which must be quite common, judging from the ambergris which they cast ashore.

BRANDÔNIO   Yes, along this coast they are very numerous, and run very large, especially in the summertime. Some of them come ashore, and from these they make fish oil. In Bahia there are some Biscayans who kill lots of them with harpoons, and they manufacture the fish oil from them, which is the trade that they have taken up.[116]

    But you are clearly mistaken in thinking that the whales cast the ambergris ashore, because they don't do so. The reason that the ambergris comes ashore is that those very whales, and some other big fish, seek it as food in the depths of the sea, where it grows along great reefs. In their struggles to tear it loose, pieces are broken off, some large and some small, which the sea throws up on the beach, where they are discovered.[117] Nonetheless, a few days ago I was assured—quite reliably—that something had happened at the Rio Grande [do Norte] border that really contradicts everything I have just said about the creation of ambergris.

ALVIANO Well, don't keep it a secret from me.

BRANDÔNIO Two trustworthy men who can be believed (for they saw this with their own eyes along the beaches of Rio Grande, on Cabo Negro[118]) declared that a settler in that same captaincy, Diogo de Almeida by name, commander of the fort, came upon a bough about as long as your arm and almost as thick, which the sea had cast up on the shore. It had two branches at one end; part of one of them had been broken off, but the other one was whole, and bore a few dead leaves resembling cypress leaves. Stuck to that piece of wood, like the resin that some trees exude, were three or four ounces of ambergris of good quality. So it appears that in the ocean depths grow trees of the kind that that bough came from and that they give off ambergris as other trees give off resin. Now if that is so, then those who maintained that it grows like the ocean reefs were mistaken, while those hit the mark who believed that it is like resin—for the bough that was discovered is ample proof of that. And since the finding of such a bough is a thing that cannot be doubted, I shall resume my discussion of the shellfish, pointing out first of all the great quantity of octopuses, crawfish, and lobsters that are caught along the reefs at the conjunction of the spring tides, when the ebb has set in and the fresh water mingles with the sea.[119]

ALVIANO And how do they catch them at that time?

BRANDÔNIO They catch them at night with lighted torches, for the shellfish, startled by the flames, let themselves be taken without even attempting to escape.

There are also many rock barnacles, and other mollusks known as limpets, periwinkles, and oysters, which are to be had in such quantity that they are almost the daily fare of the inhabitants of this land, especially of those who live close to the sea. Some of the oysters I've seen were so large—and I am not exaggerating!—that you had to cut them in pieces with a knife to be able to eat them. They grow along the shores of the tidal rivers and in among the roots, branches, and trunks of a tree they call mangrove, which I have already described.[120]

ALVIANO Do they by any chance find pearls or seed pearls in these oysters, as they do in the oysters found on the coasts of India?

BRANDÔNIO I don't believe that those I am discussing are of that kind, for the oysters from which they extract pearls in India are taken on the high seas, and the ones here are gathered in the rivers.[121] However, they do find pearls in some oysters after they have been roasted, but by that time the pearls have been ruined by the fire. But that happens only rarely. I have a pearl like that at home that I will give you.

ALVIANO I'll have a good time showing it off in the Kingdom and being able to say that pearls are found in Brazil too.

BRANDÔNIO Likewise there are many clams, and another mollusk known as *sapinhaguá*,[122] and, above all, a very strange one that has been named *sernambim*.[123]

ALVIANO What is this strange mollusk like?

BRANDÔNIO It is different from all the others, for it has blood just the way a fish has, despite its being all closed up inside its shell. This is something no similar mollusk has. But what above all is so astonishing is that at the different conjunctions of the moon this oyster has a menstrual flow as women have.

ALVIANO I'll never dare tell that to anyone in Portugal, for they would never believe me.

BRANDÔNIO Well, here I can give you all the inhabitants of this state as witnesses of the truth of what I say. You can't ask a single one of the old settlers[124] in this land who won't back up the truth of what I have said.

ALVIANO I don't doubt but what that's the truth, but still I don't wish to obligate myself to hunt for such proof.

BRANDÔNIO No one can oblige you to believe anything except what you want to believe, but what I have told you cannot be doubted. In this country there are also various kinds of crab, which are the chief food of the poor people who live here, of the native Indians, and of the Guinea slaves. This is because they are so plentiful and can be caught with little labor. One variety of them is called *uçá*,[125] another *siri*,[126] and still another *guaiá*.[127] There are also the *guaiaranha*[128] and the *aratu*,[129] which is said to be an antidote for poison, though I have never experimented with it. Also, there are some of another kind that are called *garauçá*.[130] Above all, there is the *guaiamu*,[131] which is really most amazing.

ALVIANO Well, don't make a secret of it!

BRANDÔNIO This species of crab lives on land along the saltwater rivers, in coves and grottoes they make by throwing up the earth so as to form a hole underground, the way ants fashion their hills; and there they live on the grasses and fruits that the land produces. They even make their holes in planted fields, wherein they do much damage. These crabs are caught both in their holes and outside of them. They are delicious eating and have beautiful big corals.[132] What is most amazing is that when the first rains fall in these parts, in January or February, the crabs leave their burrows in great squadrons and spread out inland for almost a league. They blanket the fields where the salt water never reaches, not even a drop of it. There they are caught in great numbers. They even proceed of their own accord to infest the houses of the people who live in those regions, it being noted that those that are caught therein are the fattest and most delicious to eat. The natives say, when they catch them this way, that the crabs "are on the loose," which is the same as saying they are lascivious.[133]

ALVIANO Amazing things these are that you tell me. If they had come to the notice of the ancients I am sure they would have written great volumes on them; yet we make little of them, as if they were not worth thinking about.

BRANDÔNIO That is because they are well known and much used among us and such things cause no surprise. But since I still have much to say about beasts, domestic and wild, we shall do well to leave the sea and turn our prow towards land—the fourth element—which we have not yet discussed in connection with animals.

ALVIANO I beg that you will do so.

BRANDÔNIO I am not ashamed now to confess to you a weakness of mine, which is that I was awfully anxious to get out of this. I didn't want to venture into the maze of the various species, different characteristics, strange shapes, and tongue-twisting names of the beasts, both wild and tamed, that live in this great Brazilian land. But, being obligated by the promise I made you, I must trample over every obstacle to get on with my task. Yet as I do so, you must understand that the memory cannot hold or the mind single out everything that should be said on such a subject. I warn you ahead of time that no matter how much I tell you there will still be twice as much left untold. And with that preliminary, let me begin with what I have at hand, starting with the Neptunian horse,[134] a swift and spirited animal. Although there are a great many of this breed, they formerly abounded in countless numbers in these American [Brazilian] fields,[135] while in those of Buenos Aires not nearly so many were raised. But these horses have cruel enemies—the Guinea slaves, who heedlessly slaughter them for food wherever they come upon them. They even steal highly prized and valuable horses right out of their stables for the same purpose.[136] Dropping that subject, I will say that the horses in this country are very heavy workers, despite their going unshod. Either because their hooves are especially hard or because the soil is not very stony, they have no need of horseshoes. It very often happens that one of these horses is used in a single afternoon in the games of jousts with staves, tilting at the ring, and running at the duck,[137] and is ridden very hard. And at times they continue this exercise three to four days in a row, never getting winded, being as sound at the end as at the beginning. Just one run like that would be enough to exhaust twenty Spanish horses. The horses here have great stamina, even though they are badly fed, ordinarily getting nothing to eat but grass—in this land called *capim*.[138] It is a wonder if they ever get a little millet, considering that you can't always find some when you want it.

ALVIANO   And how much is a horse like that worth?

BRANDÔNIO   Some exceptionally fine ones I have seen sold for 500 cruzados or less. But when a horse turns out to be a superior animal and is well tempered, it will usually bring about 200 cruzados.

ALVIANO   Are horses as long-lived here as in Portugal?

BRANDÔNIO   They are, and even more so. Why, one never thinks a horse is old here, for one that is fifteen or sixteen is as fit for all kinds of work as a four-year-old.

ALVIANO   Are there mules out here?

BRANDÔNIO   Yes, there are, but there aren't any.

ALVIANO   I don't understand that kind of talk.

BRANDÔNIO   Well, I'll explain. I said that there are mules out here, for some breeding donkeys were sent out from the Kingdom and they reproduced splendidly, but the race ended with the death of the females and there was no one who would take the trouble to send for any others, not even for a pair of them to reproduce their kind.[139] Thus, I said that there are mules out here but that there aren't any.

ALVIANO   Now I see what you mean.

BRANDÔNIO   In this land there is also a great quantity of cattle,[140] fat and well fleshed, excellent for eating, but people either don't want or don't know how to use profitably the infinite supply of milk they give. The greatest use they make of them is to turn the young bulls [by castration] into docile oxen for work in the sugar mills and the fields, and this is one of the best things to invest in in this country. I knew a man[141] who had more than a thousand head of cattle, in several different corrals,[142] and he made a big profit on them. Not everybody does so well, but they all make it a point to raise cattle, for that is a most important source of wealth.

ALVIANO   And what do a cow and calf sell for?

BRANDÔNIO   A cow, if it is a good cow, is valued in these northern captaincies at between four and five milreis, and the calf, if old enough to be harnessed to a wagon, is valued at six to seven milreis, and a grown ox is worth twelve to thirteen milreis.[143] That's the way the prices usually run. Many ewes, lambs, and she-goats are raised too. It is common for the ewes to drop two lambs to a litter and the she-goats two to three kids.[144]

ALVIANO   How strange! But with all those kinds of livestock reproducing so abundantly, surely there is no lack of cheese or of wool in this land.

BRANDÔNIO   But on the contrary they are not to be found here, for the settlers do not want to bother with them.[145] Although they might have a great quantity of sheep's wool, even if they used it just to stuff mattresses, they are quite satisfied instead to pay three or four milreis for the wool that is imported from the Kingdom. And the same thing goes for cheese. This negligence has grown so bad that, though such livestock do ever so well in this land, the people don't want to spend any time on raising them. They are quite content to raise only what they need for home use—than which nothing could be more shameful!

ALVIANO   For the sake of Brazil's honor, that is something to be quiet about.

BRANDÔNIO   From sheep and goats another kind of livestock has been developed, of which I have owned a lot. These are hybrids, born of ewes and billy goats,[146] and they have characteristics of both parents. Taking something from each parent, they are quite a different animal in their makeup and are excellent eating.

ALVIANO   I never heard tell of this new species of animal born of such a cross.

BRANDÔNIO   They are to be found here in Brazil all right, and I have had many of them, as I told you; so don't be afraid to believe it. There are also lots of fine hogs, of the same stock as those in our Portugal. Their meat is so healthful that it is prescribed for the sick.[147]

ALVIANO   Just a few days ago I visited a sick man who asked the doctor if he could eat pork, and the doctor forbade it most insistently.

BRANDÔNIO   In the early stages of an illness it was always thought wise to abstain from eating pork, but as the sickness ran its course it has not been found that pork did the patient any harm. These modern doctors want to pervert what was always approved by the ancients.[148] Perhaps they do it for no other reason than to appear learned.

ALVIANO   Many of them certainly act that way, and it's too bad for their patients. But I wish you would tell me if all of the livestock that you have talked about was native to this land and was found here by our Portuguese when they came to settle, or if all of it was sent over from Spain.

BRANDÔNIO   None of the livestock I have mentioned was found in this province, but all of it was brought over here from Portugal, except for some horses and mares that came from Cape Verde, where they were bred before being introduced here.[149] But if you want to hear about the nature and characteristics of the animals that were already here, indigenous to the country, pay attention to me and perhaps I can make you raise your eyebrows with astonishment.

ALVIANO   Tell me everything, for here I am, ready to listen to you.

BRANDÔNIO   There are many animals around here that they call *antas*.[150] They are the size of an ox, run wild, and are hunted with muskets and pitfalls. Their meat is good to eat.

ALVIANO   And is their hide like that which we make use of?

BRANDÔNIO   Exactly, but no use is made of *anta* hides, for people out here don't have the patience to tan and sew them, but let them go to waste. There are also a great many bucks, does, and boars.

ALVIANO   And is this game hunted the same way it is in Portugal?

BRANDÔNIO   No, only with muskets and arrows.[151] The hunters—who also use traps and pitfalls—go out to the places where the animals are accustomed to herd. In this way they generally catch a lot of them. Their meat is very good to eat, like that in Portugal. There are different kinds of boar, such as the one they call *taiaçu,* and another called *taitetu* or *taçuité,* depending on its size.[152] All of these species—unlike those that came from Spain—have navels on their backs, which seems to be the way nature chose to make them.

ALVIANO   That's strange, and it would be hard for an uninformed person to believe.

BRANDÔNIO   Well, there can't be any doubt about it, for it is a well-known fact. And although, as I have said, this game is killed with muskets and arrows, or traps and pitfalls, there is still another species that is hunted in a strange fashion. Now, in this the hunter goes to a spot where he knows for certain that the pack has gathered. There,

Two howler monkeys and a white-lipped peccary (*taiaçu*) with the supposed navel on its back. Cristóvão de Lisboa, *História dos animais e árvores do Maranhão* (1624; facsim. Lisbon: Arquivo Histórico Ultramarino e Centro de Estudos Históricos Ultramarinos, 1967), fol. 67. *Courtesy of the Edward E. Ayer Collection, The Newberry Library, Chicago.*

before he lets himself be seen, he selects a tree that will be easy to climb when necessary, and when he has the tree picked out he shows himself to the pack and shouts at them. As soon as they sense him, they make for him like so many lions, to tear him to pieces. But the prudent hunter quickly takes refuge in the tree, where he waits for the boars to close in. They do this at once, gnawing at the roots and trunk since they cannot reach the man perched above them. Now the ready hunter, seeing them rapt in fury, simply takes his sharp lance and sticks one of the pigs so as to draw blood. Once the others see the blood flow they rush to attack the bleeding boar, who, to defend himself, bites back at his attackers, and thus they bleed one another, deceived by the lure of the blood gushing from each one. They wage a fierce battle, in the course of which they tear each other apart with their teeth until they fall dead. Throughout all this, the hunter—safely ensconced in the tree—delightedly awaits the end of the struggle to collect the spoils. Many pigs die in that place and he has them carried off to his house, where he takes as much as he wants of them, for their meat is most delicious.[153]

ALVIANO   How pleasant and gratifying it must be to hunt that way, since so much game is caught with so little effort. Would that I might always be engaged in such sport!

BRANDÔNIO   Well, out here it is only the Indians born in this country who engage in it. Another animal, called a paca,[154] exists in great abundance. It has light and dark markings, and is much bigger than a hare. Its meat is about as fat as that of the wild pig but is much better eating. The agouti[155] is a small animal that can be tamed and will run around the house, when people don't object. There is, too, another and similar kind called coati,[156] and both kinds are good to eat. The *tatu*[157] is a beast you can see painted on some maps because of its oddity and the strange way it is put together. It carries plates of armor in the style that we use, and these are very strong. Beneath this armor its little body is sheltered. And there are lots of these, which are considered very fine for the table.

ALVIANO   During the past few days they showed me one of these beasts, and I was amazed to see what it was like.

BRANDÔNIO   I wanted to take one to Portugal, but I couldn't carry out my plan because it died at sea.

ALVIANO   It would have aroused great interest there.

BRANDÔNIO   The *jaritacaca*[158] is a dark-colored animal, the size of a little
dog, and the rarest and strangest creature in the world. If it happens
to be attacked by anyone who seeks to capture it while it is feeding
in the fields, it runs away. But when it realizes that it is cornered,
in self-defense it emits a wind that by its foul odor is able to strike
to earth, senseless, any living thing pursuing it, be it man or horse
or dog or any other kind of animal whatever, which remains stretched
out there, unconscious, for the space of three or four hours. The most
amazing thing is that the clothing, saddle, stirrups, or dog collar that
has been touched by the foul-smelling wind is no longer good for
anything, but must be thrown into the fire and burned up. And if
this has happened to a man it isn't enough for him to wash himself
once, ten times, or even twenty times with water to get rid of that
nasty smell, for it stays on him for the space of a week or ten days
until, with time, it wears off. One day when I was watching them
weigh the sugar, a man happened to come into the weighhouse. Now,
more than a week before this, he had been touched by the wind of
that animal. Although he had already washed his hair many times,
shaved off his beard, and changed his clothes, the smell that came
from him was so bad that we who were in the weighhouse had to flee
outside.[159] We didn't know what the reason for this was until he
himself explained what had happened to him.

ALVIANO   That is a stupendous thing, and so strange and rare that it
is hard to believe it. I would advise kings and princes to find a way
to breed these animals in captivity, training them not to emit that
wind except when told to do so, for by means of it they might overcome
great armies without swords ever being drawn.

BRANDÔNIO   Well, don't think that it is a joke, for that's just what
would happen if there were some way that they could make use of it.
       Many rabbits also are found here; they are like our Portuguese ones,
but not because they are native to Portugal. It seems that they must
go back to some that came from there, and from these sprang the
great number that exist today.[160] There is another, indigenous, species
that they call *sauiá*,[161] but they are smaller. Another, *punaré*[162] by
name, has a long tail and looks rather like a rat. Then there is the
preá,[163] which is excellent eating. And also another very small variety,
called *mocó*,[164] which is tamed and kept in the house because it is a
good rat catcher. There is still another kind called *reruba*.[165] All of
these are kinds of rabbit, but some are large and some are small.

ALVIANO   There aren't that many kinds in Portugal; so it seems that Brazil has an advantage here.

BRANDÔNIO   The *quatimirim*[166] is a little animal with a tail big enough to cover its whole body. When you come upon one of them you can see nothing more than its tail, for all of its body is hidden underneath. The *mocó*, or *quoqui*,[167] to use another name, is an animal the size of a baby rabbit. Nature has decreed that they have a pocket in their underbelly in which to shelter their young after birth; and when they travel they carry them tucked away inside it. When they stop, they let the young out to feed and graze in the fields. When they take to the trail again, they gather in their young once more.

ALVIANO   And does that pocket perchance open into their entrails?

BRANDÔNIO   No, for they have one skin over the other, and the little pocket is formed by the outer skin.

ALVIANO   These are amazing things you tell me, and you hold me in suspense with them.

BRANDÔNIO   The *tamanduá-açu*[168] is a brown and white animal, about the size of a six-month-old colt. Its tail is long and wide enough to cover it completely from head to foot, and its meat is very good to eat.

You find several varieties of fox here, too. They are great hunters and go after chickens particularly, which never escape once the foxes get in among them.

ALVIANO   As for foxes, it would be better if there weren't any, for they do great damage everywhere.

BRANDÔNIO   The *irara*[169] is an animal the size of a cat. It is black, and has a long muzzle and a mouth like an eyelet, and feeds mainly on ants.

ALVIANO   I don't see how it can find enough ants to live on, for they are a tiny prey.

BRANDÔNIO   It makes use of a strange device for this purpose: it goes in search of ant hills and other places where ants generally can be found. There, stretched out along the ground, it sticks out its very long tongue, which is covered with a sticky substance. Soon its tongue is swarming with ants which, one after another, come up to get the bait. When the animal feels that it has collected enough, it pulls its tongue back in with a good mouthful on it. When it has eaten that, it sticks out its tongue many more times, until it has had its fill of this fare. Thus it is not hard for it to find its food.

Guaxinim (Brazilian raccoon). *Tamanduá* (anteater). Cristóvão de Lisboa, *História dos animais e árvores do Maranhão* (1624; facsim. Lisbon: Arquivo Histórico Ultramarino e Centro de Estudos Históricos Ultramarinos, 1967), fol. 69. *Courtesy of the Edward E. Ayer Collection, The Newberry Library, Chicago.*

ALVIANO   The nature of this animal deserves attention, as does the way it obtains its food, for, though it seems difficult, that turns out to be easy enough because of the contrivance it employs.

BRANDÔNIO   There are also lots of chameleons in this country. They are called sinimbus[170] in the native language, and are big and beautiful. Green is their natural color. They will stay on a tree for the space of two or three days without leaving it. They seem to live on the wind, as people who live here have written.[171]

ALVIANO   I'd like to know if these chameleons change their color, as they are said to do.

BRANDÔNIO   Yes, they do, for I have seen many of them placed upon cloths of different colors. After they have been on them for some while, they take on almost the same color, though not quite perfectly or distinctly. The savages in this country eat them and say that their flesh is very good. The tegu[172] is a lizard; it preys terribly on chickens and is considered good eating. The *jia*[173] is an animal that resembles a frog and is about the size of a turtle. It is awfully good to eat, and whoever has one needn't go without a good supper. There is also in this land a weird animal that our Portuguese call a sloth, while the native heathen call it *aí*.[174] But since it is quite well known, I don't want to weary myself telling you about it.

ALVIANO   But I wish you would tell me about it in detail, for I know nothing about this animal, and I have not even heard of it before now.

BRANDÔNIO   This sloth is the size of a dog, though it doesn't stand so high. It has a strange face and features, and is brown or black in color. Its toes are very distinct and end in exceedingly large, sharp claws. Nature has endowed this animal with great phlegm and laziness, so much so that when it has to climb up or down a tree, even a small tree, it requires at least two days. The same thing happens on the ground when it has to move even a short way, for to lift and stretch out one foreleg and then do the same with the other one, so as to move forward, it requires at least a good quarter of an hour. Neither whips, nor cuts, nor even fire can make it move any faster, for in the same way and in the same rhythm it continues to move its limbs as if nothing had been done to it. It has such strength in them that wherever it sinks its claws in, there is no prying it loose save with the greatest labor. The sloths always carry their young clinging to

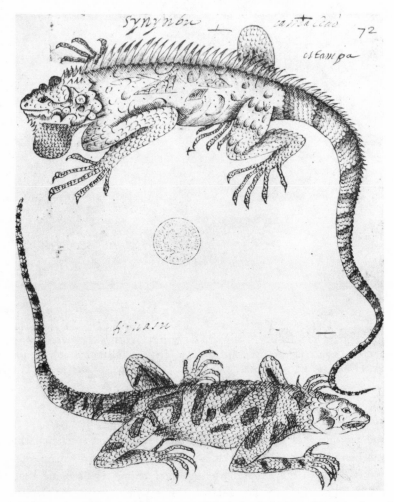

A sinimbu and a *teguaçu,* or large tegu. Cristóvão de Lisboa, *História dos animais
e árvores do Maranhão* (1624; facsim. Lisbon: Arquivo Histórico Ultramarino e
Centro de Estudos Históricos Ultramarinos, 1967), fol. 72. *Courtesy of the
Edward E. Ayer Collection, The Newberry Library, Chicago.*

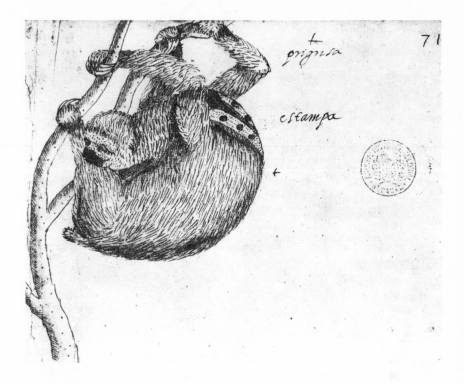

A sloth clinging to a branch. Cristóvão de Lisboa, *História dos animais e árvores do Maranhão* (1624; facsim. Lisbon: Arquivo Histórico Ultramarino e Centro de Estudos Históricos Ultramarinos, 1967), fol. 71. *Courtesy of the Edward E. Ayer Collection, The Newberry Library, Chicago.*

them while they are small. They carefully hold on to their father or mother and never let go their hold until they are grown up.

ALVIANO   Each time you tell me stranger things, so strange that the mind cannot believe they exist in this world.

BRANDÔNIO   Well, in what I'm telling you I am not straying one mite from the truth, nor is there anyone who can correct me in this. The *aguará-açu*[175] is an animal that looks like a dog. The margay[176] is like a cat—that is, a wildcat—and is very handsome with its striped coat. The *tiquaam*[177] is another variety of wildcat and is a great omen for the Indians, so much so that if they meet up with one after they have begun a journey they at once desist from it, for they are convinced that no good can come to them from it once they have seen this beast. The *eiratê*[178] is a big animal that climbs trees like a cat when it sees that there is honey in them. Once up the tree, it makes a hole in the trunk with its teeth and claws to get at the honey, which it eats to satiation without any fear of the bees' stinging it.

ALVIANO   That animal must be of the nature of a bear, being so fond of honey.

BRANDÔNIO   I don't know what kind of beast it is, but I do know that honey is its only food. The *jupará*[179] is another great hunter, itself hunted with dogs by the Indians for food. The coendou[180] is a kind of hedgehog, similar to those in Portugal, which the Indians also eat. The *guaxinim*[181] is a wild dog of medium size. The *jagararuapem*[182] is not a large animal but is a very keen and fine hunter.

ALVIANO   Since that animal is such a good hunter it must never go hungry.

BRANDÔNIO   It spends all its time hunting. You must already have seen the pretty little saki monkeys that are raised in this province and sent to Portugal, where they are much prized for their soft hair, tiny bodies, curious faces, and lively spirits.

ALVIANO   I have seen many like that, and I even have one at home, which was given to me as a present a few days ago. They make very fine pets.

BRANDÔNIO   I will admit that I am afraid to tell you about the monkeys, for there is so much to say about them that you may think I'm telling you stories. But, seeing that I am in a place where I can prove the truth of what I say, I shall tell you what I know of this subject. This land has a great number of monkeys of different kinds, some big and some small. The big ones are called *guaribas*,[183] and I will deal with them last. The smaller ones have different customs and abilities, the chief of which is their habit of going to the corn fields to steal corn when it is ripe. They take their precautions in this manner: before they come down from the trees, they choose from their number three or four lookouts, which they post in the places where they will have the best view of the field, from the tops of some high trees. These lookouts always stand their watch with a sharp eye. The other monkeys, reassured by these precautions, come down from the trees to execute their thievery, each one of them, curiously enough, contriving to make off with three or four ears of corn, which—if they are not discovered—they will carry away with them. But if by chance some people appear while the monkeys are still busy with their thievery, their lookouts give them the signal by means of certain cries. When these are heard by the rest of them, they beat a hasty retreat, ready or not. But if people come and the lookouts are careless and fail to give the signal to their brothers who are busy stealing, they all flee as best they can, and the first thing they do is to beat up the lookouts. They tear them apart with their teeth, thus giving their carelessness its proper punishment.[184]

ALVIANO   A rational person could do no more, nor could he comport himself with more forethought. I would like to know how to catch some of these monkeys, for I intend to take many tame ones back to Portugal.

BRANDÔNIO   They catch them with lassos and traps. A slave of mine used to make an ingenious trap: he'd take a jug with a narrow mouth and half fill it with corn. He'd tip it over on the ground, with some kernels of corn spilling out around the mouth. The jug was planted in a spot where the monkeys were accustomed to come to steal. As soon as one would come up to the jug, he would see the kernels of corn. After eating them he would look down the hole to see if there were any more. When he saw that there were, he would thrust his hand into the mouth of the jug. But when he wanted to withdraw it full of corn, he was unable to. For since he had put his hand in empty it would go into the hole, but now that it was full he could not draw it out again. Thus he was caught. Since he did not realize that he had to let go of the corn in order to withdraw his hand, he would do nothing but cry out. When the hunter heard these cries, he would just throw a lasso over him, break the jug, and bring the monkey home.[185]

ALVIANO   That's the way I would like to do my hunting, just for the amusement of seeing the animal caught that way.

BRANDÔNIO   I've heard tell of another stupendous thing that these same monkeys do, though I can't claim to have witnessed it, but trustworthy persons have assured me that they have. When a pack of these animals is on the trail in winter and comes to a river that is so swollen that it prevents their passage (for they cannot swim across it in the season when they are carrying their young with them), they use a wonderful strategem so as not to be obliged to interrupt their journey. Now this is that they seek out two tall trees on opposite sides of the river. They climb up the tree on their side of the river and out on a branch of it that hangs over the water. On this, one of the monkeys gets a firm grip with his hands, and lets his body hang down. Another monkey joins himself to the first one, holding on to him tightly in the same way, with his arms around the first one's chest. Then another, and afterwards many more in this way form a chain of monkeys. Since this chain is very long, they swing themselves from one side to the other until the last monkey, at the end of the chain, can catch hold of a branch of the nearest tree on the opposite side. Then, tensing themselves, they tighten up the chain little by little. When it is taut, the rest of the monkeys pass over it with their young on their backs. When all of them are on the other side, the first one, he who grasped the tree on the near side, lets go his grip and lands on the other side with his companions, for his opposite number does not let go but keeps the chain whole until the first monkey swings over as I have explained and joins all the rest of them.[186]

ALVIANO   That is such a fantastic thing that I wouldn't dare to tell it back in the Kingdom, for I am afraid that they would jeer at me.

BRANDÔNIO   Well, you will find many people here who can guarantee that it is true. *Guaribas* are another variety of monkey; they are much bigger and have beards. In their habits and in the foresight with which they run their lives they are almost human. They live together in tribes in the tops of the tallest trees deep in the forest. There they make a ceaseless racket that can be heard from far off. Anyone who didn't know the source of this would be convinced that it was made by human voices or by instruments, for that is what it sounds like. These *guaribas* always take care of each other's beards when they get too long, and in doing so they use sharp stones[187] and their teeth and nails. When men shoot arrows at them and a *guariba* suffers a slight wound, he at once pulls out the arrow sticking in his body and with flaming anger hurls it at the person who shot it at him, hoping to do just what was done to him. Afterwards he heals his wounds easily by applying some herbs known only to *guaribas*.[188] When they do happen to have a deep and mortal wound, they recognize it as such. Before dying they attach themselves to the tree where they are, tying their tails to a branch of it so that they die suspended therefrom and do not fall to the ground, so much do they hate becoming the prey of those who killed them.

ALVIANO   When these *guaribas* happen to meet a man in the woods, I should like to know if they let him pass safely or if they attack him.

BRANDÔNIO   Sometimes they let him pass, because they don't notice him, but other times they go after him, making grimaces and feints and other gestures. As a matter of fact, I know a *mameluco,* a native of this land, who came in badly frightened by them. He told me that they were closing in on him so fiercely that he thought he was done for. You also find in this country some ounces or tigers,[189] boldly striped, the size of a calf. They're great ones for attacking cattle, and generally kill lots of them.

ALVIANO   How do they kill the cattle?

BRANDÔNIO   Simply by pouncing on them and dealing them a blow on the head with a paw, but so hard that it's enough—ah, wondrous thing!—to break the skull in several places and scramble their brains. The cow or calf that this happens to dies right away without any visible wound or any sign to show how he suffered such a hurt.

ALVIANO   I'd like to know if they attack people the way they do cattle.

BRANDÔNIO   I've never heard of their killing a white man, but Indians and Guinea blacks, yes, when they get very hungry.[190] There is also another variety of this same species, smaller in body, called *suçua-rana.*[191] They usually kill calves and small animals, but they are not so dangerous as those others.

I don't want to pass over in silence the different kinds of poisonous snakes that are found throughout this province, like the *jararaca,*[192] the *surucucu,*[193] the coral snake,[194] and another that they call rattler because it has some knots in its tail that look like rattles and sound like them when it shakes them hard. All these snakes are very poisonous, and they are greatly feared because the people whom they bite die in a short while. There is another kind of snake, much bigger, which the Indians call *boiaçu.*[195] We call it a deer snake because when it captures a deer it eats its victim, swallowing it whole. These snakes hunt hanging from trees and drop down on their prey. It has happened that they have attacked and killed a victim by sticking their tails up his rectum, this being the part that they first come upon. I saw one such snake that was so big that I'm afraid to say how big it was, for fear you wouldn't believe me. People say a strange thing about them; that is, that after they die and have been eaten by animals, they are born again like the phoenix, and grow living flesh on their skeletons.[196]

ALVIANO   I consider that to be impossible, for there is no sign of its being true, since it is contrary to the laws of nature.

BRANDÔNIO   Well, I told you that I had never seen it, but I will venture to introduce you to lots of people who will tell you that they have seen it happen just as I've described it to you. And now I confess that I cannot go on any longer, nor do I dare start anything new, although there are many more land animals I could mention.

ALVIANO   You have already told me and shown me so many marvelous things about the various kinds of land animals and their habits that I don't see how there can be anything left to say, unless it be about the customs of the heathen hereabouts, which is the last of the things you promised to tell me.

BRANDÔNIO   To do that I shall have to recover my strength and breath, for the subject is as long as it is difficult. Therefore, to continue our conversation, which I am most eager to do, I shall meet you tomorrow at this same place, at the usual time.

Notes to Dialogue V

1 · In Dialogue III (sugar, brazilwood, cotton, and timber), and Dialogue IV (food crops).

2 · Since there was as yet no scientific classification of animals, Brandão, following a usage common at the time, groups the creatures according to the elements they inhabit. His difficulty with fire as a habitat was shared by earlier writers. See François de Dainville, *La géographie des humanistes,* p. 29.

3 · The salamander was a mythological reptile pictured as similar to a lizard. It was supposed to make its dwelling in fire. Brandônio's skepticism about the salamander legend typifies the growing readiness of his age to reject tradition and authority in favor of personal observation and experience.

4 · *Gallus gallus domesticus* is not native to the Americas, but originated in southeast Asia. It was Cabral who brought chickens to Brazil from Portugal in 1500. They proved to be an invaluable addition to the aboriginal food supply and rapidly spread throughout Brazil. Raymond M. Gilmore, "Fauna and Ethnozoology of South America," in Julian H. Steward, ed., *Handbook of South American Indians* (hereafter cited as *HSAI*), 6:393.

5 · The turkey was domesticated in or around the Mexican highlands and entered South America in pre-Columbian times by cultural diffusion. Brandão, like Soares de Sousa, uses the older Portuguese name for turkey, *galipavo.* This word was replaced in the course of the seventeenth century by the modern *peru,* reflecting the fact that the bird came to Brazil from

Spanish America. José Pedro Machado, *Dicionário etimológico da língua portuguesa*, s.v. "peru." Edward F. Tuttle, "Borrowing Versus Semantic Shift: New World Nomenclature in European Languages," in Fredi Chiappelli, ed., *First Images of America: The Impact of the New World on the Old* (hereafter cited as *First Images*), p. 599.

6 · "There are 22 orders with 86 families of birds in Neotropica; it is the richest bird fauna in the world and an ornithologist's paradise." Gilmore, "Fauna of South America," *HSAI*, 6:383.

7 · MS *jaqus*. The name *jacu* is used for various species of guan, especially the rusty-margined guan (*Penelope superciliaris* Tem.). The Tupi is *i* [he who] + *a* [grain] + *cu* [eat] = he who eats grains. James F. Clements, *Birds of the World: A Check List*, p. 50; James L. Taylor, *A Portuguese-English Dictionary* (hereafter cited as *Taylor*), s.v. "jacu"; Gabriel Soares de Sousa, *Notícia do Brasil* (1945), 2:89, n. 3.

8 · Also *aracuã*. MS *aquaham*. Any of various chachalacas (genus *Ortalis*). The Tupi comes from *ará* (an alteration of *güirá* [bird]) + *aquã* [swift]. Soares de Sousa, *Notícia do Brasil* (1945), 2:115, n. 6. *Taylor*, s.v. "aracuã." Undoubtedly the Tupi *aracuã* gave us the English word guan, applied to a bird of the same family.

9 · Also *motum*. Curassow—a large, turkey-like bird belonging to any one of various species of the genus *Crax*. The Tupi is *mí* [plumage] + *tu* [black]. Garcia says Brandônio's praise of the curassow is exaggerated. Soares de Sousa, *Notícia do Brasil* (1945), 2:89, n. 2; Rodolfo Garcia, ed., *Diálogos das grandezas do Brasil*, V, n. 1.

10 · Also *jaboru, iaburu*. MS *jaburu*. *Mycteria americana*. From Tupi *i* [he who has or is] + *abiru* [full], an allusion to the bird's large craw. Clements, *Birds of the World*, p. 53; Soares de Sousa, *Notícia do Brasil* (1945), 2:99, n. 4.

11 · MS *urui*. The spot-winged wood quail (*Odontophorus capueira* Spix). These birds prefer the dense forests, where they live on the ground in small bands, feeding on small fruits and insects. Aurélio Buarque de Holanda Ferreira, *Novo dicionário da língua portuguesa* (hereafter cited as *Aurélio*), s.v. "uru."

12 · Also *nhapupé, enapupê, nhã-popê, inhambuapé*. The red-winged tinamou (*Rhynchotus rufescens* Tem.). The Tupi means "he who flies low." Soares de Sousa, *Notícia do Brasil* (1945), 2:115, n. 1; *Aurélio*, s.v. "inhambuapé."

13 · Also *inamu, inambu, nhambu*. A tinamou. *Nambu*, which Brandônio mentions just below, does not—in modern nomenclature, at least—refer to a smaller tinamou, as Brandônio says it does, but is simply another form of the word *inhambu*. *Taylor*, s.v. "inhambu." Over *inhambu* in the Leyden manuscript an emendator has written *nambuuasu* [*inhambu* + *asu* (large)],

apparently in support of Brandônio's opinion that these are two different birds.

14 · Also *anu*. MS *anuns*. The smooth-billed ani (*Crotophaga ani* L.). Clements, *Birds of the World*, p. 133. Brandônio is mistaken in thinking the ani has no blood in its veins.

15 · Doubtless the jandaya conure (*Aratinga jandaya* Gmel.). Clements, *Birds of the World*, p. 122. The jandaya is celebrated in José de Alencar's romantic novel, *Iracema*, where its mournful song forecasts the human tragedy of the story.

16 · In Greek mythology, hideous and predatory creatures that were part bird and part woman.

17 · Any one of a number of thrushes. The *sabiá* is famous in song and story. Every Brazilian schoolchild knows the "Song of Exile," written by Antônio Gonçalves Dias, which begins "In my land are palmtrees, where sings the *sabiá*."

18 · Ouzel (Portuguese *melro*, as in the manuscript) can mean either thrush or blackbird. Perhaps to make clear that Brandônio is speaking here about the former, an emendator of the Leyden MS has written above *melro* the word *tordo*, a more common name for thrush.

19 · There are no nightingales in the New World, though Columbus thought he heard one on Hispaniola. Christopher Columbus, *Journal of Christopher Columbus*, translated by Cecil Jane, p. 192. The name *rouxinol* (nightingale) is used in Brazil for several song birds, but none of these is the true nightingale of southern Europe, including Portugal.

20 · It is a fact that many Brazilian birds utter raucous sounds. The opponents in the controversy about the new lands argued endlessly as to which were superior songsters, the Brazilian or the European birds. Antonello Gerbi, *The Dispute of the New World*, pp. 161–165 and Index.

21 · Perhaps the *tui-juba* (probably *Psittacula passerina* L.), a parakeet found in the Northeast of Brazil and today usually known in Portuguese as *tapa-cu* or *cu-tapado* [stuffed-up anus]. Garcia, ed., *Diálogos*, V, n. 1; *Aurélio*, s.v. "tapacu."

22 · The solitary tinamou (*Tinamus solitarius* Vieill.). Michael Walters, *The Complete Birds of the World*, p. 2; Antônio Geraldo da Cunha, *Dicionário histórico das palavras portuguesas de origem tupi*, s.v. "macucaguá."

23 · Fernão Cardim describes this striking bird with its great burnished beak. The toucan can be domesticated and is good to eat; its feathers are esteemed for their elegance. Baptista Caetano, Cardim's editor, says the name is common to various birds of the Rhamphastidae family; he suggests that it comes from Tupi *ti* [beak] + *cang* [bone] = bony beak. *Tratados da terra e gente do Brasil*, pp. 48 and 105.

24 · The blue and yellow macaw (*Ara ararauna* L.). The *canindé* is vividly

described by Léry: the plumage under its stomach and around its neck is "as yellow as fine gold"; the back, wings, and tail are blue. The beak and claws are hooked like those of a parrot. The author adds that the bird is often mentioned in native songs. The Indians made extensive use of the *canindé*'s feathers for decoration. Léry's editor, Paul Gaffarel, cites Belon, *Histoire de la nature des oyseaux* (1553), bk. 6, sec. xii, p. 297, on the method developed by the Indians for removing the feathers without damaging the feathers or the birds. Jean de Léry, *Histoire d'un voyage faict en la terre du Brésil,* 1:173 and corresponding notes, p. 213.

Above *canindé* in the Leyden MS an emendator has inserted what appears to be *curusira,* a word that has not been identified.

25 · MS *apecû.* Brandônio's assertion that this bird has four spurs is startling to every naturalist, since no New World bird is so equipped. Brandônio's bird may be the *ipecu (opicu, uapicu)*, lineated woodpecker (*Dryocopus lineatus*), described by Marcgrave, which has four toes. Clements, *Birds of the World,* p. 204; Jorge Marcgrave, *História natural do Brasil,* p. 207 and n. 576, and p. 219.

26 · MS *gurajnhete.* This is evidently Soares de Sousa's *uranhengatá,* identified by Pirajá da Silva as either the purple-throated euphonia (*Euphonia chlorotica* [= *Tanagra chlorotica violaceicollis* Cab.]) or the violaceous euphonia (*Euphonia violacea* [= *Tanagra violacea pampolla* Oberholser]). Pirajá da Silva gives the alternative forms *uraenhangatá, gurinhatá, gurinhatã* (all North of Brazil), and *gaturamo* (South of Brazil). The spellings with initial *u* and *g* are equivalent, since in Tupi *guara, guará, urá, gurá, guirá, güirá* all mean bird. Pirajá da Silva thinks the name comes from Tupi *güirá* [bird] + *nheeng* [talk] + *atã* [much]. The bird is about the size of a sparrow and has a yellow breast and neck and black wings, sides, and tail. Soares de Sousa, *Notícia do Brasil* (1945), 2:109 and n. 1. Jácome Monteiro says this bird is the most musical of all the birds in the colony. *Relação da Província do Brasil, 1610,* in Serafim Leite, *História da Companhia de Jesus no Brasil,* 8:424, "Do *guiranheenguetá.*" See Cunha, *Dicionário tupi,* s.v. *guriatã.*

27 · Also *guiratangueima.* The yellow-rumped cacique (*Cacicus cela* L.). Garcia, ed., *Diálogos,* V, n. 1; see De Schauensee, *Birds of South America,* p. 432, s.v. *"Cacicus cela."*

28 · MS *anacans.* Contrary to Brandônio's assertion, the *anacã* is a parrot—the hawk-headed parrot (*Deroptyus accipitrinus* L.). With its long, rounded tail, it looks more like a hawk than a parrot when in flight. Garcia, ed., *Diálogos,* V, n. 1; Clements, *Birds of the World,* p. 128; Rodolphe Meyer De Schauensee, *The Birds of Colombia and Adjacent Areas of South and Central America,* p. 110, s.v. "red-fan parrot"; F. Haverschmidt, *Birds of Surinam,* p. 149.

29 · Perhaps a variant of *guarainhete* (see above, n. 26); it would not be the first time that Brandônio unwittingly listed variants of the same name as if they designated different creatures or plants.

30 · In the Middle Ages it was believed that the pelican offered its breast to its young so that they might feed on its blood—a legend that gave rise to the use of the pelican in Christian symbolism to typify the Atonement. For a more detailed explanation of the myth see the *Catholic Encyclopedia*, s.v. "pelican."

31 · MS *tamatianguasu*. Presumably, *tamatião* [night heron] + *açu* [large]. *Taylor.*

32 · MS *quriquaqua*. Perhaps the buff-necked ibis (*Theristicus caudatus* Bod.). This bird is brownish gray, with white wings and breast and a long, curved beak. Its name imitates its cry. See Rodolpho von Ihering, *Dicionário dos animais do Brasil*, s.v. "curicaca," and De Schauensee, *Birds of South America*, p. 34, s.v. *"Theristicus caudatus."*

33 · MS *arasari*. Another Tupi name for this bird is *tucani* [little toucan]. Both refer to any of the toucans of the genera *Pteroglossus* Ill., *Baillonius* Cass., and *Selenidera* Gould. These are small, bright-plumaged birds with long bills. *Aurélio*, s.v. "araçari."

34 · MS *migua*. From Tupi *mbi gua* [round foot]. The olivaceous cormorant (*Phalacrocorax olivaceus* Humb.), a large water bird with a strong hooked bill. Clements, *Birds of the World*, p. 16; *Aurélio;* Haverschmidt, *Birds of Surinam*, pp. 8–9.

35 · MS *giruba*. A motmot, probably the blue-crowned motmot (*Momotus momota* L.), which has blue-green feathers. This bird, usually less than four inches long, looks like a tiny kingfisher. It burrows deeply into the banks of rivers to make its nest. Information from Field Museum of Natural History, Chicago; De Schauensee, *Birds of Colombia*, p. 169, s.v. "blue-crowned motmot."

36 · Also *piririguá*. The guira cuckoo (*Guira guira* Gmel.). The name *pirariguá* is also used for other birds, for instance the *peitica*. Clements, *Birds of the World*, p. 134; Garcia, ed., *Diálogos*, V, n. 1. See below, n. 45.

37 · The name *japu* is used for various birds of the family of the Icteridae, especially those of the genera *Gymnostinops* Scl. and *Ostinops* Cab., which have a large yellow beak and a long yellow tail. *Aurélio.*

38 · Garcia suggests in his notes to the *Diálogos* (V, n. 1) that this is the *guarajuba* or *guirejaúba* (*Conurus guarouba* Gmel). But in a note in Cardim's *Tratados*, Garcia identifies it as the *quereiuá* (*Cotinga cincta* Kuhl) (p. 105). The latter is surely the correct identification, for the *guarajuba* is a yellow bird, as its Tupi name—*guara* [bird] + *juba* [yellow]—indicates, whereas Brandônio's bird is blue.

39 · Possibly the *taquara*, a name applied to two genera of the family Momotidae: *Baryphthengus* Cab. and Hein. and *Momotus* Briss., birds that are

little known because they inhabit the jungle. Another name for *taquara* is *juruva*. Von Ihering, *Dicionário dos animais do Brasil; Aurélio*, s.v. "juruva." Brandônio mentioned a *juruva* earlier (above, n. 35), but that is apparently a different bird from the one described here. Perhaps in his time *taquara* and *juruva* designated different varieties of motmot.

40 · The red-rumped cacique (*Cacicus haemorrhous* L.). Walters, *Birds of the World*, p. 293.

41 · This bird has not been identified.

42 · MS *tucanosu*. The large toco toucan (*Rhamphastos toco*). The Tupi is *ti* [beak] + *cang* [bone] + *açu* [big]. *Taylor*, s.v. "tucanaçu." See Soares de Sousa, *Notícia do Brasil* (1945), 2:90 and n. 3.

43 · Garcia says this must be *taperá*, the brown-crested martin (*Progne tapera*), also called *andorinha* [swallow] in some parts of Brazil. Clements, *Birds of the World*, p. 274; Garcia, ed., *Diálogos*, V, n. 1.

44 · Brandônio is quite right, for the *Hirundo* is a widespread genus of swallow, found in both the Old World and the New. It is possible that the birds originally migrated from Africa to North and South America. Philip J. Darlington, Jr., *Zoogeography: The Geographical Distribution of Animals*, p. 308, s.v. "Hirundinidae."

45 · *Tapera naevia* L. (*Aurélio*) or *Empidonomus varius* Vieill. (Garcia). The *peitica* has at least fifteen popular names, among them *saci, matitaperê*, and *pirariguá*, names also applied to other birds. Garcia notes that the *peitica* retains its bad reputation today in the northern states of Brazil. *Aurélio*, s.v. "saci"; Garcia, ed., *Diálogos*, V, n. 1.

46 · Below, p. 314, and see VI, n. 46.

47 · Brandônio uses the Portuguese word *ema* (*hema*). The rhea is the three-toed South American ostrich, *Rhea americana*. The rhea is similar in appearance to the true ostrich (genus *Struthio*) of Africa and the Near East, but is smaller and more finely feathered. The MS reading, *hema*, is yet another instance of the name of an Old World creature being applied to a denizen of the New World that was thought to resemble it. The *ema* [rhea] is not to be confused with the Australian emu (*Dromiceius novaehollandiae*), which is likewise similar to the ostrich but is even smaller than the *ema*. Alfred Newton, *A Dictionary of Birds*, pp. 212–213, s.v. "emeu"; Clements, *Birds of the World*, p. 4.

Other writers of the time repeat with less skepticism than Brandão the assertion that the rhea eats metals; e.g., Marcgrave, *História natural*, p. 190. In Brazil the expression "the stomach of an ostrich" is still used of persons who can digest everything. The story that the bird uses its wings like a sail to run at great speeds is common among the chroniclers, and appears to be given some credence by Rodolpho von Ihering, *Da vida dos nossos animais: Fauna do Brasil*, p. 68. But Oliveira Pinto says (in Marcgrave, *História natural*, n. 489) that this belief has no basis in reality.

48 · Also *sariema*. MS *siriema*. Crested screamer (*Cariama cristata* L.), a red-legged bird with plumage of a dirty gray color. In spite of the seriema's resemblance to the *ema* (rhea) in both name and appearance, the two birds are not related, as Brandônio seems to think they are. Von Ihering, *Dicionário dos animais do Brasil*, s.v. "seriema"; *Aurélio*.

49 · In the sixteenth century Brazil was popularly known as "the Land of Parrots," because these birds were so numerous there.

50 · MS *coriqua*. Probably Soares de Sousa's *corica*, green with a yellow bib and a few scarlet feathers on the wings. Pirajá da Silva identifies it as *Amazona amazonica* L., and says the name is derived from Tupi *curaú*, "evil-speaking." Soares de Sousa, *Notícia do Brasil* (1945), 2:96 and n. 3. But *Aurélio* suggests it may be *Eucinetus barrabandi* Kuhl, which is green with slight yellow, scarlet, orange, blue, and black markings. The Tupi name may well have been applied to several talking birds.

51 · Also *sijá*. MS *ciia*. This is Soares de Sousa's *cuja*, which he describes as green all over and having a beak hooked downwards. His editor, Pirajá da Silva, identifies the bird as *Pionus menstruus*, a bird which retains the name *suia* in the North but is known in the South as *maitaca*. *Notícia do Brasil* (1945), 2:110–111 and n. 11. For a more detailed description of the *suia* [blue-headed parrot], see Haverschmidt, *Birds of Surinam*, p. 145, item 190.

52 · Macaw. *Ara* is a variant of *guara*, bird. Doubling a syllable in Tupi adds the idea of large size; so *arara* is "large bird."

53 · Tapirage, the process of modifying the color of parrots' feathers by rubbing a dye into the skin, is still practiced over a large part of South America. Métraux (1944) tells how the Tupinambás of coastal Brazil and certain Indians of other areas mixed a frog- or toad-skin secretion with a plant dye—usually the orange or red dye made from the annatto tree (*Bixa orellana* L.)—and rubbed it on freshly plucked areas of the parrots' skin. Other Indian groups used the fat of fish, or plant dye alone, for the same purpose. The new feathers came in most commonly yellow, but sometimes orange or red. Gilmore, "Fauna of South America," in *HSAI*, 6:397–398. The operation causes a great deal of pain to the birds, and many of them die as a result of it.

54 · The manuscript plainly reads Ireland [*Irlanda*], but this is almost certainly a mistake for Iceland [*Islanda*—an old spelling of *Islândia*]. Because *r* and *s* were easily mistaken for each other in handwriting, *Irlanda* and *Islanda* were often confused in manuscripts. Iceland at this time, along with Sweden, Norway, and Greenland, still enjoyed its great medieval reputation as a source of the most excellent falcons. See, e.g., Pietro

Martire d'Anghiera [Peter Martyr], *Decades of the Newe Worlde,* in *The First Three English Books on America* [?1511]–1555 A.D., p. 300. Ireland, on the other hand, was rarely mentioned as a breeding place for falcons. Brandão himself writes *Islanda* in a closely ensuing passage (p. 253), evidently referring to the same locality.

55 · Also *apacanim;* today *urutaurana.* Ornate hawk-eagle (*Spizaetus ornatus* Daud.). Garcia, ed., *Diálogos,* V, n. 1; Von Ihering, *Dicionário dos animais do Brasil,* s.v. "apacanim."

56 · On p. 249 Brandônio said that hunting birds are not used in Brazil because "the men don't want to take the trouble."

57 · It is not possible to identify with certainty all the falcons named by Brandônio. Falcons of the seventeenth century cannot be assigned to modern scientifically designated species, partly because Linnaeus's classification of birds had not yet come into existence and partly because falconry was beginning to lose its popularity, so that the meanings of some of the terms of the sport, including names of birds, were lost. Clado Ribeiro de Lessa, *Vocabulário de caça,* pp. 72–73.

58 · Not identified.

59 · Not identified.

60 · The *eixua guaçu* and the *eixua merim* [large and small *eixua*] were known to the author of a list of birds of prey prepared at the end of the sixteenth century, "De algumas cousas mais notáveis do Brasil," *Revista do Instituto Histórico e Geográfico Brasileiro* 148 (1923):400–401, s.v. "Pássaros de rapina." Unfortunately, the birds were not described.

61 · Also *toató, taquató.* MS *taguato.* Today a generic name for hawk. Pirajá da Silva in Soares de Sousa, *Notícia do Brasil* (1945), 2:104, n. 2.

62 · MS *quaraquara. Milvago chimachima* Vieill. This bird of prey is related to the falcons; its Tupi name is derived from its cry. It is a beautiful bird with brownish-yellow feathers tipped with white and yellow, and a black and white tail. Mary Louise Grossman and John Hamlet, *Birds of Prey of the World,* pp. 377, 378; Guilherme Piso, *História natural e médica da Índia Ocidental,* pp. 195–196.

63 · Not identified. This onomatopoetic word is likely to have been a popular local name.

64 · Also *jucurutu, nhacurutu.* MS *jaqueretu.* This is Magellan's great horned owl (*Bubo virginianus magellanicus* Gmel.). *Taylor,* s.v. "jacurutu."

65 · Also *sondais, suiná, suinara, suindara, tuidara.* MS *tuindá.* The common barn owl, *Strix flammea perlata* Licht. Von Ihering, *Dicionário dos animais do Brasil,* s.v. "suindara."

66 · MS *burahu.* Probably a local variant of *bacurau (acurau),* a name applied to a number of genera of the family Caprimulgidae. The birds, which are mainly nocturnal, are known in English as nightjars or goatsuckers.

The latter name, which is duplicated in many languages as well as in the scientific designation of the family, reflects an absurd tradition as to how the bird obtains its nourishment. The *bacurau* spends its day in sleep, perched on a tree or crouching on the ground, becoming active towards nightfall and hunting throughout the night. Brandônio appears to use *burau* for certain smaller birds of the family, which resemble martins and swallows. Wied-Neuwied makes a distinction between the little goatsuckers, which he found on the beaches of the northeast coast of Brazil, and a larger species that inhabited the woods. Marcgrave saw the birds in the neighborhood of Pernambuco, where they were known as *ibiiau.* Newton, *Dictionary of Birds,* pp. 638–643; Maximilian Alexander von Wied-Neuwied, *Travels in Brazil, in the Years 1815, 1816, 1817, Part 1,* p. 147; Marcgrave, *História natural,* p. 195, s.v. "ibiiao," and n. 516; Emil August Goeldo, *As aves do Brasil,* pt. 1, pp. 192–193.

67 · The initial *k* of this word is an anomaly, since *k* does not occur in the Portuguese alphabet. The letter appears to be an interpolation in a different hand from the rest of the manuscript. If the original word was not *kacum,* but *acum,* the bird may be a variety of the *acurau* or *bacurau* [nightjar; see above, n. 66], which has habits much like those of Brandônio's bird.

68 · MS *airire.* White-faced tree duck (*Dendrocygna viduata* L.). The Tupi name is onomatopoetic. The bird is widely distributed on rivers and lakes of South America and Africa. Von Ihering, *Dicionário dos animais do Brasil,* s.v. "irerê."

69 · Also *paturé, poteti, poteri.* MS *potori.* The masked duck (*Oxyura dominica*). These ducks are distributed in great numbers throughout South America. Clements, *Birds of the World,* p. 32; Von Ihering, *Dicionário dos animais do Brasil,* s.v. "paturi"; *Taylor,* s.v. "paturi."

70 · Also *saracura, sericora.* MS *seriquo.* The rail, any of various species of the genera *Limnopardalus* and *Aramides.* This bird lives near fresh water or in swamps. Soares de Sousa, *Notícia do Brasil* (1945), 2:115, n. 2; Francisco Augusto Pereira da Costa, *Apontamentos para um vocabulário pernambucano de termos e phrases populares,* in *Revista do Instituto Arqueológico, Histórico e Geográfico Pernambucano* 34 (1936), p. 671, s.v. "sericoia."

71 · MS *colhereiro.* The Tupi is *ajajá;* Brandônio uses a Portuguese name that designated in Portugal a bird similar to the *ajajá* and of the same family. The name *ajajá* is no longer used in Brazil, but as with many other Tupi names, it is preserved in the scientific designation of the species, *Ajaja ajaja.* Von Ihering, *Dicionário dos animais do Brasil,* s.v. "colhereiro."

72 · MS *caram.* Limpkin or courlan (*Aramus scolopaceus* Gmel.). According to *Webster's Seventh New Collegiate Dictionary* (1965), "courlan" is not derived from the Tupi but comes, through the French, from the Galibi *kurliri.*

(The Galibi are Carib Indians living in the Guianas.) The second part of the Galibi word echoes the bird's cry. Newton, *Dictionary of Birds,* s.v. "limpkin," pp. 514–515.

73 · Perhaps the *guaruru* (*taquiri, taquari*), the black-crowned night heron (*Nycticorax nycticorax* L.). De Schauensee, *Birds of Colombia,* p. 31.

74 · Perhaps the *guarirama* of Soares de Sousa—the green kingfisher (*Chloroceryle americana americana* Gmel.). Pirajá da Silva derives the name from Tupi *guará* [sea-bird] + *ariramba* [small]. Soares de Sousa, *Notícia do Brasil* (1945), 2:92 and n. 5.

75 · Soares de Sousa reported that a similar phenomenon could be observed during the summer in Bahia: the butterflies flying over the city of Salvador towards the far side of the bay, a distance of nine or ten leagues (thirty-one to thirty-four miles), in such numbers that they filled the air. Soares's editor, Pirajá da Silva, witnessed the migration in modern times. Neither writer speaks of the butterflies' drowning themselves. Garcia cites modern naturalists on this migration. Soares de Sousa, *Notícia do Brasil* (1945), 2:117 and n. 5; Garcia, ed., *Diálogos,* V, n. 2.

76 · Brandônio is evidently referring to the story about the astrologer who was so preoccupied with gazing at the stars that he failed to watch his own feet and hence fell into a well. The fable was repeated by several classical authors, including Plato, who relates it of Thales in the *Theaetetus.* It also appeared in sixteenth- and seventeenth-century collections of *facéties.* After Brandão's time, La Fontaine included the anecdote in his *Fables* (bk. II, no. 13). It is also told about various other people; a version heard on television in 1979 made the story apply to Albert Einstein. There appears to be no reason for foisting it on Aristotle except that this was a common practice with all sorts of traditional lore. The versions differ in detail, but most agree that the man was an astrologer, his attention fixed on the heavens so that he did not see where his feet were going. Brandônio, by omitting this essential element, has destroyed the point of the story.

77 · Also *acarapitanga.* MS *carapitangua.* Any of various fishes of the genus *Lutianus,* especially the red snapper, *L. aya* Bloch. The Tupi is *acará* [the name of several fishes] + *pitanga* [red]. Soares de Sousa, *Notícia do Brasil* (1945), 2:200, n.5; *Taylor,* s.v. "vermelho."

78 · MS *serra.* Any of several mackerel-like fishes of the genus *Scomberomorus,* found in tropical waters. The Portuguese name for these fish, *serra,* and the Spanish name, *sierra,* both mean "saw"; English-speaking peoples use the Spanish term.

79 · Also *camuripema, camuripim, congurupi, pirapema,* etc. MS *camoropim.* The common tarpon (*Tarpon atlanticus* Val.). *Aurélio.*

80 · In the manuscript the initial *c* appears to have been written over a *g;* the

spelling with *g—gamboa*—is the southern form of this word. A *camboa* is a shallow pond or lagoon that communicates with the sea by a narrow inlet and that is provided with a gate. At high tide the gate is opened by the pressure of the water, and the fish enter; at low tide the gate closes and the fish are caught inside.

When Manuel de Azevedo at some time prior to 1596 settled the island of Conceição in the mouth of the Paraíba River, he constructed on the island not only a fort but also a *camboa,* which proved valuable as a source of fish for the captaincy. Brandão must have seen this *camboa* many times. "Carta de data da nossa ilha da Restinga defronte de Cabedello," *Revista do Instituto Histórico e Geográfico Paraibano* 10 (1946): 179–180.

81 · Brandônio amplifies and partly repeats the description of the sea cow given on p. 30; and see I, n. 79.

82 · On Fridays and other fast days Catholics usually ate fish instead of meat. Cardim in 1585 reported that in the Jesuit *colégio*'s garden in Rio de Janeiro "the fish are varied and numerous; you just ought to see the great catches on Fridays." Cardim and other contemporaries voiced the same scruple as Alviano about eating the meat of the sea cow on fast days. *Tratados,* pp. 70–71, 309.

83 · The ten-pounder (*Elops saurus* L.). The Tupi name of this elongated fish comes from *iba* [stick] + *rana* [like]. The fish has an excellent flavor, but it is difficult to eat because of the small bones dispersed throughout the flesh. Soares de Sousa, *Notícia do Brasil* (1945), 2:206 and n. 8; Marcgrave, *História natural,* p. 154; *Taylor.*

84 · MS *gaibicuarasu.* Garcia thought this might be Soares de Sousa's *goaivicoara* (*guaibicuara, guaibi, guaimi* [*Conodon nobilis* L.]), called *roncador* [grunter] by the Portuguese in reference to the sound the fish makes in the water. Soares de Sousa, *Notícia do Brasil* (1945), 2:205 and n. 9; Garcia, ed., *Diálogos,* V, n. 3. Cf. Cunha, *Dicionário tupi,* s.v. *guaibicuaraçu.*

85 · MS *camorim.* The snook: any of various species of the genus *Centropomis.* The name *camurim* is heard in the North of Brazil; in the South the fish goes by the Portuguese name *robalo,* which properly designates a popular European fish, *Labrax lupus.* The *camurim* is a favorite of gourmets in Brazil. Eurico Santos, *Nossos peixes marinhos,* pp. 136–137, s.v. "robalo"; Soares de Sousa, *Notícia do Brasil* (1945), 2:206, n. 6; *Taylor.*

86 · Most fishes have calcium carbonate concretions in their inner ears. This stonelike material varies in amount according to the species. Brandônio's description is too brief to permit identification of the fish. Dr. Loren Woods, former Curator of Ichthyology, Field Museum of Natural History, Chicago.

87 · Also called *cambira, tainha-de-corso, tainha-seca, tainha-curimã, tainha-*

verdadeira. MS *corima*. The striped mullet (*Mugil cephalus* L.). In Pernambuco this is the best liked for food of the local mullets. Eurico Santos, *Nossos peixes marinhos*, pp. 104–105.

88 · Also *carapeua, acarapeba;* MS *carapeva*. *Diapterus rhombeus* Cuv., a mojarra. The Tupi is *cara* [short for *acara*, fish] + *peba* [flat]. Soares de Sousa, *Notícia do Brasil* (1945), 2:210, n. 6; *Taylor; Aurélio*.

89 · Also *corumbatá, curumatá, crumatá, curimatá, grumatã*. MS *curamata*. A scaly freshwater fish of the genus *Prochilodus* Agass. The Tupi is a corruption of *guiri* [fish] + *mbatã* [tender]. Costa, *Vocabulário pernambucano*, s.v. "curumatá"; Von Ihering, *Dicionário dos animais do Brasil*, s.v. "corumbatá."

90 · Three genera and a number of species of the piranha have been identified. The fish is intensely feared throughout Brazil for the reason given by Brandônio. Many stories both true and false are told of its fierce, often fatal, attacks on animals and men, which make swimming in some rivers too dangerous to be attempted. For a detailed discussion of the piranha see George S. Myers, ed., *The Piranha Book*.

91 · The third largest of Brazil's great rivers and the largest that is wholly in Brazil. It rises inland from Rio de Janeiro, in western Minas Gerais, and flows north for more than 1,000 miles into the state of Bahia and the border of Pernambuco; then it turns east to the ocean, forming the boundary between Alagoas and Sergipe.

92 · The Una River flows into the sea at Barreiros in southeastern Pernambuco. Piranhas are found in many rivers of Brazil as well as of other South American countries.

93 · MS *peixe-galo*, the Portuguese name. *Selene vomar* L. Most of the chroniclers take note of this fish, using its Tupi name in various forms: *abacatuaia* (Marcgrave), *abacatuajá* (Piso), *zabucai* (*çabucai*) (Soares de Sousa). See Soares de Sousa, *Notícia do Brasil* (1945), 2:209, n. 2; Eurico Santos, *Peixes de água doce*, p. 165.

94 · Brandônio's *salé* may be the *solé* (*Mugil curema* Val.), more commonly known as *parati*. The *solé* is a mullet common in Brazilian waters, like other fishes Brandônio discusses in this passage. Eurico Santos, *Nossos peixes marinhos*, p. 106.

95 · MS *saasu*. Amber-fish (*Seriola lalandi* Val.). A sea fish, whose Tupi name is derived from the trait Brandônio describes: Tupi *eçá* [eye] + *açu* [large]. Today the fish is called *olho de boi* [ox-eye] in Portuguese. Garcia, ed., *Diálogos*, V, n. 3; *Aurélio* and *Taylor*, s.v. "olho-de-boi."

96 · MS *sauna*. Either of two mullets, *Querimana curvidens* Val. or *Q. brevirostris* Mir. Rib. *Aurélio*.

97 · See above, n. 87.

98 · MS *mandeii*. A name common to various freshwater catfishes.

99 · The Portuguese name that Brandônio uses, *roncador*, means grunter, and is derived from the sound the fish makes in the water. The *roncador* is identified as *Condon nobilis* L. or *Bairdiella ronchus* Cuv. In all probability this is the same fish as the *gaibicuaraçu* mentioned in n. 84 above, q.v. See also *Aurélio*, s.v. "roncador."

100 · Wagener states that the *corcovado* [hunchback] resembles a carp in size and taste. Zacharias Wagener, *Zoobiblion: Livro de animais do Brasil*, p. 186 and illus. no. 10. Olivério Pinto in his commentary on the *corcovado* suggests that the fish belongs to the family of the Carangidae; he thinks it may be the *cabeçudo* [bighead], a name applied to several species of the genus *Caranx*, which is found in Bahian waters. See also Piso, *História natural e médica*, p. 147.

101 · Puffers: various species of the genus *Spheroides*. Tupi *baiacu* or *maiacu*, from *mbaecu* [something hot or poisonous]. Soares de Sousa, *Notícia do Brasil* (1945), 2:213 and n. 5.

102 · Also *tamuatá, tamboatá, cambuatá, camboatá, cambute, tambuatá*. Armored catfish (*Callichthys callichthys* L.). Edelweiss says the correct Tupi form is *camboatá*, from *caa* [forest] + *bo* [through the] + *atá* [walking], "the one who walks through the forest." Gabriel Soares de Sousa, *Notícia do Brasil* (1974), p. 468.

103 · Perhaps the fish is the *acari* (also *cari, uacari*), of the genus *Loricaria;* Soares de Sousa gives *acará*, from *aca* [shell] + *ra* [scaly]. The Portuguese word *cascudo* [hard-shelled] is another name for the *acari* in Brazil. Its body, like that of the *tamoatá*, is protected by bony plates. Soares de Sousa, *Notícia do Brasil* (1945), 2:232 and n. 11; Eurico Santos, *Peixes de água doce*, pp. 92–95.

104 · MS *jacundã*. Any of various fishes of the genus *Crenicichla* Heckel, very common in the North of Brazil. *Jacundá* is a corruption of the Tupi *nacundá*, "he who has a large mouth." Costa, *Vocabulário pernambucano*, s.v. "jacundá."

105 · *Piaba* (*piava*) is the name given in the Northeast of Brazil to certain small freshwater fish of the family Characidae, subfamily Tetragonopterinae, which are known in the South as *lambaris*. Von Ihering, *Dicionário dos animais do Brasil*, s.v. "lambari."

106 · Also *carapó, sarapó-tuvira, ituipinima. Cymnotus carapo* L. The Tupi *sarapó* means "the one who slips out of the hand." The fish is widely distributed in Brazil. *Aurélio*, s.v. "carapó" and "sarapó."

107 · Also *tarira, tariira, taraíra*. MS *tararira. Hoplias malabaricus* Bloch. Von Ihering, *Dicionário dos animais do Brasil*, s.v. "traíra." The fish moves in sluggish water from which worms find their way inside its head and there lay their eggs. Dr. Loren Woods, former Curator of Ichthyology, Field Museum of Natural History, Chicago.

108 · MS *musu*. The *muçu* is the only representative in South America of the family Symbranchidae, *Symbranchus marmoratus* Bloch. Von Ihering, *Dicionário dos animais do Brasil*, s.v. "muçum." When the ponds in the fields dry up after the rainy season, this fish burrows into the ground, where it remains for months; with the return of the water it revives. Brandônio is of course mistaken in thinking that the fish appears in fields where there never were any fish before, but he is not alone in making this mistake. Aristotle himself presented a similar theory: "Certain fishes are produced spontaneously, and do not come out of eggs or from copulation. [These] are all formed either out of mud or out of sand and the putrefying matter on the surface. This fry never grows or propagates, and as time goes on it disintegrates, to be followed by a fresh growth, so that apart from a short interval there is some of it almost all the rest of the time: it persists from the autumn [rising of] Arcturus until the spring." Aristotle, *Historia Animalium*, 2:283–285.

109 · A trammel is a net consisting of three layers, the two outer ones being coarse meshed and the middle one fine meshed and slack. The fish pass easily through either outer layer and are pocketed in the interior net.

110 · Cf. *camboa*, n. 80 above.

111 · See III, n. 122.

112 · Tupi *capim* [grass] + *guara* [eater]. The capybara (*Hydrochoerus hydrochoerus* L.) is a member of the guinea pig family and is the largest living rodent. The Portuguese call the animal a water hog because it spends so much time in the water. An adult capybara may reach four feet in length and may weigh up to 100 pounds. Hans Staden describes the animal as follows: "There is also an animal called Cativare, which lives both on land and in water, and eats the reeds growing by the water's edge, and when these beasts are alarmed they dive to the bottom. They are bigger than sheep, having a head shaped like a hare['s], only larger, and they are short-eared. They have a short tail and fairly long legs. On land they move quickly from one body of water to another. . . . The flesh tastes like pig's flesh." The fact that the capybara feeds on land established its claim to be meat rather than fish, just as Brandônio says. Hans Staden, *The True History of His Captivity, 1557*, ed. Malcolm Letts, p. 165, and p. 182, n. 92; *Aurélio*, s.v. "capivara."

113 · An example of Brandônio's logic at its lowest ebb: the high quality of the capybara's flesh is no reason for considering it meat!

114 · Cf. I, n. 79 and, for the scruple about the meat of the sea cow, p. 256, and n. 82 above.

115 · The conflict between doubting and believing, or experience and authority, so typical·of the period, recurs throughout the *Dialogues*. Usually, as in the present passage, Alviano is the doubter and Brandônio the believer,

but it is not possible to say that either speaker consistently voices either point of view. Rather, both reflect the uncertainties of their time.

116 · See p. 45, and I, n. 162.

117 · Early writers on Brazil and India reflect these and other theories about the origin of ambergris: it is the "foam" or the "filth and dung" of the whale; or it comes from a well at the bottom of the sea; or it is a plant growing on the bottom of the ocean, as Brandônio suggests. For a detailed summary of early theories of origin, see Albert Gray in his edition of François Pyrard de Laval, *The Voyage of François Pyrard, of Laval to the East Indies, the Maldives, the Moluccas and Brazil,* 1:229, n. 1. See also John [Jan] Huyghen van Linschoten, *The Voyage of John Huyghen van Linschoten to the East Indies,* 2:92–93; Duarte Barbosa, *The Book of Duarte Barbosa,* 2:106–107 and n. 3; João dos Santos, *Ethiópia Oriental, e vária história de cousas notáveis do Oriente,* bk. 1, chap. 28. For the modern scientific view see I, n. 82.

118 · Properly Ponta Negra, at least today.

119 · The spring tide occurs each month at or shortly after the new and the full moon. It is normally the highest tide of the month.

120 · On pp. 162–163 and in III, n. 165.

121 · The pearls probably came from clams. Dr. Alan Solem, Curator of Invertebrates at the Field Museum of Natural History, Chicago, graciously informed the editors that Brazil has a fauna of more than 100 different species of freshwater clams, most of which would have the potential of occasionally secreting a pearl.

122 · MS *sapimiaga.* According to L. Travassos (as cited by Von Ihering), the *sapinhaguá* is an edible mollusk; Von Ihering thinks it may be similar to the cockle. Von Ihering, *Dicionário dos animais do Brasil,* s.v. "sapinhaguá."

123 · The name *sernambim* is applied to a large number of marine bivalves, but Brandônio is evidently referring to one of several species, such as *Murex brancaris* L., *M. truncatulus* L., or *Purpura patula* L., which possess a gland that secretes a colorless liquid. By the activity of sunlight and fermentation this liquid takes on a purple color. It was used by the ancients to dye rich fabrics and vestments, an art which, according to legend, goes back to the sixteenth century B.C. See Soares de Sousa, *Notícia do Brasil* (1945), 2:235, n. 1.

Brandônio is in error about the "menstrual flow," but his mistake is understandable. Alan Solem (see n. 121 above) furnished the following explanation: Many marine clams have the habit, during appropriate phases of the moon, of sending sex products into the water, which would account for the "menstrual flow."

124 · Alviano has frequented Brazil for at least eighteen years, since he refers to something he saw there in 1600 (p. 91). Yet he does not consider

himself an old settler: see p. 105. Apparently Brandônio concurs, since he does not expect Alviano to be familiar with "the strange *sernambim*."

125 · MS *usá*. The fiddler crab (*Gelasimus stenodactylus*). Von Ihering, *Da vida dos nossos animais*, p. 194.

126 · MS *seri*. A name applied to several species of crustaceans belonging to the family Portunidae. Von Ihering, *Dicionário dos animais do Brasil*, s.v. "siri."

127 · Also *goiá, guajá, guaiá-apará, uacapará*. MS *goajá*. The generic name for crab in the Tupi language. Von Ihering, *Dicionário dos animais do Brasil*, s.v. "guaiá."

128 · MS *guoazaranha*. Spider crab. A mixed Tupi and Portuguese word: Tupi *guaiá* [crab] + Portuguese *aranha* [spider].

129 · *Aratus pisoni* Milne Edw., a small, squarish marine land crab that lives on reefs and in mangrove swamps, where it climbs easily to the top branches of the trees. It is collected by torchlight. Von Ihering, *Dicionário dos animais do Brasil*, s.v. *aratu; Aurélio;* Costa, *Vocabulário pernambucano*, s.v. "aratú."

130 · Also *goaiaüçá, quara-uçá, graüçá*. MS *garausâ*. *Oxypoda arenaria* Catesby. From Tupi *quara* [hole] + *uçá* [crab] = "crab that lives in a hole." A small reddish crab found on the beaches, in holes in the sand. In popular language in Brazil, *graüçá* came to mean "red-headed person." Soares de Sousa, *Notícia do Brasil* (1945), 2:221, n. 5.

131 · Also *guaimu, goiamu, guaiamum*. MS *guanhamu*. *Cardisoma guanhumi* Latreille. This crab measures more than half a meter in breadth. In the North of Brazil it is caught in fish traps, fattened with scraps from the table, and eventually used as food. Vicente do Salvador's account of the habits of the *guaiamu* is strikingly similar to Brandônio's: "During the first rains of winter, which are in February, when they are fattest and the females full of eggs, they come out of their holes and go wandering about the fields and roads and making their way into the houses, where they are eaten." *História do Brasil, 1500–1627*, p. 81.

132 · The ovaries, which in some crustaceans are bright red.

133 · MS *andaõ ao ata* (modern *andam ao atá*), "wander aimlessly." Many words and phrases expressing aimless movement carry the meaning "lascivious" in Brazil, especially when applied to females. Costa, *Vocabulário pernambucano*, s.v. "atôá."

134 · A small Spanish warhorse which had been used in fighting the Moors on the Peninsula, and which in America proved to be both dependable and sturdy. J. F. de Almeida Prado, *Pernambuco e as capitanias do norte do Brasil* (1530–1630), 4:57.

135 · In the wild territories between the Rio de la Plata and Patagonia roamed thousands of wild horses, descendants of Spanish animals that had been

abandoned by the Europeans. Now deteriorated in physique, they moved across the pampas in herds of as many as 10,000. Félix de Azara, *Apuntamientos para la historia natural de los quadrúpedos del Paragüay y Rio de la Plata,* 2:202–213.

136 · The "Guinea slaves" often had a hard time getting enough to eat. For the most part they had to raise their own food in the scanty free time they had left after laboring long hours for their masters. Small wonder that they stole and ate horses, filched manioc from the fields (p. 196), and, according to some accounts, drank oil from the lamps in the sugar mills or licked it from the implements.

137 · See III, n. 90. *Pato,* the game of running at the duck, in spite of being quite dangerous, was very popular, especially among the gauchos of Argentina and southern Brazil. As it was originally played, the participants, mounted on horseback, struggled for the possession of a duck [*pato*], which was buried up to its neck in the ground. To win the game it was necessary to get possession of the *pato* and then to carry it three or four miles while defending it from the other players. The participants threw themselves on their adversaries, lashing them with their whips and trying to bring down their horses with a kind of lariat having nails at one end and capable of being thrown so as to twist around a horse's foot. Later the duck was replaced by a heavy ball with handles, which is still known as the *pato.* See Azara, *Apuntamientos,* 2:225–226.

138 · A corruption of the Tupi *cáa-piy* [delicate leaf or delicate plant]. Costa, *Vocabulário pernambucano,* s.v. "capim"; *Aurélio.*

139 · A mule is the offspring of a union between a jackass (male donkey) and a mare. The "breeding donkeys" Brandônio wanted sent out from the Kingdom would have mated with each other, and their male offspring would have been bred with mares to produce mules.

140 · Cattle, as well as horses, destined for Brazil were usually taken first to Cape Verde, where they were bred and the offspring conditioned to face the rigors of life in the pastures of the Northeast. Soares de Sousa, *Notícia do Brasil* (1945), 1:301 and n. 1.

141 · According to Prado, Brandônio refers here to the wealthy Duarte Gomes da Silveira. *Pernambuco,* 4:50. See I, n. 106, and III, n. 106.

142 · The "corrals" were actually pastures, since the word at this time meant simply a place where livestock was raised. Prado, *Pernambuco,* 4:50.

143 · The prices of cattle for Pernambuco as given by Brandônio were higher than in some other parts of the country because the sugar mills in the Northeast required a constant supply of these animals. In São Paulo horses could be bought for only one-fifth or one-sixth of the price demanded in the North. See Roberto C. Simonsen, *História econômica do Brasil (1500–1820),* p. 163.

144 · In the manuscript a different hand has added *"e quatro"* ("and four").

145 · Another reason for the lack of interest in raising livestock was that pasture lands were scarce, since much of the land that would have been suitable for pasture was used for the raising of sugar cane. This created a problem because cattle were needed in the sugar-milling process.

146 · Modern science has established that a cross between two genera is virtually impossible. Nevertheless, the belief in the hybrid Brandônio describes, as well as in other non-existent hybrids, remained firmly fixed in men's minds for a long time. As late as 1937 Affonso de E. Taunay, discussing this very passage in the *Dialogues,* asserted the existence of this creature, citing two authorities. One of these, the Brazilian zoologist Candido de Mello Leitão, according to Taunay, reported that the animal was known to the Romans and was still common in France, where it was called *chabin* or *chabris.* Taunay gives no citation for Leitão's alleged statement, and no allusion to the *chabin* has been found in any of Leitão's published works. The other authority cited by Taunay is the *Dictionnaire Larousse,* which, according to Taunay, says the *chabin* is very rare but not impossible, even being abundant in Cuba, Santo Domingo, and Mexico. The reference to Larousse is wrong, for Larousse dictionaries and encylopaedias from the earliest edition (of 1897–1904) list the *chabin* only as a "mistake." Taunay may have been recalling the entry in *La Grande Encyclopédie* of 1885–1892, s.v. "chabin," which does list the creature as real and defines it as the product of the crossing of a female goat with a ram. Affonso de E. Taunay, "Monstros e monstrengos do Brasil," *Revista do Museu Paulista* 21 (1937):925–926. Believers in the *chabin* had the support of no less eminent a naturalist than Buffon, who asserted that couplings between goats and sheep do occur rather frequently, and are sometimes prolific, but that no intermediate species has resulted. Georges Buffon, *Histoire naturelle, générale et particulière* (Paris: Sanson, 1786), vol. 32, *Quadrupèdes,* tome 1:184–185.

147 · The pork was from pigs imported from Portugal, since no true pig is native to Brazil. According to Piso, pigs were better for eating when bred in Brazil from animals of Portuguese stock. "Their meat is a safe and agreeable delicacy, and preferred to that of sheep," he declared. *História natural médica,* p. 227. Anchieta wrote in 1585 that "the sick eat chicken and pork, the latter being better during the entire year in both healthfulness and taste." But this favorable opinion of pork was beginning to lose ground, as appears from Alviano's following remark. Eventually pork disappeared altogether from medically recommended dietaries. Joseph [José] de Anchieta, *Cartas, informações, fragmentos históricos e sermões (1554–1594),* p. 428; cf. Kaspar van Baerle, *Rerum per Octennium in Brasilia et Alibi Gestarum, sub Praefectura Illustrissimi Comitis*

I. Mauritii Nassaviae . . . Historia, p. 223; Luís da Câmara Cascudo, *História da alimentação no Brasil,* p. 214.

148 · In contrast to Brandônio's intellectual independence at the beginning of Dialogue I and elsewhere, in this passage he adheres to tradition and condemns "modern doctors" who prefer their own judgment to the authority of the ancients. As in society in general, so in the individual the Renaissance conflict was resolved sometimes in favor of the old, sometimes of the new.

149 · See above, n. 140.

150 · *Tapirus americanus* Gmel. The Portuguese word *anta,* which Brandônio uses, appears to be of Arabic origin. The Tupi name for the animal, *tapira,* has given us the English word tapir. One of the largest Brazilian game animals, the tapir served as a standard of comparison for unfamiliar creatures. Thus the Indians called the cow, which was brought in by the Portuguese, *tapiraçu biaguara* [big foreign tapir]. Tapirs ordinarily travel in pairs, opening wide paths through the jungle that are known as milky ways. Von Ihering, *Dicionário dos animais do Brasil,* pp. 91–93; Cascudo, *História da alimentação no Brasil,* p. 156.

151 · In Portugal men hunted the wild boar on horseback, with a pack of hounds. Earlier they had used spears, but by this time firearms must have been the most commonly employed weapons. Hence the difference Brandônio notes between Portuguese and Brazilian methods of hunting did not lie in the weaponry. Rather, he appears to be thinking of the Brazilian practice, described here, of lying in wait for the animals in places where they were accustomed to congregate, instead of chasing them on horseback as was done in Portugal. A. H. de Oliveira Marques, *Daily Life in Portugal in the Late Middle Ages,* p. 244. Cf. Dom João I's treatise on hunting, *Livro da montaria,* ed. Francisco Maria Esteves Pereira (Coimbra: Universidade de Coimbra, 1918).

152 · The animal described here is a peccary, called by the settlers *porco-do-mato* [wild pig]. The species mentioned by Brandônio are the only two to be found in Brazil. The *taiaçu* is the white-lipped peccary (*Dicotyles albirostris*), and the *taitetu* or *taçuité* is the white-collared peccary (*Dicotyles tayassu*). A number of sixteenth-century chroniclers assert, like Brandônio, that the peccary has its navel on its back, but the supposed navel is really a gland. This gland gives forth an unpleasant odor; it must be removed as soon as the animal is killed to prevent the odor's permeating the flesh. The Indians used the teeth of the peccary to file their bows and arrow shafts smooth, and the bristles as paint brushes to decorate pottery. Monteiro, *Relação,* p. 417; Von Ihering, *Da vida dos nossos animais,* pp. 53–54, "Dos porcos monteses."

153 · Prado dismissed this story as a hunter's tall tale, but several chroniclers

describe similar procedures. Oviedo saw essentially the same technique in the West Indies: "When the Christians come upon a herd of pigs they try to get up on a rock or the trunk of a tree, even if it be no more than three or four palms high, and from there they wound two or three, or as many more as they can, with lance thrusts as they pass. And sparing the dogs, they capture a few in this way. But these animals are very dangerous when encountered in herds, if there is no elevated place from which the hunter may attack them, as I have said." Cardim likewise tells how the Indians hunted pigs from trees, but like Oviedo he does not say that the hunter induced them to attack each other. Cardim, *Tratados*, p. 33; Gonzalo Fernández de Oviedo y Valdés, *Oviedo dela natural historia delas Indias*, chap. 19 (misnumbered 20), fol. 21^r. Cf. Prado, *Pernambuco*, 3:241, and Von Ihering, *Da vida dos nossos animais*, p. 54.

154 · *Cuniculus paca* L. weighs some twenty-two pounds. It lives by itself in the woods, and is hunted with dogs, which drive it into its burrow or into the water. The animal provides a delicious, whitish meat. Gilmore, "Fauna of South America," in *HSAI*, 6:372.

155 · Also *aguti, cutia, acouti.* MS *cotia*. A member of any of several species of *Dasyprocta illiger* found in Brazil. The animal is a rodent related to the guinea pig. It is about the size of a rabbit and has grizzled fur. Agoutis are easily tamed and make acceptable house pets, as Brandônio notes. Von Ihering, *Dicionário dos animais do Brasil*, s.v. "cutia"; Ernest P. Walker, *Mammals of the World*, 2:1027.

156 · Also *coatimundi*. Nose-bear (*Nasua nasua* L.). A tropical carnivore, related to the raccoon. It has a long, flexible snout. Walker, *Mammals of the World*, 2:1183.

157 · Armadillo. Monteiro (1610) observes that the armadillo is often called "armored horse" because with its covering of overlapping bony plates it resembles a warhorse caparisoned for battle. A small variety, called *tatuí*, has white meat that is as delicious as chicken. Monteiro, *Relação*, pp. 419–420.

Several maps embellished with drawings of armadillos and other exotic animals are reproduced in Wilma George, *Animals and Maps* (Berkeley and Los Angeles: University of California Press, 1969): Diego Ribero's 1529 map of the world (Museum of the Propaganda), pp. 208–209; Guillaume Le Testu's 1566 world map (Bibliothèque Nationale, Paris), pp. 196–197; Jodocus Hondius's 1599 map of Guiana (pp. 72–73).

158 · Also *jaritataca, jarataqueque, jaraticaca, jariticaca, maitacaca, cangambá,* etc. MS *jarataquaqua*. Skunk (*Conepatus chilensis amazonicus*). In the manuscript an emendator has crossed out *jara* and written *mai* above the line. Garcia, ed., *Diálogos*, V, n. 5; *Aurélio*.

159 · Monteiro (1610) asserted that the smell given off by the skunk is so

overpowering that it has proved fatal to dogs and even to some Indians. *Relação,* p. 421.

160 · The Old World rabbit is *Oryctolagus cuniculus.* The New World rabbit is various species of the genus *Sylvilagus.* The two animals are similar in appearance.

161 · MS *sauja.* This is not a rabbit at all but is the spiny rat (genus *Echimys*). There are some twenty species of this rodent in South America. *Aurélio,* s.v. "sauiá"; Walker, *Mammals of the World,* 2:1063.

162 · Also *punari.* MS *punary.* The name is applied to two rodents, *Cercomys cunicularius* Cuv. and *C. inermis.* Walker, *Mammals of the World,* 2:1058.

163 · Also *apereá, aperiá.* MS *aparias. Cavia aperea* Erxleben 1777. The Tupi means "one who is constantly met on the road." The flesh of this rodent is still regarded in the Northeast of Brazil as good eating. Soares de Sousa, *Notícia do Brasil* (1945), 2:148, n. 2; Von Ihering, *Dicionário dos animais do Brasil,* s.v. "preá."

164 · MS *moquô.* Rock cavy (*Cavia rupestris* zu Wied.). A rodent similar to the guinea pig, but a little larger. *Mocó = mo-coó = ma-coó* [animal that gnaws]. In the Northeast, which has little game, the *mocó* is hunted and consumed as food. Rodolfo Garcia, "Diccionário de brasileirismos," *Revista do Instituto Histórico e Geográfico Brasileiro,* tomo 76 (1913), pt. 1, s.v. "mocó"; Walker, *Mammals of the World,* 2:1018.

165 · Unidentified.

166 · Also *cotimirim, quatipuru, agutipuru, caxinxe, caxinguelê, serelepe, quatiaipé.* MS *aquostimerim.* Pygmy squirrel (*Guerlinguetus aestuans* L. 1766 or *Sciurus aestuans* L. 1766). The Tupi name comes from *quati* [pointed nose] + *mirim* [little]. Soares de Sousa, *Notícia do Brasil* (1945), 2:144, n. 3; Von Ihering, *Dicionário dos animais do Brasil,* s.v. "serelepe."

167 · Also *guaiquica, mucura-xixica, cuíca, chichica, quíca.* MS *quoquy.* The *mocó* mentioned here is not the same animal as the *mocó* mentioned on p. 269 and in n. 164 above, which is a cavy. Here the author is describing a marsupial—a diminutive opossum, perhaps *Peramys iheringi.* One meaning of *mocó* is "bag" or "pouch"; hence *mocó* is appropriate to an animal furnished with an abdominal pocket, like the *quoqui* described here. Von Ihering, *Da vida dos nossos animais,* p. 10.

168 · Also *tamanduá-bandeira, tamanduá-cavalo, jurumi.* MS *tamendoasu. Tamanduá-açu = tá (taxi)* [ant] + *monduá* [hunter] + *açu* [large]. The great anteater (*Myrmecophaga jubata* L.). When the *tamanduá-açu* goes to sleep, it covers itself with its long tail so that it is almost completely hidden as if under a mound of dark-colored straw. Vicente do Salvador says that even in his time (1627) only aged Indians ate it. Today nobody uses the meat as food. Soares de Sousa, *Notícia do Brasil* (1945), 2:132 and n. 1;

Von Ihering, *Da vida dos nossos animais,* pp. 17–19; Vicente do Salvador, *História do Brasil,* pp. 76–77.

169 · MS *irarâ.* English "eyra." Tupi *irara* (Guarani *eira*) means "honey-eater" or "bee-eater." The Indians used this name for the honey-eating *Tayra barbara,* but the animal referred to here is the *tamanduá-mirim* (*Tamandua tetradactyla*), the small anteater (Spanish *oso colemeneo,* honey bear), which feeds on ants, termites, and bees. Walker, *Mammals of the World,* 1:486.

170 · Also *tijibu, senembu.* MS *sinébu.* The American chameleon (*Iguana tuberculata* Laurentius). The Tupi means "he who shows a change." This is not the true chameleon, which belongs to the family of the Camaeleonidae. The sinimbu is able to inflate a sac in its throat to resemble an Adam's apple, and because of this, one of its names is *papo-vento* [wind-pouch]. In the popular speech this became *papa-vento* [wind-eater]. Von Ihering, *Da vida dos nossos animais,* p. 119.

171 · See III, n. 98. "Have written" may suggest that Brandão had a written source for this portion of his work.

172 · Also *teiú, tiú.* MS *teju.* Brandônio must be referring to the *tejuaçu,* or big tegu (*Tupinambis teguixin*), the largest of Brazilian lizards, which is regarded as a delicacy. This lizard not only eats chickens but also skillfully sucks eggs through a small hole that it makes in the shell without cracking it. Eurico Santos, *Anfíbios e répteis do Brasil,* pp. 125–129; Von Ihering, *Dicionário dos animais do Brasil,* s.v. "teiú."

173 · MS *gia.* In fact, the animal *is* a frog (*Rana gigas* Spix).

174 · MS *ahû.* According to Pirajá da Silva, *aí* is an imitation of the whistling sound uttered by the animal. Soares de Sousa, *Notícia do Brasil* (1945), 2:150, n. 1.

175 · Also *jaguaraçu, guara, caxito.* MS *aguarâ asu.* From *jaguara* [wild dog] + *açu* [big]. Though sometimes called a wolf, the *aguará-açu* is not a true wolf (*Canis*) but is a maned wolf, the Brazilian species being *Chrysocyon brachyurus* Ill. The animal resembles a red fox. It is shy, preying on birds and small animals; it also eats fruits and vegetables. In spite of its retiring nature, it bears in legend a considerable reputation as a dangerous beast. Walker, *Mammals of the World,* 2:1163; C. de Mello Leitão, *Zoo-Geografia do Brasil,* pp. 297–298; Von Ihering, *Dicionário dos animais do Brasil,* s.v. "guará."

176 · Also *gato-do-mato* (Portuguese), *maracajá.* MS *maracaiâ.* Both the English margay and the Portuguese *maracajá* come from the Tupi *maracá-yá,* "he who makes a noise like a gourd rattle." Margay is a collective name for various species of the genus *Felis* that do not exceed one meter in total length. They live in the jungle and hunt small game. Von Ihering, *Dicionário dos animais do Brasil,* s.v. "gato-do-mato." The margay's coat is partly striped and partly marked with rosettes like the jaguar's. Bran-

dônio calls it *listado,* which properly means striped but is often used for vague markings.

177 · Not identified.

178 · MS *heiratê. Tayra barbara* or *Galictis barbara,* a weasel-like animal, closely akin to the grison. *Taylor,* s.v. "irara." The Tupi means "true honey-eater." The animal was often called *irara* [honey-eater], but the *eiraté* is properly a different animal from the *tamanduá-mirim,* which, as explained above (n. 169), also commonly went by the name *irara.*

179 · MS *juparra.* Kinkajou (*Potos flavus* Schreb.). In Tupi *jupará* means "the restless one." The popular name in Portugal is *macaco da meia noite* [mid-night monkey]. Soares de Sousa, *Notícia do Brasil* (1945), 2:151, n. 1; *Aurélio.*

180 · Also *cuandu.* MS *quoandu.* The Brazilian porcupine, genus *Coendou.* The Tupi means prehensile tail. *Taylor,* s.v. "ouriço-cacheiro." Soares de Sousa, *Notícia do Brasil* (1945), 2:152, n. 2.

181 · Short for *jaguacinim, jaguacininga.* MS *guasuni.* The Brazilian raccoon (*Procyon cancrivorus* Cuv.); in Portuguese, *mão pelada* [hairless paw]. The animal lives on crabs, domestic fowl, and sugar cane. Von Ihering, *Dicionário dos animais do Brasil,* s.v. "mão-pelada."

182 · Not identified.

183 · Howler monkey. The name *guariba* is applied to the five Brazilian species of the genus *Alouatta.* Von Ihering, *Dicionário dos animais do Brasil,* s.v. "bugio."

184 · These and similar anecdotes about monkeys were current among the chroniclers and are heard even today in Brazil. Von Ihering thought the account of the lookouts worth including in his *Dicionário dos animais do Brasil* (s.v. "bugio"). Anchieta in 1560 told this same story, but applied it to parrots instead of monkeys. *Cartas,* pp. 123–124.

185 · According to Ribeiro de Lessa, monkey traps made of gourds were in common use. Denis describes how "at the season in which the sapucaya, or monkey pot, is loaded with fruit, numerous bands of monkeys throw themselves into its branches. . . . If one of them, having put his hand in the pot formed by the sapucaya, tries to pull it out filled with fruit, he becomes angry, making the most comical gestures of resistance, and struggles without being able to resign himself to abandoning part of his prize for one moment." Out of season, the fruit [*cumbuca*] was deliberately made into a trap by filling the shell with chestnuts or seeds that monkeys like. A few monkeys managed to escape the trap, and these were never çaught again; hence the proverb, applied to prudent persons who do not take business risks, "An old monkey doesn't put his hand into a *cumbuca.*" Ferdinand Denis, *O Brasil,* 1:123; Ribeiro de Lessa, *Vocabulário de caça,* p. 61, s.v. "cumbuca."

186 · This story is told in abbreviated form by Anchieta, writing in 1560. *Cartas*, p. 120.

187 · Vicente do Salvador wrote in 1627 that the *guaribas* shaved each other's beards with their teeth, but does not say they used sharp stones as tools. *História do Brasil*, p. 76. To other chroniclers it is the Indians, not the monkeys, that shaved with sharp stones.

188 · This is a common belief, though apparently a baseless one. Cf. Vicente do Salvador: "When the hunter shoots [an arrow] at one [monkey] and doesn't hit him, the monkeys all nearly die laughing; but, if he hits him and he doesn't fall, he yanks the arrow out of his body and darts it at the man who hit him, and then flees upward through the tree and, chewing leaves and putting them on the wound, cures himself, and stanches the blood with them."

Similarly Vasconcellos: "They [monkeys] are surgeons of their wounds, and know how to cure them with certain herbs, which they chew and apply to the part, with marvelous effect. If one of them is struck by an arrow, he immediately draws it out with his hand; he quickly picks the herb and applies the medication, as if he had the use of reason."

Oviedo tells this same story and asserts that the monkeys after pulling out the arrow place it carefully in the tree branches so that it cannot be used again; or they break the arrow into small pieces.

Vicente do Salvador, *História do Brasil*, p. 76; Simão de Vasconcellos, *Notícias antecedentes, curiosas, e necessárias das cousas do Brasil*, in *Chrônica da Companhia de Jesu do Estado do Brasil*, p. cxlv; Oviedo, *Natural historia*, chap. 25 (misnumbered 26).

189 · There are no ounces or tigers in Brazil; Brandônio is referring to jaguars, often designated by these names. Jaguars, however, are not striped, as true tigers are. Perhaps Brandônio is thinking of the rows of large rosettes that mark the jaguar's black or reddish-yellow coat; or perhaps he is using *listado*, properly "striped," to mean "marked," a usage that is not uncommon; Brandônio described by the same word the coat of the margay, which has similar markings (p. 274 and n. 176 above). See Walker, *Mammals of the World*, 2:1279.

190 · This was a widely diffused but erroneous folk belief, one that has not died out even in modern times. Prado cites a modern romance (*Três Sargentos* [Companhia Editora Nacional, São Paulo, 1931]), in which black women lacking in virtue are called "panther fodder." *Pernambuco*, 3:243–244.

191 · MS *susurana*. Cougar (*Felis concolor*). According to Pirajá da Silva, *suçurana* is *çooaçu* [deer] + *arana* [similar (in color)]. The English name is ultimately derived from the Tupi. Soares de Sousa, *Notícia do Brasil* (1945), 2: 129 and n. 3.

192 · *Bothrops jararaca* Wied. is a dangerously poisonous pit viper, found throughout Brazil and elsewhere in South America. It is responsible for 50 percent of the cases of snakebite in Brazil. *Taylor;* Eurico Santos, *Anfíbios e répteis do Brasil,* pp. 182–184.

193 · Also *jararacuçu, surucucutinga.* MS *saracucu.* Bushmaster (*Lachesis muta* L.). The Tupi means "that which slithers and makes disappear" (i.e., quickly destroys its victim and slips away). This is the most irascible and aggressive of venomous Brazilian snakes. It reaches as much as three meters in length. Fortunately, this dangerous serpent is quite rare. The Indians consider its flesh a flavorsome tidbit. See Eurico Santos, *Anfíbios e répteis do Brasil,* pp. 178–182; *Aurélio,* s.v. "surucutinga"; *Taylor.*

194 · There is only one genus of coral snake, *Micrurus.* It exists in Brazil in eleven species. Prado criticized Brandônio for classing the coral snake with the deadly rattler, asserting that the former is only slightly dangerous. The fact is that all the Brazilian species of coral snake are very venomous, but they rarely harm human beings, because their teeth are too small to fasten themselves in the flesh. Von Ihering, *Dicionário dos animais do Brasil,* s.v. "cobra-coral"; Prado, *Pernambuco,* 3:244.

195 · Also known as *boiuçu, sucuri, sucuriú, sucuriju, sucurijuba,* etc. MS *boasu.* The Brazilian anaconda (*Eunectes murinus* L.), one of the largest snakes in the world. The Tupi is *boa* [snake] + *açu* [big]. The snake lives mostly on fish but can devour a deer, as Brandônio remarks. Von Ihering, *Dicionário dos animais do Brasil,* s.v. "sucuri."

196 · Anchieta tells similar stories, and in even more graphic detail. He says the *sucuriuba* is toothless and kills by winding itself around its victim, inserting its tail into his anus, and swallowing him whole. When the snake ingests a large animal, such as a tapir, it cannot digest its prey and falls to the ground as if dead. It remains motionless until the stomach and its contents have putrefied. Then birds of prey tear up the stomach and devour its contents. After this the deformed snake, half consumed, begins to reconstruct itself. Its flesh grows again from one end to the other, and it regains its former shape.

Such stories met with considerable skepticism even in Brandônio's time, as Alviano's remarks illustrate, but Anchieta assures the reader that "not only the Indians but the Portuguese who have spent many years of their lives in this part of the globe affirm them *uno ore.*" Anchieta, *Cartas,* pp. 111–112 and n. 97.

Dialogue VI

The Customs of the Inhabitants

ॐ

In the final dialogue Brandônio describes some of the customs of the country, both European and native. First we are given a brief but vivid glimpse of the slave-based society of wealthy whites in Brazil. Then comes a view—much more detailed—of the Brazilian natives whom the author knows, namely, the Tupinambás of the coast. This touches on most of the aspects that would be covered in a modern ethnographic survey, including birth and marriage customs, social practices, housing, food gathering, war, government, and religion. Brandônio also analyzes what he takes to be the character of the natives. The discussion contains a considerable amount of fact along with a sampling of the fancies and prejudices—sometimes contradictory ones—about Indians that were current in his time. Some points are illustrated by incidents that Brandônio represents as drawn from his own experience.

In the conclusion, Alviano, who has already confessed his error several times, again makes a formal retraction of his earlier view that Brazil is a worthless land, and promises henceforth to celebrate its "great things." On this note, rather abruptly, the Dialogues *come to an end.*

BRANDÔNIO   As a man who every day has made long marches hastens on the last day to reach his journey's end so that he can rest from his exertions, so I—intending today to complete the discharge of my obligation in this last conversation—hurried more than usual to take up my post, where I have been waiting for you quite a while already.

ALVIANO   I must confess that a visit made me forget the time; however, if I had known that you had already arrived, I would have trampled upon the obligations of civility to come to meet you.

BRANDÔNIO   You're not late even now; but let us begin the subject in hand. Surely you will recall that I have shown you all the settlements we Portuguese have made along this Brazil coast—the cities, towns, and villages, and the captaincies found throughout its length and breadth. I have pointed out the general bounty of the land as well as some things that it lacks. I have also discussed the fair skies and even fairer climate that the whole country enjoys, its richness, its fertility, the bounteous supply of food, cattle, fowl, and fish. From these things you must have inferred, if you do not wish to be thought a heretic[1] in things Brazilian, how much mistaken you were in judging it to be a worthless land.

ALVIANO   I have already repented of my error and am much ashamed of having persisted in it. But despite all the abundance you have described, and although the soil is so fertile that it would produce a great plenty of everything, still this land suffers from the lack of many things. I recall that you attributed the blame to the general negligence and scant industry of its settlers. But you neglected to say what can be done to correct that fault.

BRANDÔNIO   I acknowledge my poor memory! I can tell you that the remedy will come when there are more people in Brazil than the working of the sugar plantations, farming, and trade now require. At that time the unemployed will of necessity look for something new to turn their hands to. Thus, some will become fishermen, others shepherds, others gardeners, and yet others weavers, and they will ply the other trades which today are not found in this land in the measure needed.[2] If this were to happen, there would no longer be a lack of anything. The land would produce more than enough, and its great fertility and bounty would be clearly recognized. And there would be little or no need for any of the things that now are brought out from Portugal.[3]

ALVIANO   Even if Brazil were able to get along perfectly well without annual supplies from Portugal, immigrants would still be needed, for it is by them that the land must be settled.

BRANDÔNIO   You are mistaken in that, for even today Brazil already has enough people to settle it and within a few years will have more than enough. Pernambuco and the other captaincies of the north are now able to put into the field more than ten thousand armed men, many of them mounted.[4]

But since we are already getting off today's subject—that is, the general customs of the country—I wish to begin by saying, briefly, something about the customs of our Portuguese. Those who are not merchants devote themselves to farming, as I have already told you.

For that reason they live in the country with their families. They have built houses to live in, some with tiled roofs and others covered with pindova palm leaves or sape grass,[5] types of foliage that are used for such roofs. Although they own houses in the towns and cities, they do not reside in them, for the country is their normal dwelling place. There they are occupied with cultivating their farms and tilling their fields, using their oxen and both Guinea and native slaves for this. The greater part of a farmer's wealth in this country consists of slaves, be they few or many. The farmers live on what the slaves raise. Usually they keep a fisherman who goes out to sea to fish for them, or else fishes in the rivers, whence he brings home enough fish for their tables.

ALVIANO   Is this fisherman a slave or a freedman?

BRANDÔNIO   He is nothing else than a slave captured from the heathen of this land or one brought from Guinea.[6] And there are also some freedmen who engage themselves for this service at a very small wage. Many people, too, keep huntsmen who bring them a great supply of game, so that with this and what they raise, with the milk from their corrals, and plenty of sugar, they are richly supplied.

ALVIANO   Tell me now, are they all accustomed to eat manioc flour?

BRANDÔNIO   Quite a few people eat bread made of wheat flour as well, which they buy from the Kingdom and knead and bake at home; otherwise they send to the houses of baker women who make their living by that. The ladies dress very well and in costly fashion,[7] and when they leave their houses they are carried in hammocks[8] slung on the shoulders of slaves.[9]

ALVIANO   Wouldn't it be better for them to use a chair or a litter, like those used in India?

BRANDÔNIO   No, for the hammock is excellent for traveling the roads. A chair would be an awkward thing to use, for it happens that the churches are off the beaten track, as are the places where the ladies must go to visit their female friends and relatives. It is their custom to take with them—besides menservants on foot or on horseback— two or three female slaves, natives either of Guinea or of this land. These women always walk close to the hammock, in the bottom of which they have laid a carpet to make it comfortable.

The gentlemen are accustomed to ride their horses everywhere,[10] and have handsome trappings for them, especially when they ride in some of the celebrations. In short, most of the gentlemen here have a noble spirit and a quick temper. They are great sticklers for their honor, on behalf of which they will dare anything.

ALVIANO   I have discerned all this very clearly in the persons with whom I have talked. Further, I have found that they all speak most elegantly.

BRANDÔNIO   That is true, and I have already told you that Brazil is an academy where one can learn correct discourse.[11] But let this be enough for now about the white men, for we have much to say about the customs of the natives of this land.

In the first place, these heathen have no king whom they obey. They simply choose some headmen,[12] in whom they recognize a certain superiority, especially in matters of warfare, for in all other matters they do whatever they please.

ALVIANO   Who has the right to choose these headmen?

BRANDÔNIO   Although some inherit the post from their fathers and grandfathers, most of them owe election to their own merits. It is sufficient for a man to be a good warrior, and to be recognized as such, for all the rest to give their obedience to him. They live in houses that they build in clearings—very long houses with thatched roofs—divided up so that every couple and its children have their own quarters or section without any partition or screen between them.[13]

ALVIANO   They must not be jealous, then, for their wives and daughters!

BRANDÔNIO   On the contrary, they are; and they go to a thousand extremes about this.[14] Formerly both men and women went around naked[15]—as they still do out in the bush—without using anything to cover their shameful parts.

ALVIANO   They must have heard tell of our father Adam, when he was in a state of grace.

BRANDÔNIO   But now the heathen who live among us wear clothes; the males have breeches and the females have long shifts of very white linen cloth;[16] and they braid colored silk ribbons into their hair. It was hard work for the Fathers of the Company to persuade them to wear clothes, for nobody could get them to resist their natural inclination, which was to go naked.

ALVIANO   And do these heathen have, perchance, any religious rites or ceremonies?

BRANDÔNIO   None at all.[17] And if they do render any sort of adoration— although we know of none—it is to the devil, to whom they give the name Juruparim.[18]

ALVIANO   If they commend themselves to such a saint it is not surprising that their works resemble him.

BRANDÔNIO   And for that reason it is generally said that the language of these heathen of Brazil lacks three important letters, which are F, L, and R—by which token they have neither Faith nor Law nor Ruler.[19] They are all exceedingly fond of war, and among themselves one tribe is always fighting another. They eat human flesh, but more for vengeance—as I shall explain later[20]—than for sustenance.

They declare that they have a tradition from their ancient forebears that Saint Thomas taught them how to use manioc, on which they now live[21]—although formerly they neither ate it nor realized its usefulness. But there is no foundation for that story.

ALVIANO   And so it must be, for we do not know or read of Saint Thomas's coming to these parts.

BRANDÔNIO   And yet God could have done that, had he been so minded, just as he made Habakkuk take food to Daniel imprisoned in the den of lions.[22] But, as I said, these Indians do not give any conclusive proof of what they say.

It is their habit to give away most liberally everything they are asked for, even though it may happen that they end up stripped—which often does happen. One cannot discern in them even a trace of covetousness.

ALVIANO   One might envy them greatly for that, which is a trait not often to be met with in our Spain.

BRANDÔNIO   Up to now I have spoken only in general of the customs of these Indians. Coming now to more specific matters, I want first of all to say that when the women of these heathen give birth to a child the first thing they do, the very instant they are delivered—and sometimes when the birth has hardly been completed—is to get into the nearest river or lagoon of cold water that they can find, and there they wash themselves over and over. After they are all cleaned up, they go home to find the husband stretched out in the conjugal hammock, just as if it were he who had borne the child.[23] There they fuss over him and he is visited by relatives and friends, while the new mother busies herself with manual tasks around the house, preparing meals and going to fetch water from the river and wood from the forest, as if she had not just had a baby.

ALVIANO   And how is it possible that the water does not harm these new mothers, when the merest draft of air harms ours in Portugal?[24]

BRANDÔNIO   Rather it serves these women as medicine and a preservative so that the birth does them no harm, accustomed as they are always to wash themselves and fish in the rivers.[25] By the way, I don't want to forget to tell you something that happened to me in this connection. While riding down a steep hill on a very rainy day, I found an Indian woman sitting in the middle of the road. She was covered all over with blood, and much more was spilled all around her. When I asked what had happened, she replied that she had been delivered in that spot and that the blood came from the birth. When I asked about the child, she told me that a sudden rush of rainwater, which came flowing by there in the ruts made by a wagon, had carried it away from her down the hill. I then spurred my horse quickly to go and rescue the child, so that it might not perish, and I found it half dead, lying crosswise in a rut, where the root of a tree had stopped it. I had a slave of mine gather it up. Later on it was turned over to another slave who was a wet nurse, and who had milk to spare; so it survived and grew up to adulthood.

ALVIANO   And the Portuguese women who dwell in this land, do they perchance follow the same custom?

BRANDÔNIO   By no means; they protect themselves from drafts just the way women do in Portugal, though they don't keep to their beds so long.

ALVIANO   There can be no more barbarous custom than that which you have described [the couvade]. I believe that its like cannot be found anywhere in the world. It is unthinkable that it should be found anywhere except among these Indians, whom I hold to be no different from brute beasts.[26]

BRANDÔNIO   Now there you are greatly mistaken, for though they follow this and other customs that they learned and inherited from their ancestors, still one meets among them people who can reason a thing out and give you a shrewd answer. They do not allow themselves to be deceived by anyone. Their sons are taught from early childhood to be warriors and to like fighting.[27] To that end they train them in the use of the bow and arrow so that, though small in body, they are great archers, and to this end they are given much practice in hunting.

Now the females, when age allows for this, serve their parents until they marry.

ALVIANO   And what is marriage like among these people?

BRANDÔNIO   The nieces are the rightful wives of their uncles, and, when the latter wish to marry, the girls cannot be denied them. So usually the uncle marries his niece, daughter of his own brother or sister.[28] The father may also give his daughter in marriage to anyone whom he thinks fit, and in this connection they have a curious gallantry. Now, if there is a young man who is in love with a certain damsel, the surest way for him to win her is to go into the forest with an axe and chop some wood, but without letting anyone know what he is up to. When he has done this, he carries the wood on his back in bundles and goes to drop it off at the hut where live the father and mother of his beloved. He continues this performance for the space of several days, and by this means he makes known his intentions. This way they never deny him the girl as his wife.[29]

ALVIANO   These people must long ago have known how Jacob won his beloved Rachel, and it seems that in this custom they wish to imitate him. And may one know whether they take more than one wife?

BRANDÔNIO   A man may take three or four, and even seven or eight, according to the strength and vigor with which he is endowed, which is the chief consideration in this regard, and also provided he is a man who can support the women whom he takes in his charge for this purpose.

ALVIANO   How is it that these women do not have quarrels among themselves caused by the jealousy that some of them surely must feel toward the others?

BRANDÔNIO   In no case would they ever think of such a thing, but rather they are quite resigned—which is much to be admired.[30] The damsels, while they are yet such, are known by their hair, which they wear cut short. But as soon as they are made women, they let it grow; and there is never any deceit on that score.[31]

ALVIANO   I approve of the custom, particularly if one can have certainty as you say. But you failed to say whether those Indian men who pretend to have given birth to children, occupying the place of the women, keep to their hammocks for many days.

BRANDÔNIO   No, just a few days so they can be visited by their friends and relatives.

Now when they pay visits to each other they have a strange custom. When they see each other, the woman of the house, or the woman who comes to visit from another village (provided she has reached maturity), seats herself at the feet of the guest, or of the man she is visiting, and there, in a most sorrowful and doleful wail, recites to him for a great while past events that befell her parents and grand-parents, misfortunes that are calculated to arouse commiseration, but without the one who hears this sad tale uttering a word, so that while it lasts he seems to be a mute.[32] After it is finished, they welcome and entertain the guest as best they can, in their own fashion.

ALVIANO   I should take it as a very evil omen, their wailing like that to me, and I would not for anything put up with it.

BRANDÔNIO   Since they all go about stripped, they protect themselves from the cold at night by building fires under the hammocks in which they sleep.[33] As the house is very long and all open on the inside and the hammocks that they string up throughout it are very numerous, there come to be in this way many fires in it, and with these they warm themselves so that they do not suffer from the cold although they are naked.

ALVIANO   And what furniture do these heathen use for their needs?

BRANDÔNIO   Nothing more than the hammock in which they sleep and a bowl made from half a gourd, in which they fetch water. There are in the community three or four clay ovens, made in the manner of *alguidares* [conical earthen vessels], in which they toast the manioc meal. And with only these they think themselves richer than Croesus with all his gold, and they live as happily and as free of covetousness as if they were masters of the world.

ALVIANO   Such contentment makes me most envious, for it seems to bespeak the Golden Age. But, nonetheless, each one of these heathen must raise enough food to live on, for without that it would not be possible for him to feed himself and his family.

BRANDÔNIO   Nor do they hoard up any food supplies, for it is their custom, at the time of sowing, to lay out their fields, where they all go together to sow and to plant food crops. They are busy with this for several days, until it seems to them that they have planted enough to last them for the whole year. In the same fashion they return to weed and cultivate the fields when necessary. When they finish that labor, they engage in hunting and fishing, killing a great quantity both of beasts and of fish, for in such exercises they are all great masters.

When they have need of manioc they send for it to the planted patches, which are common property.[34] The task of making manioc meal falls to the women, who prepare all the food in their own fashion, and always have it ready for their husbands' arrival.

ALVIANO   That is not a bad custom to have their food supply as common property, provided there is no deceit involved.

BRANDÔNIO   There is never anything like that, for no one eats more than he really needs; thus there is enough food for everybody. Also, when there is a scarcity of food, no one person can escape it.

They have another custom: when they want to go hunting or fishing, which they do in great numbers, the first man to get up before dawn makes the rounds of the clearing. With great shouts he charges the others to arise, cast off laziness, and leave their shelter, for it is already time for them to be on their way. He keeps up this exhortation for quite a while, until they all pick up their weapons and take to the trail.

ALVIANO   The function of that Indian, then, is to be an alarm clock.

BRANDÔNIO   Yes, and there is always someone who performs that function. The truth is that their headmen decree these excursions not so much by giving orders as by making a request.

ALVIANO   And do these headmen, perhaps, rule over many tribes, or what jurisdiction do they have in this office that you attribute to them?

BRANDÔNIO   In every village there is a headman,[35] who recognizes no other as his superior, unless there is one who is so great a warrior that, for the fear they bear him, they respect him. But the ordinary run of headman is obeyed by the people of his village almost in fun, for in everyday matters each man does as he pleases, even if the leader commands the contrary. But they have more respect for him in matters relating to war. It is he who settles these and makes the decisions. He determines what must be done, receives the embassies, and gives them their answer, although when it is a question of establishing the terms of peace or of renewing hostilities, the advice of the old men is respected and followed. Judging from the strength and spirit that they have and the boldness they display in attacking the enemy, these heathen would certainly be very valiant soldiers if they would obey their captains better. But the superstitions they have, and the credit they give their sorcerers,[36] are their undoing and more often than not lead them to defeat.

ALVIANO   Well, what do they consult the sorcerers for?

BRANDÔNIO   When they must decide whether to go to war, they assemble in the *carpé*,[37] a round house which for this purpose only they have built in the center of the village clearing. There they proclaim the reasons they have for making war on the enemy,[38] and the way in which they intend to proceed in it. Their sorcerer—who is any Indian man or woman who assumes this role—is always present. It is up to the sorcerer to approve or disapprove the expedition, and to foretell good or bad luck, and for this they have a procedure that is ridiculous enough.

It is this: when they declare that they will vanquish their enemies, they hold out some little nets, saying that they will stuff them all, shackled, into these nets as if they were fish. At other times, flourishing fans that they have made from palm leaves, they promise to shoo them off so that soon they will fly the field. And such stock do they take in this vaingloriousness that they believe unquestioningly that things will turn out this way.

ALVIANO   But when things turn out contrariwise for them, why do they not understand that it was all a lie?

BRANDÔNIO   Nothing suffices to rid their minds of such an error, instilled in them by their parents, although they have suffered the greatest damage from having believed their sorcerers. As proof of this I want to tell you a very curious story.

In bygone times there was one of these sorcerers who assured the Indians that henceforth the land would produce its fruits by itself, without any planting or tending. Therefore, they could all enjoy themselves, have a good time, and go to sleep, for the earth would take care to give them food at the proper time. The poor Indians had such faith in him that they did just as he advised them to do. Thus they came to suffer the most severe famine that was ever heard of in this state. Reduced to necessity, they reached the point of selling themselves, their wives, and their children for an ear of corn.[39] Surely no greater poverty can be imagined.

ALVIANO   I would compare that to the story you told me of the monkeys who thrust a hand into the mouth of an empty jug and then couldn't get it out, and were captured because they didn't know enough to let go of what they were holding. Whence I infer that folk who believe such things must be pretty much like those monkeys.

BRANDÔNIO   I have already told you that they are not lacking in sound understanding, although they are so blind toward these sorcerers (who are not blind at all!) that they cannot see through their falseness and their lies.

Once war has been decided upon, the first thing they attend to is to order the trails to be made very clean, smooth, and broad, so that they can go out by them and return the same way when they are victorious. They do the same when they are visited by an honored guest.

On the day set for their departure, their leader takes the precaution to go into the clearing before dawn, and walking around it he delivers a harangue. With great shouts he inspires all his soldiers to fight hard and to attack the enemy bravely.[40] To this end he recalls for them various great deeds and victories of their ancestors and the weakness of their enemy.

ALVIANO Our captains and generals don't do any more than that themselves when they must spur their men on.

BRANDÔNIO Well, that is a most ancient custom among these heathen. When the harangue is over, they do not prepare a lot of baggage, for each man takes with him only what he needs for a few days.[41] When this runs out they live on what they find in the fields, the forest, and the rivers. The weapons they carry are bows and arrows,[42] and short sword-clubs[43] of a strong, heavy wood. These sword-clubs utterly demolish any part of the body where their blows land. They decorate the hilts of their sword-clubs with feathers of different colors. They do the same to their heads, and with that render themselves more fearsome.[44] The round shields,[45] which they also carry with them, are decorated with paint. Made of lightweight wood, they are big enough to protect the whole body, and with them they ward off the arrows of the enemy.

ALVIANO Those are not bad weapons, and if their spirits were equal to them they could not fail to achieve great things.

BRANDÔNIO They have much spirit, as I have said. Yet if, while they are marching along with all this bravura, they chance to hear the song of a bird that I have already mentioned—a bird that is an evil omen for them—they desist from the expedition and turn around and go home.[46] And in like manner, even though they are on their way to make an attack, if, before they reach their destination, they happen to run into a few enemies and kill them, they are satisfied with this and turn around and go home, leaving the rest for another time.

ALVIANO   Now don't tell me that such people are courageous, for whoever does a thing like that cannot have this virtue.

BRANDÔNIO   Well, I'll tell you something more. When they become aware that they have been detected and therefore cannot carry out their plans, on the very spot where they realized this they drop their weapons, turn around, and go back home without them. Then the one who runs fastest in his flight and is the first to reach the village from which they set out is considered the most valiant, for they say that he is endowed with great courage and stamina, because he ran faster than his ompanions.[47]

ALVIANO   It is only to be expected that people with such mixed-up customs should make a virtue out of cowardice.

BRANDÔNIO   But I haven't finished yet; for on such occasions, in order to run faster, they prick their legs with knives until they lose a great deal of blood, thinking that in this way they become more fleet of limb to travel swiftly.[48]

ALVIANO   I cannot praise them for taking such measures only to be able to flee more rapidly.

BRANDÔNIO   They also do that to reach a destination more quickly. They always launch a battle or a skirmish with much spirit. Every warrior who during it kills an enemy with his own hands, or who helps to pin one down to be killed, even if there are six or seven persons doing that, takes a new name, and from then on he is esteemed a warrior and can mark himself.

ALVIANO   Let me hear this business of names and marking in more detail, so that I may understand you.

BRANDÔNIO   All those who have killed an enemy, or who have helped to capture one whom they later killed, take names in this fashion: at dawn the day after the battle or the attack, very early while everybody is still in his hammock, each of these warriors gets up and goes about shouting, "I will henceforth be known as So-and-So" (giving himself the name he wants), "for I have killed my enemy in the field." He repeats this many times: "And by this name I wish to be known and called hereafter."[49] They all make much over him as he goes by and applaud him, particularly the women.

By marking, I meant that they make some black marks on their bodies which from that time forward stand as military insignia. They also make the marks stand out by tracing them with fire or by pricking with a needle the part they want to mark. While it is still bleeding they apply some dark dye, and that is enough to make the mark last forever.[50]

ALVIANO I have not much praise for these warriors and their military insignia.

BRANDÔNIO Well, I can tell you something more. Although these heathen kill their enemies on the field with their sword-clubs, dealing them thrusts or such powerful blows that they split them down the middle, still, if they did not break their skulls when they killed them, well, then, the dead man has not been killed, nor can the killer boast of having killed him, nor can he take a new name or mark himself.

ALVIANO Then, according to that, a man whose skull isn't broken didn't die?

BRANDÔNIO That is what they think. They carry this to such lengths that after they have won a village or some place from the enemy, the first thing they do is to rush to the burial grounds and disinter the bodies that are there. They go around and smash all the skulls. Anyone who breaks them this way gains just as great a reputation for valor and is just as much entitled to military honors as the man who broke them fighting on the field of battle, where he ran the risk of losing his life.

ALVIANO Well, now, don't say anything more about these people being endowed with understanding, for I cannot believe you if you do.

BRANDÔNIO No one can make you believe anything but what you want to believe, or oblige me to give up telling the truth of what I have seen for myself. When they capture some of the enemy, they carry them off to their villages, where they release them from their bonds.

ALVIANO And if they are freed, why don't they escape?

BRANDÔNIO They don't escape because the villages are distant from one another. It isn't possible for them to escape without soon being discovered by their tracks, for in knowing how to follow a trail these people are better than hunting dogs. Furthermore, their senses are very keen. I have sometimes seen certain Indians who had to sense the way they should go through thick underbrush, where no trail was visible. They merely pointed an arrow directly towards their destination, and that was enough for them to fix that direction in their memory and to enable them to make their way there without the slightest error. Besides, they always keep the captives well guarded.

ALVIANO And what do they want these captives for, if not for ransom?

BRANDÔNIO   Know, then, that just the opposite is true. I can affirm—
and don't think this is a fable—that if you offered to these Indians,
as ransom for one of these captives, especially if he were a white man,
as much gold as they say Croesus had, together with all the riches of
the world, they would not give him up.

ALVIANO   That's a lot to say.

BRANDÔNIO   Well, that's the way it is, for they would rather kill him
in the village clearing, which they do in this fashion: first of all, they
order that among their own people every wish of the prisoner be
gratified, no matter what he wants or asks for. Even if he desires the
wife of the chief himself, and requests her, they do not deny her to
him. All this is for the purpose of ridding him of his melancholy and
fattening him up. And when it seems to them that he has reached
that stage, the next thing they do is to clean a broad path from the
place where the village stands down to the river bank. When the path
is ready, they let the captive know that now the time has come for
him to be killed in the clearing. They tie him with a rope underneath
his arms so that he has his arms and hands free. And they do this in
such a way that they leave two long pieces to the rope, one on each
side. With great shouts and hilarity they take him this way, by the
path that I mentioned, down to the river, in which they wash him
very thoroughly, from head to foot. Now when he has been washed
they bring him back to the village with the same songs, dances, and
merrymaking, and there, while he stands in the clearing, six or seven
strong and robust young men approach him. They pick up the ends
of the rope and hold it taut, so that the unhappy prisoner cannot
budge. For if he tries to make a movement in one direction they pull
him back in the other. In this manner they hold him in a vise, as it
were, until the executioner enters the clearing, with great arrogance
and adorned with feathers of different colors. Taking slow steps, and
with the chief warriors around him, he moves up towards the prisoner.
And when he is right in front of him, he tells him with proud words
and arrogant gestures that he has every reason to be happy that he
will die at the hands of so great and fine a warrior as he is, and that
he should be even happier that his flesh is to be buried in the bellies
of so many brave chiefs and warriors as are around him, who are
waiting only for that, and that it is much better this way than for
his flesh to be eaten and buried in the bellies of filthy creatures.

Therefore, let him take heart and get his fill of seeing the light of day.

Now, if at these words the captive appears faint of heart, he is judged by all to be a weakling and a coward. But if he snarls back at them, saying that he has relatives alive who will find a way to avenge him, and therefore dies content, then he is esteemed a brave man. But no matter how it happens, one way or the other, the executioner makes a feint at his head with a sword-club, showing that he wishes to land a blow. So that the poor fellow, frightened by this, tries to ward it off or to duck. The executioner seconds this with another blow so hard that he splits his head in two. And before the victim falls to the ground he has knocked his head into small pieces, with the many other blows he deals it.

But if it happens that the captive, at the time the blow is dealt, has been so agile and has had such strength that, with his arms and hands, which are free, he could wrest the sword-club from the executioner, he escapes death—and it is for that reason that they leave them free for him to use.

ALVIANO   That's a fine way, indeed, for the warrior-executioner to do a great deed!

BRANDÔNIO   But they do not consider it to be a trivial thing. And after the unlucky fellow has been killed that way, they turn him over to the old women, who cut him into quarters and put them on to boil and roast in big pieces, which they serve up as a delicacy to the bystanders. They divide these among them all and they eat that human flesh with great gusto, more out of vengeance than to appease their hunger.

ALVIANO   It is hard to judge whether they eat it out of vengeance or because they like it.

BRANDÔNIO   It is believed that they do it out of vengeance.[51] Now the old women put the entrails and intestines in some crocks. With much singing they dance around them, holding some rods to which they have fastened fishhooks. They cast these into the entrails and, amid great laughter, pretend that they are fishing in them.

ALVIANO   And with this barbarous cruelty are they satisfied at last?

BRANDÔNIO   They do something more yet. They have a great stock of wine all ready, and they settle down to great drinking bouts[52] that last for several days.

Execution of a prisoner of war. Theodor de Bry, *India occidentalis . . .*
(Frankfort, 1590–1624), III, 212. *Courtesy of the Edward E. Ayer Collection, The
Newberry Library, Chicago.*

ALVIANO   A few days ago, when I went to visit a friend of mine at his
plantation, some Indians kept me awake all night with their drunken
revels, during which they sang some songs such as I never heard the
like of before.

BRANDÔNIO   That is their most usual custom, for to get really drunk
they prepare a lot of wine. They make this from the juice of the sugar
cane, which they fetch from the plantations, and honey, and the fruit
of the cashew. With many men and women all together in a circle,
they keep at this singing all of one day and the whole night, without
going to sleep. They generally drink a great deal of wine all during
this time, until they drop senseless on the ground. Sometimes serious
injuries result from this.

The corpses of executed captives are prepared for a cannibal festivity. Theodor
de Bry, *India occidentalis . . .* (Frankfort, 1590–1634), III, 213. *Courtesy of the
Edward E. Ayer Collection, The Newberry Library, Chicago.*

ALVIANO   And what meters or verses do they sing during so great a
space of time?

BRANDÔNIO   Nothing more than this: the first one raises his voice and
says, "The bird is on the leaf," or "The leaf is on the water," or some
such thing, and they go on repeating this interminably, some speaking
and others replying, as long as the drinking bout lasts.[53] The women
sing soprano, since they can raise their voices higher.

ALVIANO   A costly entertainment, since they spend all of one day and
night without sleep and consume so much wine. But if, perchance,
they take any women prisoners, I would like to know if they kill
them too in the village clearing, the way they kill the men.

BRANDÔNIO   Sometimes they kill them and other times they don't—
the latter being when one of the victors takes a woman as his wife or

concubine, and thus she escapes death. It is up to the man who chose her for himself to decide her fate. He does not give her any more work to do than is given to the other women, members of his own tribe.

But the strange thing is that if one of these captive women succeeds in escaping and is at that time pregnant, and if after being safe among her own people she gives birth, the child's own grandfather, and even the mother herself, kill the newborn creature and eat it, saying that they do so to the son of their enemy, for the mother was only a pouch in which his seed grew and developed, without taking on anything of her.[54] And they practice a thousand cruelties, in other similar cases.

ALVIANO   I am not surprised at such a barbarous custom after the many others you have told me about. I think all this must spring from there not being among these people any trace of love.

BRANDÔNIO   On the contrary, there are many persons among them who have given ample proof of possessing such a sentiment in a high degree. In this connection, I want to tell you a curious tale that happened a short time ago in a captaincy of this state. There was among the Petiguares a captive woman, belonging to the Tabajaras, who are their greatest enemies. Despite the fact that a Petiguar kept her as his concubine, as time went by the others planned with the Petiguar himself (who may well have been chiefly responsible) to kill the poor Tabajara[55] girl, in order to eat her.

Now she had already become close friends with another Indian, a Petiguar girl, the sister of him who had been her lover. This girl, hearing talk among her people of the death they planned to visit on her sister-in-law and friend, and moved by the love she bore her, revealed to her what peril she was in, advising her to flee and offering to accompany her. The other girl accepted the advice and the offer. Her friend not going back on her promise, the two of them fled together. This turned out so well for them that without being dis- covered they reached a settlement of white people, round about which the Tabajaras dwelt. Thereupon, the girl who belonged to that nation betook herself to their villages. Being recognized by her parents and relatives, she recounted to them how much she owed to the other Indian girl, her friend, for having saved her from death. They all thanked her greatly for this and she stayed there, living amongst them. But not many days went by before the Tabajaras, forgetful of what had happened, attempted to do to the Petiguar girl what the

Petiguares had wanted to do to their fellow tribeswoman. They began their preparations, and the pleas of the poor Indian girl, their own relative, were not enough to save her companion from the fate that awaited her. At last, when the time was come, they led her to the clearing to be killed. On seeing this, her friend, who it seems was still mindful of the obligation she was under, turned upon her troop of relatives like a lioness and by force tore the Petiguar girl from their hands. Taking her to the house of some white people, she saved her in that way from a death which she did not deserve but which had been prepared for her. Thus did she pay back in the same coin the love that the other girl had shown her when she was determined to flee from her own people to save the life of the Tabajara girl.

ALVIANO   You must find few such examples amid so much barbarity.

BRANDÔNIO   Well, I can tell you also that although these heathen are very lascivious by nature, there are many damsels among them who have a great love of chastity. Some there are who flee absolutely from having any coupling with a male, intending rather to remain virgins. The better to do this, they train with the bow and arrow and generally wander through the fields and woods hunting wild beasts. They make great catches of these, and delighting themselves in this pursuit they scorn all others.[56]

ALVIANO   Such girls as those must have heard tell of Diana and her nymphs, and to imitate them take up hunting as an occupation. Yet I cannot bring myself to believe that they will be continent, for this is a gift of the soul and cannot be prized except by one who knows its value. Now since these girls lack such knowledge, I don't see what would make one think that they could keep to this continence.

BRANDÔNIO   Think what you will, for I cannot keep you from that, nor can I fail to praise such girls for knowing how to stay clear of the fire in that part where it burns hottest. Their unusual merit is clearly seen from another custom that the heathen have, unchaste enough! Now this is that when they are visited by some distinguished guest, especially a white man, they first of all install him in a hammock, where they seat their guests, since that is what they use for chairs, and the chief sits in another hammock. Before they open their conversation they toast one another by smoking tobacco, bringing out a *petimbabo*[57] for this purpose. After this is over, and after the guest has revealed why he came and the chief has made answer, the latter at once turns over to him a damsel or his own daughter as a wife, for him to have her as such as long as he is there. There can be no more barbarous custom than that.

ALVIANO   And do the white men accept the use of these Indian girls, they being heathen?

BRANDÔNIO   Many do not, but instead reject them and only pretend to take them, but persuade them not to tell this to the chief who gave them, for he would be much affronted by this.

After gorging themselves on the flesh of the enemies whom they kill, they take a piece of it and, after it is dried, they wrap it inside a great ball of cotton yarn, and in this manner they carefully preserve it. And when they happen to have a great drinking bout, to take greater pleasure in it, they unwrap the flesh from the ball of yarn, and separate it into many small fibers, which they pass around for everybody to eat. And this they are accustomed to do as a sign of the vengeance they took and the victory they won.

ALVIANO   I do not praise them for taking vengeance in such a manner.

BRANDÔNIO   You can know how vengeful they are, for after killing their enemies they remove their teeth and string them on cords, making a necklace of them, putting the big molars at the ends and the smaller teeth in the center. I saw one of these necklaces that weighed fourteen *arráteis* [pounds], and from that you can tell what a great number of teeth there must have been in it.[58]

ALVIANO   The gem cutters won't be giving them much money for those stones, for I think they are atrocious things to put in a setting.

BRANDÔNIO   All this they do thinking to have a greater revenge. Their vindictive nature so dominates them that, if by chance when walking down a road they stumble on some stick or stone, they do not proceed until for vengeance they have uprooted or broken the thing that hurt them. And along with being revengeful, some of them are also exceedingly cruel.

A man whom I can believe told me that he had seen one of these Indians, who was returning from an attack which he had made with many others on a certain enemy village, carrying six children, the biggest of whom was not even one year old. He had strung them up like chickens on a pole, which he carried on his shoulder, half of them in front and half behind. After walking with them thus for a great while, he put them down on a rock, and then with a small knife he proceeded to break the skull of each child, giving him little blows so that his suffering would be greater. He showed no trace of pity at the groans and cries of the poor children.

ALVIANO   Never was such cruelty told of any Polyphemus, Lestrygonian, or Scythian.[59]

BRANDÔNIO   These heathen also have the custom, to make themselves look more ferocious and bizarre, of piercing the face along the lower lip and chin, where they insert some green or white stones as ornaments, and with this they think they are very elegant gentlemen.

ALVIANO   Some devil must have taught them that habit and they use it in imitation of him, and with it give greater proof of their great barbarity.

BRANDÔNIO   Well, despite all their barbarity, they know very well how to divide the seasons of the year with great regularity, being guided in this by the fruits of certain trees when they ripen. For then they know that the time has come for the planting and other pursuits in which they engage, and they are acquainted also with almost all the stars in the heavens that we know, although they give them different names.[60]

ALVIANO   It is a great thing to find that knowledge among such people.

BRANDÔNIO   The customs I have been discussing are those of the heathen who dwell in the bush and who have no relations with, or even knowledge of, white people. But those who go about among us and are taught by the religious already live much removed from such customs, for they know their catechism, baptize their children, and are married in the form specified by the Holy Council.[61] They have only one wife, wear clothes, and also learn to read, write, and count. Some of them turn out to be skilled in singing, and thus become good at playing the shawm,[62] though they do always tend to follow their natural bent, as was seen in a case that occurred some time ago.

ALVIANO   And what was that?

BRANDÔNIO   The Fathers of the Company taught one of these Indians, in whom they sensed some abilities, to read and write, and some music and Latinity, and even a little of the liberal arts. He was very quick at everything and had good habits. They even had minor orders conferred upon him, and I think I heard it said that he also received those of the Epistle and the Gospel, in order that they might ordain him as a mass priest. But that blessed Indian, obliged by his natural bent, one morning suddenly stripped off his clothes and away he went, with some relatives of his, into the bush. There he followed his savage customs until he died, not heeding the good ones they had taught him.

ALVIANO   That alone is enough to confirm me in my opinion. But I should like to have you tell me if there is in this province more than one kind of heathen, just as among us there are Frenchmen, Englishmen, Italians, and others.

BRANDÔNIO   Oh yes, there are many kinds of them,[63] such as Aimorés,[64] Tupinambás,[65] Tabajaras,[66] Petiguares,[67] Tapuias,[68] and others.

ALVIANO   And do they all, perchance, live in such brute fashion as those of whom you have talked so far?

BRANDÔNIO   Almost all of them lead pretty much the same kind of life except the Tapuias, who are very different in this respect but not in their savagery.

ALVIANO   Well, tell me how these Tapuias live.

BRANDÔNIO   I shall resume it for you briefly, for it is already getting to be time for us to go home and conclude our conversation.[69] These Tapuias live in the bush and have no villages or regular dwellings, nor do they even plant food to eat. They all live in the open country and subsist on the honey that they take from trees or that the bees make on the ground, as well as on game, which they kill in great abundance with their arrows. For this they keep the following order: they all go together in a group to set up their shelter in the spot that seems to them to be the best, erecting for this purpose a few grass huts of little value, and from there they go out to a distance of two or three leagues around to look for honey and game. As long as they find food they do not abandon that place, but when it begins to be scarce they at once move to another site, where they do the same thing. In this fashion they carry on, always living in the fields, moving their locations without tiring themselves with working or cultivating the land, for their arrows are plow and hoe to them, and even their arrows they do not shoot with the bow as the rest of the heathen do. For taking an arrow in their hands, they insert it in a hollow cane, which they carry on a finger.[70] They make such accurate shots and with such force that it is astonishing, so that the game almost never escapes if they shoot an arrow that way. A few days ago I saw one of them make a shot without a bow, and besides hitting the mark at which it was aimed, the arrow went right through a thick door, from one side to the other. They differ also in their speech, and the rest of the heathen do not understand them, for they have such a crack-jaw language. They wear their hair long like women, and they are generally so feared by all the other heathen that one Tapuia is enough to make many other Indians flee. And thus even a small number of them will enter very large villages confidently and take anything they want, with nobody so much as raising a hand against them, and the people will even let them carry their women off, so great is the fear they have of them.

And with this it seems to me that I have reached the end of my obligation, as well as I could, leaving the field open now for you to condemn Brazil as a worthless land, as you did at the start, if you think, despite the truths about it which I have told you, that informed men can with justice call it that. Of ignorant men I take no account, for their idle talk excuses them.[71]

ALVIANO   You have me so converted to your sect that everywhere, wherever I may be, I shall proclaim of Brazil and its great things the praises that they merit.

Notes to Dialogue VI

1 · Perhaps the ominous word "heretic" reflects an underlying apprehension on the part of the New Christian author: Brandão had been twice denounced to the Inquisition for heresy.

2 · This statement seems hardly consistent with Brandônio's earlier remark (p. 23) that there are craftsmen and mechanics "of every specialty" in Brazil. According to Campos Moreno, Brazil attracted too few craftsmen and too many "bachelors," or young men of education, and so the land was full of college graduates, scriveners, magistrates, solicitors, and clergymen. Diogo de Campos Moreno, *Livro que dá razão do Estado do Brasil— 1612*, p. 115 and n. 31.

3 · Cf. Brandônio's criticism of Brazilians for not producing their own oil and cotton cloth, pp. 205–206. At the beginning of the seventeenth century Brazil imported a large number of its needs from Portugal, and Brandão is not the only writer who charged it with neglect on this score. Thus Vicente do Salvador complains that Brazil could produce ample supplies of wheat, wine made from sugar cane, oil from coconuts, cotton cloth colored with native dyes, salt both artificial and natural, iron from Brazilian mines, many species of pepper and ginger, cashew nuts, and a number of other items. *História do Brasil, 1500–1627*, p. 83.

4 · According to Capistrano de Abreu, Brandônio's figure is a "palpable exaggeration," since in all the captaincies together there were hardly that many fighting men of Portuguese origin. Brandônio said on p. 305 that

Pernambuco alone supplied 6,000 of these men-at-arms, with 800 cavalry. In 1622, four years after Brandão was writing, Pernambuco had 8,000 settlers capable of bearing arms. However, only 1,000 of these possessed suitable weapons; in that tropical climate, firearms quickly rusted and became useless unless they were meticulously cleaned and cared for. Rodolfo Garcia, ed., *Diálogos das grandezas do Brasil,* "Introdução" by Capistrano de Abreu, p. 13; Francis A. Dutra, "Matias de Albuquerque and the Defense of Northeastern Brazil, 1620–1626," *Studia* 36 (July 1973):133.

5 · Cf. IV, nn. 79 and 80.

6 · Brandão was obviously accustomed to both Indian and African slaves. At first the colonists had tried to enslave the Amerindians, but these did not hold up well in captivity. Crowded together in unsanitary slave quarters, they had little resistance to disease, especially the epidemics brought in by Europeans. Most of the Indians who did not quickly die ran away to the forest. Another difficulty was that Indian slavery was illegal after 1570, except for Indians taken in a "just war" or ransomed from other tribes who would have eaten or enslaved them. (It is true that this law was extensively abused.) By Brandão's time Indians and Africans were being used in comparable numbers, especially in his area, the Northeast. Eventually the colonists gave up trying to use Indians in the sugar mills. Thus African slaves came to form the mainstay of the plantation economy. Indian slaves were still widely used, however, in occupations to which they were well adapted, such as hunting and fishing. Charles R. Boxer, "The Colour Question in the Portuguese Empire, 1415–1825," in *Proceedings of the British Academy* 47 (1961):131–132; idem, *The Portuguese Seaborne Empire, 1415–1825,* p. 96; idem, *Salvador de Sá and the Struggle for Brazil and Angola, 1602–1686,* p. 26; Vitorino Magalhães Godinho, *Os descobrimentos e a economia mundial,* 2:582; Frédéric Mauro, *Le Portugal et l'Atlantique au XVIIe siècle (1570–1670),* pp. 152–157; João Lúcio d'Azevedo, *Elementos para a história econômica de Portugal (séculos XII a XVII),* p. 165; J. F. de Almeida Prado, *Pernambuco e as capitanias do norte do Brasil (1530–1630),* 4:71, Stuart B. Schwartz, "Indian Labor and New World Plantations: European Demands and Indian Responses in Northeastern Brazil," *American Historical Review* 83 (Feb. 1978):43–79.

7 · Cf. III, n. 91.

8 · The settlers made extensive use of the hammock as a litter, especially in the wealthy sugar-raising districts such as Pernambuco, where the wives of the sugar barons set out to visit their friends in hammocks carried by slaves and adorned with the luxurious cushions and hangings and richly embroidered canopies that Brandônio describes. According to Magalhães Godinho, this practice reflects the influence of Oriental customs. Zacharias

Wagener, *Zoobiblion: Livro de animais do Brasil*, pp. 389–390 and fig. 104; Prado, *Pernambuco*, 4:82–86; Magalhães Godinho, *Descobrimentos*, 2:583.

9 · MS: "travel on the shoulders of slaves, lying in a hammock." Another example of *hysteron proteron*.

10 · "The sugar lord of the Northeast was almost a centaur—half man, half horse," says Gilberto Freyre, *Nordeste*, p. 66. Cf. p. 264 and V, n. 137. Monteiro told how on the day the Governor, Diogo de Menezes, arrived in Olinda, "he was received by 400 horsemen, very well ordered, who could have appeared in any part of Europe." Jácome Monteiro, *Relação da Província do Brasil, 1610*, in Serafim Leite, *História da Companhia de Jesus no Brasil*, 8:405.

11 · This is a common boast of the early Brazilian writers. Cf. pp. 147–148.

12 · Here, as elsewhere, Brandônio is certainly describing the Tupinambás (the generic term applied to a wide variety of coastal Tupis). Each household in a Tupinambá village had a headman, and sometimes there was also a village headman. The principal function of the latter was to be a leader in war. In peacetime, the tribe was governed mainly by custom. Florestan Fernandes, *Organização social dos Tupinambá*, pp. 270–279; Gabriel Soares de Sousa, *Notícia do Brasil* (1945), 2:246; Hans Staden, *Warhafftiger kurtzer bericht aller von mir erfarnen håndel und sitten der Tuppin Indas derer gefangner ich gewesen bin*, in *Warhaftige Historia und beschreibung eyner Landtschafft der wilden nacketen grimmigen Menschfresser Leuthen in der Newenwelt America gelegen*, chap. 13.

13 · An Indian village might consist of from four to eight houses built around a central plaza, which was the center of the social and religious life of the community. The houses were constructed of wood on a rectangular plan and had an arched or vaulted roof thatched with palm or other leaves. There was a low door on each end and sometimes two on a side. Each house was shared by 100 to 200 individuals belonging to several families.

Cardim vividly describes the interior of a native dwelling: "The house appears an inferno or labyrinth, some are singing, others are weeping, others eating, others preparing flour and wine, etc., and the whole house blazes with the fires; and they are so congenial, that all year long there isn't a fight, and since they haven't anything locked up there are no thefts; no other people could live as they do without complaints, animosity, and even killings, which are never found among them." Fernão Cardim, *Tratados da terra e gente do Brasil*, p. 272. All the writers agree that Tupi households lived harmoniously together. See, e.g., Pero de Magalhães de Gandavo, *História da Província Sancta Cruz*, in his *Histories of Brazil*, vol. 1, fol. 34.

The houses became uninhabitable after a few years because of accumulated filth and odors. In any case the Indians could not remain long in one location because the soil around the village soon became exhausted and the game scarce. Usually a settlement was moved to another location after not more than six years.

For further details about the long houses of the Tupis and their furnishings see Estêvão Pinto, *Os indígenas do Nordeste,* 2:161–175, and Alfred Métraux, "The Tupinambá," in Julian H. Steward, ed., *Handbook of South American Indians* (hereinafter cited as *HSAI*), 3:103–104.

14 · In asserting that the Indians were intensely jealous of their wives, Brandônio agrees with several other authors, who say that adultresses were severely punished physically, sometimes even by slavery or death; see Fernandes, *Organização social,* p. 206, who cites many references. On the other hand, Soares de Sousa thought the Indians could not have taken adultery very seriously, since a husband only "pummeled" an erring wife rather than killing her (as a contemporary Portuguese would have done). Estêvão Pinto agrees that adultery was a venial sin; yet he believes that most of the Indian women were faithful to their husbands. Soares de Sousa, *Notícia do Brasil* (1945), 2:256; Estêvão Pinto, *Indígenas do Nordeste,* 2:318. Probably customs varied greatly among the different tribes.

15 · The Indians went naked except for decorations composed of feathers, bones, and stones, and for markings made by vegetable dyes, which might be from the *urucu* (see IV, n. 95) or from the juice of the fruit of the genipap tree. The missionaries devoted almost as much energy to inducing the Indians to wear clothing as to give up cannibalism.

16 · Prado notes that the "linen cloths" [*panos de linho*] worn by the women were really cotton. Prado, *Pernambuco,* 3:176.

17 · Contrary to Brandônio's assertion, the Indians did have religions, but they seem to have been reluctant to discuss them with Europeans. Hence the opinion, common among sixteenth-century Europeans, that they had no religion at all. For detailed descriptions of Indian religions see Alfred Métraux, *La religion des Tupinambá et ses rapports avec celle des autres tribus tupi-guarani;* idem, "The Tupinambá," in *HSAI,* 3:127–131; Estêvão Pinto, *Indígenas do Nordeste,* pp. 185–314.

18 · A demon to whom widely different traits were attributed in various regions, but who was greatly feared everywhere. Under the influence of the missionaries the name Juruparim came to be used in the *língua geral* for the Devil, just as Tupã, the thunder god, was sometimes identified with the Christian God. See Métraux, *Religion des Tupinambá,* pp. 57–60.

19 · This idea was a commonplace of the chroniclers, though it is wildly inaccurate. It occurs in many variants, e.g., the "Bartolozzi letter" of 1502 attributed to Vespucci; André Thevet, *Singularidades da França Antárctica a que outros chamam de América,* p. 175 and p. 29, n. 2; Christovão de Gouvêa, "Summário das armadas que se fizeram e guerras que se deram

na conquista do Rio Parahyba . . . ," *Revista do Instituto Histórico e Geográfico Brasileiro* 36 (1873), pt. 1, pp. 10–11; Pero de Magalhães de Gandavo, *Treatise on the Land of Brazil*, p. 166, and idem, *Sancta Cruz*, 1:chap. 10, fol. 33ᵛ, both in his *Histories of Brazil*; Soares de Sousa, *Notícia do Brasil* (1945), 2:244; Vicente do Salvador, *História do Brasil*, p. 85; Simão de Vasconcellos, *Notícias antecedentes, curiosas, e necessárias das cousas do Brasil*, in *Chrônica da Companhia de Jesu do Estado do Brasil*, pp. lxxv–lxxvi. See Samuel Eliot Morison, *The European Discovery of America: The Southern Voyages* A.D. *1492–1616*, p. 285.

20 · See p. 318, and below, n. 51.

21 · The history of the St. Thomas legend is summarized in Jacques Lafaye, *Quetzalcóatl and Guadalupe: The Formation of Mexican National Consciousness, 1531–1813*, tr. Benjamin Keen, pp. 177–206. See also Alfred Métraux, *A religião dos Tupinambás e suas relações com as demais tribus tupi-guaranis*, note on Sommay by Estêvão Pinto, pp. 69–70.

22 · The incident of Habbakuk bringing food to Daniel does not appear in the canonical account of Daniel in the lions' den (Daniel 6) and is rejected by many biblical scholars as apocryphal. It can be read in *Biblia sacra iuxta Vulgatam Clementiam*, ed. Alberto Colunga and Laurentio Turrado (Madrid: Biblioteca de Autores Cristianos, 1982), p. 870, where it is included in an appendix to the Book of Daniel.

23 · The couvade was the object of considerable curiosity among the early travelers to Brazil, who had evidently not encountered it elsewhere in spite of the fact that the custom is both ancient and widespread. It existed among most of the South American tribes, including all the Tupi-Guaranis. According to Soares de Sousa, the Indians explained the couvade as follows: if the father is too much exposed to the air, or if he exerts himself by working, his children will die. There is no danger for the mother, they thought, for the child sprang from the father's loins, the mother's part being only to keep the seed in her womb until birth, just as the earth holds seeds that have been planted in it. *Notícia do Brasil* (1945), 2:252 and n. 1. For details of the couvade and theories about its origin see Estêvão Pinto, *Indígenas do Nordeste*, pp. 242–244, 320; Métraux, *Religion des Tupinambá*, pp. 100–102; Fernandes, *Organização social*, pp. 158–161.

24 · The medical beliefs of the time had little place for cold air or water. Prado points out that in Portugal, where medicine as a science had fallen considerably below the level it had attained under Arabic teaching, a child "was born in an overheated room and was bundled in fantastic swaddling clothes and bonds of every size and thickness. He grew up enveloped in heavy clothing, knowing nothing of water, and so throughout his life, unless he happened to fall into a creek or a lake." Prado, *Pernambuco*,

1:120; cf. Gilberto Freyre, *Casa-Grande e senzala*, 2:508. Earlier (p. 106), Alviano told how he himself shunned cold water when ailing.

25 · "The men, women, and children, as soon as they get up go and wash and swim in the rivers, no matter how cold the weather is; the women swim and paddle canoes like men," says Cardim. Though fishing was generally regarded as a man's rather than a woman's task, women sometimes performed auxiliary functions in the activity. Léry tells how "both men and women can swim and are capable of going after game or fish under water like a dog." Cardim, *Tratados*, p. 275; Jean de Léry, *Histoire d'un voyage faict en la terre du Brésil*, 2:4; Fernandes, *Organização social*, p. 114.

In spite of the unsanitary condition of their houses (see above, n. 13), the Tupis appear to have been quite clean personally. "The fact is that the European was a filthy animal in comparison with the average Asian, African, or Amerindian," says Boxer. The women combed their hair often. Many people washed before and after every meal and rinsed their mouths after eating. They even washed their hammocks occasionally, using soaps made from various plants. (This procedure seems to have been infrequent, however, as the hammocks were allowed to become exceedingly dirty.) Charles R. Boxer, *The Golden Age of Brazil, 1695–1750*, p. 19; Estêvão Pinto, *Indígenas do Nordeste*, pp. 164–165; Yves d'Évreux, *Voyage dans le nord du Brésil fait durant les années 1613 et 1614*, pp. 106–107.

26 · Alviano's prejudice against Brazil is not easily eradicated, in spite of his apparent conversion in Dialogue IV (p. 220).

27 · Children's play consisted of small-scale activities like those of their parents. Thus they not only learned by imitation but also contributed at a very early age to the family economy; for instance, by fishing with bow and arrows scaled to size. The boys learned to make as well as to use these arms. If a child didn't want to learn, nobody compelled him. Children were not punished no matter what the fault. Estêvão Pinto, *Indígenas do Nordeste*, pp. 325–328. This permissiveness is fully in keeping with the practices of the adult society already described (see pp. 307–308, and above, n. 12).

28 · Métraux says that the preferred marriages were those between cross-cousins (with a child of the father's sister or of the mother's brother) and those between a girl and her mother's brother, or in case there was no brother, the mother's nearest male relative. Métraux, "The Tupinambá," *HSAI*, 3:111. See Joseph [José] de Anchieta, *Cartas, fragmentos históricos e sermões*, pp. 448–456; Thevet, *Singularidades*, chap. 42, p. 252 and n. 2; Fernandes, *Organização social*, pp. 140–142, 186–190. On p. 103 Brandônio thought the natives' taking their nieces to wife was evidence of Israelitish ancestry.

Consanguineous marriages were common among the Portuguese colonists as well as among the Indians. Freyre states that marriage between uncles and nieces, as well as between cousins, "has gone on for generations" among aristocratic white Brazilian families in the old rural regions. Freyre, *Casa-Grande e senzala,* 1:354.

29 · Fernandes says that men who chose wives from outside the circle of their immediate relatives had to work for the parents of their intended brides. See the sources cited in his *Organização social,* pp. 200–202.

30 · Most early writers agree that a high degree of understanding and harmony obtained within the polygamous household. Cf. VI, n. 13, and see the many citations given by Fernandes, *Organização social,* p. 207. On the other hand, Soares de Sousa asserts that "there are many jealousies among the women." *Notícia do Brasil* (1945), 2:248.

31 · Soares de Sousa says the Tupinambás believed that if a girl was deceitful as to her virginity the devil would carry her off. *Notícia do Brasil* (1945), 2:248.

32 · The "weeping welcome" has been noted in many lands and has been extensively studied by anthropologists. It is mentioned by virtually all the early chroniclers of Brazil. Métraux says the custom existed in South America only east of the Andes, especially among the Tupis.

In the form described (confusedly enough) by Brandônio, the guest, if he was a man, lay down in a hammock; the women of the house sat at his feet and tearfully lamented the sufferings he had undergone on the road as well as the misfortunes that had visited their own household during his absence. If the guest was a woman, she sat at the feet of the man of the house and treated him to a similar recital. Hans Staden, *Warhaftige Historia und beschreibung eyner Landtschafft der wilden nacketen grimmigen Menschfresser Leuthen in der Newenwelt America gelegen,* chap. 34; Soares de Sousa, *Notícia do Brasil* (1945), 2:266, 268; Cardim, *Tratados,* pp. 150–151; Léry, *Voyage,* 2:104; Métraux, *Religion des Tupinambá,* pp. 180–187; idem, "The Tupinambá," in *HSAI,* 3:114–115; Estêvão Pinto, *Indígenas do Nordeste,* pp. 265–272.

33 · The hammock was one of the important contributions of the Indians to Brazilian and world culture. Marcgrave says it was the most used article among the Tupinambás, who called it *ini.* Europeans knew it by the Arawak name *hamák.* The Indians not only slept in hammocks but were often buried in them, and both of these customs were adopted by some Portuguese.

Hammocks were made of cotton or vegetable fibers or a combination of these, some so skillfully fashioned that they looked as if woven on a loom. The Indians used no bed coverings, but fires were maintained beneath the hammocks or between each two, a practice that naturally resulted in frequent conflagrations. "Fire is their clothing, and they were very miserable without fire," Cardim reported. The fires also protected against mosquitoes, vermin, and evil spirits, as well as lighting the dwelling.

"Letter of Pedro Vaz de Caminha to King Manuel," in William Brooks Greenlee, ed. and trans., *The Voyage of Pedro Álvares Cabral to Brazil and India from Contemporary Documents and Narratives,* p. 25, nn. 1 and 2; Peter Carder, *The Relation of Peter Carder,* in Samuel Purchas, *Hakluytus Posthumus or Purchas His Pilgrimes,* 16:139; Cardim,*Tratados,* p. 272; Robert H. Lowie, "The Tropical Forests: An Introduction," in *HSAI,* 3:18; Estêvão Pinto, *Indígenas do Nordeste,* pp. 164, 169–171.

For the hammock as a conveyance used by Europeans, see p. 306, and above, n. 8.

34 · The members of a local group—that is, a village—shared an agricultural area that was cultivated in common by all the families of the settlement. Within this area each family had its private plot. Each of the women of a family (which, if polygamous, might be of considerable size) had a garden in the plot, in which she raised vegetables for the family. In cases of urgent individual need, agricultural products were shared with persons not belonging to the immediate family—a favor offered willingly, generously, and for as long as necessary, but always with the expectation that it would be reciprocated when the need arose. Thus it is inaccurate to say, with some writers both early and modern, that the Brazilian Indians practiced communal living. It is to be noted that the custom with respect to agricultural products was quite different from that for game, fish, fruits, and roots. The latter resources were available in the area at large and were free to all members of the local group without restriction. Fernandes, *Organização social,* p. 120.

35 · See p. 307, and above, n. 12.

36 · Sorcerers or magicians [Portuguese *feiticeiros*] were known to the Tupi tribes as *pajés.* A *pajé* could cure the sick and those bitten by snakes, foretell coming events, change himself into an animal, make himself invisible, and transport himself instantly from one place to another. Anyone, man or woman, could become a *pajé* by being impregnated with the magic power contained in a puff of tobacco smoke directed toward him or her by an established sorcerer. The sorcerers had great authority among the people, but, according to Soares de Sousa, they were not so much believed as feared. Métraux, *Religion des Tupinambá,* pp. 80–82; Estêvão Pinto, *Indígenas do Nordeste,* p. 296; Soares de Sousa, *Notícia do Brasil* (1945), 2:264 and n. 1.

37 · Other chroniclers spell the word *carbé* or *carbet.* The *carpé* was at first a clearing in the middle of a village, and later, by extension, a community house within the clearing where the villagers carried on social and religious activities. It was here too that the elders met to "drink smoke" and make

decisions for the group. Cf. Irving Rouse's description of the oval *carbet* in Carib villages, "The Carib," in *HSAI*, 4:551–552.

38 · Vengeance, to be exacted in blood, appears to have been the universal objective of war among the Tupi peoples. Florestan Fernandes, *A função social da guerra na sociedade tupinambá*, p. 68.

39 · After the Portuguese came, religious crises occurred among the Tupis that recall revivalistic or messianistic movements elsewhere in the world, especially among the North American Indians. The sorcerers assured the people that a Golden Age was at hand in which food would be provided for them without work. Their followers gave up hunting, fishing, and horticulture and spent their time dancing; some started off on expeditions to the Terrestrial Paradise. The result was just what Brandônio describes. These messiahs may reflect the influence of Christian ideas preached by the missionaries. Métraux, "The Tupinambá," in *HSAI*, 3:131.

40 · Orators were held in such great esteem by the Tupis that an eloquent man, if successful in warfare, might become a chief. A person who aspired to this distinction was put through a long and grueling examination, sometimes lasting all day and all night or even longer, without food or sleep. During this trial he had to prove his eloquence while his fellows tried to out-argue him or talk him down; if they did not succeed, he was recognized as a *língua* and a great man. The *língua* exhorted his tribesmen to make war, kill enemies, and carry out other manly exercises. In war he had the power of life and death over captives. A war leader needed to be a good *língua* so that he could give his men an effective pep talk before battle. See the description in the "Informação da Provincia do Brasil para nosso Padre—1585," formerly attributed to Anchieta but now generally thought to be the work of Cardim. It is found in Anchieta, *Cartas*, p. 433. See also Alfred Métraux, "The Guarani," in *HSAI*, 3:85.

The term *língua* also meant an interpreter, whether Indian or European, who served as a means of communication between the whites and the natives.

41 · In addition to food and weapons, they took along trumpetlike musical instruments, used for awakening and warning the troops, and hammocks that would be strung up between trees for sleeping. A man of importance was accompanied by his wife. He bore only his weapons, while the woman was loaded down with the hammock, food, water, and the children; in addition, according to Marcgrave, she might have a parrot in one hand and a monkey in the other. The food consisted mainly of "war meal" (see p. 195, and IV, n. 12), in waterproof satchels plaited of palm leaves. Since the principal object of war was the capture of enemies to be killed and eaten, the warriors carried ropes wound around their waists to secure the captives. On the warpath the men marched in single file, the strongest

in front. Jorge W. Marcgrave, *História natural do Brasil,* p. 272; Métraux, "The Tupinambá," in *HSAI,* 3:102; Estêvão Pinto, *Indígenas do Nordeste,* pp. 259–260.

42 · Bows varied greatly in form and material among the different tribes. There were also several types of arrow. For a description of these weapons, see Estêvão Pinto, *Indígenas do Nordeste,* pp. 132–138. The Indians were expert bowmen, says Anchieta. He asserts that they needed only to catch a glimpse of a man to hit him; no bird on the wing escaped them, and they even shot fish in the water. Anchieta, *Cartas,* p. 434.

43 · The weapon described by Brandônio is undoubtedly the *tacape,* the principal weapon of the Tupinambás, and unique in South America. The chroniclers regularly called the *tacape* "sword," as Brandônio does here, but this word does not accurately describe the weapon, and in fact the Tupis did not possess true swords. The *tacape* was really a club made of heavy wood, often *pau-d'arco* or *ipê.* It had a rounded, almost elliptical head that could be used for either blows or thrusts, and a flattened, round or oval blade with a sharp edge. The haft narrowed from the head to the hilt, which was elaborately ornamented with feathers, the latter often being of ceremonial significance. Métraux's term sword-club [*épée-massue*] is an accurate description of the weapon, and accordingly this term has been adopted for the present translation.

The *tacape* is illustrated in Staden, *Kurtzer bericht,* chap. 29. Cf. Cardim, *Tratados,* pp. 164–165; Soares de Sousa, *Notícia do Brasil* (1945), 2:74–76 and n. 7; Ferdinand Denis, *O Brasil,* p. 29; Fernandes, *Função social da guerra,* p. 31; Métraux, *Religion des Tupinambá,* p. 138.

44 · Feathers were the most important form of adornment among the Indians. They were obtained from a number of birds, including *araras, quiruás, canindés, guarás,* toucans, and rheas; after the Portuguese brought chickens to Brazil, white chicken feathers were also used. Feathers decorated headbands and other apparel as well as sword-clubs and shields, and were made into elaborate ornaments such as diadems, hats, necklaces, bracelets, garters, collars, and cloaks. The most celebrated of these artifacts were the feather capes, in which the feathers were arranged in overlapping rows like the scales of a fish. Examples of such cloaks are preserved in the principal ethnological museums of the world. For a detailed description of feathered artifacts see Marcgrave, *História natural,* pp. 270–271, and Estêvão Pinto, *Indígenas do Nordeste,* pp. 114–118.

45 · The shields might be of tree bark, of light wood, or of dried leather taken from the thickest part of the back or skin of the tapir. Some tribes used cana brava leaves. The shields were wide, flat, and round like a small German drum, or tabor. They might be adorned with feathers and painted in various colors. Shields were used primarily to ward off arrows at some

little distance, rather than in hand-to-hand fighting. Léry, *Voyage*, 2:33; Estêvão Pinto, *Indígenas do Nordeste*, pp. 142–143.

46 · See p. 251, and V, n. 45. Cf. Magalhães de Gandavo, *Sancta Cruz*, fol. 38ʳ (chap. 11): "Often when they leave their own territory very determined and eager to exercise their cruelty [on the enemy], if they happen to meet a certain bird, or some similar thing that they consider a bad omen, they go no farther on their mission, and they agree then and there to turn around, without any one of the company being opposed to this."

Métraux suggests that the bird may be the *matim tapirera* (variously classified as *Cuculus cavanus* L., *Tapera naevia* L., and *Empidonomus varius* Vieill.), which even today is regarded by the Tupinambás as a messenger from dead relatives, its call forecasting ill fortune. Garcia identified the bird as the *peitica* (cf. V, n. 45), which is identical with the *matim tapirera* according to Aurélio Buarque de Holanda Ferreira, *Novo dicionário da língua portuguesa* (hereafter cited as *Aurélio*), s.v. "saci." See Garcia, ed., *Diálogos*, V, n. 1, and Métraux, *Religion des Tupinambá*, pp. 69, 173.

47 · Fernandes points out that Brandônio's statement is probably correct so far as it is applied to small raiding bands, but is not appropriate to larger expeditions, when the warriors were accompanied by their wives and had to move more slowly in order to protect them. In every case the raiders were in haste to return to their village, because there was always danger that the enemy might organize a counterattack and surprise them. Fernandes, *Função social da guerra*, p. 141.

48 · The Tapirapés, a Tupi tribe sharing many traits with the Tupinambás, were one of a number of tribes who scratched their legs and arms with the teeth of the dogfish [*peixe cachorro*] to draw blood and thus gain strength. Charles Wagley, in correspondence with Frederick Hall. This custom is, after all, no more irrational than the almost universal blood-letting performed as therapy in Europe at the time.

49 · The custom of "taking a name" as practiced by the Tupinambás is variously decribed by the early writers. The most common version is that recorded by Brandão. Some scholars think that the purpose of taking a name was to protect the killer against attempts at vengeance on the part of the dead man; see, for example, Métraux, *Religion des Tupinambá*, pp. 163–165. Fernandes, challenging Métraux's view, adduces evidence that the practice has deeper and more complicated roots. See his extensive discussion of the question, with many citations, in his *Função social da guerra*, pp. 309–317.

50 · After a Tupi warrior had killed his enemy, he painted himself with genipap or *urucu* juice. Then his breast, arms, legs, and thighs were deeply slashed with agouti teeth, using patterns prescribed by custom. Charcoal or the juice of certain herbs was applied to the wounds to ensure that the scars

would remain for life. After the painful operation was over, the warrior lay in a hammock for several days without speaking, forbidden to break his silence for any reason whatever. He was fed a ration of cereal, water, and peanuts, but was not allowed to eat meat or fish until the scars had formed. Each new killing entitled the tribesman to a new tattoo. Thus the valor of a warrior was attested by the number of his scars. Métraux, *Religion des Tupinambá,* p. 167.

51 · Devouring the captives was the final step in the ritual of revenge that began with making war. See above, n. 38, and Fernandes, *Organização social,* pp. 236–238.

52 · Drinking bouts took place not only in connection with cannibal orgies but on many other festive occasions. Colorful accounts of these celebrations are provided by several chroniclers: e.g., Anchieta, *Cartas,* pp. 330, 434; Staden, *Kurtzer bericht,* chap. 15; Léry, *Voyage,* 1:150–153; Soares de Sousa, *Notícia do Brasil* (1945), 2:258–259. Cf. p. 104, where Brandônio is amazed that, in spite of "eating and drinking inordinately," the natives are healthy and strong.

53 · Monteiro in 1610 commented that the songs the Indians sang repeated in a single monotonous tone some aspect of the situation in which they found themselves. Monteiro, *Relação,* p. 415. Some of the traditional character of Indian song has lingered into modern times. As late as 1914 Algot Lange, a traveler in Pará, listened to a song sung by his Indian guide, and described it as "truly a sad and dreary song many times repeated *Kiri-kiri-kiri,* and so on indefinitely." *The Lower Amazon,* p. 243.

54 · The Indians thought of a mother as having no biological part in her child. Cf. n. 23 above.

55 · The term Tabajara (Tobayara) means enemy; it was applied by the Petiguares and other Tupi tribes who occupied the coastal regions to hostile tribes who lived inland. Since different tribes are called Tabajara, and since most of these tribes also have other names, much confusion existed. Métraux, "The Tupinambá," in *HSAI,* 3:96–97.

56 · The Greek legend of female warriors called Amazons has been localized in many lands. It early became one of the great myths of the New World, accepted as fact by Columbus himself and taken seriously as late as the nineteenth century by writers in good repute. The Amazon River owes its name to the currency of this legend; see I, n. 49. Estévão Pinto reviews the literature on the Amazons in his *Introdução à história da antropologia indígena no Brasil (século XVI),* p. 69, n. 19. See also Sérgio Buarque de Holanda, *Visão do paraíso; os motivos edênicos no descobrimento e colonização do Brasil,* pp. 28–41, 121; Robert Southey, *History of Brazil,* 1:604–609; Roberto C. Simonsen, *História econômica do Brasil (1500–1820),* p. 306

and n. 4; Affonso Arinos de Mello Franco, *O índio brasileiro e a Revolução Francesa: As origens brasileiras da theoria da bondade natural*, pp. 17–19.

57 · See IV, n. 108.

58 · Some of these necklaces contained from 2,000 to 3,000 teeth. Métraux, "The Tupinambá," in *HSAI*, 3:107.

59 · The Lestrygonians were an ancient people of Campania, Italy, fabled to be savages and cannibals. Odysseus encountered one of them, Polyphemus the Cyclops, who devoured several of Odysseus's companions before the hero escaped by a trick. The Scythians were herdsmen and shepherds, nomadic people of Tartary living in a kind of covered wagons. "They were filthy in their habits, never washing, fought on horseback, scalped their enemies, and drank out of their skulls." *Harper's Dictionary of Classical Literature and Antiquities.* Prado observes that Brandônio's statement about the vindictiveness and cruelty of the Indians is not exaggerated; it is reported by many of the old authors and is amply supported by recorded events. *Pernambuco*, 1:123–124. Anchieta, however, insists that the Indians were not cruel, "for ordinarily they do not torture their enemies." Rather, they either killed them in battle or executed them later after treating them well. Their death was a very easy one, says Anchieta, since the execution was usually performed by a single blow. If they do perpetrate cruelty, he adds, it is after the example of the Portuguese and French. Anchieta, *Cartas*, p. 329.

60 · Claude d'Abbéville gives the Indian names for certain stars and constellations of the southern hemisphere and relates some superstitions attached to them. He also demonstrates that the Tupis had an elementary knowledge of astronomy. Claude's information constitutes virtually all that is known of Tupi astronomy. Claude d'Abbéville, *Histoire de la mission des Pères Capucins en l'Isle de Maragnan et terres circonvoisines*, fols. 316–320; Garcia, ed., *Diálogos*, VI, n. 15.

61 · The Council of Trent, which was convened by the Roman Catholic Church in 1545 and sat until 1563. It made new regulations on marriage as well as on many other subjects.

62 · A double-reed woodwind instrument (now obsolete), similar to the oboe. The Fathers taught the Indians to play instruments so that they could take part in church services.

63 · Except for the Aimorés and the Tapuias, all the tribes mentioned by Brandônio belonged to the Tupi-speaking group. Métraux, "The Tupinambá," in *HSAI*, 3:95–103.

64 · See I, n. 170.

65 · At the end of the sixteenth century the Tupinambás occupied the coast between the Parnaíba and Pará rivers and between the Cape of São Tomé and the Bay of Angra dos Reis, as well as a narrow strip of coast from

the São Francisco River south to Camamu. In addition, they occupied some other localities that cannot be precisely identified. They lived by hunting and by cultivating manioc, maize, and beans. In spite of their common language the tribes were continually at war with one another. Métraux, "The Tupinambá," in *HSAI*, 3:95–103.

66 · See p. 321, and above, n. 55.

67 · See I, n. 104.

68 · Early writers frequently apply the term Tapuias to tribes unrelated to the Tupis, such as the Aimorés. The Tapuias belonged to a number of cultural and linguistic groups. They were nomads practicing a hunting and gathering economy. Because of the mobility noted by Brandônio, the Portuguese found the Tapuias to be redoubtable adversaries. At the same time they regarded these slippery enemies as barbarous and irrational. Robert H. Lowie, "The 'Tapuya,'" in *HSAI*, 1:553; Stuart B. Schwartz, "Indian Labor and New World Plantations," *American Historical Review* 83 (Feb. 1978):45.

69 · One of Brandônio's ill-considered stylistic inversions.

70 · Brandônio is evidently referring to the atlatl [a spear thrower] used by some Tapuia and other tribes. Attached to the contrivance was a ring, which was slipped onto a finger for easy transport. The Tupis are said to use the atlatl even today to throw fish harpoons. Robert H. Lowie, "The Tarairiu," in *HSAI*, 1:564; Julian H. Steward, "Tribes of the Montana: An Introduction," in *HSAI*, 3:526; Irving Rouse, "The Arawak," in *HSAI*, 4:532. Cf. *HSAI*, 1:554, fig. 69; 4:130.

71 · A final stylistic confusion. Brandônio must have meant "Their ignorance excuses their idle talk," a particularly contorted example of his characteristic reversals of meaning.

Appendix

The Lives and Works of the Principal Chroniclers

THE CHRONICLERS ARE ARRANGED, ROUGHLY, IN CHRONO-
logical order. This arrangement enables the reader to fit Brandão into his
place in the long line of men who wrote about Brazil during the sixteenth
and seventeenth centuries (and, in one case, the eighteenth). The chronological arrangement can be only approximate, partly because many of
the dates are uncertain and partly because an author's chronological dates
may be less significant than the dates of his works.

For detailed biographies and bibliographies of the chroniclers, the reader
should consult the two standard works on Brazilian historiography by José
Honório Rodrigues. (See Bibliography.)

PERO VAZ DE CAMINHA (dates unknown)

The distinguished line of colonial writers about Brazil begins with Pero Vaz de
Caminha, who accompanied Pedro Álvares Cabral on his voyage of discovery and
sent back to King Manuel of Portugal the first description of Brazil and its people.
Caminha's letter, dated May 1, 1500, is the earliest historical and literary document
of Brazil. Writing in the first enthusiasm of the discovery, Caminha gave an
emotional yet faithful account of this initial contact of the Portuguese with the
Brazilian land and people. His tribute began a long tradition of exaltation of the
land that found renewed expression in many a chronicle, including the *Dialogues*
attributed to Brandão.

ANDRÉ THEVET (1502–1592)

Since the French had their own territorial ambitions in Brazil, it is not surprising
that travelers of that nationality were among the chroniclers about Brazil. Thevet
was associated with a Lutheran group, sponsored by Calvin and led by Nicolas
Durand de Villegaignon, who in 1555 founded a colony on the site of present-
day Rio de Janeiro. The purpose of the project was to provide a haven for French-

men, mainly Huguenots, who wanted to enjoy liberty of conscience. Thevet was a member of the Franciscan order at the time. He had earlier traveled to the Orient. After three months in Brazil, Thevet returned to France, where he abandoned the ecclesiastical life and eventually became historiographer and cosmographer to the King of France. His *Singularities of Antarctic France, Otherwise Called America*, published in 1557, is the work of a cultured, though not an erudite, man. It is an important resource for the fauna and flora of Brazil and the life of the Indians allied to the French, with events in the French colony playing only a secondary role. Thevet was the first to describe several Brazilian animals. He also helped to popularize the contemporary concept of the "noble savage," exerting considerable influence on Michel de Montaigne himself. The early editions of Thevet's work were popular, but only briefly, because he was thought to have invented much of what he related. He retained this reputation for mendacity over several centuries, but it is now evident that he described carefully, though with some exaggeration, those phenomena which he himself had observed, but that he tended to accept uncritically almost anything he was told.

HANS STADEN (ca. 1530?–after 1555)

Perhaps in all those who traveled in Brazil during the first two centuries of colonization, whatever their country of origin and their condition in life, there was a liberal dash of the soldier of fortune. The German Hans Staden was an almost pure example of this breed. Born in Hesse and brought up a staunch Lutheran, Staden lived through a series of hair-raising adventures among the cannibals, ever supported by the firm conviction that God held his hand over him through every trial and danger.

Staden made two trips to Brazil, in 1547 and 1549. On his second visit he was taken prisoner by Tupinambá Indians and spent nearly a year in captivity, expecting to be killed and devoured in accordance with the tribal custom (see Dialogue VI). But using a number of clever ruses, Staden managed to escape this fate, and eventually he made his way back to Germany, where he published an account of his adventures, the *True History and Description of a Country of the Wild, Naked, Cruel Cannibal People Situated in the New World of America* (1557). Along with the *True History* Staden printed a treatise describing the Tupinambás and the flora and fauna of the country. This book, enriched by numerous woodcuts executed under Staden's personal supervision, still makes fascinating as well as informative reading.

PERO DE MAGALHÃES DE GANDAVO (ca. 1540?–?)

It was some seventy years after the discovery of Brazil that the true chronicle of the country had its beginning, in the *Treatise of the Land of Brazil* (ca. 1570) of Magalhães de Gandavo. Born and educated in Portugal, Magalhães occupied a place among the most distinguished humanists of the day and was a friend of Luís de Camões. He traveled to Brazil and resided there for some time, becoming a sugar mill operator and applying his learning and skills to the study and description of almost every aspect of the new land. Magalhães's purpose was to "reveal to the Kingdom [Brazil's] fertility and impel many poor people to go and live in this province, for that will bring its happiness and increase." Magalhães was the first writer to describe systematically the captaincies lining the Brazilian coast, a procedure that is followed by Brandão (though not in the same order). Magalhães recounted the principal historical events of the early colonial period; he also examined the life and customs of the Indians, the topography, the commerce, the rivers, the fauna and flora, and the economic riches of the country, especially in the area he knew best, that around Salvador—that is, the central part of the Atlantic coast.

JEAN DE LÉRY (1534–1611)

Jean de Léry was another member of Villegaignon's colonizing expedition. Himself a Lutheran, he acted at first as the recorder of the association; but dissensions soon arose among the colonists, as a result of which Léry was exiled to Indian territory. He took full advantage of his involuntary exposure to native customs, studying the Indian way of life and taking careful notes. Returning to Europe after an absence of two years, he devoted himself to the study of theology and eventually was ordained pastor.

Léry's *History of a Voyage to the Land of Brazil,* published in 1578, was written to provide Calvin with information that might be helpful to exiles from Catholic countries. In addition to describing the dissensions and sufferings of the Villegaignon expedition, Léry gave valuable information on the appearance and habits of the Indians, the Indian languages, and the flora and fauna of the country, especially of the Rio de Janeiro region.

JOSÉ DE ANCHIETA (1534–1597)

Among the most trustworthy chroniclers were the Jesuit missionaries, devoted men who not only helped to christianize the Indians and to educate both Indians and Europeans, but also left a considerable literary production. Their writings consist mainly of reports to their superiors in Rome, detailing the work of the missions and describing the country, its inhabitants, and its products. Many of these reports are truly valuable because the authors participated in the life they were picturing and because they reported their data with scholarly precision.

Outstanding among the Jesuit chroniclers was Father Anchieta, "the apostle of Brazil," whose efforts were indefatigable—and for the most part effective—in every area of missionary and educational activity. Thus he worked to pacify the Indians, helped to drive the French out of Rio de Janeiro, founded what later became the Colégio de São Vicente, and served the Company of Jesus as provincial for Brazil. Anchieta began a chronicle of the Company of Jesus in Brazil, but only fragments of this work remain. Surviving are a grammar of the Tupi language (the *língua geral* or common language), literary compositions in Portuguese, Latin, and Tupi, and a number of letters and reports, notably the "Report on Brazil and Its Captaincies" (1584), which contains much valuable historical information.

GABRIEL SOARES DE SOUSA (1540?–1591)

The most important—because the most comprehensive and reliable—of the sixteenth-century chroniclers was Gabriel Soares de Sousa. Soares de Sousa came to Brazil from Portugal as a young man and lived for seventeen years as a sugar lord in Bahia. Then he became fascinated by stories of gold and silver deposits in the back country. In the hope of obtaining royal authorization to exploit these riches as well as financial support for the endeavor, he prepared for the King a detailed report on the resources of the country, the *Descriptive Treatise on Brazil* (1587). He succeeded, eventually, in obtaining the support he sought, and in 1591 he organized an elaborate expedition from Salvador into the back country. Before he could locate any of the supposed treasure, however, he died of a fever in the wilds.

Soares de Sousa's treatise was the first attempt to produce a connected history of the Brazilian settlements. Though his historical data are raw and incomplete, they are immensely valuable, and they are supplemented with important facts about almost every phase of the Brazilian scene, especially the area around Salvador, which the author knew best. Included is information on geography, hydrography, Indian customs and language, agriculture, natural medicine, zoology, mineralogy, and timber. Soares de Sousa also offered many thoughtful suggestions about fortifying and developing the country. His presentation, though not of genuinely literary quality, is impressive in its breadth of vision. "This kingdom is capable of having built in it a great empire," Soares de Sousa declared with faith and foresight.

Soares de Sousa's work provides much the same kind of information for the central coastal area that Brandão gives for the Northeast. His treatment is more thorough and scholarly than Brandão's, but less personalized and anecdotal. Both are full of intelligent appreciation of the new land.

FERNÃO CARDIM (1548–1625)

In Brandão's own century, the seventeenth, the roster of chroniclers begins with another distinguished missionary. Fernão Cardim rose to high office in the Jesuit institutions of Rio de Janeiro and Salvador. Returning to Portugal in 1601, he was captured by English pirates and was a prisoner in England for many months. The pirates also seized his manuscripts, in which he had assembled for his religious superiors much valuable information about the new land and the labors of the Company of Jesus there, as well as about Brazilian geography, climate, ethnography, zoology, and botany. Fortunately, the work was not thrown into the sea but was taken to England, translated, and published anonymously as one of the items in the famous collection called *Purchas His Pilgrimes* (1625), about twenty-five years after its probable date of composition. There is a modern edition in Portuguese, whose title may be translated as *The Treatise on the Climate and Land of Brazil.*

JÁCOME MONTEIRO (1574–?)

Jácome Monteiro was one of a number of Jesuit chroniclers who wrote accounts of various phases of the life around them for the information of their superiors in Rome. His *Account of the Province of Brazil* (1610) contains minute descriptions of certain Brazilian fauna and products, as well as of the Indians and their customs. Monteiro concerned himself mainly with the São Paulo region, but also describes other sections of Brazil.

FRANÇOIS PYRARD DE LAVAL (ca. 1570–1621)

Pyrard de Laval was a born adventurer in the tradition of Hans Staden. As a youth he set sail for India from France in 1601, with a company of merchants who wanted to prove that the French could make the India voyage as well as the Portuguese. After nearly ten years in which Pyrard visited the maritime regions and islands of the East and traveled most of the way around the world, he returned home by way of Brazil, where he stayed only a short time. On his return to France he decided to write down his observations of the lands he had explored in order to inform his countrymen and help others who might undertake similar voyages. His book, *The Voyage of François de Pyrard of Laval* (1611), is mainly devoted to India, but includes an important short section on Brazil.

DIOGO DE CAMPOS MORENO (1566–ca. 1617)

As sergeant major of Brazil, Diogo de Campos Moreno was in a position to discuss with the authority of a government official both military and economic conditions as they existed at almost the precise date of the *Dialogues*. Campos Moreno had taken an active part in the military campaigns against the French and Indians in Ceará and Maranhão (see Dialogue I). At the order of King Manuel he wrote his *Account of the State of Brazil—1612*, dealing with the economic condition of the northern captaincies. This careful and authoritative document provides a valuable basis of comparison for the *Dialogues*, written only six years later. It consists of statistical reports on eight captaincies, from Porto Seguro to Rio Grande do Norte. Working from recent and official sources, Campos Moreno was able to provide reliable and important information on the growth of the country, the Indian wars, religious activities, resources, mills, population, military works, and income. He also gave a keen-eyed picture of the political situation, including such controversial matters as the disputes between the settlers and the Jesuits.

CLAUDE D'ABBÉVILLE (?–1632)

The French continued to cherish territorial ambitions in Brazil during the seventeenth century, but now their interest centered not on the Rio de Janeiro region but on the so-called East-West Coast. In 1612 an expedition was undertaken by Daniel de la Touche, Sieur de la Ravardière, for the purpose of establishing a colony in Maranhão, which France coveted for its brazilwood. In the expedition were four Capuchins eager to plant their faith among the Tupinambás. One of them was Claude d'Abbéville, who after remaining in Maranhão for four months returned to France and wrote his *History of the Mission of the Capuchin Fathers on the Isle of Maranhão and Adjacent Lands*. The work was published in Paris in 1612 and was an immediate success. It remains a classic of indigenous ethnography, showing an understanding of and sympathy with the Indians that were unusual at the time.

YVES D'EVREUX (1570–1630?)

One of the four Capuchins who accompanied La Ravardière to Maranhão, Yves continued his *confrère*'s history of the mission and settlement under the title *Voyage in the North of Brazil Made during the Years 1613 and 1614*. After the failure of the first mission to Maranhão, a second mission was sent out in 1614, so that Yves was able to spend four years in the place, in contrast to Claude d'Abbéville's brief four-month sojourn there. But in 1615 the French were dislodged from Maranhão by the Portuguese (an event described by Brandônio in Dialogue I). Returning to France, Yves found that the French wanted to hear no more about the disastrous expedition. Yves's book was actually given up to destruction in his publisher's office. One copy, however, was fortunately saved in part; but the work did not see the light of publication till 1864.

Yves's work shows him to have been a naive but clear-eyed observer of the Indians. It contains fundamental information about the ethnography and linguistics of the region.

VICENTE DO SALVADOR (1564–1639?)

Vicente do Salvador is the only chronicler who mentioned Brandão by name—but only as an Indian fighter, not as a writer. Vicente was one of the few chroniclers who were born in Brazil. A native of Bahia, he became a Franciscan missionary in the North of Brazil before traveling to Spain to begin his *History of Brazil, 1500–1627*, which he completed in Brazil in 1627.

Much of Vicente's information is borrowed from Soares de Sousa. He described the growth of the country and traced the growth of each settlement (though some parts of his book are incomplete because of gaps in the manuscript). He also gave detailed accounts of the wars with the Indians. In no sense is Vicente do Salvador's a typical work of history. He lacked proper sources and had no understanding of historical methodology. He simply wrote down whatever he himself found interesting—facts, anecdotes, legends, observations. But Vicente preserved a great deal of worthwhile information. He supplied many geographical and some botanical, zoological, ethnographic, and linguistic data, interspersed with popular stories and picturesque expressions. His writing is attractive because of its simple, natural style and the author's genuine love for Brazil.

Vicente do Salvador and Brandão give similar data on several matters, but there is no real evidence that the former had seen Brandão's manuscript, written some nine years before his own. For a list of the points on which the two authors coincide, see Capistrano de Abreu's "Nota preliminar" in his edition of Vicente do Salvador's work.

GEORG MARCGRAVE (1610–1643/44)

The most outstanding of the seventeenth-century scientists was a young German, who came to Brazil in 1638 in the service of the count of Nassau. While in Brazil he accumulated copious notes on botany and zoology, which were supplemented by drawings of specimens from his valuable botanical and zoological collection. He died before he had a chance to publish his work, but fortunately the notes were edited and published in Leyden in 1648 by his friend Johannes de Laet as the twelve-volume *Natural History of Brazil*. This book, written in Latin, was the first truly scholarly study of Brazil's flora and fauna. To it were added descriptions of the Amerindians and of the climate and geography of the land. This impressive work contains more than 400 woodcuts of plants, animals, insects, and fishes, most of them described here for the first time. Valuable, too, are Marcgrave's maps and drawings, but unfortunately some of these have been lost. "If he had lived to publish more of his work, he might well have been the greatest naturalist since Aristotle," said Charles R. Boxer.

WILLEM PISO (1611–1678)

Another of the brilliant young Dutchmen in Maurits's entourage was Piso, who followed the governor to Brazil as his personal physician. It may be that he had Georg Marcgrave as his assistant. In any case, Piso contributed to Marcgrave's *History* a four-volume section on tropical medicine, which made him one of the prime authorities on this subject until well into the nineteenth century. A later edition of the work, *On the Natural History and Pharmacology of Both Indies,* added the work of Jacobus Bontius, a pioneer in tropical medicine of the East Indies.

SIMÃO DE VASCONCELLOS (1597–1671)

Interest in scientific studies continued even after the Dutch had been driven out of the country. Observers writing around the middle of the seventeenth century—hence after Brandão's death—made rich additions to the knowledge of Brazilian phenomena and thus illuminate many a passage in the *Dialogues*.

Simão de Vasconcellos was born in Portugal but early moved to Bahia. Here he entered the Company of Jesus and rose to become provincial of the order for Brazil. His main literary work is the *Chronicle of the Company of Jesus of the State of*

Brazil, published in 1663 in a truly magnificent edition. Two supplements included in this work appeared separately in 1668 under the title *Primary, Curious, and Necessary Notes About Things in Brazil.*

ANDRÉ JOÃO ANTONIL (1650–1716)

Though Antonil wrote a century later than Brandão, his work is exceedingly useful to readers of the *Dialogues* because its major portion deals with the production of sugar, which was Brandão's own occupation and which he treats in some detail. Antonil's real name was João António Andreoni. An Italian Jesuit, he held important offices in his order in Bahia at the end of the seventeenth and the beginning of the eighteenth century. His *Culture and Wealth of Brazil in Its Drugs and Mines* (1711) deals with four Brazilian industries: those of sugar, tobacco, gold and silver mines, and cattle and hides.

In spite of his priestly calling, Antonil's approach was even more practical than that of Brandão. He described minutely and enthusiastically the riches of the new land and explained how these could best be exploited. Thus his description of the sugar industry constitutes a handbook for setting up and running a successful sugar mill.

Antonil's work was suppressed by the Portuguese government shortly after its publication. Some authorities believe this happened because of fear that the work would awaken the cupidity of other nations.

Bibliography

Abeyasinghe, Tikiri. *Portuguese Rule in Ceylon, 1594–1612.* Colombo, Sri Lanka: Lake House Investments, 1966.

Abreu e Brito, Domingos de. *Sumário e descripção do reino de Angola e do descobrimento da ilha de Loanda e da grandeza das capitanias do Estado do Brasil.* Edited by Alfredo de Albuquerque Felner as *Um inquérito à vida administrativa e económica de Angola e do Brasil em fins do século XVI.* Coimbra: Universidade de Coimbra, 1931.

Acosta, Joseph [José] de. *Historia natural y moral delas Indias.* Seville: Juan de León, 1590.

Agassiz, Louis, and Elizabeth Cabot Agassiz. *A Journey in Brazil.* Boston: Ticknor and Fields, 1868.

Ailly, Pierre d'. *Imago Mundi, de Pierre d'Ailly.* Edited by Edmond Buron. 3 vols. Paris: Maisonneuve Frères, 1930–1931.

Alden, Dauril. "The Growth and Decline of Indigo Production in Colonial Brazil: A Study in Comparative Economic History." *Journal of Economic History* 25 (March 1965):35–60.

———. *Royal Government in Colonial Brazil, with Special Reference to the Administration of the Marquis of Lavradio, Viceroy, 1769–1779.* Berkeley and Los Angeles: University of California Press, 1968.

———. "Yankee Sperm Whalers in Brazilian Waters, and the Decline of the Portuguese Whale Fishery (1773–1801)." *The Americas* 20 (Jan. 1964), no. 3:267–288.

———, ed. *Colonial Roots of Modern Brazil.* Berkeley and Los Angeles: University of California Press, 1973.

Alencar Araripe, Tristão de. *História da Província do Ceará desde os tempos primitivos até 1850.* 2d ed. Coleção História e Cultura. Fortaleza: Instituto do Ceará, 1958.

Almeida, Candido Mendes de. *Memórias para a história do extincto Estado do Maranhão,* vol. 2. Rio de Janeiro: Typ. do Commércio, de Brito e Braga, 1860–1874.

Anchieta, Joseph [José] de. *Cartas, informações, fragmentos históricos e sermões (1554–1594).* Rio de Janeiro: Civilização Brasileira, 1933.

Andreoni, João António. See Antonil, André João.

349

Anghiera, Pietro Martire d' [Peter Martyr]. *Décadas del Nuevo Mundo.* Translated from the Latin by A. Millares Carlo. Edited by Edmundo O'Gorman. 2 vols. Mexico: Porrúa, 1964–1965.

————. "Decades of the Newe Worlde." In *The First Three English Books on America* [?1511]–1555 A.D., edited by Edward Arber, pp. 43–398. Birmingham, England, 1885. Reprint. New York: Kraus Reprint Co., 1971.

Antonil, André João [João António Andreoni]. *Cultura e opulência do Brasil por suas drogas e minas.* Translated and edited by Andrée Mansuy. Paris: Institut des Hautes Études de l'Amérique Latine, 1965.

Aristotle. *Historia Animalium.* With an English translation by A. L. Peck. 3 vols. Loeb Classical Library. Cambridge, Mass.: Harvard University Press, 1965–.

Aurélio. See Ferreira, Aurélio Buarque de Holanda.

Azara, Félix de. *Apuntamientos para la historia natural de los quadrúpedos del Paragüay y Rio de la Plata.* 2 vols. Madrid: Viuda de Ibarra, 1802.

Azevedo, João Lúcio d'. *Elementos para a história econômica de Portugal (séculos XII a XVII).* Lisbon: Gabinete de Investigações Econômicas do Instituto Superior de Ciências Econômicas e Financeiras, 1967.

Baerle, Kaspar van. *Rerum per Octennium in Brasilia et Alibi Gestarum, sub Praefectura Illustrissimi Comitis I. Mauritii Nassaviae . . . Historia.* Amsterdam: Silberling, 1660. See also Barlaeus, Casparus, and Barléu, Gaspar van.

Barbosa, Duarte. *The Book of Duarte Barbosa.* Translated by Mansel Longworth Dames. 2 vols. Hakluyt Society, Series 2, vols. 44 and 49. London: Hakluyt Society, 1918–1921.

Barlaeus, Casparus. See Baerle, Kaspar van, and Barléu, Gaspar van.

Barléu, Gaspar van. *História dos feitos recentemente praticados durante oito anos no Brasil, e noutras partes sob o govêrno do illustríssimo João Maurício Conde de Nassau, etc.* Translated and edited by Cláudio Brandão. 2d ed. Rio de Janeiro: Imprensa Nacional, 1940. See also Baerle, Kaspar van, and Barlaeus, Casparus.

Barros, João de. *Da Ásia de João de Barros e de Diogo do Couto.* 24 vols. Lisbon: Régia Officina Typográffica, 1777–1788.

Barroso, Gustavo. *O Brasil na lenda e na cartografia antiga.* São Paulo: Companhia Editora Nacional, 1941.

Beaurepaire Rohan, Henrique de. "Chorographia da Província da Parahyba do Norte." *Revista do Instituto Histórico e Geográfico Paraibano* 3 (1911):165–365.

Bluteau, Raphael. *Vocabulário portuguez, e latino.* 8 vols. Coimbra: Collégio das Artes da Companhia de Jesu, 1712–1721.

Boxer, Charles R. "Admiral João Pereira Corte-Real and the Construction of Portuguese East-Indiamen in the Early 17th Century." *The Mariner's Mirror* 26 (1940):388–406.

————. "The Colour Question in the Portuguese Empire, 1415–1825." *Proceedings of the British Academy* 47 (1961):113–138.

————. *The Dutch in Brazil, 1624–1654*. Oxford: Clarendon Press, 1957.

————. *The Dutch Seaborne Empire: 1600–1800*. New York: Knopf, 1965.

————. *The Golden Age of Brazil, 1695–1750*. Berkeley and Los Angeles: University of California Press, 1969.

————. *The Great Ship from Amacon: Annals of Macao and the Old Japan Trade, 1555–1640*. Lisbon: Centro de Estudos Históricos Ultramarinos, 1959.

————. "Jorge de Albuquerque Coelho." *Anais da Academia Portuguesa da História*, Series 2, vol. 15 (1965):140 ff.

————. "The Portuguese in the East 1500–1800." In Harold V. Livermore, ed., *Portugal and Brazil: An Introduction*, pp. 185–247. Oxford: Clarendon Press, 1953.

————. *The Portuguese Seaborne Empire, 1415–1825*. New York: Knopf, 1969.

————. *Salvador de Sá and the Struggle for Brazil and Angola, 1602–1686*. London: Athlone Press, 1952.

————, ed. and trans. *The Tragic History of the Sea, 1589–1622*. Hakluyt Society, Series 2, vol. 112. Cambridge: University Press, 1959.

[Brandão, Ambrósio Fernandes?] *Diálogos das grandezas do Brasil*. See Garcia, Rodolfo, ed., and Mello, José Antonio Gonsalves de, ed.

Braudel, Fernand. *La Méditerranée et le monde méditerranéen à l'époque de Philippe II*. 2 vols. Paris: Colin, 1966.

Buarque de Holanda, Sérgio. *Visão do paraíso; os motivos edênicos no descobrimento e colonização do Brasil*. Rio de Janeiro: José Olympio, 1959.

Buarque de Holanda, Sérgio, director. *História geral da civilização brasileira*. Tomo 1, *A época colonial*, vol. 1, *Do descobrimento à expansão territorial*. 2d ed. São Paulo: Difusão Européia do Livro, 1963.

Burkill, Isaac H. *A Dictionary of the Economic Products of the Malay Peninsula*. 2 vols. Kuala Lumpur, Malaysia: Ministry of Agriculture and Cooperatives, 1966.

Burns, Bradford, ed. *A Documentary History of Brazil*. New York: Knopf, 1966.

Calado, Manuel. *O valeroso Lucideno e triunfo da liberdade*. 2 vols. São Paulo: Edições Cultura, 1943.

Calmon, Pedro. *História do Brasil*. 7 vols. Rio de Janeiro: José Olympio, 1959.

The Cambridge History of Africa. Vol. 4. *From c. 1600 to c. 1790*. Edited by Richard Grey. Cambridge: Cambridge University Press, 1975.

Caminha, Pero Vaz de. *A carta de Pero Vaz de Caminha*. Edited by Jaime Cortesão. Facsimile, transcription, and modernized version. Rio de Janeiro: Livros de Portugal, 1943.

————. "Letter of Pedro Vaz de Caminha to King Manuel." In William Brooks Greenlee, ed. and trans., *The Voyage of Pedro Álvares Cabral to Brazil and India, from Contemporary Documents and Narratives*, pp. 3–33. Hakluyt Society, Series 2, vol. 81. London: Hakluyt Society, 1938.

Campos Moreno, Diogo de. *Livro que dá razão do Estado do Brasil—1612.* Edited by Hélio Vianna. Recife: Arquivo Público Estadual, 1955. See also Sluiter, Engel. "Report on the State of Brazil, 1612." *Hispanic-American Historical Review* 29 (Nov. 1949):518–562.

Canabrava, Alice Piffer. *O comércio português no Rio da Prata (1580–1640).* Boletim 35, História da Civilização Americana, no. 2. São Paulo: Universidade de São Paulo, 1944.

Carder, Peter. *The Relation of Peter Carder of Saint Verian in Cornwall.* . . . In Samuel Purchas, *Hakluytus Posthumus or Purchas His Pilgrimes,* 16:136–146. New York: AMS Press, Inc., 1965.

Cardim, Fernão. *Tratados da terra e gente do Brasil.* Edited by Baptista Caetano, Capistrano de Abreu, and Rodolfo Garcia. 2d ed. Brasiliana, vol. 168. São Paulo: Companhia Editora Nacional, 1939.

"Carta de data da nossa ilha da Restinga defronte de Cabedello." *Revista do Instituto Histórico e Geográfico Paraibano* 10 (1946):179–180.

Casas, Bartolomé de las. *Apologética historia sumaria.* 2 vols. Mexico City: Universidad Nacional Autónoma de México, Instituto de Investigaciones Históricas, 1967.

Cascudo, Luís da Camara. *História da alimentação no Brasil.* Brasiliana, vol. 323. São Paulo: Companhia Editora Nacional, 1967.

Chaudhuri, K. N. *The English East India Company: The Study of an Early Joint-Stock Company, 1600–1640.* London: Frank Cass, 1965.

Chiappelli, Fredi, ed. *First Images of America: The Impact of the New World on the Old.* 2 vols. Berkeley and Los Angeles: University of California Press, 1976.

Cipolla, Carlo M. *Guns and Sails in the Early Phase of European Expansion 1400–1700.* London: Collins, 1965.

Clarke, James Stanier. *The Progress of Maritime Discovery, from the Earliest Period to the Close of the Eighteenth Century.* Vol. 1 (sole volume). London: T. Cadell and W. Davies, 1803.

Claude d'Abbéville. *Histoire de la mission des pères Capucins en l'Isle de Maragnan et terres circonvoisines.* Edited by Alfred Métraux and Jacques Lafaye. 1612. Facsim. reprint. Graz: Akademische Dr. u. Vrl., 1963.

Clements, James F. *Birds of the World: A Check List.* 2d ed. New York: Two Continents Publishing Group, Ltd., 1978.

Coaracy, Vivaldo. *O Rio de Janeiro no século dezessete.* Coleção Rio 4 Séculos, vol. 6. Rio de Janeiro: José Olympio, 1965.

Colmeiro y Penido, Miguel. *La botánica y los botánicos de la península hispano-lusitana.* Estudios Bibliográficos y Biográficos. Madrid: M. Rivadeneyra, 1858.

Colón, Fernando. *La historia de el Almirante D. Christóval Colón.* In *Historiadores primitivos de las Indias Occidentales,* ed. Andrés González de Barcia Carballido y Zúñiga, 1:1–128. Madrid, 1749.

Columbus, Christopher. *The Journal of Christopher Columbus.* Translated by Cecil Jane, with an appendix by R. A. Skelton. London: A. Blond, 1960.

Columbus, Ferdinand. *The Life of the Admiral Christopher Columbus by His Son, Ferdinand.* Translated and annotated by Benjamin Keen. New Brunswick, N.J.: Rutgers University Press, 1959.

Contarini, Gasparo. *Gasparis Contareni Cardinalis ampliss. philosophi sua aetate praeseantissimi de elementis et eorum mixtionibus libri quinque.* Geneva: Nicolaus Divitis, 1548.

Copia der Newen Zeytung ausz Presillg Landt. See *Tidings out of Brazil.*

Corrêa, Manoel Pio. *Flora do Brasil. Algumas plantas úteis, suas applicações e sua estatística, 1909.* Rio de Janeiro: Typographia da Estatística, 1909.

Costa, Angyone. *Migrações e cultura indígena.* São Paulo: Companhia Editora Nacional, 1939.

Costa, Francisco Augusto Pereira da. *Anais pernambucanos.* Vol. 2. *1591–1634.* Recife: Arquivo Público-Estadual, 1952.

———. *Apontamentos para um vocabulário pernambucano de termos e phrases populares.* In *Revista do Instituto Arqueológico, Histórico e Geográfico Pernambucano* 34 (1936): 7–763.

———. "O passo do Fidalgo." *Revista do Instituto Arqueológico, Histórico e Geográfico Pernambucano* 10 (March 1902):53–74, 171–173.

Costa, Francisco da. "Relatório sobre o trato da pimenta." In *Documentação ultramarina portuguesa,* 3:293–379. Lisbon: Centro de Estudos Históricos Ultramarinos, 1973.

Couto, Diogo do. *O soldado prático.* Edited by M. Rodrigues Lapa. Lisbon: Livraria Sá da Costa, 1937.

Cunha, Antônio Geraldo da. *Dicionário histórico das palavras portuguesas de origem tupi.* São Paulo: Editora da Universidade, 1978.

Curtin, Philip D. *The Atlantic Slave Trade: A Census.* Madison, Wis.: University of Wisconsin Press, 1969.

Dainville, François de. *La géographie des humanistes.* Paris: Beauchesne, 1940.

Darlington, Philip J., Jr. *Zoogeography: The Geographical Distribution of Animals.* London: John Wiley, 1957.

Deerr, Noel. *The History of Sugar.* 2 vols. London: Chapman and Hall Ltd., 1949–1950.

Dellon, Gabriel. *Nouvelle relation d'un voyage fait aux Indes Orientales contenant la description des isles de Bourbon et de Madagascar, de Surate, de la côte de Malabar, de Calicut, de Tanor, de Goa, etc.* Amsterdam: P. Marret, 1699.

Denevan, William M., ed. *The Native Population of the Americas in 1492.* Madison, Wis.: University of Wisconsin Press, 1976.

Denis, Ferdinand. *O Brasil.* 2 vols. in 1. Bahia: Livraria Progresso Editora, 1955.

De Schauensee, Rodolphe Meyer. *The Birds of Colombia and Adjacent Areas of South and Central America.* Narberth, Pa.: Livingstone Publishing Co., 1964.

————. *The Species of Birds of South America and Their Distribution.* Narberth, Pa.: Academy of Natural Sciences, 1966.

De Silva, Chandra Richard. "The Portuguese East India Company 1628–1633." *Luso-Brazilian Review* 11 (1974):152–205.

————. *The Portuguese in Ceylon 1617–1638.* Colombo, Sri Lanka: H. W. Cave, 1972.

————. "Trade in Ceylon Cinnamon in the Sixteenth Century." *The Ceylon Journal of Historical and Social Studies,* n.s. 3 (1973):14–27.

Diccionário histórico, geográphico e ethnográphico do Brasil. Instituto Histórico, Geográphico, Ethnográphico do Brasil. Rio de Janeiro: Imprensa Nacional, 1922.

Dicionário de história de Portugal. Edited by Joel Serrão. 4 vols. Lisbon, Iniciativas Editoriais, 1963–1971.

Diégues, Manuel, Jr. *O engenho de açúcar no Nordeste.* Documentário da vida rural, no. 1. Rio de Janeiro: Ministério da Agricultura, 1952.

Diffie, Bailey W. *Latin-American Civilization: Colonial Period.* New York: Octagon Books, Stackpole, 1967.

Diffie, Bailey W., and George D. Winus. *Foundations of the Portuguese Empire, 1415–1580.* Minneapolis: University of Minnesota Press, 1977.

"Discripción de la Provincia del Brasil." In *Documentação ultramarina portuguesa,* 2: 1–7. Lisbon: Centro de Estudos Históricos Ultramarinos, 1962.

Documentos para a história do açúcar. Vol. 1. *Legislação (1534–1596).* Instituto do Açúcar e do Álcool. Rio de Janeiro: Serviço Especial de Documentação Histórica, 1954.

Domínguez, Rafael Antonio. *Historia de las esmeraldas de Colombia.* Bogotá: Gráficas Ducal, 1965.

Dorsett, P. H., A. D. Shamel, and Wilson Popenoe. *The Navel Orange of Bahia, with Notes on Some Little-Known Brazilian Fruits.* U.S. Dept. of Agriculture, Bulletin 445. Washington, D.C.: Government Printing Office, 1917.

Downton, Nicholas. See Foster, William, ed.

Ducke, Adolfo. "Estudos botânicos no Ceará." *Anais da Academia Brasileira de Ciências* 31 (June 30, 1959):211–308.

Duffy, James. *Portugal in Africa.* Baltimore: Penguin Books, 1963.

Dutra, Francis A. "Centralization vs. Donatarial Privilege." In Dauril Alden, ed., *Colonial Roots of Modern Brazil,* pp. 19–60. Chicago: University of Chicago Press, 1973.

————. "Matias de Albuquerque and the Defense of Northeastern Brazil, 1620–1626." *Studia* 36 (July 1973):117–166.

Ellis, Myriam. *A baleia no Brasil Colonial.* São Paulo: Universidade de São Paulo, 1969.

Enciclopédia brasileira Mérito. São Paulo: Editora Mérito, 1959–1964.

Estaço da Sylveira, Symão. *Relação summária das cousas do Maranhão.* Lisbon, 1624. Facsim. reprint. Boston: Massachusetts Historical Society, 1929.

Fernandes, Florestan. *A função social da guerra na sociedade tupinambá.* 2d ed. São Paulo: Pioneira, 1970.

———. *Organização social dos Tupinambá.* São Paulo: Instituto Progresso Editorial, 1948.

Fernandes, Hamilton. *Açúcar e álcool ontem e hoje.* Coleção Canaviera no. 4. Rio de Janeiro: Instituto de Açúcar e do Álcool, 1971.

Ferrari, Sante. *I tempi, la vita, le dottrine di Pietro d'Abano, saggio storico-filosofico.* Geneva: Tipografia R. Istituto Sordomuti, 1900.

Ferreira, Alexandre Rodrigues. "Diário da viagem philosóphica pela Capitania de São-José do Rio-Negro." *Revista do Instituto Histórico e Geográfico Brasileiro* 51 (1888):5–166.

Ferreira, Aurélio Buarque de Holanda. *Novo dicionário da língua portuguesa.* Rio de Janeiro: Editora Nova Fronteira, 1975.

Ferreira Pinto, Irineu. *Datas e notas para a história da Parahyba.* Vol. 1. *1908–1916.* Reprint. João Pessoa: Editora Universitária, 1977.

Figueiredo Falcão, Luiz de. *Livro em que se contém toda a fazenda e real património dos reinos de Portugal, Índia e ilhas adjacentes.* Lisbon: Imprensa Nacional, 1859.

Flecknoe, Richard. *A Relation of Ten Years Travells in Europe, Asia, Affrique, and America.* London, 1654.

Foster, William, ed. *The Voyage of Nicholas Downton to the East Indies, 1614–15, as Recorded in Contemporary Narratives and Letters.* Hakluyt Society, Series 2, vol. 82. London: Hakluyt Society, 1939.

Freyre, Gilberto. *Casa-Grande e senzala.* 9th Brazilian ed. 2 vols. Rio de Janeiro: José Olympio, 1958.

———. *Nordeste.* 3d ed. Rio de Janeiro: José Olympio, 1961.

Galvano, António. See Galvão, António.

Galvão [Galvano], António. *The Discoveries of the World, from Their First Original unto the Year of Our Lord 1555.* Edited by Richard Hakluyt. 1601. Reprint with Portuguese text. Hakluyt Society, Series 1, vol. 30. London: Hakluyt Society, 1862.

García, Gregorio. *Origen de los indios de el Nuevo Mundo e Indias Occidentales.* Valencia: Mey, 1607.

Garcia, Rodolfo, ed. *Diálogos das grandezas do Brasil.* Bahia: Livraria Progresso Editora, 1956.

———. "Diccionário de brasileirismos." *Revista do Instituto Histórico e Geográfico Brasileiro* 76 (1913), pt. 1:633–947.

Garcilaso de la Vega [El Inca]. *Comentarios reales de los Incas.* Edited by José Durand. 3 vols. San Marcos, Peru: Universidad de San Marcos, 1959.

George, Wilma. *Animals and Maps.* Berkeley and Los Angeles: University of California Press, 1969.

Gerard, John. *The Herball or General Historie of Plantes.* London: Norton, 1597.

Gerbi, Antonello. *La disputa del Nuovo Mondo: Storia di una polemica, 1750–1900.* Milan and Naples: Riccardo Ricciardi Editore, 1955.

———. *The Dispute of the New World: The History of a Polemic, 1750–1900.* Translated by Jeremy Moyle. Pittsburgh: University of Pittsburgh Press, 1973.

Gilmore, Raymond M. "Fauna and Ethnozoology of South America." In Julian H. Steward, ed., *Handbook of South American Indians,* 6:345–464.

Glamann, Kristof. *Dutch-Asiatic Trade 1620–1740.* Copenhagen: Danish Science Press, 1958.

Glossary of Brazilian-Amazonian Terms. Compiled by Donald Farquhar, Helen Macmillan, and Bernard Siegel. Washington, D.C.: Office of the Coordinator, Inter-American Affairs, Research Division, 1943.

Greenlee, William Brooks. "The First Half Century of Brazilian History." Revised reprint from *Mid-America* 25 (April 1943):91–120.

———, ed. and trans. *The Voyage of Pedro Álvares Cabral to Brazil and India from Contemporary Documents and Narratives.* Hakluyt Society, Series 2, vol. 81. London: Hakluyt Society, 1938.

Grollenberg, L. H. *Atlas of the Bible.* New York: Thomas Nelson and Sons, 1956.

Grossman, Mary Louise, and John Hamlet. *Birds of Prey of the World.* New York: Clarkson N. Potter, 1964.

Guerra, Flávio. *Evolução histórica de Pernambuco.* Vol. 1, pt. 1. *Donatária.* Recife: Companhia Editora de Pernambuco, 1970.

———. *História colonial do Nordeste.* Rio de Janeiro: Distribuidora Record, 1963.

Guerra, Francisco. "Aleixo de Abreu (1568–1630), Author of the Earliest Book on Tropical Medicine Describing Amoebiasis, Malaria, Typhoid Fever, Scurvy, Yellow Fever, Dracontiasis, Trichuriasis and Tungiasis in 1623." *Journal of Tropical Medicine and Hygiene* 71 (March 1968):55–69.

Handbook of South American Indians. See Steward, Julian H., ed.

Hanke, Lewis. *The Imperial City of Potosí.* The Hague: Martinus Nijhoff, 1956.

———, ed. *History of Latin American Civilization: Sources and Interpretations.* Vol. 1. *The Colonial Experience.* Boston: Little, Brown, 1967.

Hargreaves, Dorothy and Bob. *Tropical Trees Found in the Caribbean, South America, Central America, Mexico.* Kailua, Hawaii: Hargreaves Co., 1965.

Harper's Dictionary of Classical Literature and Antiquities. Edited by Harry Thurston Peck. 2d ed. New York: American Book Co., 1898.

Haverschmidt, F. *Birds of Surinam.* Wynnewood, Pa.: Livingston, 1968.

Heiser, Charles B., Jr. *Seed to Civilization: The Story of Man's Food.* San Francisco: W. H. Freeman and Co., 1973.

Hemming, John. *Red Gold: The Conquest of Brazilian Indians.* Cambridge: Harvard University Press, 1978.

Herckmans, Elias. "Descrição geral da Capitania da Paraíba." *Revista do Instituto Arqueológico, Histórico e Geográfico Pernambucano* 5 (Oct. 1886):239–288.

Hobson-Jobson. See Yule, Henry, and A. C. Burnell.

Hoehne, F. C. *Botânica e agricultura no Brasil no século XVI.* Brasiliana, vol. 71. São Paulo: Companhia Editora Nacional, 1937.

Houaiss, Antônio, and Catherine B. Avery, eds., *The New Appleton Dictionary of the English and Portuguese Languages.* New York: Appleton-Century-Crofts, 1967.

Huddleston, Lee Eldridge. *Origins of the American Indians; European Concepts, 1492–1729.* Austin, Texas: University of Texas Press, Institute of Latin American Studies, 1967.

Hygino, José. "Relatórios e cartas de Gedeon Morris de Jonge." *Revista do Instituto Histórico e Geográfico Brasileiro* 58 (1895), pt. 1:237–319.

Ihering, Rodolpho von. *Da vida dos nossos animais: Fauna do Brasil.* São Leopoldo, Rio Grande do Sul: Rotermund, 1934.

———. *Dicionário dos animais do Brasil.* São Paulo: Universidade de Brasília, 1968.

Jaboatão, António de Santa Maria. *Novo orbe seráfico brasílico ou Chrónica dos frades menores da Província do Brasil.* 1761. Reprint (5 vols. in 3). Rio de Janeiro: Typ. Brasiliense M. Gomes Ribeiro, 1858–1862.

Jacobs, Herbert, ed. *Documenta Malucensia.* Rome: Institutum Historicum Societatis Iesu, 1974.

Kayserling, M[eyer]. *Christopher Columbus and the Participation of the Jews in the Spanish and Portuguese Discoveries.* Translated by Charles Gross. New York: Hermon Press, 1968.

Kellenbenz, Hermann. "Der Pfeffermarkt um 1600 und die Hansastädte." *Hansische Geschichtsblätter* 74 (1956):32.

Kiemen, Mathias C. "The Indian Policy of Portugal in America." In Lewis Hanke, ed., *History of Latin American Civilization: Sources and Interpretations.* Vol. 1, *The Colonial Experience,* pp. 253–263. Boston: Little, Brown, 1967.

Kimble, George H. T. *Geography in the Middle Ages.* London: Methuen, 1938.

Koster, Henry. *Travels in Brazil.* 2d ed. 2 vols. London: Longman, Hurst, Rees, Orme and Brown, 1817.

Labat, Jean Baptiste. *Nouveau voyage aux isles de l'Amérique.* 6 vols. The Hague: P. Husson, 1724.

Lach, Donald Frederick. *Asia in the Making of Europe.* 3 vols. Chicago: University of Chicago Press, 1965.

Lafaye, Jacques. *Quetzalcóatl and Guadalupe: The Formation of Mexican National Consciousness, 1531–1813.* Translated by Benjamin Keen. Chicago: University of Chicago Press, 1976.

Lane, Frederic Chapin. "Venetian Shipping During the Commercial Revolution." *American Historical Review* 38 (Jan. 1933):219–239.

Lange, Algot. *The Lower Amazon.* New York and London: G. P. Putnam's Sons, 1914.

Lapa, José Roberto do Amaral. *O Brasil e as drogas do Oriente.* Marília, São Paulo: Faculdade de Filosofia, Ciências e Letras de Marília, 1966.

Las Casas. See Casas, Bartolomé de las.

Le Cointe, Paul. *Árvores e plantas úteis.* 2d ed. Brasiliana, vol. 251. São Paulo: Companhia Editora Nacional, 1947.

Leite, Serafim. *História da Companhia de Jesus no Brasil.* 10 vols. Lisbon: Livraria Portugalia; Rio de Janeiro: Civilização Brasileira, 1938–1950.

―――. *Novas cartas jesuíticas (de Nóbrega a Viera).* Brasiliana, vol. 194. São Paulo: Companhia Editora Nacional, 1940.

―――. *Páginas de história do Brasil.* Brasiliana, vol. 93. São Paulo: Companhia Editora Nacional, 1937.

―――. *Suma histórica da Companhia de Jesus no Brasil (Assistência de Portugal),* 1549–1760. Lisbon: Junta de Investigações do Ultramar, 1965.

Léry, Jean de. *Histoire d'un voyage faict en la terre du Brésil.* Edited by Paul Gaffarel. 2 vols. Paris: Lemerre, 1880.

―――. *Viagem à terra do Brasil.* Translated and edited by Sérgio Milliet after the edition of Paul Gaffarel, with notes on the Tupi by Plínio Ayrosa. 2d ed. São Paulo: Livraria Martins Editora, 1951.

Leur, Jacob Cornelis van. *Indonesian Trade and Society: Essays in Asian Social and Economic History.* The Hague: Van Hoeve, 1955.

Lévi-Strauss, Claude. "The Use of Wild Plants in Tropical South America." In *Handbook of South American Indians,* 6:465–486.

Linschoten, John [Jan] Huyghen van. *The Voyage of John Huyghen van Linschoten to the East Indies, from the Old English Translation of 1598.* Edited by Arthur Coke Burnell and P. A. Tiele. 2 vols. Hakluyt Society, Series 1, vols. 70 and 71. London: Hakluyt Society, 1885.

Lippmann, Edmund Oskar von. *História do açúcar desde a época mais remota até o começo da fabricação do açúcar de beterraba.* Translated by Rodolfo Coutinho. 2 vols. Instituto do Açúcar e do Álcool. Rio de Janeiro: Leuzinger, 1941–1942.

Lisboa, Cristóvão de. *História dos animais e árvores do Maranhão.* Lisbon: Arquivo Histórico Ultramarino e Centro de Estudos Históricos Ultramarinos, 1967.

Lisboa, João Francisco. *Crônica do Brasil Colonial (Apontamentos para a história do Maranhão).* Petrópolis: Ministério da Educação e Cultura, 1976.

Loreto Couto, Domingos do. *Desaggravos do Brasil e glórias de Pernambuco.* Rio de Janeiro: Biblioteca Nacional, 1904.

Lowie, Robert H. "The 'Tapuya.'" In *Handbook of South American Indians,* 1: 553–556.

―――. "The Tarairiu." In *Handbook of South American Indians,* 1:563–574.

―――. "The Tropical Forests: An Introduction." In *Handbook of South American Indians,* 3:1–56 and plates 89 and 90 (after p. 794).

Machado, José Pedro. *Dicionário etimológico da língua portuguesa.* 2d ed. Lisbon: Editorial Confluência, 1967–.

Magalhães, Basílio de. *Expansão geográphica do Brasil Colonial.* 2d ed. Brasiliana, vol. 45. São Paulo: Companhia Editora Nacional, 1935.

Magalhães de Gandavo, Pero de. *História da Província Sancta Cruz*. 1576. With a facsimile and a translation. In idem, *The Histories of Brazil*, vol. 1.

————. *The Histories of Brazil*. Translated and edited by John B. Stetson, Jr. 2 vols. in 1. New York: The Cortes Society, 1922.

————. *Treatise on the Land of Brazil*. In idem, *The Histories of Brazil*, 2: 123–183.

Magalhães Godinho, Vitorino. *Os descobrimentos e a economia mundial*. 2 vols. in 3. Lisbon: Editora Arcadia, 1963.

Malheiro Dias, Carlos, ed. *História da colonização portuguesa do Brasil*. Edição Monumental Comemorativa. 3 vols. Porto: Litografia Nacional, 1921–1924.

Malkiel, Yakov. "Changes in the European Languages Under a New Set of Sociolinguistic Circumstances." In *First Images of America*, 2:581–593.

Marcgrave, Georg. *Historiae Rerum Naturalium Brasiliae, Libri Octo*. Antwerp: Joannes de Laet, 1648. See also Marcgrave, Jorge W.

Marcgrave, Jorge W. [Georg]. *História natural do Brasil*. Translated into Portuguese by José Procopio de Magalhães. São Paulo: Imprensa Oficial do Estado, 1942.

Marchant, Alexander. *From Barter to Slavery: The Economic Relations of Portuguese and Indians in the Settlement of Brazil, 1500–1580*. Baltimore: Johns Hopkins Press, 1942.

Marques, A. H. de Oliveira. *Daily Life in Portugal in the Late Middle Ages*. Translated by S. S. Wyatt. Madison, Wis.: University of Wisconsin Press, 1971.

————. *History of Portugal*. Vol. 1. *From Lusitania to Empire*. New York and London: Columbia University Press, 1972.

Martius, Carlos [Karl] Friedrich Philipp von. *Natureza, doenças, medicina e remédios dos índios brasileiros (1844)*. Translated and edited by Pirajá da Silva. Brasiliana, vol. 154. São Paulo: Companhia Editora Nacional, 1939.

Martius, Karl Friedrich Philipp von. *Beiträge zur Ethnographie und Sprachenkunde Amerika's, zumal Brasiliens*. 2 vols. Leipzig: Fleischer, 1867.

Martyr, Peter. See Anghiera, Pietro Martire d'.

Mauro, Frédéric. *Le Portugal et l'Atlantique au XVIIe siècle (1570–1670)*. Paris: S.E.V.P.E.N., 1960.

Meilink-Roelofsz, Marie Antoinette Petronella. *Asian Trade and European Influence in the Indonesian Archipelago Between 1500 and About 1630*. The Hague: Martinus Nijhoff, 1962.

Mello, José Antonio Gonsalves de, ed. *Diálogos das grandezas do Brasil*. 2d ed. Recife: Imprensa Universitária, 1966.

Mello Franco, Affonso Arinos de. *O índio brasileiro e a revolução francesa, as origens brasileiras da teoria da bondade natural*. Coleção Documentos Brasileiros, 7. Rio de Janeiro: José Olympio, 1937.

Mello Leitão, C. de. *Zoo-Geographia do Brasil*. Brasiliana, vol. 77. São Paulo: Companhia Editora Nacional, 1937.

Mendes de Vasconcellos, Luiz. *Diálogos do sítio de Lisboa*. In *Antologia dos economistas portugueses,* edited by António Sérgio, pp. 1–169. Lisbon: Oficinas Gráficas da Biblioteca Nacional, 1924.

Mérito. See *Enciclopédia brasileira Mérito.*

Métraux, Alfred. "The Botocudo." In *Handbook of South American Indians,* 1: 531–540.

————. "The Guaraní." In *Handbook of South American Indians,* 3:69–94.

————. *A religião dos Tupinambás e suas relações com a das demais tribus tupi-guaranis.* Translated and edited by Estêvão Pinto. Brasiliana, vol. 267. São Paulo: Companhia Editora Nacional, 1950.

————. *La religion des Tupinambá et ses rapports avec celle des autres tribus Tupi-Guarani.* Paris: Leroux, 1928.

————. "The Tupinambá." In *Handbook of South American Indians,* 3:95–133.

Monardes, Nicholas. *Primera y segunda y tercera partes de la historia medicinal de las cosas que se traen de nuestras Indias Occidentales que sirven en medicina.* Seville: A. Escrivano, 1574.

Monteiro, Jácome. *Relação da Província do Brasil, 1610.* In Serafim Leite, *História da Companhia de Jesus no Brasil,* 8:393–425. Rio de Janeiro: Civilização Brasileira, 1938–1950.

Moraes e Silva, Antônio de. *Diccionário da língua portugueza.* 8th ed. 2 vols. Rio de Janeiro: Silva Lobo, 1890–1891.

Morison, Samuel Eliot. *The European Discovery of America: The Southern Voyages A.D. 1492–1616.* New York: Oxford University Press, 1974.

Morse, Richard McGee. *From Community to Metropolis: A Biography of São Paulo, Brazil.* Gainesville: University of Florida Press, 1958.

Mun, Thomas. *A Discourse of Trade, from England unto the East-Indies.* 1621. Facsim. reprint. New York: Facsimile Text Society, 1930.

Mundy, Peter. *The Travels of Peter Mundy in Europe and Asia, 1608–1667.* 5 vols. in 6. Hakluyt Society, Series 2, vols. 17, 35, 45, 46, 55, 78. Cambridge: Hakluyt Society, 1907.

Myers, George S., ed. *The Piranha Book.* Neptune City, N.J.: T. F. H. Publications, 1972.

Neuwied. See Wied-Neuwied, Maximilian Alexander von.

New Appleton Dictionary. See Houaiss, Antônio, and Catherine B. Avery, eds.

Newe Zeytung ausz Presillg Landt. See *Tidings Out of Brazil.*

Newton, Alfred. *A Dictionary of Birds.* London: Adam and Charles Black, 1893–1896.

Nieuhof, Joan. *Memorável viagem marítima e terrestre ao Brasil.* Based on an English translation by M. Moacir N. Vasconcelos of the original Dutch version of 1682. 2d ed. São Paulo: Martins, 1951.

Nóbrega, Manuel da. *Cartas do Brasil (1549–1560).* Rio de Janeiro: Officina Industrial Gráphica, 1931.

Nova gazeta da terra do Brasil (Newe Zeytung ausz Presillg Landt, 1515). Translated and edited by Rodolpho R. Schuller. With a facsimile. Rio de Janeiro: Officinas Gráphicas da Biblioteca Nacional, 1914. See also *Tidings Out of Brazil*.

Novinsky, Anita. *Cristãos novos na Bahia*. São Paulo: Perspectiva, Editora da Universidade de São Paulo, 1972.

Novo Michaelis dicionário ilustrado. 2 vols. 2d ed. São Paulo: Edições Melhoramentos, 1961.

Nowell, Charles E. *The Great Discoveries and the First Colonial Empires*. Ithaca: Cornell University Press, 1954.

———. *A History of Portugal*. Princeton: Van Nostrand, 1952.

Oliveira, Nicolau de. *Livro das grandezas de Lisboa*. Lisbon: Impressão Régia, 1804.

Orta, Garcia d'. *Colóquios dos simples e drogas da Índia*. Edited by O Conde de Ficalho. 2 vols Lisbon: Imprensa Nacional, 1891–1895.

———. *Colóquios dos simples e drogas e cousas medicinais da Índia*. 1563. Facsim. Lisbon: Academia das Ciências de Lisboa, 1963.

Oviedo y Valdés, Gonzalo Fernández de. *La historia general delas Indias*. Seville: Cromberger, 1535.

———. *Oviedo dela natural historia delas Indias*. Toledo: Remõ de Petras, 1526.

Parkinson, John. *Paradisi in Sole: Paradisus Terrestris*. 2d impression, much corrected and enlarged. London: Richard Thrale, 1656.

Parry, John Horace. *The Age of Reconnaissance*. Cleveland and New York: World Publishing Co., 1963.

———. *The Discovery of the Sea*. New York: Dial Press, 1974.

———. *The Spanish Seaborne Empire*. New York: Knopf, 1970.

Paschoa, António Gonçalvez. "Descripção da cidade e barra da Paraíba." In *Documentação ultramarina portuguesa*, 1:17–19. Lisbon: Centro de Estudos Históricos Ultramarinos, 1960.

Pearson, Michael Naylor. *Commerce and Compulsion: Gujarati Merchants and the Portuguese System in Western India, 1500–1600*. Ann Arbor, Mich.: University Microfilms, 1972.

Peckholt, Theodor. *Volksbenennungen der brasilianischen Pflanzen und Produkte derselben in brasilianischen (portugiesischen) und von der Tupisprache adoptirten Namen*. Milwaukee: Pharmaceutical Review Publishing Co., 1907.

Pequeno dicionário brasileiro da língua portuguesa. 7th ed. Revised by Aurélio Buarque de Hollanda Ferreira. Rio de Janeiro: Editora Civilização Brasileira, 1948.

Pereira da Costa, Francisco Augusto. See Costa, Francisco Augusto Pereira da.

Peter Martyr. See Anghiera, Pietro Martire d'.

Pico della Mirandola, Giovanni. *De Astrologia Disputationum lib. 12*. In *Opera Omnia*, 2. Basel, 1572–1573.

Pinto, Estêvão. *Os indígenas do Nordeste*. Vol. 2. Brasiliana, vol. 112. São Paulo: Companhia Editora Nacional, 1938.

————. *Introdução à história da antropologia indígena no Brasil (século XVI)*. Mexico City: Instituto Indigenista Interamericano, 1958.

Pinto, João Pereira de Castro. "A Parahyba nos tempos coloniaes." *Revista do Instituto Histórico e Geográfico Paraibano* 1 (1909):21–38.

Pinto, Luiz. *Síntese histórica da Paraíba, 1501–1960.* Rio de Janeiro: Gráfica Ouvidor, 1960.

Pinto, Olivério Mário de Oliveira. *Catálogo das aves do Brasil e lista dos exemplares existentes na coleção do Departamento de Zoologia.* Part 2. *Ordem Passeriformes.* São Paulo: Departamento de Zoologia, Secretária da Agricultura, Indústria e Comércio, 1944.

————. *Catálogo das aves do Brasil e lista dos exemplares que as representam no Museu Paulista.* Part 1. *Aves não Passeriformes. . . . Revista do Museu Paulista* 22 (1938).

Pires, Tomé. *The Suma Oriental of Tomé Pires . . . and the Book of Francisco Rodrigues (1512–1515).* 2 vols. Hakluyt Society, Series 2, vols. 89 and 90. London: Hakluyt Society, 1944.

Piso, Guilherme [Willem]. *História natural do Brasil ilustrada.* Translated and edited by Alexandre Correia. With the original Latin text. São Paulo: Companhia Editora Nacional, 1948.

————. *História natural e médica da Índia Ocidental.* Translated and edited by Mário Lôbo Leal. Rio de Janeiro: Instituto Nacional do Livro, 1957.

Piso, Willem. See Piso, Guilherme.

Prado, J. F. de Almeida. *A Bahia e as capitanias do centro do Brasil (1530–1626).* Brasiliana, vols. 247, 247A, 247B. São Paulo: Companhia Editora Nacional, 1945–1950.

————. *A conquista da Paraíba (séculos XVI a XVIII).* Brasiliana, vol. 321. São Paulo: Companhia Editora Nacional, 1964.

————. *Pernambuco e as capitanias do norte do Brasil (1530–1630).* Brasiliana, vols. 175, 175A, 175B, 175C. São Paulo: Companhia Editora Nacional, 1939–1942.

Prestage, Edgar. *The Portuguese Pioneers.* London: Adam and Charles Black, 1933.

Primeira visitação do Santo Officio às partes do Brasil: Confissões de Pernambuco, 1594–1595. Edited by José Antonio Gonsalves de Mello. Recife: Universidade Federal de Pernambuco, 1970.

Ptolemaeus, Claudius. *Tratado da sphera . . . de Claudio Ptolomeo.* Translated and edited by Pero Nunes, 1537. Facsim. Munich: J. B. Obernetter, 1915.

Purseglove, John William. *Tropical Crops: Dicotyledons.* 2 vols. New York: Wiley, 1968.

Pyrard de Laval, Francisco [François]. *Viagem de Francisco Pyrard, de Laval, contendo a notícia de sua navegação às Índias Orientais, Ilhas de Maldiva, Maluco e ao Brasil.* Translated into Portuguese and edited by Joaquim Heliodoro da Cunha Rivara. Revised by A. de Magalhães Basto. 2 vols. Porto: Livraria Civilização,

1944. [This edition is not textually reliable because it is based on a late and unsatisfactory French edition.]

Pyrard de Laval, François. *Traité et description des animaux, arbres, et fruicts des Indes Orientaux observez par l'autheur.* In *Voyage de François de Pyrard, de Laval.*

———. *Voyage de François Pyrard, de Laval.* 3d ed. 2 vols. in 1. Paris: S. Thiboust, 1619.

———. *The Voyage of François Pyrard of Laval to the East Indies, the Maldives, the Moluccas and Brazil.* Translated and edited by Albert Gray. 2 vols. in 3. Hakluyt Society, Series 1, vols. 76, 77, 80. London: 1887–1890.

Record, Samuel J., and Robert W. Hess. *Timbers of the New World.* New Haven, Conn.: Yale University Press, 1943.

Ribeiro, João Pedro. *Dissertações chronológicas e críticas sobre a história e jurisprudéncia ecclesiástica e civil de Portugal.* Lisbon: Academia Real das Sciéncias de Lisboa, 1857.

Ribeiro de Lessa, Clado. *Vocabulário de caça.* Brasiliana, vol. 239. São Paulo: Companhia Editora Nacional, 1944.

Rocha Pitta, Sebastião da. *História da América portuguesa.* 3d ed. Bahia: Livraria Progresso Editora, 1950.

Rodrigues, José Honório. *Historiografía del Brasil, siglo XVI.* Translated from Portuguese into Spanish by Antonio Alatorre. Historiográficas IV. Mexico City: Instituto Panamericano de Geografía e Historia, 1957.

———. *Historiografía del Brasil, siglo XVII.* Translated from Portuguese into Spanish by Antonio Alatorre. Mexico City: Instituto Panamericano de Geografía e Historia, 1963.

Rogers, Francis M. *The Travels of the Infante Dom Pedro of Portugal.* Cambridge: Harvard University Press, 1961.

Rosário, António do. *Frutas do Brasil numa nova, e ascética monarchia. . . .* Lisbon: A. Pedrozo Galram, 1702.

Rouse, Irving. "The Arawak." In *Handbook of South American Indians,* 4:507–546.

———. "The Carib." In *Handbook of South American Indians,* 4:547–565.

Russell-Wood, A. J. R. *Fidalgos and Philanthropists: The Santa Casa da Misericórdia of Bahia, 1550–1755.* Berkeley and Los Angeles: University of California Press, 1968.

Sacrobosco. See Thorndike, Lynn. *The Sphere of Sacrobosco and Its Commentators.*

Salas, Alberto Mario. *Las armas de la Conquista.* Buenos Aires: Emecé Editores, 1950.

Sampaio, Alberto José de. *A alimentação sertaneja e do interior da Amazônia.* Brasiliana, vol. 238. São Paulo: Companhia Editora Nacional, 1944.

Sampaio, Francisco Antônio de. "História dos reinos vegetal, animal e mineral do Brasil, pertencente à medicina." *Anais da Biblioteca Nacional [do Rio de Janeiro]* 89 (1969).

Santos, Eurico. *Anfíbios e répteis do Brasil.* 2d ed. Rio de Janeiro: F. Briguiet, 1955.

———. *Nossos peixes marinhos.* Rio de Janeiro: F. Briguiet, 1952.

———. *Peixes de água doce.* Rio de Janeiro: F. Briguiet, 1954.

Santos, João dos. *Ethiópia oriental, e vária história de cousas notáveis do Oriente.* Évora: Convento de S. Domingo, 1609.

Sauer, Carl O. *Agricultural Origins and Dispersals.* 2d ed. Cambridge, Mass., and London: M.I.T. Press, 1969.

———. "Cultivated Plants of South and Central America." In *Handbook of South American Indians,* 6:487–543.

Sauer, Jonathan D. "Changing Perception and Exploitation of New World Plants in Europe, 1492–1800." In *First Images of America,* 2:813–832.

Schery, Robert W. *Plants for Man.* New York: Prentice-Hall, 1952.

Schwartz, Stuart B. "Free Labor in a Slave Economy." In Dauril Alden, ed., *Colonial Roots of Modern Brazil,* pp. 147–197. Berkeley and Los Angeles: University of California Press, 1973.

———. "Indian Labor and New World Plantations: European Demands and Indian Responses in Northeastern Brazil." *American Historical Review* 83 (Feb. 1978): 43–79.

———. "Magistracy and Society in Colonial Brazil." *Hispanic American Review* 50 (1970):717.

———. *Sovereignty and Society in Colonial Brazil: The High Court and Its Judges, 1609–1751.* Berkeley and Los Angeles: University of California Press, 1973.

Simonsen, Roberto C. *História econômica do Brasil (1500–1820).* 3d ed. Brasiliana, Grande Formato, vol. 10. São Paulo: Companhia Editora Nacional, 1957.

Sluiter, Engel. "Dutch Maritime Power and the Colonial Status Quo, 1585–1641." *The Pacific Historical Review* 11 (1942):29–41.

———. "Report on the State of Brazil, 1612." *Hispanic American Historical Review* 29 (Nov. 1949):518–562. [An annotated edition of Diogo de Campos Moreno, *Livro que dá razão do Estado do Brasil—1612.*]

Smith, Robert C. "Colonial Towns of Spanish and Portuguese America." In *History of Latin American Civilizations,* vol. 1, *The Colonial Experience,* edited by Lewis Hanke, pp. 283–292. Boston: Little, Brown, and Co., 1967.

Soares de Sousa, Gabriel. *Notícia do Brasil.* Edited by Pirajá da Silva. 2 vols. Biblioteca Histórica Brasileira, 16. São Paulo: Livraria Martins Editora, 1945.

———. *Notícia do Brasil.* With commentaries and notes by Francisco Adolfo de Varnhagen, Manuel Augusto Pirajá da Silva, and Frederico G. Edelweiss. São Paulo: Empresa Gráfica da "Revista dos Tribunais," 1974.

Soeiro, Susan A. "The Social and Economic Role of the Convent: Women and Nuns in Colonial Bahia 1677–1800." *Hispanic American Historical Review* 54 (May 1974):209–232.

Southey, Robert. *History of Brazil.* 3 vols. London: Longman, 1810–1819.

Souza, Bernardino José de. *Dicionário da terra e da gente do Brasil.* 5th ed. Brasiliana, Grande Formato, vol. 19. São Paulo: Companhia Editora Nacional, 1961.

———. *O pau-brasil na história nacional.* Brasiliana, vol. 162. São Paulo: Companhia Editora Nacional, 1939.

Staden, Hans. *Hans Staden: The True History of His Captivity, 1557.* Translated and edited by Malcolm Letts. New York: McBride, 1929.

———. *Warhafftiger kurtzer bericht aller von mir erfarnen händel und sitten der Tuppin Indas derer gefangner ich gewesen bin.* 1557. Facsim. reprint. In *Warhaftige Historia und beschreibung eyner Lantschafft der wilden nacketen grimmigen Menschfresser Leuthen in der Newenwelt America gelegen.*

———. *Warhaftige Historia und beschreibung eyner Lantschafft der wilden nacketen grimmigen Menschfresser Leuthen in der Newenwelt America gelegen.* Frankfurt am Main: Wegner, 1925.

Steensgaard, Niels. *Carracks, Caravans and Companies: The Structural Crisis in the European-Asian Trade in the Early 17th Century.* Copenhagen: Scandinavian Institute of Asian Studies, 1973.

Steward, Julian H. "Tribes of the Montaña: An Introduction." In *Handbook of South American Indians,* 3:507–533.

———, ed. *Handbook of South American Indians.* Smithsonian Institution, Bureau of American Ethnology Bulletin no. 143. Washington, D.C.: U.S. Government Printing Office, 1946–1959.

Studart Filho, Carlos. *O antigo Estado do Maranhão e suas capitanias feudais.* Fortaleza: Imprensa Universitária do Ceará, 1960.

Sturtevant, E. Lewis. *Sturtevant's Notes on Edible Plants.* Edited by U. P. Hedrick. New York Dept. of Agriculture, 27th Annual Report, vol. 2, pt. 2. Albany, N.Y.: J. B. Lyon Co., 1919.

"Summário das armadas que se fizeram e guerras que se deram na conquista do Rio Parahyba . . . ," *Revista do Instituto Histórico e Geográfico Brasileiro* 36 (1873), pt. 1, pp. 5–89.

Sylveira, Symão Estaço da. See Estaço da Sylveira, Symão.

Symcox, Geoffrey W. "The Battle of the Atlantic, 1500–1700." In *First Images of America,* 1:265–277.

Taunay, Affonso de E. "Monstros e monstrengos do Brasil." *Revista do Museu Paulista* 21 (1937):911–1044.

Tavernier, Jean Baptiste. *Travels in India.* Translated and edited by V. Ball. 2 vols. London: Macmillan, 1889.

Taylor, James L. *A Portuguese-English Dictionary.* Stanford, Cal.: Stanford University Press, 1958.

Teixeira de Oliveira, José. *História do Estado do Espírito Santo.* Rio de Janeiro: Coutinho, 1951.

Thevet, André. *The New found Worlde, or Antarctike, wherein Is Contained Wonderful and Strange Things. . . .* Translated by Thomas Hacket. London: Bynneman, 1568.

———. *Singularidades da França Antárctica a que outros chamam de América.* Translated and edited by Estêvão Pinto. Brasziliana, vol. 229. São Paulo: Companhia Editora Nacional, 1944.

———. *Les singularitez de la France Antarctique, autrement nommée Amérique.* Paris: Héritiers de Maurice de la Porte, 1557.

Thomson, James Oliver. *History of Ancient Geography.* Cambridge: Cambridge University Press, 1948.

Thorndike, Lynn. *The Sphere of Sacrobosco and Its Commentators.* Chicago: University of Chicago Press, 1949.

Tidings out of Brazil. Translated by Mark Graubard from *Copia der Newen Zeytung ausz Presillg Landt,* with commentary and notes by John Parker. Minneapolis: University of Minnesota Press, 1957. See also *Nova gazeta da terra do Brazil.*

Tilmann, Jean Paul. *An Appraisal of the Geographical Works of Albertus Magnus and His Contributions to Geographical Thought.* Michigan Geographical Publications, no. 4. Ann Arbor: University of Michigan, 1971.

Tuttle, Edward F. "Borrowing Versus Semantic Shift: New World Nomenclature in European Languages." In *First Images of America,* 2:595–611.

Varnhagen, Francisco Adolfo de. *História geral do Brasil antes da sua separação e independência de Portugal.* 5 vols. Vol. 1, 4th ed.; vols. 2–5, 3d ed. São Paulo: Companhia Melhoramentos, [1927?].

Varthema, Ludovico di. *The Travels of Ludovico de Varthema in Egypt, Syria, Arabia Deserta and Arabia Felix, in Persia, India, and Ethiopia, A.D. 1503 to 1508.* Translated by John Winter Jones and edited by George Percy Badger. Hakluyt Society, Series 1, vol. 32. London: Hakluyt Society, 1863.

Vasconcellos, Simão de. *Chrônica da Companhia de Jesu do Estado do Brasil.* 2d ed. 2 vols. Lisbon: A. J. Fernandes Lopes, 1865.

———. *Notícias antecedentes, curiosas, e necessárias das cousas do Brasil.* In *Chrônica da Companhia de Jesu do Estado do Brasil,* 1:xxv–clvi.

Vat, Odulfo van der. "The First Franciscans of Brazil." *The Americas* 5 (July 1948): 18–30.

Vianna, Hélio. *História do Brasil.* 2 vols. São Paulo: Edições Melhoramentos, 1961–1962.

Vicente do Salvador. *História do Brasil, 1500–1627.* 5th ed. Revised by Capistrano de Abreu, Rodolfo Garcia, and Venâncio Wílleke. São Paulo: Edições Melhoramentos, 1965.

Vicente Vianna, Francisco. *Memória sobre o Estado da Bahia.* Bahia: Typographia e Encardernação do "Diário da Bahia," 1893.

Wagener, Zacharias. *Zoobiblion: Livro de animais do Brasil.* Brasiliensia Documenta 4. São Paulo: Emprêsa Gráfica da "Revista dos Tribunais," 1964.

Wagley, Charles, and Eduardo Galvão. *The Tenetehara Indians of Brazil.* 1949. Reprint. New York: Columbia University Press, 1969.

Walker, Ernest P. *Mammals of the World.* 2d ed., revised by John L. Paradiso. 3 vols. Baltimore: Johns Hopkins Press, 1968.

Waters, David Watkin. *The Art of Navigation in England in Elizabethan and Early Stuart Times.* London: Hollis and Carter, 1958.

Webster's Seventh New Collegiate Dictionary. 1965.

Wheeler, John. *A Treatise of Commerce.* Edited by George B. Hotchkiss. Facsim. reprint. New York: Facsimile Text Society, Columbia University Press, 1931.

Wied-Neuwied, Maximilian Alexander von. *Travels in Brazil, in the Years 1815, 1816, 1817, Part 1.* Translated from the German. London: Henry Colburn, 1820.

Wightman, W. P. D. *Science of the Renaissance: An Introduction to the Study of the Emergence of the Sciences in the Sixteenth Century.* Edinburgh: Oliver and Boyd, 1962.

Wiznitzer, Arnold. *Jews in Colonial Brazil.* Morningside Heights, N.Y.: Columbia University Press, 1960.

Yule, Henry, and A. C. Burnell. *Hobson-Jobson: A Glossary of Colloquial Anglo-Indian Words and Phrases.* Edited by William Crooke. London: John Murray, 1903.

Yves d'Évreux. *Voyage dans le nord du Brésil fait durant les années 1613 et 1614.* Edited by M. Ferdinand Denis. Biblioteca Americana. Leipzig and Paris: A. Franck, 1864.

Index

The following sample entry illustrates how the Index should be read:

ants   213–215, 270. I, n. 27; IV, n. 14

This means that ants are discussed on pp. 213 to 215 and on p. 270, and that there is a note, No. 27, on this subject at the end of Dialogue I. When an item is mentioned both in the text and in an accompanying note, the index usually cites only the textual reference, since the text will guide the reader to the appropriate note.

abacatuaia   V, n. 93
abati   198. IV, n. 27
abati-mirim   IV, n. 27
abatupitá   IV, n. 66
Abreu, Aleixo de   II, n. 65
Abreu, Capistrano de   viii, 347
Abyssinia   II, n. 20
açabengita   160
   "academy" of good manners   5, 148, 307
acarapeba   V, n. 88
acarapitonga   V, n. 77
acari   V, n. 103
acouti   V, n. 155
acum   V, n. 67
acurau   V, nn. 66, 67
Adam's apple   215
advantages of Brazil   22
Afonso IV, King of Portugal   I, n. 23
Africa   98. See also Angola, Guinea
agouti (*aguti*)   268. V, n. 155; VI, n. 50
Agua dos Meninos   I, n. 164
aguará-açu   274

ague   111
agutipuru   V, n. 166
aí   272
Aimorés   46, 325. I, nn. 170, 174; VI, n. 68
aipim   IV, 16
airire   V, n. 68
ajajá   V, n. 71
   "alarm clock"   312
albacor   256
Albertus Magnus   87. II, n. 16
Albuquerque, Duarte Coelho de   38
Albuquerque, Jerônimo de   29. I, nn. 54, 70, 72, 83, 143
Albuquerque Coelho family   I, nn. 125, 134
aldeias   I, n. 165
Alencar, José de   I, n. 81
Alentejo   195
alfavaca   212
Algarve   97, 149
alguidar   311
alqueire   197, 202

Alvarado, Pedro de   I, n. 16
Álvares, Fernão   I, n. 68
Álvares, Nuno   10
Alviano
    attitude toward Brazil   VI, n. 26
    residence in Brazil   II, n. 24
Alvor   149
Amazon River   15, 25, 27, 28. I, nn.
    49, 54
    fish in   I, n. 55
    sources   I, nn. 58, 59, 64
Amazons   VI, n. 56
ambare   217
amber   200
amber-fish   V, n. 95
ambergris (amber)   31, 132, 134, 138,
    152–155, 260, 261
amendoim   202
American hog-plum   217
anacã   250
anbou   IV, n. 147
Anchieta, José de   8, 343
ancients   85, 88, 89
angelim   160
Angola   20, 47, 104, 149, 158, 202. I,
    nn. 19, 36; II, n. 26; III, n. 131
Anghiera, Pietro Martire d'   II, n. 40
Angola pea   IV, n. 43
ani   249
annatto   IV, n. 95; V, n. 53
anta   266
anteater   V, nn. 168, 169
ants   213–215, 270. I, n. 27; IV,
    n. 114
anu   V, n. 14
apacanim   V, n. 55
aparias   V, n. 163
apê   217
apecu   250
apereá   V, n. 163
appendicitis   108–109
aquaham   V, n. 8
aquê   200
aquostimerim   V, n. 166
araçá   109, 220
    a. açu   220

araçari   251
Araçuagipe   35
araquã   248
arara   252
arare   257
arariba   209
arasari   V, n. 33
araticu   217
aratu   262
Araújo, António de   I, n. 64
Ardas (Ardras, Adras)   II, n. 69
ariri   IV, n. 48
Aristotle   96, 97, 98, 255. II, nn. 1, 6,
    16, 30; IV, n. 76
armadillo   V, n. 157
armored catfish   V, n. 102
astrolabe   II, n. 38
astrology   25. I, n. 45
Atahualpa   I, n. 16
atlatl   VI, n. 70
authority vs. experience   V, nn. 3, 115
Averroës   87. II, n. 6
Avicenna   II, nn. 8, 14, 16
Azeredo, Marcos de   19. I, n. 8
Azevedo, Manuel de   V, n. 80
Azores   20. I, 18; II, n. 29

Bab el Mandeb   100
bacupari   220
bacurau   V, nn. 66, 67
Bahia de Todos os Santos (Bahia,
    Salvador)   6, 42–45, 344
Baía de São Marcos   I, n. 67
baiacu   257
Baiagate   134
Balboa, Núñez de   I, n. 16; II, n. 46
balsam   110
banana   216
Banda   134
Bantus   III, n. 131
Barbadoes cherry   IV, n. 164
Barbosa Machado, Diogo   vii
Barcia Carballido y Zúñiga, André
    González de   vii
barley   200
Barradas, Constantino   I, n. 90

Barros, Cristóvão de   I, nn. 145, 146
Barros, João de   I, n. 68; III, n. 2
barter   32. I, n. 98
Basques   45
bathing as remedy   106
Bathsheba   99
batiputá   205
Bay of All Saints (Bahia)   6
bees   210
beiju   196
bejupirá   255
Belém, Santa Maria de   I, nn. 54, 107, 166
Benedictines   39, 45
Bengal   134
Bengalese walking stick   208
benzoin   134
berjacotes   216
betun   IV, n. 108
bicho de pé   112
biguá   251
birdlime   210
birds   248–254
  b. of prey   252–254
bird-songs   V, n. 20
Bishop of Brazil   32. I, n. 182
Bisnaga   134
black-crowned night-heron   V, n. 73
blacks
  cause of physical characteristics   90–96
  economic function   5, 91
  exclusion from society   I, n. 29
  numbers in Brazil   91. II, n. 21
boar   266–268
boiaçu   278
Boipeva   45. I, n. 145
boiuçu   V, n. 195
bonito   256
Bontius, Jacobus   347
Borborema Mountains   I, n. 105
Botelho, Diogo   I, n. 162
Botocudos   I, n. 170
bottle cod   IV, n. 44
bows   314
bow-wood   160. III, n. 147

Brandão, Ambrósio Fernandes   vii–viii, 9
Brazil as refuge   25
Brazil cherry   IV, n. 161
Brazilian anaconda   V, n. 195
Brazilian raccoon   V, n. 181
brazilwood (brazil)   4, 25, 31, 33, 136, 150–152, 209. I, nn. 48, 171
brown-crested martin   V, n. 43
bubonic humor   111
Buenos Aires   263
buff-necked ibis   V, n. 32
bullock's heart   IV, n. 130
buraem   160
burahu   V, n. 66
buranhém   III, n. 154
burapiroca   160
buraquií   160
burau   253
buri-do-campo (-da praia)   IV, n. 48
bushmaster   V, n. 193
butter   203, 207
butterflies   254–255

cabaraíba   160
cabeçudo   V, n. 100
Cabedelo   I, nn. 102, 112
Cabo Branco   32. I, n. 86
Cabral, Antônio Teixeira   40
Cabral, Pedro Álvares   3, 24, 25, 98, 341. I, nn. 41, 42, 171; II, n. 51
çabucai   V, n. 93
cachaça   204. IV, n. 64
cacique   V, nn. 27, 40
Cadamosto, Alvise da   I, n. 20
Cairo   138
cajá   217
calabash   28, 202
Calvin, John   341, 343
camaçarim   160
camará   160
  c. açu   212. IV, n. 103
Cambay   134
cambira   V, n. 87
camboa   V, n. 110
camboatá   V, n. 102
cambucá   220

cambuí IV, n. 163
cambute V, n. 102
Caminha, Pero Vaz de 3, 8, 341. I, n. 27
Camões, Luís de 342
campinas 199
Campo Tourinho, Pero de I, n. 171
Campos Moreno, Diogo de 8, 345. I, nn. 37, 151
Campos Moreno, Martim Soares I, n. 81
camucim 40. I, n. 142
camurim 256
camuripema (camuripim, camoropim) V, n. 79
camurupim 255
Canaan 94
canafístula 160, 217–218
Canary Islands 20, 98, 204
cangambá V, n. 158
canindé 250
Caõ, Diogo I, n. 19
Cape of Good Hope 100. II, n. 48
Cape St. Augustine 39, 102, 161. I, n. 128
Cape Verde 20, 266
capim 264
Capuchinhos I, n. 134
capybara 259–260
cará 203. IV, n. 55
caracara 253
caracatá (caraguatá, caraoatá, caravatá, caroá, caroatá, garoatá, gravatá) IV, nn. 35, 73
caram V, n. 72
carão 254
carapeba 256
carapitanga (carapitangua) 255. V, n. 77
carapó V, n. 106
caravel I, n. 30
Cardim, Fernão 8, 344
cari V, n. 103
carimã 197
Carmelites 39, 45. I, nn. 117, 135, 167
carpé 313

carrack III, n. 21
Cartagena 19
Carthage 97
Carthaginians 97, 98
Carvalho, Feliciano Coelho de 31, 35. I, nn. 83, 101, 106; II, n. 70
casabanana IV, n. 112
Cascais, marquess of I, n. 121
cashew 203, 204, 210, 217
Castejón, Francisco I, n. 102
Castelbranco, Afonso de 42. I, n. 152
Castelbranco, Duarte de, count of Sabugal III, n. 162
Castelo Branco, Francisco Caldeira de I, n. 54
Castilians 19, 20, 33
Castro e Sousa, Álvaro Pires de I, n. 121
catizal IV, n. 9
cattail 161, 206
caxinguelê V, n. 166
caxinxe V, n. 166
caxito I, n. 80; V, n. 175
Ceará 345
cedar 160
Ceylon (Sri Lanka) 134
chabin V, n. 146
chabris V, n. 146
chachalaca V, n. 8
Cham II, n. 27
chameleon 272. V, n. 170
Chanaã II, n. 27
cheese 265
chichica V, n. 167
chickpeas 203
Chile 19
China 134
ciia V, n. 51
cinnamon 134
cipó 200, 207
cities and town, principal I, n. 52
citron 216
citrus fruit trees 215
Claude d'Abbéville 8, 345, 346
climate II, n. 60
climbing plants 212–213

cloth   132, 134, 205–206, 207
cloves   134
coati   268
coatimundi   V, n. 156
cobia   255
cochineal   21
cockfish   257
coconut oil   205
Coelho, Duarte   5
coendou   275
coffee senna   II, n. 67
coir   207–208
colégios, Jesuit   I, nn. 129, 133
colbereiro   V, n. 71
"Coloma," Cristóvão   100
comandá-guaçu   IV, n. 41
comandaí (comandá-mirim)   IV, n. 42
Comilão   152
comixá   220
common bean   200
compass   II, n. 38
Conceição   37. V, n. 80
conduru   160. III, n. 144
Congo   20, 107. I, nn. 19, 21; III, n. 131
Congo pea   IV, n. 43
congurupi   V, n. 79
consulage   135
conto
   de oro   III, n. 16
   de reis   III, n. 16
copaiva   110, 161
Copaoba Mountains   34, 162, 215. I, nn. 105, 106
coral snake   278. V, n. 194
corcovado   257
corica (coriqua)   V, n. 50
corima   V, n. 87
Correia de Sá, Martim   I, n. 178
Cortés, Hernán   I, n. 16
corumbatá   V, n. 89
Cosmos   I, n. 140
cotimirim   V, n. 166
cotton   155–156, 205
cougar   V, n. 191

Council of Portugal   45, 137. I, n. 159; III, n. 48
courlan   V, n. 72
cowhage cherry   IV, n. 164
crab   262–263. V, nn. 125, 127, 128
craftsmen   VI, n. 2
crauá, croá, cruá   IV, n. 112
crested screamer   V, n. 48
Cricoré River   I, n. 174
Cruz dos Militares, church of   I, n. 178
crypto-Jew   5, 10. I, n. 5
cuandu   V, n. 180
cuja   V, n. 51
cujujuba   249
Cunha, Aires da   I, n. 68
cunhatainape   251
curassow   V, n. 9
curica   251
curicaca   250
curimá   256, 257
curimatá   256
curiquaqua   V, n. 32
curlews   254
curuá   213. IV, n. 103
curubá   IV, n. 112
curumatá   V, n. 89
curusira   V, n. 24
custard apple   IV, n. 130
cu-tapado   V, n. 21
cutia   V, n. 155

daisies   201
Daniel   308
David, King   99
deer snake   278
degredados   148. III, n. 97
diamonds   132
Diana   322
Dioscorides   157. II, n. 16
disadvantages of Brazil   I, n. 25
discovery of Brazil   24
disease of the worm   II, n. 65
diseases and remedies   105–112
doença do bicho   II, n. 65
dog caper   IV, n. 44
dolphin   255

Domingues, Pero   I, n. 64
doves   249
drumstick tree   IV, n. 149
ducks   254
Dutch   137, 139. III, nn. 49, 54
Dutch East India Company   6
dyeing feathers. See tapirage
dyes   209–210

Earthly Paradise   I, n. 75; II, nn. 14,
   57
earthquakes   113
East Indies   160. I, n. 2; IV, n. 92
East-West Coast   I, nn. 54, 68
eicajeru   220
Einstein, Albert   V, n. 76
eiratê   275. IV, n. 61
eixua   253
El Inca   II, n. 2
El Mina   II, n. 52
Elysian Fields   203, 204
ema   V, nn. 47, 48
embira   207, 208
Emerald Mountains   I, n. 8
emeralds   18, 19. I, n. 6
emu   V, n. 47
entradas   I, n. 156
erva santa (tobacco)   106
Escobar, Pero   I, n. 21
Espírito Santo   46, 47
Ethiopia   90
euphonia   V, n. 26
Extremo River   152
eyra   V, n. 169
Ezion-Geber   II, nn. 41, 48

falcons   252–253. V, nn. 54, 55, 56,
   57, 58, 59, 60, 61
False St. Ignatius bean   IV, n. 67
famine foods   201
farmers   306
Faro, Francisco de, count of
   Vimieiro   47. I, n. 184
favorable climate   24, 49, 104, 105,
   108, 112, 113

Feast of the Discovery of the True
   Cross   I, n. 42
Fenton, Edward   II, n. 50
figs   216
Figueira, Luís   III, n. 2
Filipéia of Our Lady of the Snows   33. I,
   nn. 86, 95
fish
   catching   30, 259
   in Amazon River   I, n. 55
fishes   254–263
fishhooks   27
fish oil   260
Flores Valdés, admiral Diego   100. I, n.
   102; II, n. 50
food crops   193–203
forts   31
fowls, domestic   248
fowls, wild   248–252
foxes   270
Franciscans   37, 39, 45. I, nn. 107,
   118, 134
freedmen   306
free trade   192
French   29, 31, 33, 34, 343, 345. I,
   n. 156
fruits   215–220

Gades (Cadiz)   II, n. 30
gaibicuaraçu   256. V, n. 99
Galen   II, n. 16
Galileo   II, n. 4
Galvão, António   II, n. 53
Gama, Vasco da   I, n. 41
gamboa   V, n. 80
games, equestrian   264
ganbiapiruera   253
gangorra   140
gaquara   254
garapa   204. IV, n. 64
gararina   254
garataurana   252–253
garateuma   250
garauçá (garausâ)   262. V, n. 130
García, Gregorio   II, n. 29
Garcia, Rodolfo   viii

Garcilaso de la Vega   II, n. 2
garden
   flower g.   212
   ornaments   15
   vegetable g.   210
garlic pear   160
garuatá   IV, n. 142
gato-do-mato   V, n. 176
genipap   209. VI, n. 50
geremu   IV, n. 51
Ghana   II, n. 52
ginger   193, 208
giruba   V, n. 35
Giuntini, Francesco   II, n. 11
goaiaüçá   V, n. 130
goaivicoara   V, n. 84
goajá   V, n. 127
goatsucker   V, n. 66
goiá   V, n. 127
Goitacás   I, n. 174
gold   132
Gold Coast   II, n. 52
gold mines   47, 48
Golden Age   30, 311. I, n. 78
goldenshower senna   IV, n. 149
Gonsalves de Mello, José Antonio   xiii,
   9, 11, 14
Governor General   32
governors of Brazil   133
governors of the Kingdom   I, n. 159
grains of Paradise   IV, n. 91
Grão-Pará   I, n. 64
grapefruit   215
grapes   213–215
gravatá   200, 217
green kingfisher   V, n. 74
grexiuruba   220
grumatá   V, n. 89
grumixama   IV, n. 155
grunts   257
guabiroba   217
guaiá   262
guaiamu   262–263
guaiaranha   262
guaibi   V, n. 84
guaimi   V, n. 84

guaiquica   V, n. 167
guan   V, nn. 7, 8
Guanabara Bay   I, n. 177
guanandim   161
Guanches   98. II, n. 37
guandu   202
guanhamu   V, n. 131
guapeva   IV, n. 67
guapuronga (guapuranga)   220. IV, n. 159
guaquaqua   253
guara   V, n. 175
guarainhete (uraenhangatá
   uranhengatá)   250. V, nn. 26, 29
guarajuba   V, n. 38
guariba   275, 277–278
guarirama   V, n. 74
guaruru   V, n. 73
guasuni   V, n. 181
guava   109, 216
guaxa   251
guaxinim   275
Guinea (Guinea Coast)   49, 88, 90, 92,
   93, 95, 96, 104, 105, 107. I, nn. 19,
   20, 21, 84
Guinea corn   IV, n. 26
Guinea grains   IV, n. 91
Guinea pepper   IV, n. 91
guira cuckoo   V, n. 36
guiranheenguetá   V, n. 26
guiratangueima   V, n. 27
guirejaúba   V, n. 38
gums   210
gunpowder   17
guoazaranha   V, n. 128
guurainghaetá   250
gurajnhete   V, n. 26
guti, güti, goti   IV, n. 141

Habakkuk   308
hake   255
Hall, Frederick Arthur Holden   ix, xi–
   xiii
Ham   94, 96
hammock   306, 311. VI, n. 8
harpy   249. V, n. 16
hawk. See birds of prey

heiratê   V, n. 178
hemp   206
herbs   211
Herckmans, Elias   II, n. 106; IV,
   n. 115
Hercules   20
heresy   VI, n. 1
hicambu   220
High Court   15, 32, 42–45. I, nn. 151,
   160, 161, 181
   criticism of   I, n. 151
Hiram, King of Tyre   99. II, n. 41
Hispaniola   100. II, nn. 31, 48
holy wood   160
honey   203, 204, 206, 210, 275
honey and butter   I, n. 78
horse   263–264, 266, 306
House of Mercy   146, 150
house of retirement   I, n. 139
houses   207
howler monkey   V, n. 183
Huguenots   342
hunting
   of animals   266–268
   of birds   249, 253
hybrids   265
hyvourahés   III, n. 154

ibá-mirim   220
ibiiau   V, n. 66
ibiracui   III, n. 151
ibirarema   160
ibn-Sina   II, n. 9
icaco plum   220
Iceland   252, 253
Igaraçu   I, n. 140
Ilheta de Pessegueiro   97
Ilhéus   45, 46. I, nn. 169, 170
inambu   V, n. 13
inamu   V, n. 13
Indians   27, 268, 272
   as fisherman   30
   astronomy   VI, n. 60
   attitude toward adultery   VI, n. 14
   birth practices   308–309
   burial practices   I, n. 144

cannibalism   308, 323
character   308
conversions   324–325
couvade   308, 309, 310
cruelty   323, 324
customs   307–326
decorations   VI, n. 15
dress   307
education   309. I, n. 107; VI, n. 27
evangelization of   35
family relations   310
feathers   314
festivals   105–106
fires   311
food production   311
function in society   I, n. 29
furniture   311
government   VI, n. 12
headman   307. VI, n. 12
health   II, n. 60
houses   311
language   308. I, n. 57
longevity   104. II, n. 57
marriage customs   309, 310. VI,
   n. 28
music   320. VI, n. 53
nakedness   VI, n. 15
omens   274–275, 314
oratory   VI, n. 40
origin   96–103. II, nn. 29, 56
ornaments   324
religion   307–308. VI, nn. 17, 39
scientific knowledge   324
sharing   VI, n. 34
spiritlessness   20
taking a name   215
treatment of prisoners   316–318
tribes. See Aimorés, Goitacás, Parecis,
   Petiguares, Tabajaras, Tapirapés,
   Tapuias, Tupinambás
victory celebrations   318, 319
villages   VI, nn. 12–15
vindictiveness   323
warfare   314–316
   vengeance as objective   VI, n. 35
weapons   314

weeping welcome 310–311
indigo 21, 132, 208–209
ingá 217
inhambu 211–212, 249
inhambuapé V, n. 12
inhame 203. IV, n. 55
inhanduroba 205
Inquisition 10. I, n. 5; VI, n. 1
ipecu V, n. 25
irara 270–272. V, n. 178
irarê 254
Ireland V, n. 54
ironwood 160
Isidore of Seville II, n. 16
Israelites 103
Itamaracá 32, 37, 134, 150, 192
Itanhaém I, n. 183
Itapagipe, Fort I, n. 164
ituipinima V, n. 106

jabiru stork 248
Jaboatão III, n. 120
jabotá IV, n. 67
jabutapitá IV, n. 66
jabuticaba IV, n. 151
jacaranda 160
jacaré 260
jack 256
jackfruit 217
Jacob 310
jacu 248
jacundá 257
jacurutu 253
jagararuapem 275
jaguacinim V, n. 181
jaguar V, n. 189
jaguaraçu V, n. 175
Jaguaribe 31, 161
jamacaru 217
jamaracaú IV, n. 137
jambul 217
janamacará IV, n. 137
jandaya parakeet 249. V, n. 15
jangada (boat) 154, 161, 259. III,
   n. 122
jangada (tree) 161

japu 251
jaqueretu V, n. 64
jararaca 278
jararacuçu V, n. 193
jarataqueque V, n. 158
jaritacaca 269
jatobá 160. IV, n. 101
jerimu 202
   j. pacova 202
Jesuits 39, 40, 45, 307, 343, 344,
   345. I, nn. 107, 118, 129, 165
jewfish 255
jia 272
jimson weed 205
joambo (*jambool*) IV, n. 147
João III, King of Portugal 28. I, n. 67
João VI, King of Portugal I, n. 46
João Pessoa I, nn. 86, 95
Jonge, Gedeon Morris de IV, n. 7
jucurutu V, n. 64
juhuapupe 249
Junctinus (Giuntino) 88. II, nn. 12, 16
jupará 275
juquiri IV, n. 88
jurumu IV, n. 51
juruni V, n. 168
Juruparim 307
juruva 251. V, n. 39
jutahi (*jutahy*) III, n. 138; IV, n. 101

kacum 253
Kaffirs 204
kapok 206. IV, n. 76
kingfisher 251
kinkajou V, n. 179

laborers I, nn. 32, 33
ladino III, n. 130
lake, source of major rivers 27
lambari V, n. 105
Land of Holy Cross 98
lanti III, n. 157
Laval, François Pyrard de 345
lavradores 256
Leitão, Martim I, nn. 95, 96
lemon 215

Lencastre, Álvaro de, duke of Aveiro   I,
   n. 171
lentils   203
León Pinelo, Antonio Rodríguez de   vii
Léry, Jean de   8, 343
letter of safe-conduct   I, n. 157
Leyden MS of *Dialogues*   vii–viii. I,
   nn. 1, 145
liana   212
liberty chests   III, n. 22
lignum vitae   160
lima beans   201
lime   215
limpkin   V, n. 72
lineated woodpecker   V, n. 25
Lisbon MS of *Dialogues*   vii–viii. I,
   nn. 1, 145
livestock   21, 32, 264–265, 278
love bird. See *tuim*
Luanda   I, nn. 19, 84
Lucan (Marcus Annaeus Lucanus)   87. II,
   nn. 5, 16
lumber   159–163
lupines   203

macambira   IV, n. 35
maçaranduba   160, 217
macaw   V, nn. 24, 52
macaxera   196
mace   III, n. 26
mackerel   255
macugagá   250
macujé   217
macunã (*macuna, mucuná*)   200. IV, n. 39
Madeira   205. I, n. 18; II, nn. 29, 37
Magalhães de Gandavo, Pero de   8,
   342–343
maís   198
maitaca   V, n. 51
maize   198
malaguetta   193
malaria   111
mal do bicho (disease of the worm)   106.
   II, n. 68
mallards   254
mameluco   107, 278

manatee   I, n. 79
mandacaru   IV, n. 137
mandi (*mandeii*)   257. V, n. 98
maned wolf   V, n. 175
mangaba   217
mangrove   162–163, 261
maniçoba   200
manioc   32, 47, 193–197, 306, 311
manioc press   IV, n. 10
manjericão   212
manjerióba   II, n. 67
Manuel I, King of Portugal   3, 24, 138,
   341, 345
maracajá   V, n. 176
maracujá   212, 213. IV, nn. 103, 113
   m. açu   213
   m. mexira   213
   m. mirim   213
   m. peroba   213
Maranhão   29, 30, 31, 162, 345, 346.
   I, n. 80
Maranhão River   28
Marcgrave, Georg   8, 347
maré (*marí*)   IV, n. 37
margay   274
marinheiro   IV, n. 37
masa   202
Mascarenhas Homem, Manuel   31. I,
   nn. 70, 83
masked duck   V, n. 69
massango   IV, n. 46
massapê   199
matim tapirera   VI, n. 46
matitaperê   V, n. 45
mborici   IV, n. 164
measles   107
medicinal plants   157–159
medicinal springs   211
Mello Leitão, Candido de   V, n. 146
melro   V, n. 18
Mendez, Diogo   I, n. 45
Menezes, Diogo de   I, nn. 14, 105
Menezes, Francisco de Sá de   45
merchandising   146
midnight monkey   V, n. 179
milho zaburro   IV, n. 26

military capability of Brazil 305. V, n. 4
millet 200, 264
Mina 100. I, n. 84
Minas Gerais I, nn. 187, 189
mines
 Minas Gerais I, n. 187
 Peru I, n. 10
 São Paulo I, n. 189
mingau 197. V, n. 34
mining 21
missionary motive for settlement III, n. 2
mocó (*quiqui*) 270. V, n. 167
mocó (rock cavy) 269
mocotó IV, n. 36
Moctezuma I, n. 16
mocugê (*mucugê*) IV, n. 146
Mohammed 203
mojarra V, n. 88
mollusks 261, 262
Molucca Islands (Ilhas de Malaquo) 100, 134. II, n. 47
monkey traps V, n. 185
Monsanto, count of 37. I, nn. 121, 184
monsoon I, n. 154
Montaigne, Michel de 342
Monteiro, Jácome 345
moon 112
moquô V, n. 164
Moraes, Manuel de viii
moray eel 255
mordexim 110
motmot V, nn. 35, 39
motum V, n. 9
Moura, Alexandre de I, n. 72
muçu 259
mucura-xixica V, n. 167
mule 264
mullet 255
Mundus Novus II, n. 40
munguba (*mungubeira*) 15, 160, 206. I, n. 2
mureci (*morosi, murici*) IV, n. 164
musk 132, 134
mutum 248

nambu 249. V, n. 13
names for Brazil 24, 25
Natal I, n. 83
natural da terra III, n. 98
navigation 133–134
naxenim 202
needlefish 256
New Christians 5, 10. I, nn. 5, 151
New World 108, 132
nhacurutu V, n. 64
nhambi IV, n. 106
nhambu V, n. 13
nhandiroba IV, n. 67
nhã-popê (*nhapupe*) V, n. 12
Nieuhof, Joan IV, n. 32
nightingales 249
nightjar V, n. 67
nitta tree 160, 210
Noah II, nn. 27, 43
"noble savage" 342
Nóbrega, Father Manuel da I, nn. 37, 156, 165
no-eye pea IV, n. 43
Nombre de Dios I, n. 66; II, n. 50
nose-bear V, n. 156
Nunes, Pedro II, n. 12
nutmeg 134

ochre 210
oil 205
oiti 217
oiticoró 217
okra 220
olandi III, n. 157
Old Christians I, n. 151
Olinda 5, 6, 39, 91
olivaceous cormorant V, n. 34
Ophir 99, 100, 102. II, nn. 41, 45, 55
opicu V, n. 25
opinions of Brazil
 favorable I, nn. 25, 75
 unfavorable I, nn. 25, 75
orange 215
orchard 215
Orecha, Pedro de I, n. 162
Orellana, Francisco de I, n. 49

Orient: Portuguese conquests I, nn. 15, 17
ornate hawk-eagle V, n. 55
ounce 278
Our Lady of the Conception (house of retirement) I, n. 139
Our Lady of the Rosary (church) I, n. 117
ouvidor-geral I, n. 153. See superior crown magistrate
owl V, nn. 64, 65

paca 268
pacapiá IV, n. 67
paina 206
pajamarióba 106
palitos 141. III, n. 71
palms
   coconut 205, 207–208, 220
   hearts of 208
   pindova 207, 306
Panama I, n. 66; II, n. 48
panelas 135
panha IV, n. 76
"panther fodder" V, n. 190
papaya 220
paper-making 17
papo-vento (*papa-vento*) V, n. 170
Pará 25–27, 28, 48, 105, 162
Paraíba 32, 33–37, 134, 150, 192, 211. I, n. 99
Paraíba, Administrator of 37, 40
Paraíba River 98
parati V, n. 94
Paraupaba, Lake I, n. 64
Parecis IV, n. 71
Parnaíba River I, n. 104
parrot-foot grass IV, n. 45
parrots 4, 251. V, n. 28
pataca 47
pati IV, n. 148
paturé V, n. 69
paturi 254
pau d'hástea 162
pau-ferro 160
payemannióba II, n. 67

Peachtree Island 97
peanut 202. IV, n. 47
pearls
   Brazil 261–262
   India 132
peas 201
peccary IV, n. 63; V, n. 152
peiti 217
peitica 251. V, n. 36; VI, n. 46
peixe-galo V, n. 93
pele de lixa 107
pelican 250
pepper 133
   Brazil 138–139, 208. IV, n. 91
   India 133, 134, 137, 138, 192–193
   malaguetta 208
   red 193
Pepper Coast IV, n. 91
pequeá (*pequi, pequiá*) IV, n. 62
Pernambuco 5, 32, 33, 38–41, 134, 149, 150, 192, 198–199, 211, 305. III, n. 109
Persian grass IV, n. 45
Peru, trade routes to I, n. 66
peruleiro 27, 149
Peter Martyr. See d'Anghiera, Pietro Martire
Peter of Padua (of Abano) 87. II, n. 7
Petiguares 33, 34, 40, 321, 322, 325. I, nn. 83, 95
petim, pitim, petun IV, n. 108
petimbabo 322. IV, n. 108
petroglyphs 35–37
Phoenicians 96, 97
piaba 257
piçandó 202. IV, n. 38
pig 204, 265
pigeon pea IV, n. 43
pikes 161–162
pindova. See palms
pine nuts 109, 205
pineapple 216
piqui (*piquia, piquiá*) 160, 204, 220. IV, n. 62
piranha 256–257
pirapema V, n. 79

pirariguá 251. V, n. 45
pirates 29, 31, 33. I, nn. 74, 103
piron 253
Piso, Willem 8, 347
pita 206
pitanga 220
pitomba 217
pit viper V, n. 192
Pizarro, Francisco I, n. 16
Pizarro, Gonzalo I, n. 49
plague 108
Pliny II, n. 16
Point Jesus 39
poisons and antidotes 157–159
  tapioca as poison 196
pole wood 162
pomegranate 216
Ponta Negra V, n. 118
population 305
porcelain 134
porco-do-mato V, n. 152
porcupine, Brazilian V, n. 180
pork 265–266
Porto Seguro 46. I, n. 171
Portuguese
  conquests in Orient 20
  exploration 20
  motives for exploration I, n. 10
  potato 202
    as purgative 109
poteri (*potori*) V, n. 69
poteti V, n. 69
Potosí I, n. 66
preá 269
precious stones 18, 134. I, nn. 5, 6;
  III, n. 5
profitability of Brazil and India
  compared 134–140
Ptolemy (Claudius Ptolemaeus) 87. II,
  nn. 4, 6, 8, 16
puffer V, n. 101
punaré (*punari*) 269. V, n. 162
purges 4, 109–110
purging cassia IV, n. 149
pygmy squirrel V, n. 166

quadrant II, n. 38
quail 249
quaiquaiai 252
quaraquara V, n. 62
quara-uçá V, n. 130
quatiaipé V, n. 166
quatimirim 270
quereiuá V, n. 38
quíca V, n. 167
quiinha-apûã IV, n. 91
quince 216
Quintilian II, n. 23
quirejuabe 251
quiri 161
quiripiranga III, n. 158
quoandu V, n. 180
quoqui 270

rabbit 269–270
Rachel 310
Raíz I, n. 105
rattlesnake 278
Ravardière, Seigneur de la. See Touche,
  Daniel de la
Real River I, n. 145
Recôncavo I, n. 147
Red Sea 99, 100
red snapper V, n. 77
refuge, Brazil as I, n. 46
Relação. See High Court
reruba 269
resin 210
rhea 251. V, n. 48
Ribero, Diego V, n. 157
rice 197–198
Rio de Janeiro 6, 46, 47, 341, 343,
  344
Rio de la Plata 19, 47, 149. I, n. 58
Rio Doce I, n. 173
Rio Grande (do Norte) 31, 32. I, nn.
  70, 86; II, n. 70
River of the Amazons. See Amazon River
robalo V, n. 85
Robertus Anglicus II, n. 12
rock cavy V, n. 164
Rodrigues, José Honório 341

roncador   V, nn. 84, 99
rose apple   IV, n. 147
roseate spoonbill   254
rosewood   III, n. 143
rubies (of India)   132
rye   200

Sá, Mem de   I, nn. 171, 177
saaçu   257
sabiá   249
saci   V, n. 45
Sacrobosco, Johannes de (John of
   Holywood)   88. II, nn. 12, 16, 18
Saint Benedict, Order of   35
Saint Thomas   308
salamander   248
salé   257
Sale, Antoine de la   III, n. 1
Salvador da Bahia de Todos os Santos   I,
   n. 148
Santa Clara of the Exile   I, n. 139
Santa Cruz   I, nn. 40, 171
Santa Catarina   I, n. 102
Santarem, João de   I, n. 21
Santiago, Bento Dias de   9. III, n. 119
Santo Amaro   I, nn. 171, 183
Santo Antônio, Fort   I, n. 164
Santos Reis Magos, Fort   I, nn. 70, 83
São Bento, monastery and church of   I,
   n. 107
São Domingos River   I, n. 99
São Filipe, Fort   I, nn. 72, 102
São Francisco, Fort   I, n. 131
São Francisco River   45, 257. I, nn. 58,
   145
São Jorge, Fort   I, n. 131
São Jorge (São Jorge da Mina)   II, n. 52
São Luís   29
São Luís, Fort   I, n. 72
São Mateos River   I, n. 173
São Paulo   47–48, 345. I, n. 156
São Tomé   20, 105. I, n. 21
São Vicente   25, 47, 48
sape grass   207, 306
sapimiaga   V, n. 122
sapinhaguá   262

sapotaia   202. III, n. 148; V, n. 185
sapucaya   160, 208, 217
sapupira   160
saracucu   V, n. 193
saracura   V, n. 70
sarapó   257
sardines   256
Sardinha, Pedro Fernandes   I, n. 90
sariema   V, n. 48
Sarmiento de Gamboa, Pedro   II, n. 50
sauiá   269
saúna   257
scriptures   II, n. 28
sea cow   30, 256
sea turtle   259
sebipira   III, n. 145
senembu   V, n. 170
sensitive plant   208
serelepe   V, n. 166
Sergipe-del-Rei   41
seri   V, n. 126
sericóias   254
sericora (seriquo)   V, n. 70
seriema   251
sernambim   262
serra   V, n. 78
sesame   202
settlers
   criminal elements   III, n. 97
   extravagance   146
   motives for immigrating   III, n. 2
   negligence   19, 21, 22, 23, 24, 48,
      159, 198, 200, 203, 204, 205,
      206, 207, 208, 209, 210, 211,
      212, 213, 215, 220, 265. I, n. 28;
      III, n. 37; IV, n. 114; VI, n. 3
   occupations   23
   preference for coast   I, n. 13
sharks   255, 256
shellfish   260, 261, 262, 263
ship-building   161–162
ships   133
shrimp   259
sierra   255
sijá   V, n. 51
silk   132, 134

Silveira, Duarte Gomes da 35, 150, 264. I, n. 106; III, n. 106; V, n. 141
silver 132, 145
sinimbu 272
siri 262
siriema V, n. 48
slaves 23, 144, 147, 207, 259, 263, 278, 306. I, n. 35; V, n. 136
  economic importance II, n. 22
  number in Brazil III, n. 100
  short life I, n. 36; VI, n. 6
slaves, Indian
  intolerance of captivity I, n. 36; VI, n. 6
sloth 272–274
smallpox 107, 108. I, nn. 16, 83; II, n. 70
snakes 278–279
snook V, n. 85
Soares de Sousa, Gabriel 8, 344, 346. I, n. 107
Sofala 100
solé V, n. 94
Solomon, King 99
sondais V, n. 65
sorcerers 312–314
soursop IV, n. 130
Sousa, Gaspar de 29. I, nn. 69, 72, 148
Sousa, Luís de I, n. 89
Sousa, Pero Lopes de I, n. 123
Sousa, Tomé de 6. I, nn. 147, 165
South Sea 100. II, n. 46
Souza, Francisco de 47. I, n. 181
Souza, Lopo de 47. I, n. 184
Souza, Martim Afonso de I, nn. 9, 184
Spain
  as geographical term I, n. 38
spices 134, 138
spiny rat V, n. 161
spot-winged wood quail V, n. 11
squash 202
Staden, Hans 342, 345
stonefish 256
stowage privileges 134
Strait of Gibraltar 97

Strait of Magellan 100. I, n. 102; II, n. 48
strangler fig 160
striped mullet V, n. 87
suçuarana 278
sucupira III, n. 145
sucuri V, n. 195
sucurijuba V, nn. 195, 196
sugar 19
  as medium of exchange I, n. 98
  chest I, n. 155
  kinds 145
  processing 140–143
  profitability 19, 32, 132–136
  tithes on 32
sugar barons (*senhores de engenho*) 143–144, 146
sugar cane, 5, 17, 21
sugar mills I, nn. 163, 171
  division of profits 144–145
  exemptions 136
  number of III, n. 65
  requirements 143–144
sugar planters I, n. 34; III, n. 64
suia 252. V, n. 51
suiná (suinara, suindara) V, n. 65
suindá 253
suis I, n. 154
superior crown magistrate 42. I, n. 160
superstitions I, n. 111
Surinam cherry IV, n. 164
surmullets 256
surucucu 278
surucucutinga V, n. 193
susurana V, n. 191
swallows 251. V, n. 44
sweetsop IV, n. 130
sword-club VI, n. 43
swordfish 256
Sylveira, Symão Estaço da I, nn. 75, 77

Tabajaras 321, 325. I, n. 95
tabua 161
taçuité 266
taguató (toató, taquató) 253. V, n. 61
taiá 202

taiaçu 266
tainha-curimã V, n. 87
tainha-de-corso V, n. 87
tainha-seca V, n. 87
tainha-verdadeira V, n. 87
taioba 202, 212
taitetu 266
tamanduá-açu 270
tamanduá-bandeira V, n. 168
tamanduá-cavalo V, n. 168
tamanduá-mirim V, nn. 169, 178
tamarind 216
tamatianguasu V, n. 31
tamatião-açu 250
tamboatá V, n. 102
tamoatá 257
tamoatarana 202
tapa-cu V, n. 21
taperá V, n. 43
tapioca 195–196
tapir V, n. 150
tapirage 252. V, n. 53
Tapirapés VI, n. 48
Tapuias 325–326. I, nn. 57, 156; IV,
   n. 61; VI, n. 70
taquara V, n. 39
taquari (taquiri) V, n. 73
taqueira 212
taraba 251
tarpon V, n. 79
Tarshish 99
tatajuba (tatagiba, tataíba) 209, 220. IV,
   nn. 53, 96
tattoo 315–316
tatu 268
tatuí V, n. 157
tegu 272
teiú (teju, tiú) V, n. 172
Teixeira, Bento viii
tejuaçu V, n. 172
temiú-catu IV, n. 133
Tenochtitlán I, n. 16
ten-pounder V, n. 83
Terrestrial Paradise 88
Thevet, André de 8, 341–342
three-spike goosegrass IV, n. 45

three-toed South American ostrich V,
   n. 47
Three Wise Men, Fort of the I, n. 70
Tierra del Fuego II, n. 49
tiger. See ounce
tijibu V, n. 170
timber 155–157
timbó 207
tinamou V, nn. 12, 13, 22
Tinharé I, n. 169
tiquaam 274
tiquaran 251
titarimbó 208
tobacco 106, 212, 322. I, n. 98; II,
   n. 66
   "drinking smoke" VI, n. 37
topazes, from India 132
Tordesillas (Tordesilhas), Treaty of 4
tordo V, n. 18
Torres, Tomás de I, n. 45
torrid zone: habitability 15, 85–89,
   103, 105
toucan 250
   toco t. V, n. 42
Touche, Daniel de la, Seigneur de la
   Ravardière 29, 346. I, n. 71
trade 144–147, 149–150
trade guilds I, n. 32
traditionalism, Portuguese III, n. 63
traíra 259
Trancoso, Gonçalo Fernandes 152
trapiche 140, 141
traveling salesmen 147
Treasury Council III, n. 48
trellises 212, 213, 215
tucanaçu 251
tucani V, n. 33
tucuma 205–206
tuidara (tuindá) V, n. 65
tui-juba V, n. 21
tuim 252
Tupã VI, n. 18
Tupi-Guarani language I, n. 57
Tupinambás (Tupis) 2, 325, 342, 343.
   I, n. 144; VI, n. 12

uacapará V, n. 127
uacari V, n. 103
uapicu V, n. 25
uaxua IV, n. 153
ubacropari IV, n. 154
ubaperungua IV, n. 159
ubarana 256
uçá 262
uchi (uxi, uxipuçu) IV, n. 153
uiti IV, n. 141
umari 200
umbu (imbu) IV, n. 158
Una River 257
Urganda 207
Uriah 99
urn burial 41
uru 249
urubu 254
urucu 209. VI, n. 50
uruinduba III, n. 156
urundeúva 161
urutaurana V, n. 55
usá V, n. 125
usury 147
uti 220
utim IV, n. 141
uvaia 217

Vasconcellos, Simão de 8, 347–348
Vatablo "Parisiense" (Franciscus
    Vatablo) 99–100. II, nn. 45, 46
Vaux, Charles des I, n. 71
vegetables 211–212
Venice 138

Vera Cruz I, n. 40
vermin 111, 112
Vespucci, Amerigo 97, 98. II, nn. 32,
    40, 56
Vicente do Salvador 8, 13, 346–347. I,
    nn. 37, 151
Villegaignon, Nicolas Durand de 341,
    343
Vossius, Isaac vii

Waldseemüller, Martin II, n. 32
war meal 195
wealth of Brazil 132. I, n. 14
West Indies 19, 20, 28, 94, 95, 96,
    198. I, n. 7; II, n. 40; IV, n. 92
whales 45, 260
whaling industry I, n. 162
wheat 198–200
    w. flour 306
white-faced tree duck V, n. 68 ·
whitewood 160
wildcat 274
wine 204–205, 207
woodpecker 250
wood pigeon 249
wool 206, 265
wounds, treatment of 110–111

yellow wood 160
Yves d'Evreux 346

zaburro 198
Zaire River I, n. 19

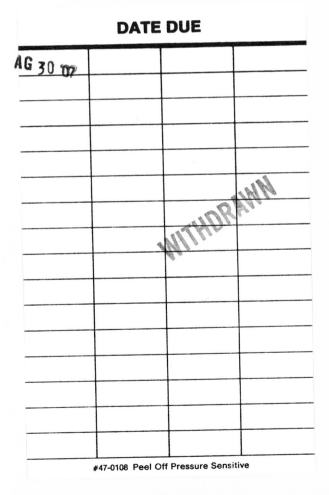

DATE DUE

AG 30 02			